This book is dedicated to Herbert Passin,
Professor Emeritus at Columbia University,
distinguished East Asian scholar,
and a dear friend.

*Confucianism
and the Family*

SUNY Series in Chinese Philosophy and Culture
David L. Hall and Roger T. Ames, Editors

Confucianism
and the Family

EDITED BY

Walter H. Slote
and
George A. De Vos

State University of New York Press

Published by
State University of New York Press, Albany

For information, address State University of New York Press,
State University Plaza, Albany, N.Y., 12246

Production by Diane Ganeles
Marketing by Patrick Durocher

Library of Congress Cataloging-in-Publication Data

Confucianism and the family / edited by Walter H. Slote and George A. De Vos.
        p.   cm. — (SUNY series in Chinese philosophy and culture)
      Includes bibliographical references and index.
      ISBN 0-7914-3735-3 (alk. paper). — ISBN 0-7914-3736-1 (pbk. :
   alk. paper)
      1. Confucianism—Asia.   2. Family—Asia.   3. Asia—Social life and
   customs.   I. Slote, Walter H.   II. De Vos, George A.   III. Series.
   BL1844.A78C64   1998
   299'.5121783585—dc21   97-26846
                                                                        CIP

10 9 8 7 6 5 4 3 2 1

Contents

Preface

This study is based upon the premise that the family constitutes the central element of those societies that have been profoundly influenced by the Confucian, and later Neo-Confucian, mandate. The power of the doctrine, the extent of its influence, and its incorporation into the lives of so many for so long a period of time, attests to its enduring fit between the culture and the psychological character of the people. But as time passes, so do forms of governance and conduct, and so it has been with Confucianism. Modern technology, the impact of Western influences, and massive shifts in the internal social and political balance have brought about rapid changes. It therefore is an appropriate moment to look into the nature of the family in the societies that constitute the "Confucian core"—namely maintained China, Taiwan, Korea, Japan, and Vietnam. Singapore, because of its large Chinese population and its current emphasis upon Confucian values, has also been included.

The particular form in which Confucianism is expressed varies from society to society, and from one historical period to another. There are, however, essential characteristics that remain consistent among all. Both are addressed in this volume. While we place our emphasis on Confucianism, we are fully aware that there are other influences that have had a profound impact on the development of these societies. These include Buddhism, Taoism, Shinto, folk religions, and more recently, Western Christianity as well as Marxist, socialist, and democratic ideologies.

The issues have been examined from diverse perspectives. The authors come from related but distinct disciplines—anthropology, sociology, religion, philosophy, history, psychiatry, psychology, and psychoanalysis. Far from producing a cacophony of tongues, the result seems a companionable and stimulating mix.

Perhaps the most distinctive feature of our venture is the emphasis in a number of the chapters on the psychocultural aspects of the Confucian family. To the best of our knowledge, this is the first time that this area has been brought into focus. Consideration is given to such factors as motivation, psychodynamics, interpersonal relationships, intrapsychic processes, character structure, the individual and society as an interrelated and mutually interacting synthesis, and above all, the unconscious as a primary determinant of behavior.

The book is organized under five headings: Introduction, Historical Dimensions, Hierarchy and Gender, Contemporary Exigencies, and Psycho-cultural Continuities.

In an introductory overview Wei-Ming Tu, Walter Slote, and Francis Hsu present an investigation of the family as the nucleus of society both from experiential and structural points of view. Tu explores the initial historical-social context of Confucius, with reference to what biographical knowledge we have. With exceptional cogency he guides us through the vicissitudes of Confucian thought in the subsequent cultural history of China.

Slote investigates the interpersonal and intrapsychic dynamics within the Confucian family. Although the formal authority of the father as head of the family is readily observable, he places particular emphasis upon the subtle power of the mother. This subject is further pursued by Haejoang Cho, as are the increasing degrees of empowerment of women within the family in Asia, as elsewhere, and Slote analyzes intrafamilial tensions and the manner in which Confucian family interaction often calls for the suppression of affect, and its consequences. These tensions are explored in some depth in a later chapter by Bou-Yong Rhi, who examines the neurotic forms of coping that periodically appear in response to the exigencies of a form of family life still subject to a rigid employment of differences in formal status.

Finally, Slote introduces the theme of change as an evolving process in Asia. Several chapters of the final section of the volume are directly devoted to problems of continuity and transition as they have been occurring in Singapore and Taiwan as well as in Vietnam, Korea, and Japan.

Hsu emphasizes cultural variations within social structure, particularly those that separate Asian traditions from those of the Christian world or Islam. He diagrams the manner in which present social organization interacts with past cultural heritage in one direction, and with individual behavior in the other. For Hsu one must continually consider those abiding concerns that keep societies "glued" together. In Confucian Asia, filial piety is a focal point of reference. Yet, despite espousing similar virtues, Japanese and Chinese culture have continued to be organized differently. The Japanese employ nonkinship criteria in cementing social belonging. This leads to significant variances in social organization, which in turn influence the behavior of individual Japanese or Chinese in a dissimilar way, especially in the economic and occupational patterning of their related cultures.

The major historical section of the book provides a condensed review of the Confucian tradition as it has developed in the various societies under consideration. In tracing Confucianist thought in Korea and its development in relation to the family, John Duncan focuses on the political changes that preceded the Choson dynasty. He takes us into the social background of the period and critically reviews alternative interpretations explaining the rise of Neo-Confucianism: those pursuing a materialist-structuralist analysis emphasized the economic, social, and class interests represented in the emerging scholar-official; a second view is that the younger scholar-officials reacting to the corruption and decadence of the previous Koryo period sought to carry out a radical reconstruction of Korean society along the line of Confucian ideals.

Juxtaposed in Duncan's chapter are the pros and cons of a more structuralist versus an ideological interpretation of Confucian development within Korean society. Duncan, conversant with both approaches, gives us a detailed exposition that also centers on the family as the primary social unit. He delineates the way in which family structure was transformed by the exogamy increasingly practiced by the elite in the capital. This practice was brought about by a need to maintain the power of one's family in a society composed of Yangban (elite) drawn from diverse regions. Once instituted, this practice gradually spread to local clan seats where endogamous unions had previously preserved family status. As a result, partial bilateral inheritance evolved toward a more sinicized form of family structure, not only in inheritance practices, but in other features of a Confucian nature as well.

In chapter 5, Nguyen Ngoc Huy recounts a history of Chinese political pressure and concomitant Confucian intellectual and social influence in Vietnam that is intertwined with local cultural features continuing into recent times. While accepting their Confucian and Buddhist religious institutions, the Vietnamese opposed the Chinese military/political incursions, thereby intensifying their distinct national identity. Despite sinic social and religious influences, the Vietnamese maintained an indigenous uniqueness within their family institutions. For example, their gender relationships granted women almost equal rights, for example, a divorced woman who remarried retained her property independent of the husband's family.

In a final historical chapter, George De Vos concentrates on Tokugawa Japan because of its major Confucianist influences as they were blended with indigenous religious and social adaptations of Buddhist thought. In the Tokugawa period Confucian thought was used both to justify the legitimacy of the Shogunate, and to maintain a Japanese moral certainty and intellectual integrity against the power of the West and its scientific and material superiority. Education during the Meiji period (1867–1912) extended the Confucian family practices of the Samurai and wealthy merchants to the common folk. Throughout, the Japanese maintained their own idiosyncratic cultural distinctions that made their adaptation of Confucian thought intrinsically Japanese.

In the same chapter, De Vos appraises the adaptation of Japanese Confucianists to the pressures of Western science. The importance of Confucianism in Japanese modernization, in contrast to its conservative function in countries such as Korea, was exemplified by the manner in which Confucian thought and patterns of family life evolved as the basis for social ethics during the Meiji period. It was incorporated into a universal public education in which scientific rationality was also essential. This brief historical review sets the stage for the final chapter (chapter 17), in which De Vos explores, from the point of view of developmental psychology, the inner experiences of those who continue to be socialized within the Confucian family ethos in Japan.

In part III, we directly address what is perhaps the major issue making Confucianism so problematical for many who might want to view it as a sustaining ethical base for contemporary social life. Can a modern Confucian society modify itself toward horizontal forms of equal status within the family? Can forms of hierarchy inherited from the past be transmuted into new forms within modern societies? How are current experiences compatible with a Confucian sense of morality and self-development?

Tu surveys the essential nature of hierarchy as part of Confucian tradition in his discussion of "the three bonds." A wife's status was determined not only by her husband's position, but by her own family's prominence. Furthermore, woman's fate in the role of wife and mother remained inevitably intertwined with the economic and societal situation of her children. In chapter 7, Tu discusses the actual power wielded by women in the ordinary day-to-day situation.

In chapter 8, Stephen Young explores the tensions concerning gender status in present-day Vietnam. Historically, he traces some of the enduring features of Vietnamese culture that differ from the paradigms brought from China. There was, and is, more individualism in Vietnam, validated not through a concept of power internal to the self, but through ideas that conceptualize fatalism and destiny. Although the individual achieves autonomy in the sense of not being subject to others, this does not eventuate in a sense of internalized initiative. Power is primarily located in the forces of destiny; not within the person. Rather than emphasizing Confucian personal initiative, the Vietnamese have emphasized a concept of fate that resembles "karma," which is congenial to Buddhist tradition. In part V, Slote returns to this theme in chapter 16, as does De Vos in chapter 17. There is definitely a cultural difference between concepts of destiny in Vietnam and the experience of power within the self found in the Japanese tradition.

Yim assesses male-female family roles in Korea in relationship to the ancestors and to the supernatural. Benign concepts of family continuity are formally ritualized in ancestor worship, sustaining the patriarchal continuity of man as the head of the household. In Korea, but not in Japan or China, women's roles takes on a more complementary ritual function in relation to the dead, who remain part of the social life of the living. Through domestic acts of worship, the women seek to placate the ghosts and malevolent beings who might cause ill to a family by means of their periodic use of shamanistic ritual practices. This role division is clearly marked; it demonstrates that women negotiate with power but their forms of meditation are not an accredited part of Confucianism.

A question that may occur to one observing the cultural continuity of Confucianism is whether, in China or elsewhere, it could ever be considered a total encompassing religion? Do Taoist, Buddhist, or folk practices supplement what remains incomplete in Confucianism itself? Some human emotions and forms of belief seem not to receive sufficient recognition within the basically rational orientation of Confucian thought. What is notably absent in this-worldly Confucianism is any dealing with supernatural forces. There is no tolerance of magical practices that help humans negotiate with the metaphysical. Rather, ancestors are worshipped as benign beings that symbolize and maintain family continuity. Confucianism is not considered a religion by some because it lacks a capacity within itself to deal with fear and anxiety, usually symbolized by various beliefs in the supernatural. Confucian practice leaves little place for any sense of awe or dread directed toward a potentially threatening mystical world.

Cho, in chapter 10, reflects upon the problems of power within the contemporary Confucian patriarchy of Korea. Empowerment for a woman occurs in the status position of mother; not in her horizontal transactions as wife. The vertical, hierarchical, and generational is emphasized over the companionate possibilities of family life. She probes the aspects of matrifocality and family continuity; mother power and the "overdependence" between men and women.

In chapter 11, Lebra examines the *Ie* or household as it has reflected a Japanese form of Confucian hierarchy, allowing women to realize, in age-grading patterns, some instrumental and expressive forms of fulfillment. During young womanhood, there was social suppression of her rights and personal needs. Eventually, a sense of internal empowerment occurred with the changing status that age afforded, but a true sense of fulfillment was to be realized only toward the end of her lifespan. In considering some of the recent dilemmas in the contemporary woman's role, Lebra raises the question of whether or not Confucianism may be dying in modern Japan. Certainly, Confucian gender ideology is gradually becoming outmoded.

Kwang-Kyu Lee in Korea and Eddie Kuo in Singapore look at the urban environment and its pressures as a new family lifestyle takes shape. How does modernization and its exigencies allow for any form of Confucian continuity? Problems of urban housing are a paramount issue. Small apartments make living with a son more complex and continuation of formal ritual very difficult. Furthermore, there are blandishments toward a more fashionable way of life as introduced by the ever-present mass media.

The last four chapters comprising part V are devoted directly to the more psychocultural perspective of this book. David Jordan, as a result of his analysis of contemporary writings about filial piety, seeks out some of their derivative psychological implications in modern Taiwan and sketches representations of nurturance, duty, and the proper use of education. He studies the manner in which self-sacrificing exemplars are still depicted, and the models in which identification eventually occurs with parental figures. In present-day Taiwan there are fewer rewards for filial self-sacrifice. Instead, a more secular view underscores the appropriateness of gratitude for early nurturance, rather than the formalized duty owed to a parent due to his status. This focus on gratitude discussed by Jordan brings us closer to the pattern of family continuity found in the Japanese who also tend to be organized around a similar emphasis on gratitude for parental care. The Japanese concern themselves with love of parents, not duty toward them. Rhi takes us inside the psychiatric facilities of modern Korea. He provides illustrations of how the tensions within the hierarchical family such as the status of mother-in-law over daughter-in-law, or the demands of responsibility faced by a first son, can take their toll when not met by an effective form of psychological coping. Patterns of psychogenic illness reveal forms of stress that may be surmounted, but often leave residual damage.

Following this chapter, Slote extensively develops a theme previously touched on by Young, namely a continuing pattern of fatalism that is a central part of the experience of self in many Vietnamese. In the final chapter, De Vos conjoins the Confucian heritage of Japan to considerations of developmental psychology. He evaluates the experience of intrapsychic power as it relates to concepts of causality, and proposes that the family patterns of "propriety" as socialized in early childhood created not only a sense of age-graded self-discipline, but also moral and aesthetic sensibilities.

We wish to express our deep appreciation to the East Asian Institute, Columbia University, and to the Center for Korean Studies, University of California, Berkeley, for the support that they have given this project. We also wish to thank Kim Seong-Jin, former president of the International Cultural Society of Korea for his generous assistance in initiating this study, and to the Korea Foundation.

WALTER H. SLOTE
GEORGE A. DE VOS

I

Introduction

1

Confucius and Confucianism

Wei-Ming Tu

The Confucian Ethos

Confucianism, a generic Western term that has no counterpart in Chinese, is a worldview, a social ethic, a political ideology, a scholarly tradition, and a way of life. Although Confucianism is often grouped together with Buddhism, Christianity, Hinduism, Islam, Judaism, and Taoism as a major historical religion, it is not an organized religion. Yet, it has exerted a profound influence on East Asian political culture as well as on East Asian spiritual life. Both in theory and practice, Confucianism has made an indelible mark on the government, society, education, and family of East Asia. It is an exaggeration to characterize traditional Chinese life and culture as "Confucian," but Confucian ethical values have, for well over 2,000 years, served as the source of inspiration as well as the court of appeal for human interaction at all levels—between individuals, communities, and nations in the Sinic world.

Confucianism did not have an organized missionary tradition, but by the first century B.C., it had spread to those East Asian countries under the influence of Chinese literate culture. The age of Confucianism, in the centuries following the Confucian revival of Sung times (A.D. 960–1279), embraced Choson dynasty Korea from the fifteenth century and Tokugawa Japan from the seventeenth century. Prior to the introduction of Western powers into East Asia in the mid-nineteenth century, the Confucian persuasion was so predominant in the art of governance, the form and content of elite education, and the moral discourse of the populace that China, Korea, and Japan were all distinctively "Confucian" states. Moreover, Vietnam and Singapore in Southeast Asia have also been under Confucian influence.

The story of Confucianism does not begin with Confucius (Latinized form of K'ung-fu-tzu, Master K'ung; 551–479 B.C.). The Chinese term *Ju-chia*, which is inadequately rendered as Confucianism, literally means the "family of scholars," signifying a genealogy, a school, or a tradition of learning. Confucius was not the founder of Confucianism in the sense that Buddha was the founder of Buddhism and Christ was the founder of Christianity. Nor did Confucius live up to the highest Confucian ideal, the sage-king. Throughout Chinese history, followers of Confucian tradition openly acknowledge that only the legendary sage-kings such as Yao and Shun fully embodied the Confucian idea of "inner sageliness and outer kingliness."

Confucianism is a historical phenomenon. The emergence of the Confucian tradition as a way of life, its elevation to the status of a state cult, its decline as moral persuasion, its continuous influence in society, its revival as a living faith, its metamorphosis into a political ideology, its response to the impact of the West, and its modern transformation, can all be analyzed as integral parts of East Asian culture. The Confucians do not have an internalist hagiographic interpretation of their past narrative. Indeed, a distinctive feature of Confucianism is its expressed intention to regard the everyday human world as profoundly spiritual. By regarding the secular as sacred, the Confucians try to refashion the world from within according to their cultural ideal of the unity between human community and Heaven.

The period of 550–200 B.C., historically known as the age of the "hundred philosophers," was a golden age in classical Chinese thought. Contending vigorously in proposing solutions to the pressing problem of bringing order out of chaos and in giving meaning to human life under constant threat of brutal warfare, four major schools of thought emerged as four substantially different responses to the decline and fall of the glorious Chou civilization, an elaborate "feudal" ritual system that had provided economic well-being, political order, social stability, and cultural elegance in China proper for several centuries.

The Taoists, who developed a philosophy of nature and spiritual freedom, advocated a total rejection of human civilization, which they believed to be the source of suffering. The Moists were concerned about the aggressiveness of the newly arisen hegemonic states, the wastefulness of the aristocratic style of life, and the pervasive injustice. They organized themselves into military units to bring about love and peace through self-sacrifice. The Legalists accepted the inevitable disintegration of the "feudal" ritual system and allied themselves to the centers of power. The Confucians opted for a long-term solution to the collapse of the Chou dynasty through education as character-building. They believed that one could attain true nobility through self-cultivation and inner enlightenment. Their ideal humanity (sagehood) and their practical model (the nobleman) were not only prophets and philosophers but also teachers and statesmen. This combination of theory and practice made them men of spiritual vision and political mission who shared a common faith and creed.

For several centuries, Confucius was counted as one of the philosophers and Confucianism one of the schools in the Chinese world of thought. It took a few generations of concerted effort by the followers of Confucius to establish the "scholarly tradition" advocated by Confucius as the dominant intellectual force in China. However, Confucianism never existed alone as the exclusive orthodoxy of the state and the attempt to promote Confucianism as the state ideology at the expense of other schools in the second century B.C. was short-lived. Rather, the gradual expansion of the Confucian cultural movement into different layers of an alien despotic polity and various echelons of society enabled the tradition to become truly influential. The carriers of the Confucian tradition were the scholars. They were men of action as well as ideas. Through their efforts, the Confucian persuasion penetrated virtually all dimensions of life in traditional China.

A viable way of life for so many and for so long, Confucianism has sometimes been viewed as a philosophy and sometimes as a religion. As an all-encompassing humanism that neither denies nor slights Heaven, it is not only the faith and creed of the Chinese scholars but a way of life in East Asia; so deeply ingrained in the fabric of society and polity that it is often taken for granted as naturally human. East Asians may profess themselves to be Shintoists, Taoists, Buddhists, Muslims, or Christians, but rarely, if ever, do they cease to be Confucians.

The Life and Thought of Confucius

Confucius considered himself a "transmitter" rather than a "creator"; he consciously tried to reanimate the old order to attain the new. He proposed that we retrieve the meaning of the past by breathing vitality into the seemingly outmoded rituals. Confucius's love of antiquity was motivated by his strong desire to understand why certain rituals, such as the ancestral cult, reverence for Heaven, and the mourning ceremonies, had survived for centuries. His journey into the past was a search for roots, roots of humanity grounded in the deepest needs for belonging and communication. He had faith in the cumulative culture. The fact that traditional ways had declined did not diminish their great potential for innovation in the future. In fact, Confucius's sense of history was so strong that he saw himself as a conservationist responsible for the continuity of the cultural values and the social norms that had worked so well for the Chou civilization.

The Historical Context

The scholarly tradition envisioned by Confucius can be traced back to the sage-kings of antiquity. Although the earliest dynasty confirmed by archaeology to date was the Shang dynasty (c. twenty-third century B.C.), the history that Confucius claimed to have been relevant was much earlier. Confucius may have initiated a cultural process known in the West as Confucianism, but he and those who followed him considered themselves part of a tradition, later identified by Chinese historians as Ju-chia, "scholarly tradition," which had its origins two millennia previously when, legend has it, the sage-kings Yao and Shun formed a moral community by their exemplary teaching.

Confucius may have dreamed of the golden age of Yao and Shun as "great harmony," but his hero was the Duke of Chou (d. 1094 B.C.), who was said to have helped to consolidate and refine the "feudal" ritual system, thus enabling the Chou dynasty to survive in relative peace and prosperity for more than five centuries. Inspired by the statesmanship of the duke, Confucius's lifelong dream was to be in a position where he could emulate the duke by putting into practice the political ideas that he had learned from the ancient sage-kings. Although Confucius never realized his political dream, his conception of politics as moral persuasion became more and more influential.

The idea of Heaven, unique in Chou cosmology, was compatible with the concept of the Lord-on-High in the Shang dynasty. The Lord-on-High may have referred to the progenitor of the Shang royal lineage so that the Shang kings could claim their position as divine descendants as the emperors of Japan later did, but Heaven to the Chou kings was a much more generalized anthropomorphic God. They believed that the Mandate of Heaven (the functional equivalent of the will of the Lord-on-High) is not constant and that there is no guarantee that the descendants of the Chou royal house will be entrusted with kingship, for "Heaven sees as the people see and heaven hears as the people hear"; the virtues of the kings are essential for the maintenance of their power and authority.

This emphasis on benevolent rulership, as evidenced in the pronouncements of numerous bronze inscriptions, was both a reaction to the collapse of the Shang dynasty and an affirmation of a deep-rooted worldview. Although the Chou military conquest, which may have occurred in 1045 B.C., was the immediate cause for the downfall of the Shang dynasty, the Chou conquerors strongly believed that the last Shang king lost the Mandate of Heaven because of his indulgence in debauchery. Since the Mandate of Heaven was never wedded to a particular lineage and since the only guarantee for the preservation of the Mandate was the superior performance of the rulers, the Chou kings were apprehensive of losing the trust of the people. The rhetoric of benevolent rulership was also predicated on the worldview that since one is intimately connected with one's ancestral line—which, for the royal household, extends virtually to all members of the nobility—one acts on behalf of a community, and that the mutuality between Heaven and the human community further demands that the kings, as Sons of Heaven, conduct themselves in the spirit of filial piety not only toward their own ancestors but toward Heaven as well.

Partly because of the vitality of the "feudal" ritual system and partly because of the strength of the royal household itself, the Chou kings were able to control their kingdom for several centuries, but in 771 B.C. they were forced to move their capital eastward to present-day Lo-yang to avoid barbarian attacks from Central Asia. The real power then passed into the hands of feudal lords. However, since the surviving line of the Chou kins continued to be recognized in name, they still managed to exercise some measure of symbolic control.

The "feudal" ritual system was based on blood ties, marriage alliances, and old covenants as well as newly negotiated contracts and was an elaborate system of mutual dependence. The appeal to cultural values and social norms for the maintenance of interstate as well as domestic order was predicated on a shared political vision: authority lay in the universal kingship, which was heavily invested with ethical and religious power by the Mandate of Heaven. Organic social solidarity was achieved not by legal constraint but by ritual observance.

By Confucius's time, the "feudal" ritual system had been so fundamentally undetermined that political crises precipitated a profound sense of moral decline: the center of symbolic control could no longer hold the kingdom from total disintegration. Archaeological and textual evidence shows that the period witnessed unprecedented economic growth (e.g., the use of iron for agricultural implements, the availability of metallic coinage, commercialization, and urbanization) and the loosening of the kinship bonds of rigidly stratified society. Both contributed to a major restructuring the political order.

Confucius's response was to raise the ultimate question of learning to be human; in so doing he attempted to reformulate and revitalize the institutions that, for centuries, had been vital to political stability and social order: the family, the school, the local community, the state, and the kingdom. Confucius did not accept the status quo, which held that wealth and power spoke the loudest. He felt that virtue, both as a personal quality and as a requirement for leadership, is essential for individual dignity, communal solidarity, and political order.

The Life of Confucius

If the English-speaking community were to choose one word to characterize the Chinese way of life for the last two thousand years, the word would be "Confucian." It assumed that no other person in Chinese history has so profoundly influenced the thoughts and actions of his people, as a teacher of humanity, as a transmitter of culture, an interpreter of history, and as a molder of the Chinese minds. The other religious philosophies, notably Taoism and Buddhism, have also significantly shaped the Chinese character; but Confucian values and norms have never ceased to be defining characteristics of the

Chinese way of life. Many Chinese have professed to be Taoist, Buddhist, Muslim, and Christian, but seldom have they abandoned their Confucian roots. From the time that Confucianism was generally accepted by the Chinese populace (second century B.C.), it has become an integral part of Chinese society as a whole and of what it means to be Chinese.

Considering Confucius's tremendous importance, his life seems starkly undramatic, or as a Chinese expression has it, "plain and real." The plainness and reality of Confucius's life, however, illustrate his humanity not as revealed truth but as an expression of self-cultivation, the ability of human effort to shape his own destiny. The faith in the possibility of ordinary human beings' becoming awe inspiring sages and worthies is deeply rooted in the Confucian heritage, and the insistence that human beings are teachable, improvable, and perfectible through personal and communal endeavor is typically Confucian.

Although the facts about Confucius's life are scanty, they provide us with an unusually precise time frame and historical context. Confucius was born in the twenty-second year of the reign of Duke Hsiang of Lu (551 B.C.). The traditional claim that he was born on the twenty-seventh day of the eighth lunar month has been questioned by historians, but the twenty-eighth of September is still widely observed in East Asia as Confucius's birthday. It is an official holiday, "Teachers' Day," in Taiwan.

Confucius was born in Ch'u-fu in the small feudal state of Lu in modern Shantung Providence, which was noted for its preservation of the traditions of ritual and music of the Chou civilization. His family name was K'ung and his personal name Ch'iu, but he is referred to as either "K'ung Tzu" or "K'ung Fu-tzu' ("Master K'ung") throughout Chinese history. The adjectival "Confucian," conveniently derived from the Latinized Confucius, is not a meaningful term in Chinese; nor is the term "Confucianism," which was coined as recently as the eighteenth century in Europe.

Confucius's ancestors were probably members of the aristocracy who had become virtually poverty-stricken commoners by the time of his birth. His father died when Confucius was only three years old. Instructed first by his mother, Confucius then distinguished himself as an indefatigable learner in his teens. Toward the end of his life he recalled that by the age of fifteen his heart was set upon learning. An historical account notes that, even though he was already known as an informed young scholar, he felt that it was appropriate to inquire about everything while visiting the Grand Temple.

Confucius served in minor government posts managing stables and keeping books for granaries before he married a woman of similar background when he was nineteen. It appears that he may have already acquired a reputation as a multitalented scholar at an early age. He had just turned twenty when he named his newborn son "Carp," allegedly after the gift of the Lu king had sent him. Confucius's mastery of the six arts—ritual, music, archery, charioteering, calligraphy, and arithmetic—and his familiarity with the classical traditions, notably poetry and history, enabled him to start a brilliant teaching career in his thirties.

We do not know who Confucius's teachers were. There is a story that he sought instructions on ritual from the Taoist master, Lao Tzu, that is obviously apocryphal, but it is well known that he made a conscientious effort to find the right masters to teach him, among other things, ritual and music. Confucius is known as the first private teacher in China, for he was instrumental in establishing the art of teaching as a vocation, indeed a way of life. Before Confucius, aristocratic families had hired tutors to educate their sons, and government officials had instructed their subordinates in the necessary techniques, but he was the first person to devote his whole life to learning and teaching for the purpose of transforming and improving society. He believed that all human beings could benefit from self-cultivation. He inaugurated a humanities program for potential leaders, opened the doors of education to all, and defined learning not merely as the acquisition of knowledge, but also as character-building.

For Confucius, the primary function of education was to provide the proper way of training noblemen (chun-tzu), a process that involved constant self-improvement and continuous social interactions. Although he emphatically noted that learning is "for the sake of the self" (the end of which is self-knowledge and self-realization), he found public service a natural consequence of true education. Confucius confronted learned hermits who challenged the validity of his desire to serve the world; he resisted the temptation to "herd with birds and animals" to live apart from the human community and opted to try to transform the world from within. For decades, Confucius was actively involved in the political arena hoping to put his humanist ideas into practice through governmental channels.

In his late forties and early fifties, Confucius served first as a magistrate, then as an assistant minister of public works, and eventually as minister of justice in the state of Lu. It is likely that he accompanied King Lu as his chief minister on one of the diplomatic missions. Confucius's political career was, however, short-lived. His loyalty to the king alienated him from the power holders of the time, the big Chi families, and his moral rectitude did not sit well with the king's inner circle, who enraptured the king with sensuous delight. At fifty-six, when he realized that his superiors were uninterested in his policies, he left the country in an attempt to find another feudal state to render service. Despite his political frustration, he was accompanied by an enlarging circle of students during this self-imposed exile of almost thirteen years. His reputation as a man of vision and mission spread. A guardian of a border post once characterized him as the "wooden tongue for a bell" of the age, delivering Heaven's prophetic note to awaken the people (Analects 3.24).

Indeed, Confucius was perceived as the heroic conscience who knew realistically that he might not succeed, but fired by a righteous passion, continuously did the best he could. At the age of sixty-seven, he returned home to teach and to preserve his cherished classical tradition by writing and editing. He died in 479 B.C. at the age of seventy-three. According to the Records of the Historian, seventy-two of his students mastered the "six arts" and those who claimed to be his followers numbered three thousand.

The Analects *as the Embodiment of Confucian Ideas*

The *Analects (Lun-yu)*, the most revered sacred scripture in the Confucian tradition, was probably compiled by the second generation of Confucius's disciples. Based primarily on the Master's sayings, preserved in both oral and written transmissions, it captures the Confucian spirit in form and content in the same way that the Platonic dialogues underscore the Socratic pedagogy. The *Analects* has often been viewed by the critical modern reader as a collection of unrelated conversations randomly put together. This impression may have resulted from the mistaken conception of Confucius as a mere commonsense moralizer who gave practical advice to students in everyday situations. If we approach the *Analects* as a sacred scripture centered around a sagely personality that is intended for those who want to revive and reanimate an historical moment, a sacred time, we come close to what has been revered in China for centuries. The *Analects* is a communal memory, a literary device on the part of those who considered themselves beneficiaries of the Confucian way to continue the memory and to transmit a form of life as a living tradition. The purpose in compiling these digested statements centering around Confucius is not to present an argument or to record an event but to offer an invitation for its readers to take part in an ongoing conversation. Dialogue is used to show Confucius in thought and action, not as an isolated individual, but as a center of relationships. Actually the sayings of the *Analects* reveal the inner person of Confucius—his ambitions, his fears, his joys, his commitments, and above all, his self-image. Confucians for centuries learned to reenact the awe-inspiring ritual of participating in a conversation with Confucius through the *Analects*.

One of Confucius's most significant personal descriptions is a short autobiographic account of his own spiritual development found in the *Analects*:

> At fifteen I set my heart on learning; at thirty I firmly took my stand; at forty I had no delusions; at fifty I knew the Mandate of Heaven; at sixty my ear was attuned; at seventy I followed my heart's desire without overstepping the boundaries of right. (2.4)

Confucius's life as a student and teacher exemplified the Confucian idea that education is a ceaseless process of self-realization. When one of his students reportedly had difficulty describing him, Confucius came to his aid: "Why did you not simply say something to this effect: he is the sort of man who forgets to eat when he engages himself in vigorous pursuit of learning, who is so full of joy that he forgets his worries and who does not notice that old age is coming on?" (7.18).

Confucius was deeply concerned that the culture *(wen)* he cherished was not being transmitted and that the learning *(hsueh)* he propounded was not being taught. However, his strong sense of mission never interfered with his ability to remember silently what had been imparted to him, to learn without flagging, and to teach without growing weary (7.2). What he demanded of himself was strenuous: "It is these things that cause me concern: failure to cultivate virtue, failure to go deeply into what I have earned, inability to move up to what I have heard to be right, and inability to reform myself when I have defects" (7.3). What he demanded of his students was the willingness to learn: "I do not enlighten anyone who is not eager to learn, nor encourage anyone who is not anxious to put his ideas into words" (7.8).

The community that Confucius created through his inspiring personality was a scholarly fellowship of like-minded men of different ages and different backgrounds from different states. They were attracted to Confucius because they shared his vision and in varying degrees took part in his mission to bring moral order to an increasingly fragmented polity. This mission was difficult and even dangerous. The Master himself suffered from joblessness, homelessness, starvation, and, occasionally, life-threatening violence. Yet his faith in the survivability of the culture that he cherished and the workability of the approach to teaching that he propounded was so steadfast that he convinced his followers as well as himself that Heaven was on their side. When Confucius's life was threatened in K'uang, he said:

> Since the death the King Wen [founder of the Chou dynasty], does not the mission of culture *(wen)* rest here in me? If Heaven intends this culture to be destroyed, those who come after me will not be able to have any part of it. If Heaven does not intend this culture to be destroyed, then what can the men of K'uang do to me? (9.5)

This expression of self-confidence may give the impression that there was presumptuousness in Confucius's self-image. However, Confucius made it explicit that he was far from attaining sagehood and that all he really excelled in was "love of learning" (5.28). To him learning not only broadened his knowledge and deepened his self-awareness but also defined who he was. He frankly acknowledged that he was not born of knowledge (7.20) and that he did not belong to the class of men who could innovate without possessing knowledge (7.28). Rather, he reported that he used his ears widely and followed what was good in what he had heard, and used his eyes widely and retained what he had seen in his mind. His learning constituted "a lower level of knowledge" (7.28). This level of knowledge is presumably accessible to the majority of the human community. In this sense, Confucius was neither a prophet with privileged access to the divine nor a philosopher who has already seen the truth, but a teacher of humanity who is an advanced fellow traveller on the way to self-realization.

As a teacher of humanity, Confucius stated his ambition in terms of human care: "to bring comfort to the old, to have trust in friends, and to cherish the young" (5.26). Confucius's vision of the way to develop a moral community began with a holistic reflection on the human condition. Instead of dwelling on abstract ideas such as the state of nature, Confucius sought to understand the actual situation of a given time and use that as a point of departure. His aim was to restore trust in government and to transform society into a moral community by cultivating a sense of human caring in politics and society. To achieve that aim, the creation of a scholarly community, the fellowship of *chun-tzu* (noblemen), was essential. In the words of Confucius's disciple, Tseng Tzu, the true nobleman "must be broad-minded and resolute, for his burden is heavy and his road is long. He takes humanity as his burden. Is that not heavy? Only with death does his road come to an end. Is that not long?" (8.7). However, the fellowship of *chun-tzu*, as moral vanguards of society, did not seek to establish a radically different order. Its mission was to reformulate and revitalize those institutions that were believed to have for centuries maintained social solidarity and enabled people to live in harmony and prosperity. An obvious example was the role and function of the family.

It was related in the *Analects* that when Confucius was asked why he did not take part in government, he responded by citing a passage from an ancient classic, the *Book of Documents,* "Simply by being a good son and friendly to his brothers a man can exert an influence upon government!" to show that what one does in the confines of one's private home is politically significant (2.21). This is predicated on the Confucian conviction that the self-cultivation of each person is the root of social order and that social order is the basis for political stability and universal peace. This assertion that family ethics is politically efficacious must be seen in the context of the Confucian conception of politics as "rectification" *(cheng).* The rulers are supposed to be moral exemplars who govern by moral leadership and exemplary teaching rather than force.

The government's responsibility is not only to provide food and security but also to educate the people. Law and punishment are the minimum requirement for order; social harmony can only be attained by virtue through ritual performance. To perform ritual is to take part in a communal act to promote mutual understanding.

One of the fundamental Confucian values that ensures the integrity of ritual performance is filial piety. Confucius sees filial piety as the first step toward moral excellence. He seems to contend that the way to enhance personal dignity and identity is not to alienate ourselves from the family but to cultivate our genuine feelings for our parents. To learn to embody the family in our minds and hearts is to enable ourselves to move beyond self-centeredness, or to borrow from modern psychology, to transform the enclosed private ego into an open self. Indeed, the cardinal Confucian virtue, *jen* (humanity), is the result of self-cultivation. The first test for our self-cultivation is our ability to cultivate meaningful relationships with our family members. Filial piety does not demand unconditional submissiveness to parental authority but recognition of and reverence for our source of life.

The purpose of filial piety, as the Greeks would have it, is "human flourishing" for both parent and child. Confucians see it as an essential way of learning to be human. They are fond of applying the family metaphor to the community, the country, and the universe. They prefer to address the emperor as the son of Heaven, the king as ruler-father, and the magistrate as the "father-mother official" because they assume that implicit in the family-centered nomenclature is a political vision. When Confucius responded that taking care of family affairs is itself active participation in politics, he made it clear that family ethics is not merely a private and personal concern because the public good is realized by and through it.

In response to his best disciple, Yen Hui, Confucius defined humanity as "conquer yourself and return to ritual" (12.1). This interplay between inner spiritual self-transformation (the Master is said to have freed himself from four things: "opinionatedness, dogmatism, obstinacy, and egoism" [9.4]) and social participation enabled Confucius to be "loyal" *(chung)* to himself and "considerate" *(shu)* of others (4.15). Understandably, the Confucian "golden rule" is "Do not do unto others what you would not want others to do unto you!" (15.23). Confucius's legacy, laden with profound ethical implications, is captured by his "plain and real" appreciation of learning to be human as communal enterprise:

> A man of humanity, wishing to establish himself, also establishes others, and wishing to enlarge himself, also enlarges others. The ability to take an analogy of what is near at hand can be called the method of humanity.

Formation of the Classical Confucian Tradition

According to Mo Tzu (fl. 479–438 B.C.), shortly after Confucius's death, his followers split into eight distinct schools all claiming to be the legitimate heir to the Confucian legacy. Presumably each school was associated with or inspired by one or me of Confucius's disciples. Yet the Confucians did not exert much influence on the intellectual scene in the fifth century B.C. Although the mystic Yen Hui, the faithful Tseng Tzu, the talented Tzu Kung, the erudite Tzu-hsia, and others may have generated a great deal of enthusiasm among the second generation of Confucius's students, it was not at all clear at the time that the Confucian tradition would emerge as the most powerful persuasion in Chinese history.

Mencius (371–289 B.C.?) complained that the world of thought in the early Warring States period (403–222 B.C.) was dominated by the collectivism of Mo Tzu and the individualism of Yang Chu (440–360 B.C.). Judging from the historical situation a century after Confucius's death, the disintegration of the Chou "feudal" ritual system and the rise of powerful hegemonic states clearly showed that the Confucian attempt to moralize politics was not working and that wealth and power spoke the loudest. The hermits (the early Taoists) who left the mundane world to create a spiritual sanctuary in nature in order to lead a contemplative life and the realists (the proto-Legalists) who played the dangerous game of assisting ambitious kings to gain wealth and power so that they could influence the political process were actually setting the intellectual agenda. The Confucians refused to be identified with the interest of the ruling minority because their social consciousness impelled them to serve as the conscience of the people. They were in a dilemma. They wanted to be actively involved in politics but they could not accept the status quo as the legitimate arena in which authority and power were exercised. In short, they were in the world but not of the world; they could not leave the world, nor could they effectively change it.

Mencius: The Paradigmatic Confucian Intellectual

Mencius is known as the self-styled transmitter of the Confucian Way. Educated first by his mother and then allegedly by a student of Confucius's grandson, Mencius brilliantly performed his role as a social critic, a moral philosopher, and a political activist. He argued that cultivating a class of scholar-officials who would not be directly involved in agriculture, industry, and commerce was vital to the well-being of the state. In his sophisticated argument against the physiocrats (those who advocated the supremacy of agriculture), he intelligently employed the idea of the "division of labor" to defend those who "labor with their minds," and observed that "service" is as important as "productivity." To him, Confucians serve the vital interests of the state as scholars not by becoming bureaucratic functionaries but by assuming the responsibility of teaching the ruling minority the "human government" (jen-cheng) and the kingly way (wang-tao). Understandably, in his dealing with feudal lords, Mencius conducted himself not merely as political adviser but also as a teacher of kings. Mencius made it explicit that a true man cannot be corrupted by wealth, subdued by power, or affected by poverty.

To articulate the relationship between Confucian moral idealism and the concrete social and political realities of his time, Mencius criticized the pervading ideologies of Mo Tzu's collectivism and Yang Chu's individualism as impractical. Mo Tzu advocated "universal love," but Mencius contended that the result of the Moist admonition to treat a stranger as intimately as one would treat one's own father would be to treat one's own father as indifferently as one would treat a stranger. Yang Chu, on the other hand, advocated the primacy of the self. Mencius contended that excessive attention to self-interest will lead to political disorder. Indeed, in the Moist collectivism, "fatherhood" cannot be established and, in Yang Chu's individualism, "kingship" cannot be established.

Mencius's strategy for social reform was to change the language of profit, self-interest, wealth, and power into a moral discourse with emphasis on rightness, public-spiritedness, welfare, and exemplary authority. However, Mencius was not arguing against profit. Rather, he instructed the feudal lords to opt for the great benefit that would sustain their own profit, self-interest, wealth, and power in a long-term perspective. He urged them to look beyond the horizon of their palaces and to cultivate a common bond with their ministers, officers, clerks, and the seemingly undifferentiated masses. Only then, he contended, would they be able to maintain their own livelihood. He encouraged them to extend their benevolence and warned them that this was crucial for the protection of their own families.

Mencius's appeal to that which is common to all people as a mechanism of government was predicated on his strong "populist" sense that the people are more important than the state and the state is more important than the king, and that the ruler who does not act in accordance with the kingly way is unfit. In an apt application of the Confucian principle of the "rectification of names," Mencius concluded that an unfit ruler should be criticized, rehabilitated, or, as the last resort, deposed. Since "Heaven sees as the people see; Heaven hears as the people hear," revolution, or literally "to change the Mandate" in extreme cases, is not only justifiable, but a moral imperative.

Mencius's "populist" conception of politics is predicated on his philosophical vision that human beings are perfectible through self-effort and that human nature is good. While he acknowledged biological and environmental factors in shaping the human condition, he insisted that we become moral simply by willing to be so. According to Mencius, the reason that willing entails the transformative moral act is that our nature's propensity to be good is automatically activated whenever we decide to bring it up to our conscious attention. As an illustration, Mencius built his idea of the human government on the assertion that every human being is capable of commiseration:

> No man is devoid of a heart sensitive to the suffering of others. Such a sensitive heart was possessed by the former kings and this manifested itself in humane government. With such a sensitive heart behind humane government, it was as easy to rule the world as rolling it on your palm. (IIA.6)

Mencius continued to observe that each human being is endowed with four feelings: commiseration, shame, modesty, and right and wrong. These feelings, like fire starting up or as a spring coming through, serve as the bases for cultivating the four cardinal virtues: humanity, rightness, ritual, and wisdom. The message is that we become moral not because we are told we must be good but because our nature, the depth-dimension of humanity, spontaneously expresses itself as goodness.

Mencius taught that we all have the inner spiritual resources to deepen our self-awareness and broaden our networks of communal participation. Biological and environmental constraints notwithstanding, we always have the freedom and the ability to refine and enlarge our Heaven-endowed nobility (our "great body"). Mencius's idea of degrees of excellence in character-building vividly illustrates this continuous refinement and enlargement of our selfhood:

> He who commands our liking is called good *(shan)*.
> He who is sincere with himself is called true *(hsin)*.
> He who is sufficient and real is called beautiful *(mei)*.
> He whose sufficiency and reality shine forth is called great *(ta)*.
> He whose greatness transforms itself is called sagely *(sheng)*.
> He whose sageliness is beyond our comprehension is called spiritual *(shen)*.

Furthermore, Mencius asserted that if we fully realize the potential of our hearts, we will understand our nature, and by understanding our nature, we will know Heaven. This profound faith in the human capacity for self-knowledge and for understanding Heaven by tapping spiritual resources from within enabled Mencius to add an "anthropocosmic" dimension to the Confucian project. Learning to be fully human, in this Mencian perspective, entails the cultivation of human sensitivity to embody the whole universe as one's lived experience.

All the ten thousand things are there in me. There is no greater joy for me than to find, on self-examination, that I am true to myself. Try your best to treat others as you would wish to be treated yourself, and you will find that this is the shortest way to humanity. (VIIA.4)

The Confucian nobleman, as envisioned by Mencius, is an exemplary teacher, a political leader, a meaning-making thinker, and a prophetic intellectual.

Hsun Tzu: The Transmitter of Confucian Scholarship

If Mencius brought Confucian moral idealism to fruition, Hsun Tzu (fl. 298–238) conscientiously transformed the Confucian project into a realistic and systematic inquiry on the human condition with special reference to ritual and authority. Widely acknowledged as the most eminent of the notable scholars who congregated in Chi-hsia, the capital of the wealthy and powerful Ch'i state in the mid third century B.C., Hsun Tzu distinguished himself in erudition, logic, empiricism, practical-mindedness, and argumentation. His critique of the so-called "twelve philosophers" gave an overview of the intellectual scene of his time. His penetrating insight into the shortcomings of virtually all the major currents of thought propounded by his fellow thinkers helped to establish the Confucian school as a forceful political and social persuasion. His principal adversary, however, was Mencius and he vigorously attacked Mencius's view that human nature is good as naive moral optimism.

True to the Confucian and, for that matter, Mencian spirit, Hsun Tzu underscored the centrality of self-cultivation. He outlined the process of Confucian education, from nobleman to sage, as a ceaseless endeavor to accumulate knowledge, skills, insight, and wisdom. He believed that unless social constraints are well articulated, we are prone to make excessive demands to satisfy our passions. As a result, social solidarity, the precondition for human flourishing, is undermined. The most serious flaw in the Mencian commitment to the goodness of human nature is the practical consequence of neglecting the necessity of ritual and authority for the well-being of society. By stressing that human nature is evil, Hsun Tzu singled out the cognitive function of the mind (human rationality) as the basis for morality. We become moral by voluntarily harnessing our desires and passions to act in accordance with societal norms. This is alien to our nature but perceived by our mind as necessary for both survival and well-being.

Like Mencius, Hsun Tzu believed in the perfectibility of all human beings through self-cultivation, in humanity and rightness as cardinal virtues, in humane government as the kingly way, in social harmony, and in education, but his view of how this could actually come about was diametrically opposed to Mencius's. The Confucian project, as shaped by Hsun Tzu, defines learning as socialization. The authorities of ancient sages and worthies, the classical tradition, the conventional norms, the teachers, the governmental rules and regulations, and political officers are all important for transforming human nature. A cultured person is by definition a fully socialized participant of the human community who has successfully sublimated his instinctual demands for the public good.

Hung Tzu's tough-minded stance on law, order, authority, and ritual seems precariously close to the Legalists whose policy of social conformism was designed exclusively for the benefit of the ruler. His insistence on objective standards of behavior may have ideologically contributed to the rise of authoritarianism, which resulted in the dictatorship of the Ch'in (221–206 B.C. As a matter of fact, two of the most influential Legalists, the theoretician Han Fei (d. 233 B.C.) from the state of Han and the Ch'in minister Li Ssu (d. 208 B.C.), were his pupils. Yet, Hsun Tzu was instrumental in the continuation of the Confucian project as a scholarly enterprise. His naturalistic interpretation of Heaven, his sophisticated understanding of culture, his insightful observations on the epistemological aspect of the mind and social function of language, his emphasis on moral reasoning and the art of argumentation, his belief in progress, and his interest in political institutions so significantly enriched the Confucian heritage that he was revered by the Confucians as the paradigmatic scholar for more than three centuries.

The Confucianization of Politics

The short-lived dictatorship of the Ch'in marked a brief triumph of Legalism, but in the early years of the Western Han (206 B.C.–A.D. 8), the Legalist practice of the absolute power of the emperor, complete subjugation of the peripheral states to the central government, total uniformity of thought, and ruthless enforcement of law was replaced by the Taoist practice of reconciliation and non-interference. This practice is commonly known in history as the Huan-Lao method, referring to the art of rulership attributed to the Yellow Emperor (Huang Ti) and the mysterious "founder" of Taoism, Lao Tzu. A few Confucian thinkers such as Lu Chia and Chia I made important policy recommendations, but before the emergence of Tung Chung-shu (c. 179–104 B.C.) the Confucian persuasion was not particularly influential. However, the gradual Confucianization of Han politics must have begun soon after the founding of the dynasty. The decisions of the founding fathers to allow the reinstitution of the feudal system and the first emperor to implement an elaborate court ritual opened the gates to Confucian influence on the basic structure of the Han government. The imperial decision to redress the cultural damage done in the book-burning fiasco of the Ch'in by retrieving the lost classics through extensive search and oral transmission indicated a concerted effort to make the Confucian tradition as integral part of the emerging political culture.

By the reign of the Martial Emperor (Wu Ti, 141–87 B.C.), who was by temperament a Legalist despot, the Confucian persuasion was deeply entrenched in the central bureaucracy through such practices as the clear separation of the court and a government that was often under the leadership of a scholarly prime minister, the process of recruiting officials through the dual mechanism of recommendation and selection, the family-centered social structure, the agriculture-based economy, and the educational network. Confucian ideas, which were also firmly established in the legal system as ritual, became increasingly important in governing behavior, defining social relationships, and adjudicating civil disputes. Yet it was not until the prime minister Kung-sun Hung (d. 121 B.C.) had persuaded the Martial Emperor to formally announce that the Ju school alone would receive state sponsorship, that Confucianism became an officially recognized imperial ideology and state cult.

As a result, Confucian classics became the core curriculum for all levels of education. In 136 B.C., the Martial Emperor set up at court five Erudites of the Five Classics and in 124 B.C. assigned fifty official students to study with them, thus creating a de facto imperial university. By 50 B.C., the student enrollment at the university had grown to an impressive three thousand, and by A.D. 1, a hundred men a year were entering government service through the examinations administered by the state. In short, those with a Confucian education began to staff the bureaucracy. In A.D. 58, all government schools were required to make sacrifices to Confucius, and in A.D. 175, the court had the approved version of the classics, which had been determined by scholarly conferences and research teams under imperial auspices extending over several decades, and which were carved on large stone tablets. These stelae were erected at the capital and are today well-preserved in the national museum of Hsi-an. This act of committing to permanence and to public display the precise content of the sacred scriptures symbolizes the completion of the formation of the classical Confucian tradition.

The Five Classics

A concrete manifestation of the coming of age of the Confucian tradition is the compilation of the Five Classics. By including both pre-Confucian texts, *Book of Documents* and *Book of Poetry* and contemporary Chin-Han material such as certain portions of the *Book of Rites,* it seems to have been an ecumenical attempt to establish the core curriculum for Confucian education. The Five Classics can be described in terms of five visions: metaphysical, political, poetic, social, and historical. The metaphysical vision, symbolized by the *Book of Changes (I Ching)*, combines divinatory art with numerological technique and ethical insight. According to the philosophy of change, the cosmos is a great transformation occasioned by the constant interaction of two complementary as well as conflicting vital energies, *yin* and *yang*. The universe, which resulted from this great transformation, always exhibits organismic unity and dynamism. The nobleman, inspired by the harmony and creativity of the universe, must emulate the highest ideal of the "unity of man and Heaven" through ceaseless self-exertion.

The political vision, symbolized by the *Book of Documents (Shu Ching)*, addresses the kingly way in terms of the ethical foundation for a humane government. The legendary Three Emperors (Yao, Shun, and Yu) all ruled by virtue. Their sagacity, filial piety, and work ethic enabled them to create a political culture based on responsibility and trust. Through exemplary teaching, they encouraged the people to enter into a "covenant" with them so that social harmony could be achieved without punishment or coercion. Even in the Three Dynasties (Hsia, Shang, and Chou), moral authority, as ritualized power, was sufficient to maintain political order. The human continuum, from the undifferentiated masses, via the enlightened people and the nobility, to the sage-king, formed an organic unity as an integral part of the great cosmic transformation. Politics means "rectification" and the purpose of the government is not only to provide food and maintain order but also to educate.

The poetic vision, symbolized by the *Book of Poetry (Shih Ching)*, underscores the Confucian value of the common human feelings. The majority of the verses express emotions and sentiments of persons and communities from all echelons of society on a variety of occasions. The internal resonance, the basic rhythm, of the poetic world characterized by the book is mutual responsiveness. The tone as a whole is honest rather than earnest and evocative rather than expressive. The social vision, symbolized by the *Book of Rites (Li Chi)*, defines society not as an adversary system based on contractual relationships, but as a community of trust with emphasis on communication. The society organized by the four functional occupations— the scholar, farmer, artisan, and merchant—is, in the true sense of the word, a cooperation. As a contributing member of the cooperative enterprise, each person is obligated to recognize the existence of others and to serve the public good. By the principle of "the rectification of names," it is the king's duty to act kingly and the father's duty to act fatherly. If the king or father fails to behave properly, he cannot expect his minister or son to act in accordance with ritual. It is in this sense a chapter in the *Rites* entitled "The Great Learning" specifies, "From the Son of Heaven to the commoner, all must regard self-cultivation as the root." This pervasive "duty-consciousness" features prominently in all Confucian literature on ritual.

The historical vision, symbolized by the *Spring and Autumn Annals (Ch'un-ch'iu)*, emphasizes the significance of collective memory for communal self-identification. Historical consciousness is a defining characteristic of Confucian thought. By defining himself as a transmitter and as a lover of antiquity, Confucius made it explicit that a sense of history is not only desirable but is necessary for self-knowledge. Confucius's emphasis on the importance of history was in a way his reappropriation of the ancient Sinic wisdom: reanimating the old is the best way to attain the new. Confucius may not have authored the *Spring and Autumn Annals,* but it seems likely that he applied moral judgment to political events in China proper from the eighth century to the fifth century B.C. In this unprecedented political criticism, he assumed a godlike role in evaluating politics by assigning ultimate "praise and blame" in history to the most powerful and influential political actors of the period. This practice inspired not only the innovative style of the Grand Historian, Ssu-ma Ch'ien (d.c. 85 B.C.) but was widely employed by others writing dynastic histories in imperial China.

The Five Classics, as five visions—metaphysical, political, poetic, social, and historical—provide a holistic context for the development of Confucian scholarship as a comprehensive inquiry in the humanities.

Tung Chung-shu: The Confucian Visionary

Like the Grand Historian, Tung Chung-shu (c. 179–104 B.C.) also took the *Spring and Autumn Annals* absolutely seriously. However, his own work, *Luxuriant Gems of the Spring and Autumn Annals* is far from being a book of historical judgment. It is a metaphysical treatise in the spirit of the *Book of Changes.* A man extraordinarily dedicated to learning (he is said to have been so absorbed in his studies that for three years he did not even glance at the garden in front of him and with a strong commitment to moral idealism (one of his often-quoted dicta is "rectifying rightness without scheming for profit; enlightening his Way without calculating efficaciousness"), Tung was instrumental in developing a characteristically Han interpretation of the Confucian project.

Despite the Martial Emperor's pronouncement that Confucianism alone would receive imperial sponsorship, Taoist, yin-yang cosmologists, Moists, Legalists, shamanists, seances, healers, magicians, geomancers, and others all contributed to the cosmological thinking of the Han cultural elite. Indeed, Tung himself was a beneficiary of this intellectual syncretism, for he freely tapped the spiritual resources of his time in formulating his own worldview. His theory of the correspondence between man and nature, which involves a forced analogy of the four seasons, twelve months, and 366 days in a year to the four limbs, twelve sections (three in each limb), and 366 bones in the human body, is predicated on an organismic vision in which all modalities of being are interconnected in a complex network of relationships. The moral to draw from this metaphysics of consanguinity is that human actions have cosmic consequences.

Tung's inquiries on the meaning of the "Five Agents" (metal, wood, water, fire, and earth), the correspondence of man and the numerical categories of Heaven, and the sympathetic activation of things of the same kind, as well as his studies of cardinal Confucian values such as humanity, rightness, ritual, wisdom, and trustworthiness enabled him to develop an elaborate worldview integrating Confucian ethics with naturalistic cosmology. What Tung accomplished was not merely a "theological" justification for the emperor as the "Son of Heaven." Rather, his theory of mutual responsiveness between heaven and man provided the Confucian scholars with a higher law to judge the conduct of the ruler. As a matter of fact, his rhetoric of "portents of catastrophes and anomalies" specified that floods, droughts, earthquakes, comets, eclipses, and even benign but unusual natural phenomena such as "growing beards on women" are celestial signs warning against man's wicked deeds. Later these acted as an effective deterrent to the whims and excesses of the monarchs. Tung offered the Confucian intellectuals an interpretive power with far-reaching political implications.

Tung's mode of thought reflects the scholarly penchant for prognostication, divination, and numerological speculation prevalent during his time. Known as adherents of the "New Texts" school, these scholars, basing their arguments on the reconstructed classical texts written in the "new script" of the Han, were intensely interested in exploring the "subtle words and great meanings" of the classics in influencing politics. The Usurpation of Wang Wang (9–23) was in part occasioned by the popular demand of the Confucian literati that a change in the Mandate of Heaven was inevitable. Despite Tung's immense popularity, his worldview was not universally accepted by Han Confucian scholars. A reaction in favor of a more rational and moralistic approach to the Confucian classics, known as the "Old Text" school, had already set in before the fall of Western Han. Yang Hsiung (c. 53 B.C.–A.D. 18), in *Model Sayings,* a collection of moralistic aphorisms in the style of the *Analects,* and the *Classic of the Great Mystery,* a cosmological speculative in the style of the *Book of Changes,* presented an alternative worldview. This school, claiming its own recensions of authentic classical texts allegedly rediscovered during the Han period and written in an "old" script before the Ch'in unification, was widely accepted in the Easter Han (25–220). As the institutions of the Erudites and the imperial university expanded in the Eastern Han, the study of university expanded in the Eastern Han, the study of the classics became more refined and elaborate. Confucian scholasticism, like its counterparts in Talmudic and biblical studies, became too professionalized to remain a vital intellectual force.

Yet Confucian ethics exerted great influence on government, schools, and society at large. Toward the end of the Han, as many as 30,000 students attended the imperial university. All public schools throughout the land offered regular sacrifices to Confucius and he virtually became the patron saint of education. Many Confucian temples were also being built. The imperial courts continued to honor Confucius from age to age; a Confucian temple eventually stood in every one of the 2,000 counties. As a result, the teacher, together with Heaven, Earth, the emperor, and parents, became one of the most respected authorities in traditional China.

Confucian Ethics in the Taoist and Buddhist Context

Incompetent rulership, faction-ridden bureaucracy, a mismanaged tax structure, and the domination of eunuch power toward the end of the Eastern Han, first prompted widespread protests by the imperial university students. The high-handed policy of the court in imprisoning and killing thousands of them and their official sympathizers in 169 may have put a temporary stop the intellectual revolt, but the downward economic spiral made the peasant's life unbearable. A peasant rebellion, led by Confucian scholars and by Taoist religious leaders of faith-healing sects, combined with open insurrections of the military to bring down the Han dynasty and thus put an end to the first Chinese empire. With the breakdown of the imperial Han system, not unlike the decline and fall of the Roman empire, "barbarians" invaded from the north. The northern China plains were fought over, despoiled, and controlled by rival "barbarian" tribes, and a succession of states was established in the South. This period of disunity, from the early third to the late sixth century, marked the decline of Confucianism, the rise of Neo-Taoism, and the spread of Buddhism.

The prominence of the Taoist and Buddhist persuasions among the cultural elite and the populace in general, however, did not mean that the Confucian tradition had disappeared. In fact, Confucian ethics was by then virtually inseparable from the moral fabric of Chinese society. Confucius continued to be universally honored as the paradigmatic sage. The outstanding Taoist thinker, Wang Pi (226–249), argued that Confucius, by not speculating on the nature of the Tao, had a superior experiential understanding of it than Lao Tzu did. The Confucian classics remained the foundation of all literate culture and sophisticated commentaries were being produced throughout the age. Confucian values continued to dominate in such political institutions as the central bureaucracy, the recruitment of officials, and local governance. The political forms of life were distinctively Confucian too. When a "barbarian" state adopted a Sinicization policy, notably the case of the Northern Wei (386–535), it was by and large Confucian in character. In the South, systematic attempts were made to strengthen family ties by establishing clan rules, genealogical trees, and ancestral rituals based on Confucian ethics.

The reunification of China by the Sui (581–618) and the restoration of lasting peace and prosperity by the T'ang (618–907) gave a powerful stimulus to the revival of Confucian learning. The publication of a definitive, official edition of the Five Classics with elaborate commentaries and subcommentaries, and the implementation of Confucian rituals at all levels of governmental practice, including the compilation of the famous T'ang legal code, were two outstanding examples of Confucianism in practice. An examination system was established based on literary competence. It made the mastery of Confucian classics a prerequisite for political success and was, therefore, perhaps the single most important institutional innovation in defining elite culture in Confucian terms.

Nevertheless, the intellectual and spiritual scene of the T'ang was dominated by Buddhism and, to a lesser degree, by Taoism. The philosophical originality of the dynasty was mainly represented by monk-scholars such as Chi-tsang (549–623), Hsuan-tsang (596–664), and Chih-i (538–597). An unintended consequence in the development of Confucian thought in this context was the prominent rise of some of the metaphysically significant Confucian texts, notably *Chung-yung (Doctrine of the Mean)* and *I-chuan (The Great Commentary of the Book of Changes)*, which appealed to some Buddhist and Taoist thinkers. A sign of a possible Confucian turn in the T'ang was Li Ao's (died c. 844) essay on "Returning to Nature," which foreshadowed some salient features of Sung (960–1279) Confucian thought. However, the most influential precursor of a Confucian revival was Han Yu (768–824). A great essayist, he attacked Buddhism from the perspectives of social ethics and cultural identity with telling effectiveness. He discussed and provoked interest in the question of what actually constitutes the Confucian Way. The issue of *Tao-t'ung,* the transmission of the Way or the authentic method to repossess the Way, has stimulated much discussion in the Confucian tradition since the eleventh century.

The Confucian Revival

The Buddhist conquest of China and the Chinese transformation of Buddhism, a process of the introduction, domestication, growth, and appropriation of a distinctly Indian form of spirituality, lasted for at least six centuries. Since Buddhist ideas were introduced to China via Taoist categories and since the development of the Taoist religion benefited by modelling itself on Buddhist institutions and practices, the spiritual dynamics in medieval China was characterized by Buddhist and Taoist values. Against this background, the reemergence of Confucianism as the leading intellectual force involved both a creative response to the Buddhist and Taoist challenge and an imaginative reappropriation of classical Confucian insights. Furthermore, after the collapse of the T'ang empire, the grave threats to the survival of Chinese culture from the Khitans, the Jurchens, and later the Mongols prompted the literati to protect their common heritage by deepening their communal critical self-awareness. To enrich their personal knowledge as well as to preserve China as a civilization-state, they explored the symbolic and spiritual resources that made Confucianism a living tradition.

The Sung Masters

The Sung dynasty (960–1279) was militarily weak and substantially smaller than the T'ang in size, but its cultural splendor and economic prosperity were unprecedented in human history. The Sung "commercial revolution" produced social patterns including flourishing markets, densely populated urban centers, elaborate communication networks, theatrical performances, literary groups, and popular religions that remained in many ways unchanged into the nineteenth century. Technological advances in agriculture, textiles, lacquer, porcelain, printing, maritime trade, and weaponry demonstrated that China excelled not only in the fine arts but also in the hard sciences. The decline of the aristocracy, the widespread availability of printed books, the democratization of education, and the full implementation of the examination system produced the gentry—a new social class noted for its literary proficiency, social consciousness, and political participation. The outstanding members of this class, such as the classicists Hu Yuan (993–1059) and Sun Fu (992–1057), the reformers Fan Chung-yen (989–1052) and Wang Anshih (1021–86), the writer-officials Ou Yang-hsiu (1007–72) and Su Shih (1036–1101), and the statesman-historian Ssu-ma Kuang (1018–86) contributed to the revival of the Confucian persuasion in education, politics, literature, and history, and collectively to the development of a literati style, a way of life informed by Confucian ethics.

Nevertheless, the Confucian revival, understood in traditional historiography as the establishment of the lineage of the "Learning of the Tao" (Tao-hsueh), is traced through a line of thinkers from Chou Tun-i (1017–73) by way of Shao Yung (1011–77), Chang Tsai (1020–77), Ch'eng Hao (1032–85), Ch'eng I (1033–1107), and finally to the great synthesizer Chu Hsi (1130–1200). These thinkers developed an inclusive humanist vision that integrated personal self-cultivation with social ethics and moral metaphysics in a holistic philosophy of life. In the eyes of the Sung literati, this new philosophy authentically reanimated the classical Confucian insights and successfully applied them to the concerns of their own age.

Chou Tun-i ingeniously articulated the relationship between the "great transformation" of the cosmos and the moral development of the person. In his metaphysics, humanity, as the recipient of the highest excellence from Heaven, is itself a center of "anthropocosmic" creativity. He developed this all-embracing humanism by a thought-provoking interpretation of the Taoist diagram of the Great Ultimate *(t'ai-chi)*. Shao Yung further elaborated on the metaphysical basis of human affairs insisting that a disinterested numerological mode of analysis was most appropriate for understanding the "supreme principles governing the world." Chang Tsai, on the other hand, focused his attention on the omnipresence of the "vital energy" *(ch'i)*. He also advocated the oneness of principle *(li)*, comparable to the idea of natural law, and the multiplicity of its manifestations while the principle expresses itself through the "vital energy." As an article of faith, he pronounced in the *Western Inscription:* "Heaven is my father and Earth is my mother, and even such a small being as I finds a central abode in their midst. Therefore that which fills the universe I regard as my body and that which directs the universe I consider as my nature. All people are my brothers and sisters, and all things are my companion."

This theme of mutuality between Heaven and man (in the gender-neutral sense), consanguinity between man and man, and harmony between man and nature was brought to fruition in Ch'eng Hao's definition of humanity as "forming one body with all things." To him, the presence of the Heavenly Principle *(T'ien-li)* in all things as well as in human nature enables the human mind to purify itself in a spirit of reverence. Ch'eng I, following his brother's lead, formulated the famous dictum: "Self-cultivation requires reverence; the extension of knowledge consists in the investigation of things." However, by making special reference to the "investigation of things" *(ko-wu)*, he raised doubts about the appropriateness of focusing exclusively on the inner illumination of the mind in Confucian self-cultivation, as his brother seemed to have done. The school of the Mind as advocated by Ch'eng Hao and the school of the Heavenly Principle as advocated by Ch'eng I became two distinct modes of thought in Sung Confucianism.

Chu Hsi, clearly following Ch'eng I's School of Principle and implicitly rejected Ch'eng Hao's School of Mind, developed a pattern of interpreting and transmitting the Confucian Way that for centuries defined the Confucian project not only for the Chinese but for the Koreans and the Japanese as well. If, as quite a few scholars have maintained, Confucianism symbolizes a distinct form of East Asian spirituality, it is the Confucianism shaped by Chu Hsi. Master Chu virtually reconstituted the Confucian tradition giving it new meaning, new structure, and new texture. He was more than a synthesizer; through conscientious appropriation and systematic interpretation, he gave rise to a new Confucianism, known as Neo-Confucianism in the West, but often referred to as the School of the Heavenly Principle *(Li-hsueh)* in modern China.

"The Doctrine of the Mean" and "The Great Learning," two chapters in the *Book of Rites* had become independent treatises and, together with the *Analects* and *Mencius,* had been included in the core curriculum of Confucian education for centuries before Chu Hsi's birth. However, by putting them in a particular sequence, *The Great Learning,* the *Analects, Mencius,* and *The Doctrine of the Mean,* synthesizing their commentaries, interpreting them as a coherent humanistic vision, and calling them the four books, Master Chu fundamentally restructured the priority of the Confucian scriptural tradition by placing the Four Books above the Five Classics. The Four Books became the central texts for both primary education and civil service examinations in traditional China from the fourteenth century on. Thus, they have exerted far greater influence on Chinese life and thought in the last six hundred years than any other book.

As an interpreter and transmitter of the Confucian Way, Chu Hsi identified which early Sung masters, both as his own spiritual fathers and as true bearers of the sagely teaching, rightly belonged to the authentic lineage of Confucius and Mencius. His judgment, later widely accepted by governments in East Asia, was based principally on philosophical insight. Chou Tun-i, Chang Tsai, and the Ch'eng brothers, the select four, were Chu Hsi's cultural heroes. Shao Yung and Ssu-ma were originally on this august list, but Chu Hsi apparently changed his mind, perhaps because of Shao's excessive metaphysical speculation and Ssu-ma's obsession with historical facts.

Up until Chu Hsi's time, the Confucian thinking of the Snug masters was characterized by a few fruitfully ambiguous concepts, notably the Great Ultimate, the Heavenly principle, vital energy, nature, mind, and humanity. Master Chu defined the process of the "investigation of things" as a rigorous discipline of the mind to probe the underlying principle in things so that vital energy can be transformed, and enlightened humanity (as manifestation of nature and the Great Ultimate) realized. Accordingly, he recommended a twofold method of study: to cultivate a sense of reverence and to pursue extensive knowledge. This combination of morality and wisdom make his pedagogy an inclusive approach to humanist education. Reading books, sitting quietly, practicing rituals, physical exercise, calligraphy, arithmetic, and empirical observation all have a place in his pedagogical program. Chu Hsi reestablished the White Deer Grotto in present Kiangsi as an academy. It became the intellectual center of his age and provided an instructional model for all schools in East Asia for generations to come.

Chu Hsi was considered the preeminent Confucian scholar in Sung China, but his interpretation of the Confucian Way was seriously challenged by his contemporary, Lu Hsiang-shan (Chiu-yuan, 1139–93). Claiming that he appropriated the true wisdom of Confucian teaching by reading Mencius, Lu criticized Chu Hsi's theory of the "investigation of things" as a form of fragmented and ineffective empiricism. Instead, he advocated a return to Mencian moral idealism by insisting that establishing the "great body" is the primary precondition for self-realization. To him, the cultivation of the mind as a quest for self-knowledge provided the basis upon which the investigation of things assumed its proper significance. Lu's face-to-face confrontation with Master Chu in the famous meeting at the Goose Lake Temple in 1175 further convinced him that the Confucian project as Chu Hsi had shaped it was not Mencian. Although Lu's challenge remained a minority position for some time, his School of the Mind later became a major intellectual force in Ming China (1368–1644) and Tokugawa Japan (1600–1867).

Confucian Learning in Chim, Yuan, and Ming

For approximately 150 years, from the time the Sung court moved its capital to the South and reestablished itself there in 1127, northern China was ruled by three conquest dynasties, Liao (947–1125), Hsi-hsia (990–1227), and Chin (1115–1234). Although the bureaucracies and political cultures of both Liao and Hsi-hsia were under Confucian influence, no discernible intellectual developments helped to further the Confucian tradition there. The situation in the Jurchen Chin dynasty was entirely different. Despite the paucity of information about the Confucian renaissance in the Southern Sung, the Chin scholar-officials continued the classical, artistic, literary, and historiographic traditions of the North and developed a richly textured cultural form of their own. Chao Ping-wen's (1159–1232) combination of literary talent and moral concerns and Wang Jo-hsu's (1172–1248) productive scholarship in classics and history, as depicted in Yuan Hao-wen's (1190–1259) biographic sketches and preserved in their collected works, compared well with the high standards set by their counterparts in the South.

As the Mongols reunited China in 1279, the intellectual dynamism of the south profoundly affected the northern style of scholarship. The harsh treatment of scholars by the conquest Yuan (Mongol) dynasty (1271–1368) seriously damaged the well-being of the scholarly community and the prestige of the scholar-official class. Nevertheless, outstanding Confucian thinkers emerged throughout the period. Some opted to purify themselves so that they could repossess the Way for the future; some decided to engage themselves in politics to put their teaching into practice.

Hsu Heng (1209–1281) took the practical approach. Appointed by Khubilai, the Great Khan in *Marco Polo's Description of the World,* as the president of the Imperial Academy and respected as the leading scholar in the court, Hsu conscientiously and meticulously introduced Chu Hsi's teaching to the Mongols. He assumed personal responsibility for educating the sons of Mongol nobility to become qualified teachers of Confucian classics. His erudition and skills in medicine, legal affairs, irrigation, military science, arithmetic,

and astronomy enabled him to function as an informed adviser to the conquering dynasty. He set the tone for the eventual success of the Confucianization of
separate of Yuan bureaucracy. In fact, it was the Yuan court that first officially
adopted the Four Books as the basis of the civil service examination, a practice
that was religiously observed until 1905. Thanks to Hsu Heng, Chu Hsi's teaching prevailed in the Mongol conquest, but the shape of the Confucian project
envisioned by Master Chu was significantly simplified.

The hermit-scholar Liu Yin (1249–93), on the other hand, allegedly
refused Khubilai's summons in order to maintain the dignity of the Confucian
Way. To him, education was for self-realization. Loyal to the Chin culture in
which he was reared and faithful to the Confucian Way that he had learned
from the Sung masters, Liu Yin rigorously applied philological methods to
classical studies and strongly advocated the importance of history. Although,
true to Chu Hsi's spirit, he took seriously the idea of the investigation of
things, he put a great deal of emphasis on the cultivation of the mind. Liu Yin's
contemporary, Wu Cheng (1249–1333), further developed the School of the
Mind. He fully acknowledged the contribution of Lu Hsiang-shan to the
Confucian tradition, even though as an admirer of Hsu Heng he considered
himself a follower of Chu Hsi. Wu assigned himself the challenging task of
harmonizing the difference between Chu and Lu. As a result, he reoriented
Chu's balanced approach to morality and wisdom to accommodate Lu's existential concern for self-knowledge. This prepared the way for the revival of
Lu's School of the Mind in the Ming (1368–1644).

The thought of the first outstanding Ming Confucian scholar, Hsueh
Hsuan (1389–1464), revealed the turn toward moral subjectivity. Although a
devoted follower of Chu Hsi, Hsueh's *Records of Reading* clearly shows that he
considered the cultivation of "mind and nature" to be particularly important.
Two other early Ming scholars, Wu Yu-pi (1391–1469) and Ch'en Hsien-
chang (1428–1500) helped to define Confucian education for those who
studied the classics not simply as preparing for examinations but as cultivating
the "body and mind." They cleared the way for Wang Yang-ming (1472–1529),
the most influential Confucian thinker after Chu Hsi.

Wang Yang-ming allied himself with Lu Hsiang-shan's learning of the
mind as a critique of excessive attention to philological details characteristic
of Chu Hsi's followers. He advocated the precept of "uniting thought and
action." By focusing on the transformative power of the will, he inspired a
whole generation of Confucian students to return to the moral idealism of
Mencius. His own personal example of combining teaching with bureaucratic
routine, administrative responsibility, and leadership in military campaigns
demonstrated that he was a man of deeds. Yet, despite his competence in
practical affairs, his primary concern was moral education, which he felt had
to be grounded on the "original substance" of the mind. He later identified

this as the "good conscience" *(liang-chih)*, a primordial existential awareness that every human being possesses. He further suggested that "good conscience," as the Heavenly Principle, underlies all beings from the highest forms of spirituality to grass, wood, brings, and stone. Because the universe consists of vital energy informed by "good conscience," it is dynamic process rather than a static structure. Human beings must learn to regard Heaven and Earth and the myriad things as one body by extending their good conscience to embrace an ever-expanding network of relationships.

Wang Yang-ming's "dynamic idealism," as Wing-tsit Chan characterizes it, set the Confucian agenda for several generations in China. His followers, such as the conscientious communitarian Wang Chi (1497–1582), who devoted his long life to building a community of the like-minded, and the radical individualist Li Chih (1527–1602), who proposed to reduce all human relationships to friendship, broadened the Confucian project to accommodate a variety of lifestyles. Among Wang's critics, Liu Tsung-chou (1578–1645) was the most brilliant. His *Human Schemata (Jen-p'u)* offers a rigorous phenomenological description of human mistakes as a corrective to Wang Yang-ming's moral optimism. Liu's student Huang Tsung-hsi (1610–95), compiled a comprehensive biographic history of Ming Confucians based on Liu's writings. One of Huang's contemporaries, Ku Yen-wu (1613–82) was also a critic of Wang Yang-ming. He excelled in his studies of political institutions, ancient phonology, and classical philology. While Ku was well-known in his time and honored as the patron saint of "evidential learning" in the eighteenth century, his contemporary, Wang Fu-chih (1619–92), was discovered two hundred years later as one of the most sophisticated original minds in the history of Confucian thought. His extensive writings on metaphysics, history, and the classics made him one of the most thorough critics of Wang Yang-ming and his followers.

The Age of the Confucian Persuasion: Chosŏn Dynasty Korea, Tokugawa Japan, and Ch'ing China

Among all the dynasties, Chinese and foreign, the long-lived Chosŏn (Yi) in Korea (1392–1910) was undoubtedly the most thoroughly Confucianized. Since the fifteenth century when the aristocracy *(yangban)* defined itself as the carrier of Confucian values, the penetration of Confucian persuasion in court politics and in elite culture has been unprecedented. To this date, as manifested in political behavior, legal practice, ancestral veneration, genealogy, village schools, and student activism, Confucian tradition's vitality is widely felt in South Korea.

The single most important Korean Confucian, Yi T'oegye (1501–70), helped shape the particular character of Chosŏn Confucianism through his creative interpretation of Chu Hsi's teaching. Critically aware of the philosophical turn engineered by Wang Yang-ming, T'oegye transmitted the Chu Hsi legacy as a response to the advocates of the School of the Mind. As a result, he made Chosŏn Confucianism at least as much a true heir to Sung learning as Ming Confucianism was. Indeed, his *Discourse of the Ten Sagely Diagrams,* as an instructional aid for educating the king, offers a succinct depiction of all the major concepts in Sung learning. His exchange of letters with Ki Taesung (1527–72) in the famous Four-Seven debate, which discussed the relationship between Mencius's *four* basic human feelings, that is, commiseration, shame, modesty, and right and wrong, and the *seven* emotions such as anger and joy, raised the level of Confucian dialogue to a new height in intellectual sophistication. Yi Yulgok's (1536–84) challenge to T'oegye's representation of Chu Hsi's Confucian project, from the perspective of Master Chu's thought itself, significantly enriched the repertoire of the Learning of the Principle. The leadership of the central government combined with the numerous academies set up by the aristocratic families and institutions such as the community compact system and the village schools, made the Learning of the Heavenly Principle not only a political ideology but also a common creed in Korea (see chapter 4 below).

Chu Hsi's teaching, as interpreted by T'oegye, was introduced to Yamazaki Ansai (1618–82) in Japan. A distinctive feature of Yamazaki's thought was his representation of native Shintoism in Confucian terminology. The diversity and vitality of Japanese Confucianism was further evidenced in the appropriation of Wang Yang-ming's dynamic idealism by the Samurai-scholars, notably Kumazawa Banzan (1619–91). However, it is in Ogyu Sorai's (1666–1728) determination to return to its pre-Confucian sources to rediscover the original basis of Confucian teaching that one finds a true exemplification of independent-mindedness of Japanese Confucians. Indeed, Ogyu's brand of "ancient learning" with particular emphasis on philological exactitude foreshadowed a similar scholarly movement in China by at least a generation. Although Tokugawa Japan was never as Confucianized as Yi Korea had been, virtually every educated person in Japanese society was exposed to the Four Books by the end of the seventeenth century (see chapter 6).

The Confucianization of Chinese society reached its apex during the Ch'ing (1644–1912) when China was again ruled by a conquest (Manchu) dynasty. The Ch'ing emperors outshone their counterparts in the Ming by presenting themselves as exemplars of Confucian kingship. They consciously and ingeniously transformed Confucian teaching into a political ideology, indeed a mechanism of symbolic control. Jealously guarding their imperial prerogatives as the ultimate interpreters of Confucian truth, they substantially undermined the ability of the scholars to transmit the Confucian Way by imposing harsh measures, such as literary inquisition. Understandably, Ku Yen-wu's classical scholarship, rather than his insights on political reform, inspired the eighteenth-century evidential scholars. Tai Chen (1130–1200), the most philosophically minded philologist among them, couched his brilliant critique of Sung learning in his commentary on the "The Meanings of the Terms in the *Book of Mencius.*" Tai Chen was one of the eminent scholars appointed by the Ch'ien-lung emperor in 1173 to compile an imperial manuscript library. This massive scholarly attempt, *The Complete Library of the Four Treasures,* symbolized the grandiose design of the Manchu court to give an account of all the important works of the four branches of learning—the classics, history, philosophy, and literature—in Confucian culture. The project comprised more than 36,000 volumes with comments on about 10,230 titles, employed as many as 15,000 copyists and lasted for twenty years. Ch'ien-lung and the learned scholars around him may have enclosed their cultural heritage in a definitive form, but the Confucian tradition was yet to encounter its most serious threat.

Modern Transformation

At the time of the Opium War (1839–42), East Asian societies had been Confucianized for centuries. The continuous growth of Mahayana Buddhism throughout Asia and the presence of Taoism in China, shamanism in Korea, and Shintoism in Japan did not at all undermine the power of Confucian influence in government, education, family rituals, and social ethics. In fact, Buddhist monks were often messengers of Confucian values, and the coexistence of Confucianism with Taoism, shamanism, and Shintoism actually characterized the syncretic East Asian religious life. The impact of the West, however, like the combination of the Mongol military conquest and the age-long Buddhist influence compressed into one generation, has so fundamentally undermined the Confucian roots in East Asia that it is widely debated whether or not Confucianism can remain a viable tradition in modern times.

The gradual erosion of the Chinese intellectual's faith in the ability of Confucian culture to withstand the impact of the West may be witnessed in Lin Tse-hsu's (1785–1850) moral indignation against the British, followed by Tseng Kuo-fan's (1811–72) pragmatic acceptance of the superiority of Western technology, K'ang Yu-wei's (1858–1927) sweeping recommendation for political reform, and Chang Chih-tung's (1837–1909) desperate eclectic attempt to save the essence of Confucian learning, which eventually led to the anti-Confucian iconoclasm of the so-called May Fourth movement (1919). The triumph of Marxism-Leninism as the official ideology of the People's Republic of China (1949) relegated the Confucian rhetoric to the background.

Nevertheless, the modern Chinese intelligentsia has maintained unac-
knowledged, sometimes unconscious, continuities with the Confucian tradition at every level of life: behavior, attitude, belief, and commitment. Indeed,
Confucianism is still an integral part of the "psychocultural construct" of the
contemporary Chinese intellectual as well as the Chinese peasant.

The rise of Japan and other newly industrialized Asian countries (South
Korea, Taiwan, Hong Kong, and Singapore) as the most dynamic region of
sustained economic development since the Second World War has generated
much scholarly interest. Labelled the "Sinic World in Perspective," "The Second
Case of Industrial Capitalism," the "Eastasia Edge," or "the Challenge of the Post-
Confucian States," this phenomenon raises intriguing questions about how the
typical East Asian institutions still laden with Confucian values, such as paternalistic government, an educational system based on competitive examinations, the
family with emphasis on loyalty and cooperation, and local organization informed
by consensus have adapted themselves to the imperatives of modernization.

Some of the most creative and influential intellectuals in contemporary
China have continued to think in Confucian terms. Hsiung Shih-li's ontologi-
cal reflection Liang Shu-ming's cultural analysis, Fung Yu-lan's reconstruction
of the Learning of the Principle, Ho Lin's new interpretation of the Learning
of the Mind, T'ang Chun-i's philosophy of culture, Hsu Fu-kuan's social criticism, and Mou Tsung-san's moral metaphysics are noteworthy examples. To be
sure, articulate young intellectuals in the People's Republic of China today are
criticizing their Confucian heritage as the embodiment of authoritarianism,
bureaucratism, nepotism, conservatism, and male chauvinism, but the establishment of the Confucian Foundation, the publication of *Confucian Studies,* and
the concerted effort to rebuild Confucius's birthplace, Qufu, into a "holy land"
clearly indicate that a revival of Confucian studies is under way. Indeed, some
of the most seminal minds in mainland China, Taiwan, Hong Kong, Singapore,
and North America have persuasively articulated the relevance of Confucian
humanism to mainland China's modernization. The upsurge of interest in
Confucian studies in South Korea, Taiwan, Hong Kong, and Singapore for the
last four decades has generated a new dynamism in the Confucian tradition,
though Confucian scholarship in Japan remains unrivaled. Confucian thinkers
in the West, inspired by religious pluralism and liberal democratic ideas, have
begun to explore the authentic possibility of a "third epoch" of Confucian
humanism, signifying that its modern transformation, as a creative response to
the challenge of the West, is a continuation of its classical formulation in the
times of Confucius, Mencius, and Hsun Tzu and its medieval elaboration
represented by Chu Hsi, Wang Yang-ming, Yi T'oegye, and Yamazaki Ansai. The
new Confucian humanism, though rooted in the East, draws its nourishment
from the West as well as from Asia.

References

(1960). *The Chinese Classics.*

(1962). *Confucian Personalities.*

(1966). *Confucianism in Action.*

(1966). *Reflections on Things at Hand.*

(1967). *The I Ching.*

(1975). *Self and Society in Ming Thought.*

(1975). *The Unfolding of Neo-Confucianism.*

(1979). *Principle and Practicality: Essays in Neo-Confucianism and Practical Learning.*

(1982). *Yuan Thought: Chinese Thought and Religion under the Mongols.*

(1985). *The Rise of Neo-Confucianism in Korea.*

(1986). *Instructions for Practical Living and Other Neo-Confucian Writings* by Wan Yang-ming.

Alitto, G. S. (1979). *The Last Confucian: Liang Shu-ming and the Chinese Dilemma of Modernity.*

Bonner, J. (1986). *Wang Kuo-wei: An Intellectual Biography.*

Ch'i-yun, C. (1975). *Hsun Yueh: The Life and Reflection of an Early Medieval Confucian.*

Ch'ien, E. T. (1986). *Chiao Hung and the Restructuring of Neo-Confucianism in the Late Ming.*

Chan, W. ([1953] 1969). *Religious Trends in Modern China.*

————. (1969a). *An Outline and Annotate Bibliography of Chinese Philosophy* (revised ed.).

————. (1969b). *Source Book in Chinese Philosophy.*

————. (1986). *Chus Hsi and Neo-Confucianism.*

————. (1971). *Liang Ch'i-ch'ao and the Intellectual Transition in China, 1890–1907.*

————. (1987). *Chinese Intellectuals in Crisis: Search for Order and Meaning, 1890–1911.*

Ching, J. (1976). *To Acquire Wisdom: The Way of Wang Yang-ming.*

————. (1977). *Confucianism and Christianity.*

Confucius. (1979). *Analects.* Penguin.

Creel, H. G. (1960). *Confucius and the Chinese Way.*

Dardess, J. W. (1983). *Confucianism and Autocracy: Professional Elites in the Founding of the Ming Dynasty.*

de Bary, W. T. (1981). *Neo-Confucian Orthodoxy and the Learning of the Mind-and-Heart*.

———. de Bary, W. T. (1983). *The Liberal Tradition in China*.

de Bary, W. T., et. al., eds. (1960). *Sources of Chinese Tradition*.

Dubs, H. (1927). *Hsuntze: The Moulder of Ancient Confucianism*.

Eber, I. (1986). *Confucianism: The Dynamics of a Tradition*.

Egan, S. C. (1987). *A Latterday Confucian: Reminiscences of William Hung, 1893–1980*.

Elman, B. A. (1985). *From Philosophy to Philology*.

Fairbank, J. K. (1957). *Chinese Thought and Institutions*.

Fingarette, H. (1972). *Confucius—The Secular as Sacred*. New York: Harper & Row.

Furth, C. (1976). *The Limits of Change: Essays on Conservative Alternatives in Republican China*.

Gardner, D. K. (1986). *Chu Hsi and the Ta-hsueh: Neo-Confucian Reflection on the Confucian Canon*.

Gernet, J. (1985). *China and the Christian Impact: A Conflict of Cultures*.

Graham, A. C. (1958). *Two Chinese Philosophers: Ch'eng Ming-tao and Ch'eng Yi-ch'uan*.

Kung-ch'uan, H. (1970). *A History of Chinese Political Thought*.

———. (1975). *A Modern China and a New World: K'ang Yu'wei: Reform and Utopian, 1858–1927*.

Levenson, J. R. (1968). *Confucian China and Its Modern Fate: A Trilogy*.

Liu, J. T. C. (1967). *Ou-yang Hsiu: An Eleventh-Century Neo-Confucian*.

Lo, W. W. (1974). *The Life and Thought of Yeh Shih*.

Louie, K. (1981). *Critiques of Confucius in Contemporary China*.

Mencius. (1970). *Mencius*. New York: Penguin.

Metzger, T. A. (1977). *Escape from Predicament: Neo-Confucianism and China's Evolving Political Culture*.

Mote, F. (1971). *Intellectual Foundations of China*.

Mungello, D. E. (1977). *Leibniz and Confucianism: Search for Accord*.

Munro, D. (1969). *The Concept of Man in Early China*.

Needham, J. (1956). *Science and Civilization in China*.

Nivison, D. S. (1966). *The Life and Thought of Chang Hsueh-ch'eng*.

Pound, E. (1959). *The Confucian Odes: The Classical Anthology Defined by Confucius*.

Richards, I. A. (1932). *Mencius on the Mind.*

Schwartz, B. I. *The World of Thought in Ancient China.*

Shryock, J. K. (1966). *The Origin and Development of the State Cult of Confucius.*

Thompson, L. G. (1985). *Chinese Religion in Western Languages: A Comprehensive and Classified Bibliography of Publications in English, French, and German through 1908.*

Tillman, H. C. (1982). *Utilitarian Confucianism: Ch'en Liang's Challenge to Chu Hsi.*

Tsung-hsi, H. (1987). *The Records of Ming Scholars,* ed. Julia Ching.

Tu, W. (1976). *Neo-Confucian Thought in Action: Wang Yang-ming's Youth.*

———. (1979). *Humanity and Self-Cultivation: Essays in Confucian Thought.*

———. (1984). *Confucian Ethics Today: The Singapore Challenge.*

Tung-mei, F. (1981). *Chinese Philosophy: Its Spirit and Its Development.*

Waley, A. (1956). *Three Ways of Thought in Ancient China.*

Weber, M. (1951). *The Religion of China: Confucianism and Taoism.*

Wei-ming, T. (1976). *Centrality and Commonality: An Essay on Chung-yung.*

Wilheim, H. (1977). *Heaven, Earth, and Man in the Book of Changes.*

Wright, A. F. (1953). *Studies in Chinese Thought.*

———. (1960). *The Confucian Persuasion.*

Yu-lan, F. (1952–53). *A History of Chinese Philosophy.*

Yu-shen, L. (1979). *The Crisis of Chinese Consciousness.*

2

Psychocultural Dynamics within the Confucian Family

Walter H. Slote

Whatever its form, the family constitutes the core unit in all societies. The relationship between family and society is reciprocal: given a benign governance, to the extent that the family functions well, the society flourishes, to the extent that the family functions poorly, the society declines. It is around this conviction that this study was organized.[1]

In the investigation of this premise, the Confucian family—a term that shall be used for the sake of brevity and that encompasses family systems in China, Taiwan, Singapore, Vietnam, Korea, and Japan—offers a particularly rich source of data. It will be noted that I have confined my observations to Confucianism. Although all the societies under consideration have socioreligious derivatives in Buddhism, Taoism, various folk religions and, to a lesser extent Christianity, Confucianist values have been integrated within the psychological substructure of the individual to a far greater degree than Taoist and Buddhist values. This holds true for native folk beliefs, a potent force for many, but less applicable to our discussion. In support of this position, de Bary (1988), in his preface to *East Asian Civilizations,* stated, "Taoism and Buddhism . . . had less of a role in defining those institutions and ideas most involved in the civil liberties of East Asia as a whole and their modern transformation [than did Confucianism]." In a similar vein, De Vos (1989) stated, "Confucianism is an ethico-religious tradition that has shaped the culture of China for 2,500 years. Its influence subsequently spread to Korea, Japan, and Vietnam. Although still not directly visible in the social consciousness of modern Japanese, it still profoundly shapes primary family life experiences."

In its traditional format, Confucianism was rigidly authoritarian and bolstered by a social matrix that was essentially totalitarian. As such, the legal (but not the psychological) power of males and rulers approached the absolute. The rights of women and children were minimal, and during various historical periods they were essentially nonexistent. Class structure was rigidly set, and in spite of civil service examinations, which hypothetically were open to all (hypothetically, because only the more affluent had the funds to allow their sons to be economically unproductive during the years required for study), it was exceedingly difficult to transcend class limitations.

The social and political climate of Asia has changed. The future of Confucianism in any approximation to its traditional orthodox form appears very bleak indeed. It was appropriate for its day, but that day is past. However, when we approach the family as an institution, we are still in the midst of a transitional period in East Asia in which Confucian thought, if not ideology, is still extremely influential.

Nevertheless, the Confucian family is gradually modifying and adapting itself to an increasingly egalitarian perspective. Although pockets of relative traditionalism do exist, particularly in the clan villages and lineages in certain parts of Korea and Taiwan, external form and ancient style for the most part have disappeared. However, the substance of Confucianism, particularly in terms of interpersonal relationships and ethical values, is still alive and flourishing. This issue of form versus substance is of great consequence; formal adherence to many Confucian practices may have died out, but core patterns remain and have been effectively maintained, to one degree or another, in all the societies considered in this volume.

The Confucian family traditionally has been defined by its value system: age grading; the generational sequence; the dutiful bonding between parents and siblings; the security brought to its members by a complex but highly effective extended family system; the common core of intensely structured values; an ethical code and a morality widely disseminated and known to all; a role definition in which everyone had a specified assignment; industriousness, discipline, and the elevated position given to learning—all of which are extremely valuable and relevant for modern life. Although designed to ensure family harmony, the implementation of these qualities was far from universally benign, and certain of them posed a pattern of intrapsychic conflict that bears investigation.

Having originated from a common religious and philosophical base, a traditional format, and a stable demographic heritage, it seems reasonable to propose that homologous psychological processes might be found, to one degree or another, in all the societies we are studying. The analysis of certain interpersonal and intrapsychic dimensions would seem to bear this out. This chapter is an attempt to define some of these elements. One caveat: I am aware of the profound differences that exist from culture to culture, society to society, individual to individual. Yet if one searches beneath outward style, certain congruent qualities emerge. Harry Stack Sullivan, a very talented psychoanalyst, long ago observed that we are all more human—and more alike—than not. And those from Confucian societies would seem to be more alike than most.

In a family system that was arbitrary, in which the members were thrust into stereotypic categories that included assignment of status, role, and behavior, and in which individual differences were not only disregarded but were essentially not considered as a viable issue, a core question arises: what held the Confucian family together and what were the internal dynamics, the nature of the interpersonal relationships, and the consequences for society at large.

Power in the Family

Although the gains for those in power and those designated for power were great, the hierarchical social structure was also designed to reward the passive acceptance of the status quo by subordinates. Indeed, there were rewards, minimal though they might have been, on all the steps of the social ladder, primarily in terms of a sense of intrapsychic security through the assurance that one's destiny was determined elsewhere by an all-knowing and benign authority.

Psychologically, authorities were always endowed with a celestial aura, whether it be Confucius, Buddha, Lao-tze, or their image bestowed upon the ruling elite. And inasmuch as the governing structure was always religiopolitical, reciprocally each bolstered the other. Historically, there were occasional revolts against leadership; yet there were never revolts against the system that established and maintained the hierarchical structure and, incidentally, kept those who were oppressed, oppressed.

People always seem to need gods to transcend their own human frailties and offer, in the next world, what cannot be found in this one. The Venerables had the advantage of having been born human and, upon death, having ascended to heavenly status. Thus, not only had they been actual people, fellow humans, demonstrably fallible during their years on earth as were the rest of their fellow mortals, but they also became symbols for the ultimate potential and conceivable achievement of mankind. In that sense, in varying degrees, their mantle fell on all those in authority—emperor, ancestor, father, village elder, and so on.

These were societies based on the image of the ultimate benevolent father: omniscient, omnipotent, and protective; by derivation precisely in the same sense that during certain stages of psychosocial development the child sees the parent as an all-fulfilling and all-powerful godlike figure. Although Confucianism was vague when it came to defining heaven, and Confucius was never addressed as a god, nor did he himself make such claim, there is little doubt that in the minds of the people he was so considered. De Vos (chapter

17) is right when he defines Confucianism as a religion in that it carried the same emotionally expressive propensities as did those religions that are more formalized, with their specific deities and promised eternal rewards.

A more personal factor of Confucianism is that of the inconceivability of alternate possibilities. One tends to view both one's inner and outer worlds within the parameters set by one's own culture. To transcend these limitations, into which we are inculcated from birth, is extremely difficult and rarely achieved. It is particularly so if no other models are available, thus leaving an innovative individual the daunting task of plowing the first furrow. As we are all aware, there are few who have been able to do so, and it is often they who have changed the course of human history. This is especially true for traditional cultures, such as those we are studying, where values were essentially identical and universally maintained, where propriety and an ethical code was precisely defined and rigidly enforced, where deviation was severely punished, and where the rewards for compliance were considerable both in this world and in the next.

These cultural limitations were reinforced by a pattern of child rearing that was essentially the same for all. Not only was there a code of proper conduct that was extensively applied but, especially during the early formative years, all children were socialized in much the same way. Thus the children heard only an echo of themselves in each other and in the parents of their peers. As in all human endeavor, individual differences based upon personality and character applied to all, but the external structure, the defining characteristics of the culture, permitted extremely limited variation.

Not only was the permitted perception of the external world restricted, but so was the way in which the people defined their own particular inner universe and identified themselves (Slote, chapter 16). If all of one's fellows live with identical values, regard life with attitudes that reflect only a prevailing norm, and speak with the same voice, it is exceedingly difficult for most to act, think, and feel otherwise. The content of one's actions, the mode of ideation, and the nature of emotional expression were censored, in fact dictated, by Confucian assignment. To put this in context, it must be realized that all cultures impose this dictum, but few with the stringency that has been exacted here.

It is of particular significance to note that this tendency toward cultural conformity has greatly decreased during the present era and has resulted in a dramatic broadening of perspective within both the individual and the social order—again a reciprocal process.

Mothers and Fathers

Although all Confucian societies are male dominant, within the home it was the mother who was the primary force. It was she who ran the household and brought up the children. Her nurturance, supervision, and sanctioning were daily and continuous. Although the father in East Asian societies had full legal authority, he happily retreated from the fray and was quite content to invade the inner courtyard as infrequently as possible. In general the father was a feared and distant figure who, following the Confucian model set by his own father and his father's father before him, had been admonished to teach, direct, and discipline the children. Displays of affection were permitted toward the little ones, especially the girls—at least until they entered puberty—but not otherwise.

The father was the ultimate disciplinarian, and his discipline could be severe. A Vietnamese informant vividly remembered an elderly father ordering his fifty-year-old son to lie on the floor, arms outstretched, and beating him with a switch. It was a great loss of face for the son, who never forgave his father, and the father was secretly criticized by the other members of the family. But although such action was rare, it was within the authority of the father to do so. At the same time, many of the fathers who followed the traditional role paid a heavy price. For example, as restraints have lessened, fathers in Korea are now increasingly free to care for the children and to be warm and affectionate to them in public. Nevertheless, all my adult male informants, the products of previous generations, carried the image of their fathers as stern and remote, although the women occasionally had warmer memories. Parenthetically, grandfathers are permitted much greater latitude in expressing affection toward their grandchildren. It is common to see them assuming the care of the little ones, walking hand in hand down village lanes, chatting away together and obviously taking great delight in their new-found freedom to be openly affectionate—testimony to the emotional price they paid for the restraints imposed upon them in the past when they were fathers.

All humankind needs love, a primary emotional necessity, and the forced withholding of affection in following their assigned role was a serious sacrifice for the fathers and, of course, for their wives and their children as well. This pattern is scarcely confined to the Confucian societies. I well remember two elite Venezuelan informants, from a previous research project, who had studied in the United States, remarking how impressed they had been to see American fathers playing in the park with their children, and wistfully adding that this never had happened with their fathers. Or my own East-European Jewish grandfather, who, upon the birth of my first child, undertook to instruct me in the proper role of a father. He told me that being a father was very difficult; being a mother was very easy. This was scarcely my notion of parenting, and when I asked why it was so, he answered that a father had to teach and discipline; all the mother had to do was to love. Although he was a stern taskmaster to his children, he spoke to me with sadness.

The primary emotional tie was between mother and son, not husband and wife (Cho, chapter 10), a condition that perpetuated itself from one generation to the next. The mothers turned to the children, especially the sons and in particular the eldest son, for the comfort and devotion that they did not find in the husbands. Although in recent years there are indications of change, it has been slow and the primary relationship between mother and son is still firmly entrenched.

Thus for the son the mother tended to remain the most significant woman throughout life, a classically Oedipal situation. The difference between East and West in this respect is that in the East Asian societies it is culturally supported, maintained, and reinforced; in the West it is not. The result has been that most males, particularly in the past, were not able to replace the mother with a contemporary woman of equivalent significance.

The men were frequently abusive and demeaning toward their wives, diminishing the women's spirit and the vitality and spontaneity of the relationship. In all these societies the men spent a great deal of time in each others' company and turned to prostitutes, extramarital relationships, and entertainers (geisha, *kisang, Chi,* a *dao*) for the emotional and sexual gratification that they could not find—or did not allow themselves to find—with their wives. Most marriages remained distant, formal, and frequently hostile; both parties withdrawn, unfulfilled, and despairing of ever finding the emotional sustenance that every human requires. Psychologically, as difficult as the situation was for the women, it was equally so for the men. A son's tie to his mother, prolonged as it was long past the normal developmental sequence, resulted in a dependency that later, particularly after the mother's death, was transferred to the wife. The catch was that it could not be acknowledged and had to be submerged. The man had a role to play, and it did not include any show of uncertainty and inadequacy. Thus, he was faced with a seminal intrapsychic conflict, one that tended to remain unresolved.

The mothers, in the service of their own unfulfilled needs, were extremely possessive of the children—of all ages—particularly the sons because the daughters married out and essentially were lost to the family, and they could be wondrously innovative in their manipulative devices for retaining control. The one that particularly impressed me, and that was clearly the most effective, was the use of martyrdom. This is an operation that is common to mothers in many cultures, but never have I seen it employed with such finesse, with such vigorous and extraordinarily effective results. When it served the purpose, the mothers portrayed themselves as weak, helpless, bereft of resources, and at the mercy of others. The central issue was suffering, because without pain it would have had no impact. The children were made to feel guilty for their misdeeds—which usually consisted of not doing what their mothers wanted them to do, and inasmuch as the mothers were the primary transmitters of the Confucian code, the restraints upon independence were many. The primary ingredient was power and dominance; the effect was to reduce the child (and husband and whoever else was on the receiving end) to impotence—helpless, frustrated, furious, and floundering. In psychoanalytic terms, it is a castrating maneuver that leaves the child drained and exhausted, and very hesitant to take the mother on again. Thus, its effect was cumulative. The Confucian mother was extremely resourceful in the use of resourcelessness.

Far from being powerless, the women were quite able to exploit the men's weaknesses and express their disapproval through a myriad of strategic devices, not the least of which was persistence. Many were the husbands, who, after being harangued for hours in bed, finally, in desperation, agreed to whatever their wives wanted. Of the more routine forms of disapproval (I submit that haranguing is not universal) coldness, withdrawal, and silence seem to have been particularly effective.

Martyrdom was frequently coupled with another psychological mechanism that I find myself at a loss to define. If the situation was serious enough, the mothers wove a web of accusations and hurt feelings that could escalate until the children were distraught. The mother carved out a position in which she was aggrieved and, ostensibly, completely innocent. Some transgression, either in fact or fantasy, was chosen and magnified to the point where the original issue was often obliterated. There was always a marked paranoid quality to the accusations, but one had the distinct feeling that it was more the exploitation of a self-serving paranoid perception rather than a truly incorporated paranoid reaction, because when the issue was finally resolved—and it was not always in favor of the mother—instant peace reigned, and the issue was dropped. I have always had the sense that it was a conscious device, to be applied or withdrawn at will.

The issue is again power, domination, and the centrality of the mother. I have seen it used only in the most serious situations, such as which of the children the mother will live with after the death of the father, or if a son or daughter appears to be interested in a potential mate of whom the mother disapproves, or an envious wife whose husband relates too closely with a family member with whom she is in competition, proving that it is far from confined solely to offspring. It is particularly difficult for the children to extricate themselves. I have also encountered such maneuvers a number of times both in social situations (in which, fortunately, I was a bystander) and with analytic patients. As I shall indicate later in this volume (chapter 16), one finds, in those growing up in a Confucian culture, an ego structure and self-image that is based upon a concept of the integrated family. One may reject the family, a rare but not unheard-of occurrence, but one never loses the sense of family as the basic unit of which the personal self is but a part. It is a matter of soup versus a slice of pie. In the West, we tend to regard ourselves as one part of a whole, that is, a slice that is related to the other but who maintains his/her individuality; in the East, on a deeply buried unconscious level, one is part of a vast barley or lentil soup in which the ingredients swirl around each other and in which one's identity and sense of self is inextricably established only within the context of the whole. Autonomy, as defined in the West and as a personal, culturally supported goal, is essentially inconceivable for most East Asian societies. The inevitable result is that the family assumes a crucial, life-determining significance. The individual is not an "I," rather he/she is an inextricable part of an encompassing "we."

Shame, a matter of major significance, is a further consideration. In all Confucian societies, the transgression of social mores affects not only the transgressor, but the family as well. Each pays a price. The result is that the burden of proper conduct weighs heavily upon everyone. If one acts improperly, there is collective loss of face: the child because his or her misconduct is not only a personal matter, but reflects upon all; the elders because if a child acts improperly and it becomes public knowledge, they suffer in the eyes of their peers. The implication is that it evidences a parental character flaw: had they been more conscientious, the misbehavior would not have occurred. Thus the child not only carries responsibility for his own behavior, but for family status. Moreover, if the transgression is serious, the shame can extend throughout succeeding generations, cursing the children with a blemished heritage.

Although the family tended to be harmonious on the surface, on a deeper level it was under great strain. There were very few culturally acceptable outlets for the tensions that are present within all families, and that, in the Confucian family, were exacerbated by the defined role behavior that was demanded. The inevitable intrapsychic conflicts had few legitimized modes of expression. One that did exist for the women was found in the mother-in-law/daughter-in-law relationship. The mother-in-law traditionally has been extremely punitive toward her elder son's young wife, who inevitably lived in the parental home. Not only was the daughter-in-law young and undoubtedly more attractive than the mother, but she was also the son's sexual partner and consequently represented a serious threat to the mother's intimacy with her son and to the Oedipal tie. Moreover, the mother's frustrations and suppressed resentment arising from the constraints imposed by her position as a woman and the indignation over her previous treatment at the hands of her own mother-in-law, could legitimately be expressed toward her son's wife. The young wife was consoled by the fact that one day she would be the mother of sons, eventually a mother-in-law, and ultimately a grandmother—the most honored status (and one that carries with it the freedom to act and speak with abandon—frequently very loudly).

Although incest is an absolute taboo in all cultures, it would be quite reasonable to assume that incestuous fantasies, deeply repressed, are relatively frequent among those women who turn to their children for the affection that is not forthcoming from their husbands. I have no direct supporting clinical data from the mothers (nor do I expect to obtain it), but I believe that there would have to be a good many dissociated incestuous fantasies on the part of both mother and son. As for the sons, I have collected dreams, recalled from the adolescent years, that involved a male informant's having sexual intercourse with his mother. Others also admitted to such dreams, but said that they could not recall the content. Furthermore, the famous Chinese ghost stories—very popular among the Chinese and Vietnamese—served as a lascivious stimulant for some very tantalizing sexual imagery. These tales told of a young man's being seduced by an older, beautiful woman who, after a night of exquisite debauchery, revealed herself as a malevolent ghost and killed the dreamer (incest retribution). Again, these repressed incestuous churnings constitute a powerful force in maintaining the tie between mother and son and, therefore, son and family.

Intrafamilial Dissonance

Sibling rivalry and sibling envy was a major factor in the Confucian household, although it was rarely acknowledged and was forcefully disapproved. Divisive as it may have been, it contributed to the preoccupation with the family. A sophisticated American university-educated Korean friend repeatedly referred to the family as an authoritarian unit. She stated "You have to obey the family. It is like a military system. In all the families, after the father dies, the first son has total control. The second son has to obey him even though he may be resentful under the surface. However, he cannot let others know how he feels." Asked if she considered this good or bad, she responded, "I think that is good because there is order in the house."

It most certainly did result in order, but it also resulted in a good deal of suppressed intrafamilial dissonance. Once the mother and father died, the family very often drew far apart, while maintaining proper, but distant, contact. This was particularly common when the family had emigrated and the extended family and community were no longer present to serve as a unifying support system. Under these circumstances, internecine hostilities often broke out into the open and, for a while, open warfare would result. More commonly, the siblings simply drifted apart and reunited primarily on ceremonial occasions, such as death anniversaries.

It was usually the mother, although occasionally the father, who was at the hub of the destructive competition between siblings. On the several occasions where I have seen it played out, the mothers willingly entered the fray, ostensibly as arbitrator and peacemaker but, in fact, primarily acting to exacerbate the issue and to draw the children, both young and adult, closer to them. One dramatic example comes to mind. A younger brother, talented and successful, in a most aggressive manner, challenged his elder brother (ten years his senior) for supremacy in the family, which was Vietnamese. The older brother was my patient. The father had died shortly after arriving in the United States, and the first son had succeeded him as head of the household. What was most impressive in the encounter was not only the amount of open hostility expressed, but that ultimately the issue between the brothers became secondary to a complex joust over which son the mother would support. The conflict resolved itself into who was to be chosen as the favorite child. Each son put great pressure on the mother to decide in his favor, recapitulating a pattern that had been established early on. The mother finally handled it by arranging a secret pact with both sons in which each considered himself the winner. The brothers continued to be estranged, but the mother's dominant position as the central figure in the family was preserved. It is highly unlikely that this issue would have arisen in Vietnam, but in the United States, where sibling autonomy is accepted and hierarchical roles are less supported, it is an increasingly familiar occurrence.

Emotional Suppression

The three predominant psychological processes that derived from Confucian authoritarianism were fear, dependency, and hostility: dependency was built into the hierarchical system, and it was maintained throughout life—there was always someone who was superior, whether through age or position; fear, because it is a universal reaction to authoritarian domination; hostility, primarily in the form of a deep-seated resentment, because we are always resentful of those we fear and upon whom we are dependent. All three emotions were seriously restrictive as long as they remained unresolved, and thus each played a major role in maintaining the stability, although not the integrity, of family and nation.

Of the three, I believe that fear, and here I am specifically referring to fear of authority, has been most significant. It is rarely acknowledged: respect, deference, and submission as responses to authority are euphemistically presented as synonyms and commonly discussed; fear is not. Confucianism was based upon authoritarianism, and filial piety was the principal instrument through which it was established and maintained. Domination, and in this instance absolute domination, is always accompanied by fear on the part of the subordinate. It has been, in fact, the modus through which the Confucian hierarchical relationship was maintained. All who are repressed are fearful of those who repress them. The fact that there were significant compensations for acquiescence does not eliminate the response. Essentially we are dealing with subconscious processes, rarely available to conscious awareness and then only

under unusual provocation. As discussed below, substantive data for this observation is found in the Rorschach and Thematic Apperception Test protocols
(Slote, chapter 16) in which the fear of authority, and in particular the parent,
is clearly defined.

Overt hostility was universally suppressed, subject to cultural restraint
and strong disapproval. A child might be seething inside, but it was forbidden
for him/her to reveal how he felt. Not only was the expression of anger
toward a parent forbidden, but the conscious awareness of hostile impulses was
also stringently prohibited. The source of this was filial piety, which, together
with ancestor worship (Tu, chapter 7; Young, chapter 8; Jordan, chapter 14;
Slote, chapter 16), constituted the central underpinning of the Confucian ethic.
Thus, the dissociation of any awareness of antagonism, either toward or from
the parent, was rigorously enforced from early childhood. I have seen two-
year-olds who could get mad at a stranger (me) but not at their parents, who
were actually responsible for their frustration. Historically, it made for a stable
society; psychologically, it was the source of inner turmoil. With two exceptions, which were hedged and qualified almost to extinction, none of my
informants ever acknowledged any negative feelings toward their mother or
father (expressed more convincingly in regard to the mother). Concomitantly,
the culture demanded that they suppress all memories of anger, in any of its
various forms, on the part of the parent; again most firmly in reference to the
mothers. This was dramatically refuted in the Rorschachs, where parents were
seen as headless pigs attacking each other, bleeding lions battling, dangerous,
malevolent, and punitive—all manifestations of the unconscious, diametrically
opposite to the way they were consciously perceived. The result was that much
of the hostility toward the parent, which could not be admitted into consciousness, was both internalized and displaced on to the husbands, wives,
children, and select others. On a number of the occasions where I have seen
it expressed, it has taken the form of what I can only describe as murderous
rage. The fury and hatred that poured forth was impressive. These occurrences
were not common, but neither were they rare. Considering the cultural taboo
on overt animosity, the intensity with which it was expressed on these occasions leads one to hypothesize that the degree of suppression and the degree
of expression are linked—scarcely an uncommon phenomenon. Yet, divisive as
it may have been, it contributed to a preoccupation with the family and
therefore constituted a significant tie.

Childhood Transitions

Children in Confucian families—all Confucian families—were expelled
from the womb not once, but twice. The first at birth, the second at 6 to 7

years of age. The timing of the second varied depending upon the society, but the issue was universal.

In the vanity that is the province of males everywhere, the Confucian men consoled themselves with the belief that they were the center of the home. Although this position was supported by legend, poetry, and the sayings of the sages, it was not true: it was the children who were the primary focus and who received the greatest attention. Throughout infancy and childhood they were adored, fussed over, and cherished. Their needs were instantly responded to and, depending upon mothers' level of exhaustion and periodic impatience, usually with good humor. The quality of the mothering was impressive. The mothers clearly found their role satisfying. The young children were rarely spoken to harshly and there seemed to be a minimum of irritability and other forms of hostility expressed. Mothers seldom worked outside the home, and the mothering role was one that was highly esteemed and approved by the community.

The nature and manner of child rearing varied from society to society—for example, there were observable differences between the permissible behavior set by Japanese mothers and Korean mothers—but the primary proposition holds. There were remarkably few limits placed upon the children. When questioned, the parents explained that the young ones were not yet capable of "thinking" and therefore they could not be expected to understand discipline. In short, during the early years, restraints of any sort were minimal, and discipline was rare and muted when it did occur.

Example 1: On the broad unpaved lane in front of our *yogwan* (native inn) near Pusan in Korea is a mother, her six-year old son, and her eighteen- or twenty-month-old toddler. Mother wants to go to the right where shops abound; youngster wants to go to the left where there are interesting trees and bushes. Baby goes left; mommy indicates right. Baby insists on left. Mommy, instead of becoming adamant, starts playing a running game with her recalcitrant little one. Older brother joins in and begins to corral little brother. Peals of laughter. Everybody running around. Little one acquiesces—happily.

Example 2: I am having lunch with friends on the terrace outside their penthouse in Manhattan. Mutual Japanese friends are visiting with their sons, $2^1/_2$ and 4 years old. Adults are preoccupied with talk; children apparently feel neglected and irritated about it. Suddenly, crash! Through the window hurtles a heavy ashtray thrown by son 1. Glass everywhere, but no serious censorship of the young one. Big clean-up. Adults settle down. Again crash! Through another window sails a second ashtray, thrown by son 2. The mildest of reprimands, although the parents are obviously extremely embarrassed.

There is much to be learned from examples such as these, but this is not the forum for it. What is revealed is the freedom—some might call it license—that is permitted the child in the Confucian household, perhaps in its extreme form in Japanese families.

But at age six or seven, life dramatically changed. Abruptly, the full brunt of Confucian propriety—the complex, precisely defined code of ethical conduct, of right and wrong—was imposed. The child rebelled—or cowered—but the discipline was implacable, because no matter how painful it might have been for the parent, the honor of the family was involved. The Koreans refer to this age and the young ones as "the terrible sevens." My sense is that it is terrible for everyone concerned, both parent and child: the children furious, confused, feeling desperately rejected; the mothers unhappy, guilt-ridden, but determined. Japan is an exception. The social institutions, not the mothers, enforce the stringent code of social and personal propriety. Thus the mothers retain their position as nonrestrictive and all-condoning. This particularly holds true for the sons.

In the West, the identity crisis occurs during early adulthood. In Erikson's definition, if all goes well, it takes place somewhere between ages 18 to 25. In the East, it occurs at age 6 or 7. The switch from indulged childhood to child/adulthood is abrupt, and there is no intervening adolescence to serve as gradual preparation. The early years constitute a period of virtually unrestrained power and self-determination for the child that, psychologically, has to be equated against the dramatically limited independence assigned in the ensuing years. It is because of these polarities that it remains so significant. The consequence is a sadness, a longing for the lost nirvana that extends throughout life—a yearning repressed and relegated to the unconscious. Of all the forces that tie the Confucian child to the family, this is perhaps the strongest and most abiding.

Changes in the Family

In spite of the rigidness of the past and the difficulties presented by the changes that the Confucian family is now undergoing, we find an impressive accommodation to the socioeconomic demands of today's world, and a flexibility that most would not have anticipated. Of equal importance, it is being done in a manner that increasingly addresses the psychological needs of the people. The result is that we now hear the prediction, with mounting frequency, that the twenty-first century will be the Asian century, in the sense that the twentieth has been the American, and the nineteenth the European.

Considering the radical changes that the family has been undergoing in the West in terms of structure, intrafamilial relationships, the evolving role of women, the increasing frequency of one-parent homes, and the imposition of new sociopolitical formulations, it seemed an appropriate time to look elsewhere for suggestions, if not solutions. This is a moment in history that warrants our searching for alternate forms; we have much to learn from each other.

Note

1. At the outset I would like to point out two potentially confusing considerations. Unless specifically qualified, the term "child" refers to both the young and adult
child—the offspring—a term that I dislike and tend to shun. Furthermore, in order to
avoid an ungainly use of tense, I have, in general, used the past. All languages present
problems, but unlike some Sinic languages where tense is not employed but is inferred
by context, in English it is difficult to indicate that something has not only taken place
in the past but is still occurring in the present. As a result I have settled on the use of
"was," "has been," and so on. Let it be understood that unless otherwise stated, for our
purposes the past is also the present.

References

Caudill, W. and Plath, D. W. (1986). "Maternal Care and Infant Behavior in Japan and
America." In *Japanese Culture and Behavior*, T. Lebra and W. Lebra. Honolulu:
University of Hawaii Press.

Cohen, M. L. (1976). *House United, House Divided*. New York: Columbia University
Press.

De Bary, W. T. (1981). *Neo-Confucian Orthodoxy and the Learning of the Mind-and-Heart.*
New York: Columbia University Press.

———. and J. K. Haboush, eds. (1985). *The Rise of Neo-Confucianism in Korea,* New
York: Columbia University Press.

———. (1988). *East Asian Civilizations.* Cambridge: Harvard University Press.

———. (1991). "Confucian Hierarchy vs. Class Consciousness in Japan." *Minority Status
and Social Cohesion: The United States and Japan.* Berkeley: University of California Press.

De Vos, G. (1993). "A Cross-Cultural Perspective: The Japanese Family as a Unit in
Moral Socialization." In *Family, Self and Society: Toward a New Agenda for Family
Research,* ed. D. Hansen. 1993 Erlbaum Assoc., Hilldale, N.J.

Erickson, E. H. (1986). *Identity, Youth and Crisis.* New York: W. W. Norton.

Hsu, F. L. K. (1959). "The Family in China: The Classical Form." In *The Family: Its
Function and Destiny,* ed. R. N. Anshen. New York: Harper.

Janelli, Roger and Dawnhee Yim (1982). *Ancestor Worship and Korean Society.* Stanford,
CA: Stanford University Press.

Jordan, D. (1986). "Folk Filial Piety in Taiwan: The Twenty-Four Filial Exemplars." In
The Psycho-Cultural Dynamics of the Confucian Family: Past and Present, ed.,
W. Slote. International Cultural Society of Korea, pp. 47–112, Seoul.

Nathanson, Donald L., ed. (1987). *The Many Faces of Shame.* New York: Guilford Press.

Schwartz, B. I. (1985). *The World of Thought in Ancient China.* Cambridge: Harvard University Press.

Slote, W. (1972). "Psychodynamic Structures in Vietnamese Personality." In *Mental Health Research in Asia and the Pacific,* vol. 2: *Transcultural Research in Mental Health,* ed. W. Lebra. Honolulu: University of Hawaii Press.

————. (1986a). "Rearing Kids Confucian Style." *Columbia* 11.4. February.

————. (1986b). "The Intrapsychic Locus of Power and Personal Determination in a Confucian Society: The Case of Vietnam." In *The Psycho-Cultural Dynamics of the Confucian Family: Past and Present,* ed., W. Slote. International Cultural Society of Korea, pp. 303–26, Seoul.

————. (1992). "Oedipal Ties and the Issue of Separation-Individuation in Traditional Confucian Societies." *Journal of the American Academy of Psychoanalysis* 20.3.

————. (1993). "Koreans Abroad in Therapy: Implications for the Homeland." In *Overseas Koreans in the Global Context,* ed. K. K. Lee and W. Slote. Seoul: ASKA, Seoul National University.

Tu, W. M. (1979). *Humanity and Self-Cultivation: Essays in Confucian Thought.* Berkeley, CA: Asian Humanities Press.

————. (1986). "An Inquiry on the Five Relationships in Confucian Humanism." In *The Psycho-Cultural Dynamics of the Confucian Family: Past and Present,* ed., W. Slote. International Cultural Society of Korea, pp. 175–96, Seoul.

Wolf, A. P. (1966). "Childhood Association, Sexual Attraction, and the Incest Taboo." *American Anthropologist* 68: 883–98.

————. (1968). "Adopt a Daughter-in-Law, Marry a Sister: A Chinese Solution to the Problem of the Incest Taboo." *American Anthropologist* 70: 864–74.

Wolf, M. (1968). *The House of Lim.* New York: Appleton, Century Crofts.

————. (1972). *Women and the Family in Rural Taiwan.* Stanford, CA: Stanford University Press.

3

Confucianism in Comparative Context

Francis L. K. Hsu

Chinese Cultural-Historical Differences from the West

Let me begin by pointing out a few spectacular but usually unnoticed facts in the world.

Christianity originated from the periphery of Asia about one century before it was introduced to Europe in any significant way. Whereas it was rapidly adopted in Europe, it found very few adherents in Asia. By 1949, after at least three centuries of intensive Western missionary efforts (the last century with the help of military and economic penetration), less than one percent of Chinese were even nominally Christian. In Japan, despite the optimism of Jesuit missionaries such as St. Francis Xavier, the numbers of coverts to Christianity was even smaller and has remained so. When Prime Minister Hatoyama took office in 1954, he went to worship at the great Ise Shrine. Asked by Western reporters why he, a Christian, did this, he replied, "It is something Japanese." This calls to mind the fact that, in the early thirties, when Generalissimo Chiang Kai-Shek became a Methodist, Western missionaries, especially Methodist ones, were jubilant. Judging by European experiences, in which quite a few kings successfully forced the Lutheran, Anglican, or Catholic faith on their subjects when they themselves embraced these creeds, Westerners thought it would be only a short time before most Chinese would become Methodist, or at least Christian. They were, of course, disappointed.

A second spectacular fact is that today nearly all the world's missionaries and missionary movements are of Western origin. The Jews have not proselytized since the sacking of the Second Temple. In contrast, the Moslems regard proselytizing as essential to their faith. But Islamic fervor for proselytization seems to be coterminous with Arab political and military fortune in the non-Arab world. Their proselytizing efforts were not unlike those of Japanese who forced Shintoism on the people of Manchuria, Taiwan, and the Caroline Islands when these populations were under Japanese colonial rule. Once they no longer ruled, the Japanese were far more interested in exporting automobiles, cameras, and watches than in saving foreign souls. Only the proselytizing efforts of the Christian West have been aggressive, sustained, and global in scope. And, in spite of the loss of their colonies, Portuguese and Belgian missionaries have been no less diligent and ubiquitous since World War II than their American and British counterparts.

On the other hand, even when the Chinese empire extended far and wide under Han, T'ang, and Ming, no Chinese court had ever attempted to spread Confucianism or any other Chinese belief or ethics system, and I know of no individual Chinese who ever received a call from above to do the same.

In fact, the evidence points to the contrary. In A.D., 730, during the T'ang dynasty, a Tibetan king and son-in-law of the emperor asked for various Chinese classics and histories. The request was refused. When the request was refused a second time, and after the death of his Chinese queen the Tibetan ruler invaded China with a force of 400,000 warriors. During the same dynasty, some 3,000 Chinese Buddhist monks went on foot in small groups to India, not to spread the wisdom of any Chinese holy man, but to learn and to bring back to China the true teachings of Buddha in their original form.

A third spectacular fact is the differing manifestations of Buddhism, which reached Japan via China and Korea. The majority of Chinese worshipped some Buddhist deities at one time or another, and built temples and pagodas everywhere. But the Chinese never had the idea of congregation as in the West. They simply did not "belong" to any temple. Instead, the Chinese approach to gods is like the American approach to supermarkets. Americans will go to Jewel stores for meat, Safeway stores for produce, and Dominics stores for fruit—all depending upon which one has the better products or prices. And just as Americans do not classify themselves as Jewelists, Safewayans, or Dominicans, most Chinese are not known as Confucians, Buddhists, or Taoists.

In a way, the Japanese are as polytheistic as the Chinese; they worship many gods and spirits; they deify human beings such as General Nogi in Nogi Shrine in Tokyo or Anjin and Hime in Dojoji in Wakayama. But instead of going to many different religious "supermarkets," the Japanese confine themselves largely to two "main stores": Shinto and Buddhist. And they practice the institution of *danka*, i.e., congregation, but a congregation of households, not individual members as in the West.

The late Dr. Hu Shih, an eminent Chinese philosopher, wrote in his autobiography that when he was growing up, the sign "No Monks or Priests" was always prominently posted on the gate to his parents' home. There was nothing peculiar about Dr. Hu's parents. The same sign was on the gates to many, many Chinese homes everywhere. Buddhism played no real part in Chinese life except for funerals, memorials for the dead, or relief of disasters such as cholera epidemics. It came, therefore, as a shock to me, when I spent the 1964–65 year in Japan, to find quite a few photos of family get-togethers with obosan (monks) included.

The Chinese-Japanese contrast in Buddhism does not stop with the matter of congregation. Zen Buddhism is known in China as Ch'an Chung, and it went to Japan as such; but when Prof. Derk Bodde of the University of Pennsylvania read the first version of my book *Americans and Chinese,* one of the corrections he suggested was to change my spelling of Ch'an to Zen. Why? The Western world knows this variety of Buddhism far better in its Japanese name than its Chinese counterpart. Today the world knows the name of Daisetzu Suzuki, but no single Chinese savant of the subject has reached comparable fame. Zen has flourished in Japan much more than in China. It remained but a concern for a few learned clergy and lay scholars in China before 1949. But in today's Japan it is even incorporated as part of the initiation training of young executives in many modern business corporations.

A final fact that I will point out concerns the behavior and influence of rulers in different societies. King Ashoka of India, after being converted to Buddhism, ordered edicts engraved on stone all over his domain in order to "missionize" his subjects. Some Chinese emperors became devout Buddhists, including one who went to great trouble and expense and against the advice of his chief minister to bring a small fragment of Buddha's bones to China. None, however, made any move to spread the Buddhist faith among his subjects. Instead, ancestor worship became a single major concern. For example, the founder of the Han dynasty had his own ancestral temples erected in every province of the empire and tried to make the people do homage to his forebears:

> From his death in 195 B.C. to 40 B.C. every deceased emperor had his temples in the capital city provinces. From the third emperor to the eighth, each erected his temples during his lifetime. By about the middle of the first century A.D., there were 176 imperial temples and 30 temples for empresses and crown princes throughout the empire, which required 24,455 victuals and sacrifices annually, 45,129 temple guards, and a government staff of 12,147 in charge of sacrificial ceremonies and music. (Ho 1968, 16–17).

In spite of the fact that Chinese emperors called themselves Sons of Heaven and desired to deify their ancestors and, of course, themselves, such temples among the people were abolished about 40 B.C. The Chinese norm has been for each dynasty to establish its own ancestral temple that housed the souls of all successors to the throne after their demise. The ancestral temple of each dynasty remained the object of the exclusive ritual concern of its own imperial descendants, exactly as the ancestral temple of each clan among the common people was the exclusive concern of that clan's descendants and of no one else. The Chinese emperors never succeeded in making their subjects worship them as spirits or the soul of their imperial ancestors, in contrast to the Japanese who worship Amaterasu at Ise as a matter of course.[1]

Why Do Differences Develop?

Why do such great differences develop when the same religious creed goes from one society to another?

To answer this question, I must briefly outline my ideas on how human beings live their lives. Please think of three terms arranged vertically one above another, as follows.

Cultural Heritage

Social Organization

Individual Behavior

The cultural heritage of each society consists of all that has come down from the past and is still practiced, written down, or remembered. It consists of ideas, ethical systems, and religious teachings, scientific or empirical theories, artifacts such as the Great Wall, the wheel, jet planes, the atom bomb, and all the technology that is necessary for their construction and operation.

Social organization consists of networks of human relationships and the way the human beings in them relate, or are expected to relate, to each other. Family, clan, village, tribes, as well as schools, PTA, labor unions, the Ku Klux Klan, and churches are all examples.

Except perhaps in very rare cases, every individual is born with certain potentials, but no predetermined pattern of behavior. He acquires particular patterns of behavior by being nurtured, guided, encouraged, or even forced by this social organization. The process by which the individual is gradually initiated as an acceptable and functioning member of his society is known as socialization and acculturation. What needs to be underlined here is that the cultural heritage of every society contains far more than what its social organization normally transmits to its members. The social organization censors what is transmitted, especially to the new members. Thus, although Jesus enjoins his followers to "turn the other cheek," no Christian society I know of has ever taught that way of responding to adversaries. And although the monumental works of Joseph Needham on *Science and Civilization in China* drew all of its primary sources from Chinese writings, most who were born, raised, and completed college in China, including myself, were largely ignorant of those writings. The Chinese social organization, even under Western impact, did not encourage its youth to study them, despite China's desire at the time to imitate the West or Japan as a way out of her century of weakness and humiliation.

In each society, the social organization selects, rearranges, or warps the contents of its cultural heritage whether of indigenous or exogenous origin. However, contrary to Western notions, I find that rationality occupies only a minor position in human life. Instead, I think what powerfully guides the human activities of individuals, and especially of groups, are nonrational (as distinguished from irrational) factors, whether in business or politics, in race relations or gasoline crises, in buying a home or joining a club, in finding a mate or treating parents. To elucidate this, we need to go to the two kinds of glues that link human beings together.

Social Adherence

We all know the household paste that is made by heating a mixture of flour and water. Two materials stuck together by household paste can be separated easily by soaking them in water. We also know Elmer's Glue or epoxy. Epoxy is the stuff advertised as being able to glue anything to anything. It is so strong that it can join diving boards together. Two boards once joined by epoxy cannot be separated without destruction of one or the other.

Elmer's Glue is comparable to what drew Romeo and Juliet together. When one dies, the other has to go. And household paste is comparable to what brought *The Midnight Cowboy* in the movie by that name and any of his women together for a little while. I submit that, in social life, the two kinds of glue, namely Elmer's Glue and household paste are, respectively, affect and role. The second is a matter of utility, the first that of feeling. Role is calculable and is what we often buy and sell; but affect is far less exact—and is what we claim money cannot buy.

We know role behavior in terms of skilled or unskilled labor, white collar or blue collar, dentists and diamond cutters, housekeepers and politicians, and countless others. As each society grows in complexity, the number and variety of roles grow with it. Role differentiation is the major indicator of societal development. For example, in today's conditions, each candidate for national office in the United States is supported by an army of experts including speech writers, public relations people, technicians, and foot soldiers beyond the imagination of the small-town politicians of yesteryear. Giant corporations in the United States and elsewhere often have more diversified personnel and more workers and specialists on their payrolls than many small member states of the United Nations.

On the other hand, while our roles have evolved in number and precision with the complexity of industrial society, our affect has not. Mankind still has the same feelings as his ancestors who lived thousands of years ago: love, hate, rage, despair, endurance, hope, anxiety, forbearance, loyalty, betrayal, and so forth. The list is not long and many of the terms used to describe them are similar to each other, or even partially or wholly subsumable under each other. This is why great literature (fiction, poetry) and great art (painting, sculpture), the universal conveyors of affect everywhere, tend to survive the ages. We moderns feel the same agony and joy, the same loyalty and duplicity, as the ancients. We can relive their lives through what they have written and, were they alive today, they would be able to discuss with us our problems with our children, parents, friends and enemies, employers and employees, sweethearts and spouses.

By contrast, old books of science and technology are useless to us except as curiosities or material for histories of science and technology. Not only the ancients, but our fathers and even our older brothers would have found catching up with our present generation's developments in science and technology impossible or, at the very least, extremely arduous.

Up to this point, my distinction between role and affect seems no different from that between instrumentality and expressiveness—a distinction made popular by Talcott Parsons among social scientists. But its differences from that of Parsons are profound.

In Parsons's scheme, instrumentality is primarily linked with the father, while expressiveness with the mother (Parsons and Bales 1955, 45–54). In my view, both role and affect can be equally linked to both parents in the socialization process. For instance, quite a few examples in *Twenty-Four Examples of Filial Piety,* (Jordan, chapter 14), the well-known Chinese tale, portray a son's devotion to and sacrifices for his father or both parents, as well as a daughter's devotion to and sacrifices for her mother, mother-in-law, or father. In Japan, General Nogi, who served gloriously as commander-in-chief of the Japanese forces under Emperor Meiji in the Russo-Japanese War, committed *hara-kiri,* upon the latter's demise, to follow his master in the other world.

Role and affect are not isolated from each other. Except for extremes such as the case of Romeo and Juliet, or most parents and their babies, role and affect usually overlap. There is no scarcity of cases in which one is so committed to a usual role type activity (such as going to the office or workshop) that it turns into, for the individual, an affect activity (such as what happens to workaholics).

However, an even more fundamental distinction between my formulation and that of Parsons is the fact that affect or feeling determines role selection and performance. Whenever there is a choice, affect determines what one chooses to do, how well one does it, and how truly one enjoys the fruit of what one has done. Affect determines how people feel about themselves, about each other, and about the rest of the world. Affect determines their priorities; it shapes the way they conduct themselves and relate to each other and the rest of the world.

From this point of view, affect is far more important than role in human affairs. Anthropologists, including myself, who have explored the question of guilt and shame in cultures did, of course, underscore this fact to a certain extent (e.g., Benedict 1946; Piers and Singer 1953; Hsu 1949, 1963; and De Vos 1973), but more have concerned themselves with role. Since Ralph Linton's exposition of the importance of status and role in social relations (Linton 1936, 113–31), there has been a proliferation of terms such as role model, role playing, role image, and role expectation in sociology and anthropology literature. But hardly any work that gives comparable importance to affect.

Many systems of values (philosophies, religious creeds, ethics, whatever) are known throughout human history in diverse lands, but such systems will be of importance as driving and guiding forces in any living society only if they are interwoven with its members' patterns of affect. Otherwise, systems of human values, no matter how rational, lofty, or well thought out, will remain dead artifacts, no more than the stone tools archaeologists uncover in prehistoric sites. They will adorn the halls of museums, but they will have no bearing on how living people conduct their business, politics, or interpersonal relations. It is affect that makes human values (philosophies or religious or ethics) real and enduring. It is affect that led the organizers of many a Japanese conference to give participants each a *bento* (box of food) to take home as they left the dining hall after a nights' festivity of cocktails, speeches, and a delicious dinner, no less than the reason for General Nogi to commit *hara-kiri* upon Emperor Meiji's demise.

From the evidence at our disposal, role changes in many societies have been enormous since the dawn of human history, but changes in affective patterning in all societies have been minor if they took place at all. In the Western world today, we have more theories about human emotion than did the ancients, but not more substance or variety of affect itself. What we need to realize is that resistance or willingness to change, technical or otherwise, in each society comes not from role but from affect. The more affect is invested in a role activity, the more that role activity will resist change.

However, although Western scholars never seem to hesitate to declare what they find and feel as universal, the pattern of affect that links and repels Westerners and persists among them is not the same as that which links and repels men and women in other societies and persists among them.

The same machines tend to have the same requirements whoever their builders or operators may be. The same plants tend to grow the same way in the hands of either Japanese or American or Korean or Chinese gardeners. I have observed that even dogs, regardless how far some groups have interfered with their breeding and training, behave with certain regularity the world over. But human beings with unlike cultural heritages and social organizations live, work, enjoy, struggle, and die in drastically different ways and for very diverse reasons.

I will not detail the spectacular differences between Western novels, drama, and art on the one hand and their Chinese counterparts on the other. I have done that elsewhere. Instead, I will explicate my view here by pointing out one outstanding psychological characteristic of Western and American novels and drama: the satisfaction of individualistic ambitions without reference to social consequences. There are characters in search of identity such as Holden Caulfield in *Catcher in the Rye;* characters who go it alone to prove themselves by conquest such as Captain Ahab in *Moby Dick* or the "Old Man" in *The Old Man and the Sea;* or characters who strive to be something they can never be such as Herzog in *Herzog.* There are other manifestations such as *On the Road* or *Papillon,* but they can mostly be subsumed under the categories already named.

How different are these modern novels from ancient narratives? Writers about the West and especially the United States often are impressed by how much and how rapidly changes have occurred. But an examination of three of the most classical of Western epics, the *Iliad, Agamemnon,* and the *Odyssey,* and their great popularity inside and outside of the American schools, make it clear that the more narratives change, the more they express the same Western pattern of affect.

What was the central concern of these ancient epics? Briefly, a woman named Helen was seduced. Not her husband but her husband's brother was determined to secure her return by destroying the culprit and his people. He gathered together an armada of ships with some 200,000 men. To secure the necessary wind, he threw his eldest daughter into the sea. By his distant campaign, he indeed destroyed Troy in spite of many problems in his own ranks, but upon return he was murdered by his wife and her lover. Odysseus, one of his generals, nearly did not make it home. The effects of the expedition were so disastrous that the Achaeans, as the then inhabitants of today's Greece were known, were subsequently driven from their homeland and replaced by such other peoples as the Thessalians and Dorians. That was why Homer wrote the *Iliad* in Asia Minor and was buried, allegedly, on a small Mediterranean island called Ios. Had Agamemnon's people been Chinese, they would have asked him, I suspect, "Is the trip necessary?"

The Chinese simply do not have narratives based on characters in search of identity, characters who go it alone, characters who strive to be something they can never be, or characters who roam from one place to another having sexual experiences, stealing cars, conning people but with no other purpose in life than self-gratification. Even in *Chin P'ing Mei* (the title of the English translation is *Golden Lotus*), which is sometimes known as a Chinese pornographic novel, the villainous character Hsi Men Ch'ing suffered a premature death due to his sexual excesses and escapades and the book concluded with the reward of a son to his long-suffering but virtuous wife. The Chinese writers have been so oblivious to individual adventures and triumphs that even the hero in *Ching Hua Yuan,* the Chinese equivalent of *Gulliver's Travels,* went through his many bizarre travel experiences with his brother-in-law and a friend.

This Chinese concern with the individual's place in the group, the need for collectivity, and the consequences of the individual's actions on the collectivity has also been a central theme in the art and literature that have proliferated in China since 1949. The main difference is that the concern in pre-Communist China for family, clan, filial piety to parents, and loyalty to particular emperors has now been replaced by an effort to join hands with socialism and to catch up with the industrially advanced societies of the West.

Filial Piety: Cardinal Virtue

With their social organization centered in family and kinship, the Chinese have traditionally held on to filial piety as their cardinal virtue. This is to say, all other virtues, from honesty to love of spouse, from devotion to the ruler to interest in abstract principles, were either subordinated to this cardinal virtue or modified by it, defined in terms of it or even eliminated by it. Thus, for example, the worthiness of one's wife was first of all judged by whether she pleased one's parents; duties to the political state came after one's mourning and other obligations to parents.

After Sun Yat-sen engineered the Revolution of 1911, and especially in the Chinese Renaissance of 1919 led by Hu Shih, Chinese intellectuals attacked filial piety and Confucianism. The same line was echoed by foreign missionaries, whose theme was that filial piety must be removed for China's modernization and progress.

However, this same filial piety travelled from China to Japan, via Korea, some fifteen centuries ago. It was not imposed or even exported by its originator. Instead, Korea and Japan voluntarily sent students to China who systematically learned a language that bore no resemblance to theirs, and brought it back to Korea and Japan, where it subsequently became a central part of Japanese and Korean education and was emulated and sanctioned by rulers of both countries. For example, Japanese rulers awarded citations and material benefits to citizens for exemplary filial behavior. *The Chinese Scripture of Filial Piety (Hsiao Ching)*, was essential reading for Japanese scholars. Not being content with the Chinese stories entitled *Twenty-Four Examples of Filial Piety (Er Shih Ssu Hsiao)*, of which Jordan in chapter 14 gives us an excellent exposition, the Japanese created a body of literature on filial piety of their own, one example of which is *Biographies of Japanese Filial Children (Fu San Ko Shi Dan*, 1684), featuring fifty-one stories.

How then could the Chinese and Japanese respond so differently to Western pressures since the middle of the nineteenth century? How could the same doctrine prevent China from industrializing and modernizing but serve as no impediment to the development of Japan?

The easiest way out would be to say that the Japanese later discarded this doctrine. Another way would be to sidetrack the issue and see the presence of Emperor Meiji in Japan and the absence of any far-sighted ruler in nineteenth-century Chinas as the deciding factor. A third way would be to say that Japanese and Chinese values were dissimilar to begin with.

My view is that the ethic of filial piety imported by Japan was the same as that in China, but the human networks through which it found concrete expressions in the two societies were and are different. Furthermore, even today Japan has not discarded the ethic of filial piety. Japan has never experienced an anti-filial piety movement comparable to that of China. On the contrary, the ethic of filial piety was and is at the core of the human foundation of Japanese industrialization and modernization.

Chinese-Japanese Differences

The ethic of filial piety in China was rooted in the father-son relationship. One popular misconception is that filial piety is a one-sided affair, through which fathers exploit their sons and give nothing in return. That is not true. The son owes to his father absolute obedience, support during his lifetime, mourning after he passes away, burial according to social station and financial ability, provision for his soul's needs in the other world, and glory for the father by doing well or even better than he. But the father must provide for his sons when they are young, educate them in the ancestral tradition, finds mates for them, and leave them good names and inheritances as well as he can. Fathers and sons have to do these things not merely because they owe them to each other, but because they are both obligated to the generations that went before and those yet to come. This was why I termed the relationship one of father-son identification (Hsu 1948, 236) and later developed the notion of continuity as one of its primary attributes (Hsu 1961). From that central point of reference, the ethic of filial piety extends to mothers, to collateral kinsmen in the patrilineal line, to wider relatives, and marginally to members of one's local community.

Confirmed by a Chinese kinship structure that embodies all patrilineal consanguine relatives both horizontally and hierarchically, the ethic of filial piety was highly limited in the effective range of its operation. This gave the Chinese a high degree of kinship solidarity but prevented them from strong and enduring alliances outside of it.

The Chinese did have the notion of "transferring filial piety to devotion to emperor," but they gave it only scanty and sporadic expression. There were a few instances of such a transfer according to popular legends. The mothers of several generals in the first decades of the Christian era allegedly committed suicide because they wanted to free their sons from filial duties so that the young men could support the rebel leader who later founded the Eastern Han dynasty (Chu 1967, 64–65, 80). A high official in the Ming dynasty decided to challenge the corrupt power of the emperor's favorite eunuch in spite of the fact that the spirits of his ancestors "advised" him against it in an apparition. However, the overwhelming Chinese trend was for the individual to place his filial and kinship duties before all else—a fact that led Dr. Sun Yat-Sen erroneously to conclude that the Chinese are like a tray of loose sand, and some Western observers to speak of them as individualists. They are neither loose sand nor individualists. They cohere too well within the kinship boundary as they define it, and concern themselves too little with what goes on outside it. They could not, under the circumstances, develop a positive attitude and zeal toward, or affective involvement in, wider issues or more distant peoples.

Iemoto in Japan

However, when the ethic of filial piety was transplanted to Japan, it was incorporated into a different human network from that of China. It is impossible to describe, within the limited space of this paper, all the structural differences between Chinese and Japanese kinship systems. This was done elsewhere (Hsu 1971, 1975). Here we shall note the following general features that distinguish the Japanese system from its Chinese counterpart:

1. *Unigeniture*—one son inheritance, in contrast to the Chinese who practiced equal division of inheritance among the sons for untold centuries.

2. *Frequency of nonconsanguine adoption*—For the Chinese even adoption of the daughter's husband is not desirable and is infrequently practiced. In Japan not only is the adoption of sons-in-law frequent, but adoption of totally unrelated outsiders is common.

3. *Lineal emphasis in naming*—According to Chinese custom the names of all males on the same generational level (father's and his brothers' sons, etc.) possess one character in common; by contrast the Japanese tendency was for the names of inheriting sons to share one character in common with that of the father but not with those of his brothers. Although the rule was not absolute, it was generally observed. In the case of the Tokugawa family, it was followed until the end to the Shogun power.

4. *Parental retirement*—The Japanese father and mother retire from active power once the inheriting son and daughter-in-law take over. They even retire into separate living quarters, variously called *inkyo ya* or *hanare*, and manage their own cooking and other housekeeping chores. This is entirely contrary to Chinese custom.

5. *Dozoku*—often erroneously translated as clan, but whose basis has little in common with its Chinese counterpart. The Chinese clan is a kinship group, consisting of males who can trace themselves to a common ancestor—together with their spouses. *Dozoku* usually begins with a kinship core of *honke*, the main household of the eldest son, which collects client units or *bunke,* the branch households of younger sons or others. Moreover, *bunke* may at times be fabricated out of fictive kinship relationship and have no consanguine or affined ties at all. On the other hand, they always live in the same contiguous area and work on some common land. The Chinese clan members may be scattered in distant areas but their genealogical relationship remains their primary link, whereas Japanese brothers who move away from each other cease to be members of the same *dozoku.*

There are differences between Chinese and Japanese kinship patterns in the disposal of the dead, in rites of ancestor worship, in notions of female virginity, and so on. But enough has been said to indicate the basic differences between Chinese and Japanese kinship networks to make our point. In the Chinese social organization, kinship predominates. Kinship is the principal criterion for replenishing membership, for regulating behavior and, outside the imperial examinations in which only a tiny fraction of the population at large could succeed, for advancement in status. In the Japanese situation, the content of the father-son–based filial piety still dominates, but the human arena in which it operates is different. In other words, the social structure to which the same content applies has shifted.[2]

The ethic of filial piety governs the conduct of Japanese fathers and sons. But with unigeniture or one-son inheritance, the structural continuity of that relationship is secured on one son and his father. When and if economic necessity leads the inheriting son to seek clients, and likewise the noninheriting sons to seek patrons, they will both do so within the same frame of reference. They form the structure of *dozoku*, incorporating nonrelatives if convenient and suitable, but they behave toward each other according to the ethic of filial piety. The head of *dozoku* and his clients in it form a lasting hierarchy as a "parent part" or *oyabun*; he has permanent obligations toward his clients' "child parts" or *kabun*, just as they have eternal duties toward him. The bond is rarely dissolved, even when they are not related at all by blood or marriage. The relationship is buttressed by rituals of ancestor worship, including offerings to the souls of the *dozoku's* founder and his wife and care of their tombs. The giant modern Soka Gakai is no exception in this regard. The members of the group, especially those of *oyabun* toward *kabun* and vice versa, embody all the essential feelings and attitudes inherent in the structure of the Chinese father-son relationship, but the criteria for membership and its continuation, and for advancement in the *dozoku* are not essentially those of kinship; instead, they are economic and territorial.

Japanese Nonkinship Criteria

The nonkinship criteria for inheritance in group membership made the development of *iemoto* possible in Japan but not in China. The Chinese clan structure is a logical extension of the Chinese type of kinship in which all sons inherit equally. Its essential criterion for membership is consanguine and only marginally through adoption (Hsu 1963, 60–92). After having extended as far as clans, the Chinese social organization could not go further in its development. Hence, throughout Chinese history there were no large-scale extrakinship inheritance group organizations, except some bandit or gangster organizations that operated outside the law.

In Japan, professional groups with the inheritance of the "house founder" *(iemoto)* role became a form of human combination far more commensurate with the *dozoku* than with the Chinese clan. *Iemoto* has no counterpart in China or the West. Whereas in the *dozoku,* productivity in the land is the common objective, the foundation of *iemoto* consists of such things as the practice of a craft or skill (flower arrangement, Kabuki, judo, calligraphy, etc.) or the pursuit of an objective (business, manufacturing, political gain, religion, etc.). The nature of the relationship between master and disciple in the *iemoto* is the same as between the head of the *dozoku* and his clients: unquestioned obedience to authority, permanent mutual obligations and duties, and care for the souls of masters who have passed away.

Since *iemoto* is not, as is *dozoku,* tied to the land, its organizational boundaries and membership can be expanded greatly—almost indefinitely. The core relationship in the *iemoto* is that of the master and his voluntary disciples. As the master collects more disciples, each accomplished disciple can start his own branch establishment by collecting disciples of his own. The peers of the disciples will in turn each start his own establishment with disciples, and so the process goes on. Thus a giant organization develops (often nationwide and even international) where the original master and his establishment do not function separately; instead they are interlinking components of the whole. Takeyoshi Kawashima, the noted Japanese sociologist, even compares *iemoto* organization with that of the armed forces with clearly defined ranks, duties, and obligations as well as demarcated places for work and encampment (Kawashima 1957, 332–69).

Structurally, *iemoto* is one more step removed from the kinship base. It depends primarily on nonkinship criteria for recruitment, although the succession of the headship of the *iemoto* is often from father to son or to son-in-law. But the attitudes and feelings for the maintenance and success of the *iemoto* organization are the same as those in the kinship organization: lasting loyalty, devotion, obedience to the master, inheritance not only of the trade but also the style of its practice, discouragement of intraorganizational competition that would be disruptive to the organization as a whole, and lack of horizontal mobility, so that, once affiliated, one does not change master or organization. From the point of view of the individualist West, most of these conditions are easily seen as retarders rather than facilitators of industrial development. But where individualism is absent and man is trained to please his parents and superiors as well as to enjoy their authority and succor—all elements of the content of filial piety—these conditions induce hard work beyond the call of duty and deep dedication to the organization as a whole, both of which compensate for the lack of intraorganizational competition. Under the circumstances the nonkinship criteria for recruitment in the *iemoto* is at least a partial check against the risks of functional incompetence (Hsu 1971, 1975).

Organizational Differences

The structural framework of the premodern *dozoku,* and especially the *iemoto,* provided a ready-made basis for modern organizations such as today's industrial corporations, educational institutions, political parties and religious networks. The contemporary content of the ethic of filial piety still provides the main ingredients which go into the feelings or affective base, which determine attitudes, just as was the case in premodern *dozoku* and *iemoto.* This is why Japanese industrial workers, though making threatening noises biannually for bonus demands, rarely go on actual strike. This is why even Japanese executives and school and college teachers seldom change their places of employment.[3] On the contrary, they tend to be devoted to their employers and to the organizations of which they are a part. This state of affairs prompted one veteran Japanese diplomat, Ichiro Kawasaki, to say that once a Japanese secures a regular position in a firm or government, he is like a man who has stepped on an escalator. For the rest of his working life all he has to do is keep his place in it and he will rise automatically as time goes on (Kawasaki 1969, 97). Policies of early retirement help thin the ranks at the top. Recent reports of gains in leadership positions by Japanese women in some political parties, and the fact that even in the 1960s some female office employees publicly announced that they would no longer serve tea, are of course, signs for change. But these, too, in my view, will remain minor ripples.

In the light of this analysis we can more readily appreciate the significance of one of the outstanding differences between ancestor worship in China and Japan. For the Chinese, ritual duties are entirely confined to his actual ancestors. By extension he also has some small ritual obligations to the so-called or putative "first ancestor" of his trade. For example, Chinese actors took Emperor Ming Hwang of the T'ang dynasty as their "first ancestor" because he loved operas, and Chinese traders took Minister Fan Li of the Spring and Autumn period as their "first ancestor" because he was a merchant of great wealth, and so forth. But the ancestral spirits of the Chinese reigning emperors were the *private* concern of the emperor and his descendants alone. The people had nothing to do with them. In fact, the people were forbidden to have any interest in them. For the Japanese, on the other hand, the great ancestral shrine of Ise is a national institution at which millions of Japanese pay homage to their common ancestress, Amaterasu.

In a sense we may regard the entire Japanese people as forming something of a giant *iemoto,* with the emperor as its head of the *honke,* while the various organizations (giant and small, business, industrial, religious, military, and social) are but subordinate establishments, *bunke* or branches, within this national pyramid.

The ethic of filial piety is central in both Chinese and Japanese society. The difference is that in China the sphere of its most intense expression was confined by kinship boundaries. There was no structural device to link the kinship organization with the wider political state. Therefore, it was the confining nature of Chinese social organization that narrowly defined the sphere of affective links of the Chinese individual, not the ethic of filial piety, that prevented China from rapid and effective responses to the challenge of the West, in contrast to Japan, where the nature of the social organization allowed the same ethic new and different structural avenues of expression.

Once this is understood, we are in a better position to evaluate Robert Bellah's explanation that "China was characterized by the primacy of integrative values where Japan was characterized by primacy of political or goal-attainment values" (Bellah 1957, 188). Were China merely characterized by the primacy of integrative values, the Chinese would not have been described as "a tray of loose sands" by Dr. Sun Yat-Sen. The Chinese would have shown far more devotion to their emperors in dynastic times than they did, and far more patriotic fervor in the face of Western pressure than they did. On the other hand, were Japan merely characterized by the primacy of goal-attainment values (to use Western terms), the Japanese would have been far more "individualistic" and far less pliant to authority and group pressure than they are today. Yet the Chinese seem to be far more individualistic than the Japanese, while the Japanese have been far more effectively patriotic than the Chinese.

The truth is, China and Japan did not have fundamentally different values. The ethic of filial piety, whether we examine the Chinese family or clan or Japanese *dozoku* or *iemoto,* is both integrative and goal oriented. But China and Japan offered two different structural channels into which the ethic of Confucianism and filial piety were conducted. An integrative value that is confined to organizations depending solely on kinship affiliation as criteria for recruitment has no chance to affectively invest role performances organized to serve the larger purpose of industrial empires or nationalism. The emotionally invested goals to be attained are similarly limited to such things as pleasing the parents, enlarging the family graveyards, and glorifying the family name. But given larger human groupings with kinship as well as nonkinship criteria for recruitment, the integrative and goal-attainment components of the same ethic of filial piety became assets, rather than stumbling blocks, for industrialization and modernization. Consequently, Japanese industrialization and modernization are founded on a human equation quite dissimilar to that of their Western counterparts.

Although filial piety operates in *iemoto* and other Japanese institutions, it is not called by that name. Ruth Benedict, in her "Schematic Table of Japanese Obligations and Their Reciprocals" specifies different kinds of *on* (*ko on, on* received from the emperor; *oya, on, on* received from parents, etc.), *gimu,* and *giri* (Benedict 1946, 116). *On, gimu,* and *giri,* as well as their derivations in her list, were traditional terms still more or less used in Japan, though some Japanese, especially urban dwellers, tend erroneously to claim they are now obsolete. It is true that they are not used as frequently as before; and often they are given somewhat altered meanings.[4] Also college-educated executives in modern corporations may also use imported terms instead—such as "company spirit." But if we look beneath the names given we shall find that the emotional content of Japanese human relationships persists everywhere. It is my contention that this affective content is expressed through the ethic of filial piety that was exported to Japan from China.

Filial Piety: A Shared Tradition

Earlier I commented on the fact that some Japanese have created for themselves tales similar to those of the Chinese, an example of which is *Fu Sang Ko Shi Dan.* However, the Japanese, with their somewhat different patterns of affect rooted in their type of kinship system, have naturally made changes.

In the Chinese version of a story, one young man, Tze-chien, was mistreated by his stepmother. He had to wear a winter coat stuffed with flowers of dried reeds, while his stepmother's two sons wore coats lined with real cotton. One wintry day the whole family went out in a horse cart. The father noticed that Tze-chin shivered all over while his two stepsons sat comfortably and upright. Not receiving a satisfactory explanation from Tze-chien, the father angrily hit him with the whip with which he was driving. The whip broke the cloth of the boy's coat and revealed that it was stuffed with flowers of dried reed. This father now turned his anger to his second wife and threatened to divorce her. Tze-chien begged his father to desist from that action because he did not want to ruin his stepmother's life. He was too filial to his stepmother to allow such an occurrence.

In the Japanese version there is a boy (whose name is not reported) in Shin Ju whose stepmother had an extramarital liaison. She and her lover often corresponded with each other. His father became suspicious and one day found a pile of their correspondence. Because the father was illiterate, he asked his son to read the letters to him. The son, of course, at once knew what was going on. However, he did not want to cause a rift between his father and his stepmother. So, instead of reading to his father what was really in the letters, he faked it by saying they were exchanges between relatives on family matters. Thus he saved the marriage of his father and stepmother. When his stepmother learned about this episode, she sent a *waka* (short poem) to the son and the filial boy replied to his stepmother in another *waka:*

> *Stepmother to filial boy:*
> When I tried to cross the Kiso rapids in Shinano province,
> On a single log bridge,
> It was indeed dangerous.
> My secret was almost exposed.

> *Filial boy to stepmother:*
> Though I was never in the womb,
> Of my stepmother in Shinano province,
> I wholeheartedly think of her,
> As my real mother.

To the Chinese, the intrusion of the Japanese type of motif into a collection of filial piety stories would have been highly incongruous, for a common Chinese saying is:

> Licentiousness tops all evils;
> Filial piety is the first of all good deeds.

Notes

1. Ho offered the following not-so-plausible explanation of why the imperial temples were abolished after 40 B.C.: "For since Western Han times, the emperor's charisma had been generally taken for granted and an elaborate system of imperial temples was no longer needed. Curing the past millennium when imperial prestige enhanced almost progressively, there gradually had come into being a rich folklore which, if it did not outright regard the emperor as god, nevertheless portrayed him as divinely ordained" (Ho 1968, 17). There is no evidence that the Chinese emperor's charisma and prestige "had been generally taken for granted." Far from it. The ruling house in China was destroyed and replaced by new dynasties some eleven times before the republican revolution of 1911. This is in sharp contrast to Japan, where today's Emperor Hirohito is the direct descendant of the original founder of the one and only imperial line. In spite of this, the common people in Japan still pay homage at the great Ise shrine. This Sino-Japanese difference lies in the closed nature of the Chinese kinship system in contrast to the more open nature of its Japanese counterpart. As indicated below, the imperial shrine of each Chinese ruling dynasty was not open to the people just as the clan temple of each Chinese clan was the sole concern of its own present members and future descendants.

2. Content is the qualitative mode of interaction among individuals making up a social system, while structure is the spatial and temporal web of duties and responsibilities which join the roles of the system together. For fuller explanation see Hsu 1959, 790–805 and Hsu 1963, 27–28.

3. Some recent occurrences may prompt the conclusion that Japan is changing. I think these changes are superficial.

4. As when the term *giri* is now used among forest and other workers to refer to "obligations between near-equals related on a basis of mutual advantage" (John Bennett and Iwao Ishino 1963, 194).

References

Bellah, R. (1957). *Tokugawa Religion*. Glencoe, IL: The Free Press.

Benedict, R. (1946). *The Chrysanthemum and the Sword*. Boston: Houghton Mifflin.

Bennett, J. and I. Ishino. (1963). *Paternalism in the Japanese Economy*. Minneapolis: University of Minnesota Press.

Chu, C. (1967). "Wang Mang Kan Liu Hsiu Ch'uan Shue Ti Fen Hsi" (The Legend of Wang Mang's Pursuit Liu Hsiu). *Bulletin of the Institute of Ethnology* (Academica Sinica) 23: 37–104.

De Vos, G. (1973). *Socialization for Achievement: Essays on the Cultural Psychology of the Japanese*. Berkeley: University of California Press.

Ho, P. T. (1968). "Salient Aspects of China's Heritage." In *China in Crises*, ed. P. T. Ho and T. Tsou. Chicago: University of Chicago Press.

Hsu, F. L. K. (1949). "Suppression versus Repression: A Limited Psychological Interpretation of Four Cultures." *Psychiatry* 12.3: 223–42.

———. (1959). "Structure, Function, Content, and Process." *American Anthropologist* 61: 790–805.

———. (1963). *Clan, Caste, and Club.* Princeton, NJ: Van Nostrand.

———. (1968). "Chinese Kinship and Chinese Behavior." In *China in Crises*, ed. P. T. Ho and T. Tsou. Chicago: University of Chicago Press.

———. (1971a). *Under the Ancestor's Shadow*, rev. ed. Stanford: Stanford University Press. (Originally published in 1948 by Columbia University Press)

———. (1971b). "Japanese Kinship and Iemoto" (three chapters written especially for the Japanese translation of *Clan, Caste, and Club*). *Hikaku Bunmei Shakai Ron [Sociology of Comparative Cultures]*. Tokyo: Baifukan.

———. (1975). *Iemoto: The Heart of Japan.* Cambridge, MA: Schenkman.

Kawasaki, I. (1969). *Japan Unmasked.* Rutland, VT and Tokyo: Charles E. Tuttle Company.

Kawashima, T. (1957). *Ideorogi Thoshite no Kazoku Seido (The Family System as an Ideology).* Tokyo: Iwa Nami Shoten.

Linton, R. (1936). *The Study of Man.* New York: Appleton-Century-Crofts.

Parsons, T. and R. F. Bales. (1955). *Family: Socialization and Interaction Process.* Glencoe, IL: Free Press.

Piers, G. and M. B. Singer. (1953). *Shame and Guilt: A Psychoanalytic and Cultural Study.* Springfield, IL: Charles C. Thomas.

II

Historical Dimensions

4

The Korean Adoption of Neo-Confucianism: The Social Context

John Duncan

Strife between Buddhism and Confucianism was a major issue in Korea at the time of the change of dynasties from Koryò to Chosòn. After the founding of the new dynasty, Neo-Confucianism, or more specifically Chu Hsi Learning, replaced Buddhism as the official state orthodoxy in Korea. It is only natural, therefore, that scholarly efforts to explain the significance of the Korean adoption of Neo-Confucianism have focused on the relationship between Neo-Confucianism and the founding of the Chosòn dynasty. While this approach has helped to illuminate the political and social importance of Neo-Confucianism in the early Chosòn period, it has also obscured the spread of Neo-Confucianism among the Korean aristocracy well before Yi Sòng-gye and his supporters overthrew the Koryò dynasty in 1392.[1]

One of the consequences of this inability to appreciate the significance of the late Koryò Neo-Confucianism has been a failure to investigate the social background of the introduction and spread of Neo-Confucianism in Korea in the late thirteenth and fourteenth centuries. There can be no question that Neo-Confucian ideas influenced the ways in which late Koryò dynasty Koreans thought and behaved, and we cannot doubt that the innate beauty and power of Neo-Confucian ideas, as well as the general prestige of things Chinese, did much to attract Koreans to the new thought. On the other hand, however, the speed with which the Korean ruling class adopted Neo-Confucianism and certain unique features of fourteenth-century Korean thought indicate that the Koreans had their own reasons for finding Neo-Confucianism attractive.

This chapter will set forth the proposition that the medieval Korean aristocracy had, over the centuries, gone through a process of change in the

75

nature and structure of its family that made the aristocrats of the late Koryŏ particularly receptive to the Neo-Confucianism's revived emphasis on family and social ethics.

Conventional Interpretations

There are two major interpretations of the significance of Neo-Confucianism in fourteenth-century Korea. One is the belief that Neo-Confucianism came to the fore as an ideology that expressed the economic, social, and political class interests of a "newly rising scholar-official" *(sinhung sadaebu)* class that seized power with the founding of the Chosŏn dynasty in 1392. The other is the view that the introduction of Neo-Confucian ideas inspired a group of younger scholar-officials frustrated with the corruption and the decadence of the late Koryŏ to overthrow the dynasty and carry out a radical reconstruction of Korean society along the lines of an ideal Confucian model.

The Class Ideology Interpretation

According to the advocates of this interpretation, a new class of scholar-officials rose to challenge the established Koryŏ aristocracy in the late fourteenth century. These scholar-officials are held to have challenged the Buddhism of the aristocracy with their own ideology, Neo-Confucianism or, as it is commonly called in Korea, Chu Hsi Learning (Chuja-hak) (Yi Ki-baek 1976, 200–201). Chu Hsi Learning assertedly protected the scholar-officials' social and economic interests as locally based small and medium size landlords in conflict with the capital-based large landlords of the old Koryŏ aristocracy (Mun Ch'or-yong 1982, 122–23).

This interpretation presents some problems. The argument that Neo-Confucianism represented the interests of a new class of medium and small size landowners against the interests of the large landowners is difficult to accept for a number of reasons. To begin with, nowhere in the writings of the late Koryŏ and early Chosŏn is any attempt to rationalize or justify the social position of the locally based medium to small landlords. Furthermore, to the extent that ideologies reflect material interests, it is difficult to imagine how the relations of production for a medium-size landlord would differ from the relations of production for a large-size landlord. In either case, the means of production was the land and the relations of production were landlord-tenant and landlord-slave relations. Adherents of the class ideology interpretation endeavor to distinguish between the aristocracy and the scholar-officials on the grounds that the former were absentee landlords while the latter were resident landlords. Even if this assertion were true, once the scholar-officials took office and moved their residence to the capital, they also would have in effect become absentee landlords. At any rate, the residence of the landlord would not change the essential nature of the landlord-tenant and landlord-slave relationship. If the new scholar-officials were in fact landlords, there would appear to be no basis in their economic foundations for distinguishing between their thought and that of the landlords of the established aristocracy.

If the scholar-officials represented a genuinely new social element rising up to overthrow an established Buddhistic aristocracy, they would have needed to challenge the Buddhist underpinnings of Koryò society. Chong To-jòn did criticize the Buddhist doctrine of the transmigration of souls, which has frequently been cited as providing justification for aristocratic privilege in his *Pulssi chappyòn (Discourses on Buddha)*, but he did so not on the grounds that karma provided a false justification for hereditary social status but rather on metaphysical grounds, saying that the interaction of *yin* and *yang* and the five agents give rise to a continual going and coming between the dying and the borning that did not allow the pause needed for the personality (*chongsin*, literally spirit) of a deceased person to receive a new form (Song Ch'ang-han 1978, 235). Neither Chong nor any other thinker of the fourteenth century attacked the basic class structure of Koryò society. To the contrary, the brunt of the reformers' attack on Buddhism was directed, as Yi Sang-back has shown, at the great wealth of the Buddhist temples. The late Koryò-early Chosòn attack against Buddhism was motivated more by the need for funds for military and other state expenditures than by class antagonisms (Yi Sang-baek 1949, 163–76).

The argument that Neo-Confucianism was the ideology of a new scholar-official class that eventually overthrew the Koryò aristocracy can be questioned on yet another ground: the social backgrounds of the leading exponents of Neo-Confucianism. The most prominent Neo-Confucianists of the late Koryò period were high officials, closely identified with the Koryò royal family and aristocracy.[2] It is difficult to understand how, under the new scholar-official scenario, such stalwarts of the old regime could have introduced and propagated the ideology of their class enemies. Furthermore, a recent study of the social backgrounds of the officials of the early Chosòn dynastic government has shown that the overwhelming majority of the high-ranking officials of the early Chosòn were from old well-established Koryò aristocratic families (Duncan 1989). The leading Korean exponents of Neo-Confucianism in the fourteenth century were full-fledged members of the aristocracy. The attempt to explain the spread of Neo-Confucianism as the ideology of a new class of scholar-officials rising to power in the late fourteenth century fails to satisfy because there was no such class.

The Radical Confucianization Theory

The primary alternative to the class conflict interpretation is the argument that the late Koryŏ discovery of Neo-Confucianism inspired the Koreans to reject Buddhist beliefs and remodel their society along Confucian lines. This view is anchored in the assumption that Koryŏ was a static Buddhist society that had changed little during the centuries prior to the introduction of Neo-Confucianism in the late thirteenth century. Typical of this conception of the relationship between thought and society in Koryŏ is the view of Yi Pyŏng-do, who describes a coexistence between Buddhism and Confucianism, where Buddhism provided the philosophical foundations of society while Confucianism concerned itself with little beyond administrative technology and belles lettres (Yi Pyŏng-do 1961, 227).

The leading spokesperson for the radical Confucianization approach is Martina Deuchler, who believes that the founding of the Chosŏn marked the beginning of the Confucian transformation of Korean society. Deuchler characterizes Neo-Confucianism as in "impulse to social action" and provides the following succinct statement of the radical Confucianization argument: "Above all, the establishment of the Yi (Chosŏn) dynasty was a moral and intellectual venture that set out to prove itself by transforming Korea into a Confucian society" (Deuchler 1980, 73). She describes three stages in the Confucianization of Korean society. The first stage, belonging to the late Koryŏ, featured a pragmatic search by a group of reform-minded scholars and officials for a cure for social disorder and an effort to find that cure in close imitation of Chinese social institutions. The second, in the early Chosŏn, was marked by an "increasingly differentiated view of the Confucian mission" as some scholars, such as Yang Song-ji, began to assert the need to preserve native customs. Deuchler's third stage, in the sixteenth century, was the development of philosophical Neo-Confucianism, which provided the Koreans with a means to rationalize the retention of native customs and to integrate those customs with the Chinese values the Koreans had been assimilating since the beginning of the Chosŏn dynasty (Deuchler 1980, 96–99).

Deuchler as done much to illuminate the influence of Neo-Confucianism on early Chosŏn society, but there are problems with her interpretation that suggest there is much more involved in the history of Confucianism and society in Korea than the revolutionary reorganization of society according to an imported ideal. Deuchler herself ultimately does more to describe the Koreanization of Neo-Confucianism than the Confucianization of Korea. Her third stage in the Confucianization of Korean society was a process by which the Koreans supplemented the constant *ye* (proper ritual behavior) of "heavenly principle" *(i* or *li)* with a variable *ye* that "adjusted itself to time and geographic location." The Koreans used this concept of a variable *ye* to justify the retention of aristocratic aspects of the native Korean social order. The end result of all this, Deuchler says, was the mid-sixteenth-century emergence of a "coherent and well integrated system" that combined Chinese values and native Korean social customs (Deuchler 1980, 96–97). This compromise with indigenous tradition suggests, however, that in the end Deuchler's idealist reformers failed in their attempt to remake Korean society according to the classical Chinese model, that Korean social interests were stronger than imported ideals.

One source of Deuchler's difficulty may be her assumption that Koryŏ was a static Buddhist society. While she does recognize the presence of some form of Confucianism during the Koryŏ, Deuchler appears to follow the old view that Koryŏ Confucianism was nothing more than literary fashion and administrative techniques that had little or no influence on society. Despite such views, however, there is evidence that some Confucian social values had already begun to take root among the central aristocracy during the early Koryŏ dynasty. The use of the common generational name (*haengnyol* or *tollim cha*), a typically Confucian custom employed to identify generations in a line of descent, occurred among the central officials as early as the late eleventh century.[3] There is also evidence that some officials observed the Confucian three-year mourning period in twelfth-century Koryŏ: Yom Sin-yak, who passed the examinations during King Injong's reign (1123–46), is said to have observed the three-year mourning period at his father's graveside (*Koryo-sa* [KRS] 99:29a). This type of evidence not only raises serious questions about the notion that pre-Chosŏn dynasty Korea was an unchanging society based solely, or even primarily, on Buddhist principles, it also suggests that the relationship between Confucianism and society in Korea has a long and complex history that predates the founding of the Chosŏn dynasty by hundreds of years.

Features of Fourteenth-Century Korean Neo-Confucianism

Although modern scholars entranced with the sophisticated Nature and Principle Learning (Sòngni-hak) of the mid-Chosòn dynasty have tended to neglect the Neo-Confucian thought of the fourteenth century, in recent years as number of scholars have begun to study the actual features of late Koryŏ–early Chosòn Neo-Confucian thought. As a result, it has become increasingly clear that the primary concern of fourteenth-century Korean Neo-Confucianists lay in social ethics: the application of the Five Relations and the *Chu Hsi Family Rites (Chu-tzu chia-li)* to Korean society (Duncan 1988, 338–48).

Whereas Deuchler explains this interest in social ethics as the consequence of a search for a model to remake a corrupt society, other scholars argue that late Koryŏ Neo-Confucianism reflected the practical ethics-oriented Yüan dynasty Neo-Confucianism from which it was drawn. (Mun ch'or-yong 1982, 115–17). Although there can be no doubt that the Korean range of thought was very much limited to the ideas to which they were exposed, it is safe to assume that the Koreans accepted Yüan Neo-Confucianism uncritically.

The writings that we have from the fourteenth-century Koreans contain no expositions on the merits and deficiencies of Yüan scholarship. Nonetheless, it is possible to discern some significant differences between Yüan and late Koryŏ Neo-Confucianism. Although the Yüan dynasty was the time when Chu Hsi's interpretations became official orthodoxy, there was a very strong Merit and Profit *(kung-li)* presence in the Yüan during the early to mid fourteenth century (Dardess 1973), the period during which the Koreans were actively borrowing from the Yüan. Yet there is scant evidence of Merit and Profit influence on the Koreans.[4] Another important feature of Yüan Neo-Confucianism was the concept of the true Confucian *(chen-yu)* who was both a scholar of ethics *(yu)* and a bureaucrat or clerk *(li)*, a concept that appears to have been developed to justify Chinese service in a government where moral suasion was of little use and where higher-level decision making was the monopoly of the Mongols, leaving only clerical *(li)* positions for the Chinese (Langlois 1981, 137–38). No such use of the term "true Confucian" appears in Korean writings, although there is one reference in fourteenth-century Korean writings to the relationship between the Confucian and the clerk. This appears in an anecdote contained in Yi Che-hyŏn's *Yogòng p'aesol* about Ch'u Chok, then magistrate of Yongju. When a station clerk asked Yi Che-hyŏn if Ch'u Chok was of Confucian *(yu)* or clerk *(li)* origin, Yi answered, "He always has his brush and inkstone, and sometimes sits alone, reading out loud and whistling, so he appears to be a Confucian" (*Yogòng p'aesol* chonjip 2:15b). This suggests that a clear distinction between the Confucian and the clerk persisted in Korea, where the native royal family remained on the throne and the officials of the dynastic government did not experience the same limitations and frustrations as their Chinese counterparts.

These differences between Yüan and Koryŏ Neo-Confucianism indicate that the fourteenth-century Koreans were selective in what they borrowed from Chinese Neo-Confucianism. There is evidence to suggest that the Koreans' reasons for ignoring certain aspects of Yüan Neo-Confucianism while emphasizing social ethics had less to do with the innate attractiveness of individual concepts than with the applicability of those ideas to Korean society.

The Social Background

The fourteenth-century Korean concern with social ethics was no accident. It was the result of a prolonged process of change that had transformed the local warlord-aristocrats of the tenth century into the capital-based aristocrat-officials of the late Koryò. This process entailed significant change in the internal structure of the aristocratic family, change that required explanation and justification. Neo-Confucianism, with its revived emphasis on the Three Bonds and the Five Relations, provided the necessary explanation.

There has been disagreement among anthropologists and other scholars who study change in family structure about whether it is change in the family that causes change in larger social entities or whether change in the large entities causes change in the family. For example, there is considerable debate about whether the nuclear family arose in Western European societies because of the effects of the industrial revolution on rural society, or whether the rise of the nuclear family was a precondition of the industrial revolution (Wrigley 1978, 71–85).

In the case of Koryò dynasty Korea, it appears that it was change in the relationship of the larger social entities that initially induced change in the aristocratic family. The first Koryò kings were essentially no more than first among equals in a warlord confederation that exercised only tenuous control over local aristocrats throughout the country. By the mid-tenth century, the Koryò kings had successfully elevated themselves above the warlords and had initiated a policy of solidifying the crown's power that featured active recruitment of local aristocrats to serve as officials of the dynastic government. Many local aristocrats responded to the incentives of prestige, power, and financial reward and relocated to the capital. Once in the capital, these aristocrat-officials found the structure of their families transformed by the new setting in which they worked and lived.

The rate of change in early Koryò was moderate, if not slow. Nonetheless, by mid-dynasty the new family type was clearly established at the capital. The process accelerated and spread to the countryside in the wake of the military revolt of 1170 and the Mongol invasions of the thirteenth century so that by the end of the Koryò dynasty a new lineage group had established itself as the dominant aristocratic family type.

The Locally Based Family of Early Koryò

The locally based members of the Koryò aristocracy were the descendants of the local strongmen of the late Silla era. These warlord-aristocrats had developed their own local governments during the chaotic years before the fall of Silla and they exercised almost total control over their localities. Even after the founding of the Koryò dynasty, these local strongmen were able to maintain much of their autonomy, as reflected in the irregular prefecture-county (kun-hyòn) system of Koryò where social status was bound to geographic location (Hatada 1972, 3–40). As a consequence, the local aristocratic families of early and mid-Koryò settled permanently in their clan seats (pon'gwan), where, as hereditary local officials, they enjoyed high social status, exercised political control, collected taxes and corvee, and even directed local military and quasi-military units. Their marital relations also functioned to bolster and preserve their position in the local social order as they typically married members of their own families or neighboring local aristocrats (Ho Hùng-sik 1981, 402–4).

The locally based early Koryò aristocratic family exhibited characteristics of matrilineal as well as patrilineal descent. While the children took the father's surname and, as seen in early Koryò tombstone incriptions, seem to have traced their primary line of descent through the male side, under the resident son-in-law *(teril sawi)* system, couples lived with the wife's family until their children were grown. Inheritances were divided equally among children without regard to sex. Even ancestral memorial services alternated between sons and daughters (Ch'oe Chae-sòk 1982, 228). This relatively equal treatment of males and females was reflected in dynastic policy, which did not discriminate between the children of sons and the children of daughters in extending special privileges to merit subject progeny (Ch'oe Chae-sòk 1982, 204).

Although the early Koryò dual-lineage family appears to be basically a continuation of the Silla family type (Yi Kwang-gyu 1977, 396–98), it was closely integrated with the early Koryò sociopolitical order. Robin Fox points out that lineage principles develop out of residence locations. That is, the patrilineal principle arises as a result of patrilocal residence and the matrilineal principle as a result of matrilocal residence (Fox 1967, 95–96). If we apply Fox's line to Korea, it follows that the matrilineal features of the early Koryò family derived from the resident son-in-law system and that the maintenance of those matrilineal features was dependent on the continuation of the permanently settled, closely intermarried family pattern where the wife's family was not only close by, but also of equal status with the husband's family, so that she could enjoy the protection of her family (or her side of the family) and draw on its authority to enhance her own power within the marital relationship. Also, under the early Koryò system a family's status and prestige was dependent not so much on the efforts of individual members as on the family's continued participation in the closely entwined pattern of local life that guaranteed the continuing prestige of the local aristocrats; the role of individual males as family heads was not as important as it would be under more mobile circumstances. The dual-lineage aristocratic family of early Koryò was part of a complex, interdependent local social and political order.

The Transformation

The Koryò dynasty, anxious to ensure the loyalty of the locally based aristocracy, actively recruited their sons to serve in the central government.

This was particularly true after the establishment of the government service examination system in the mid-tenth century, with the result that there was a steady stream of men flowing into the capital from the provinces. Once these men arrived in the capital, they tended to remain and establish capital-based lines of descent.

This movement of local aristocrats into the capital did not entail the wholesale relocation of entire clans, but rather the branching out of local aristocrats from their clan seats to the capital. Yi Su-gòn has shown in his recent study of the early Chosòn Rusticated Scholars in southeastern Korea that this kind of branching out was a general phenomenon. Yi has noted, as an example, that the Kyòngju local aristocrats had bifurcated into capital and local official lines in the early Koryò, with the provincial branches continuously providing new blood for the central officialdom (Yi Su-gòn 1982, 29). Another concrete example of this can be found in the Andong Kwòn. While one line of the clan descended from Kwòn Kyun-han, that represented by Kwòn Chwa-sòm and his son Kwòn Chok, was establishing itself in the capital in the late eleventh and early twelfth centuries, another line stayed in Andong as local officials (Pak Kyong-ha 1974, 79).

The separation of central family branches from their provincial origins brought about changes in lifestyles and attitudes. One visible and important change was in marriage patterns. As noted earlier, while in their clan seats the local aristocrats customarily married within their own clans. By contrast, the marriage pattern of the central aristocrats appears to have been almost exclusively exogamous (Ho Hùng-sik 1980, 402). Inasmuch as nearly all the central families had once been local aristocrats themselves, it seems probably that when Koryò aristocrats left their clan seats and established themselves at the capital, they abandoned their tradition of endogamy in favor of exogamous marriages with other central official families.

The source materials documenting this change are limited. Clan genealogies contain little, if any, information on marriages in the early and mid Koryò period and what they do show is suspect, since Chosòn dynasty compilers may have edited their clans' genealogies to conform with the values of their Confucian orthodoxy. The *Koryò-sa* biographies also have little in the way of marriage data. There is, however, one largely neglected source of detailed information on marriage relationships: tombstone inscriptions. There are approximately 150 extant tombstone inscriptions for Koryò central official families, with dates ranging from the early eleventh century to the end of the dynasty. These tombstones typically identify the mothers and wives, sons and daughters, and often even the sons- and daughters-in-law of the descendants. The overwhelming majority of these tombstones are for men of prominent, well-established central aristocrat clans such as the Haeju Ch'oe, the Kyòngwòn Yi, the Suju Ch'oe, the Andong Kwòn, or the Andong Kim. The marriage relationships for these established members of the central aristocracy were invariably exogamous.

There are, on the other hand, tombstones for nine central officials who were new arrivals from the countryside. Of these nine tombstones, four—those for Ham Yu-il, Yi Tòk-su, Yi Mun-t'aek, and Pak Kang-su—indicate that the decedent's mothers and fathers were of the same clan. Nonetheless, once they had arrived in the capital all four of these men married women from other clans, and their children also all married outside the clan (Han'guk kùmsòk chonmun [hereafter HGKS] 3:845–46, 869, 935, 1084).

The new central officials' rejection of endogamy in favor of exogamy cannot be simply attributed to exposure to Confucian ethics in the capital. Many of these men came to the capital as graduates of provincial Confucian schools and passers of the local examinations *(hyanggong)*, making it impossible to believe that they had not been exposed to Confucian social and family ethics before arrival at the capital. A more probable explanation for the change in marriage patterns is that men new on the capital scene were anxious to secure their position by entering into marriage alliances with other central official families. This tended to draw newly arrived officials and their immediate families into the web of capital society and away from their insular clan seat origins.

By the mid-eleventh century the practice of exogamy became so entrenched at the capital that aristocrats were seeking to have it codified. This trend began with a 1046 edict prohibiting the appointment to official positions of the offspring of marriages between first cousins. The strictures were broadened to include second cousins in 1096, but just five years later the restrictions were removed for both first cousins and second cousins. There were subsequent attempts to restrict endogamy in 1116, 1134, and 1147. There is some question as to how successful these efforts were (Yi Kwang-gyu 1977, 62–63), but it is significant that each successive try widened the scope of restriction.

Why, when exogamy was already standard practice among capital-based families, did the officials of the dynastic government make repeated efforts to establish legal strictures against endogamy? The answer can be found in the way restrictions were to be enforced. As seen in the 1046 edict, the dynasty chose not to punish directly the bride and the bridegroom, but rather to prohibit their offspring from holding central offices. Since the children of the central aristocrats came from exogamous unions, this edict would have had little effect on them; it would, however, have had made it much more difficult for the sons of local aristocrats, many of whom were products of endogamous marriages, to gain positions in the dynastic government. In short, it was a way for the central aristocracy to reduce competition for the limited number of positions available in the dynastic government.

Although these Confucian marriage practices may have been used for practical political and social purposes by the early Koryò aristocracy, by the late Koryò they had become virtually unquestionable ethical requirements. The strength of the late Koryò central officialdom's belief in exogamy is illustrated by the inscription on the 1347 tombstone of Madame Ch'oe, wife of Lim Yun of the Ònyang Kim clan. The tombstone states: "One daughter [of Ch'oe and Kim Yun] married Grand General Kim Hwi-nam. Hwi-nam is a Haeyang man. He is not of the same clan as the Ònyang Kim, so there is no abomination" (HGKS 3:1179). Exogamy was clearly becoming an absolute value among the central aristocracy of the late Koryò.

If exogamy had become the rule among the central aristocrats, what then of locally based families in late Koryò? The storms that broke over the Korean peninsula during the latter half of the Koryò dynasty in the Mongol invasions and the Wako raids forced the local aristocracy to change in order to survive. Their clan seats devastated, many of them were forced to relocate to the capital or to other localities in the provinces (Ho Hùng-sik 1978, 264). Whichever the case, these aristocrats were now deprived of the privileges they had enjoyed as hereditary leaders of their clan seats and forced to survive on their own in new locations.

Did this uprooting of the local aristocrats lead them toward exogamy in the same way relocation to the capital had? The evidence here is mixed. On the one hand, Ho Hùng-sik found in his study of the families of the *Kukpo Hojòk* (National Treasury Family Register, dating from the late fourteenth century) that some local officials were still practicing endogamy quite late in the Koryò dynasty (Ho Hùng-sik 1977, 34–35). On the other hand, Ho's examination of the marriage relationships of the Hamgyong Province-based family of Sim Kyong-jong revealed that the marriage partners of the Sim were local aristocrats from various areas throughout the country, including the Kongju Yi, the Chonju Yi, and the Tongnae Chong (Ho Hùng-sik 1978, 262–63).

The apparent conflict between the two sources of evidence can be explained. Families still identified as local officials in late Koryò, such as those seen in the *Kukpo Hojòk,* were very probably families with clan seats in areas where the local social order had suffered minimal disruption and the old system, including marriage patterns, still survived. On the other hand, in areas where the Koryò local order had been destroyed or where there had been much migration, such as northeastern Korea, the newly relocated families would have been unable to continue the marriage patterns of the past, even if they had wanted to. Furthermore, they doubtless found it advantageous to marry with a number of other families in order to consolidate their social position in their new location, just as capital-based families found it necessary to forge marriage alliances with other central official families. As Ho says, "That there was little endogamy [in the northeastern area] was due less to early influence from Chinese family ethics than to the gathering of many families from various places to live together in one area" (Ho Hùng-sik 1978, 264). The practice of endogamy was clearly on the wane in the late Koryò, well before Neo-Confucianism became the officially sanctioned orthodoxy.

Another major change in the late Koryò ruling class family was the rise in status of the male head of family and the corresponding fall of the wife. The Koryò woman, in comparison to her Chosòn descendants, enjoyed a great deal of power and freedom. She had her own property, enjoyed equal inheritance rights with her brothers, was free to divorce and remarry, and shared ancestor worship *(chesa)* duties with her male siblings. Her subsequent loss of status is generally attributed to the influence of Neo-Confucianism, but in the context of the general downward trend in the status of women throughout premodern Korea, from the Silla dynasty when women ruled as queens to the late Chosòn when women's power and freedom were severely circumscribed, it can be seen as part of a long-term historical trend whose beginnings far predated the introduction of Neo-Confucianism in the late Koryò dynasty.

The increased geographic mobility of the late Koryò aristocratic family was an important cause of the rise in the status of the male head of family. This mobility worked to elevate the male head in two major ways. First, once a household left its clan seat to move elsewhere, the wife could no longer benefit from the support and protection of her own immediate relatives, unless her family happened to move along with her and her husband. While such cases probably did exist, nuclear families accounted for the greatest proportion of the families in the *Kukpo Hojòk* (Ho Hùng-sik 1977, 91–92), suggesting that late Koryò family movement generally involved husband, wife, and children. Without the constant, tangible reminders of her own family's status—or in the case of endogamy, her own support from within the family—the wife was on weaker ground in defending her position within the family.

Second, deprived of its fixed position within the settled, closely inter-woven society of its clan seat, the mobile aristocratic family of late Koryò was much more dependent on the success of its male members in obtaining posts in the government or otherwise providing for the family. Indirect evidence of this is a trend for the difference in age between husband and wife to increase near the end of the Koryò dynasty (Ho Hùng-sik 1980, 305). In a situation where the status and prosperity of the family was dependent on the husband's success in a competitive and unsettled situation, men would have been likely to postpone marriage until they felt capable of providing for a family, while prospective brides would have sought men who had already achieved a degree of status and security. The importance of the ability of its male members to provide for the family meant that the family—including the wife—had to muster its resources and its support to ensure the success of its men. The increasing importance of the role of the male family head in providing for the family resulted in higher status for men, within and without the family.

As a consequence of this process, by the end of the Koryò dynasty a new family type had emerged in the aristocracy, both in the capital and in the provinces. In contrast to the locally settled, closely intermarried, endogamous family of early Koryò where women enjoyed comparatively great power and freedom, the late Koryò family was geographically mobile and limited in size to the members of the immediate family, with the male head of family responsible for leading the family and taking care of social and economic affairs. Although the male head of family still did not exercise all the authority his mid- and late-Chosòn descendants did, the late Koryò aristocratic family was already well on its way to becoming the patriarchal family typical of the Chosòn dynasty long before Neo-Confucianism permeated Korean society. Within this context, such late Koryò-early Chosòn efforts to promulgate Neo-Confucian practices as the 1390 edicts requiring eldest sons (of official families) to carry out ancestor worship ceremonies according to the provisions of the *Chu Hsi Family Ritual* must be seen not as initial attempts to remold Korean family life but rather as an attempt to formalize and justify a family system that had already taken shape within the Koryò central aristocracy.

Discussion

The Koryò dynasty transformation of the aristocratic family from a locally based, highly endogamous entity whose status derived from its traditional position as local rulers to a mobile, exogamous unit whose prestige depended largely on the success of its male head in securing a post with the dynastic government must have introduced stresses and strains into family relationships. Most obvious in this regard is the relationship between husband and wife. Although the decline of the Korean aristocratic woman from her position of relative equality at the beginning of the Koryò dynasty to a position of near-total Confucian subservience was not complete until the mid-Chosòn dynasty (Ch'oe Chae-sòk 1972, 99–150), there is evidence that the status of women had already deteriorated badly by the end of the Koryò dynasty.

Early Koryò marriage practice had been strictly monogamous, but by the end of the dynasty polygamy was not uncommon among aristocratic families. While the spread of polygamy may be attributable to Mongol influences (Ho Hùng-sik 1977, 97), it could not have happened without the rise in status for men and the corresponding fall in status for women that had already occurred during the preceding centuries. Some sense of women's attitude toward this trend can be found in an anecdote relayed to us by Yi Che-hyòn. According to Yi, near the end of the thirteenth century a high-ranking official named Pak Yu advanced a proposal that officials be allowed to take more than one wife, justifying his suggestion with arguments about numerology and the surplus of women over men. Pak's proposal appears to have met stiff resistance from the women of the capital. Yi tells us, "All women, base and noble, were either angry or worried. On the day of a Buddhist lantern ceremony, Pak was part of the procession that followed the king through the streets. One old woman recognized Pak and said, 'The one who suggested that men be allowed to accumulate wives is that old beggar.' All those who heard shook their fingers at Pak" *(Yogòng p'aesol,* chonjip 2:14a).

The anger of women toward Pak Yu for his suggestion of polygamy suggests resistance to their loss of status. We do not, unfortunately, have any writings by women from the Koryò period to tell us what their feelings were, but it seems very likely that until such time as the paternalistic Confucian family value system was internalized by women, most probably in the early to mid-Chosòn dynasty, the changing roles of men and women must have given rise to considerable stress and tension within the Korean aristocratic family.

Finally, it may be useful to note that the way in which the late Koryò aristocracy was predisposed to accept and use Neo-Confucian social values to reinforce an already emerging new family type may help to explain why Deuchler's early Chosòn reformers were ultimately unable to recreate faithfully the Chinese model in Korea. It seems possible that, despite their lofty rhetoric and appeals to hoary Chinese antiquity, the reformers' real purpose was not to remake Korean society according to a Chinese model but rather to use Neo-Confucianism to give direction to and justification for a social system that had already begun to take shape before Neo-Confucianism was introduced to Korea.

Notes

1. Neo-Confucianism, introduced to Korea by An Hyang in 1286, had by the mid-fourteenth century gained wide acceptance among the officials of the Koryo dynastic government, including such luminaries as Yi Che-hyon, Kwon Pu, U T'ak, and Yi Saek. In fact, close examinations of the individuals involved in the factional fighting leading up to the overthrow of the Koryo dynasty reveals that the struggle was not between Neo-Confucianists and Buddhists but rather between two groups of Neo-Confucianists, with Chong To-jon and Cho Chun on one side and Chong Mong-ju and Yi Saek on the other (Duncan 1988, 398–412).

2. One of the greatest late Koryo Neo-Confucianists, Yi Che-hyon, was a particular favorite of King Ch'ungson; Yi Che-hyson's clan was closely intermarried with other powerful late Koryo clans such as the P'ap'yong Yun, the Munhwa Yu, and the Andong Kwon. Another important late Koryo Neo-Confucianist, Yi Sung-in, was a member of the same clan as the notorious late Koryo aristocrat Yi In-im; his clan was also closely intermarried with members of the late Koryo aristocracy, including the Yangch'on Ho, the Kyongju Yi, and Namyang Hong.

3. One clan that followed this practice was the Inju Yi clan, where the given names of Yi Cha-yon's grandsons all began with the character *cha* as in Yi Cha-ui, Yi

Cha-ryang, Yi Cha-gyom, and so on. Another was the Haeju Ch'oe clan, where Ch'oe Ch'ung's sons' given names all began with the character *sa*, as in Ch'oe Sa-ch'u, Ch'oe, Sa-gil, and Ch'oe Sa-ryang (*Koryo-sa* [hereafter KRS] 95:1aff.; 95:9 aff.).

4. The practical arguments advanced by such fourteenth-century Korean reformers as Cho Chun or Chong To-jon can all be found within the practical side of Chu Hsi (Langlois, 183–84); the typical Merit and Profit phrase "rich country and strong army" (*puguk kangbyong*, or *fu-kuo ch'iang-ping* in Chinese) does not appear in fourteenth-century Korean writings; Wang An-shih is mentioned only rarely, and such Merit and Profit stalwarts as Ch'en Liang and Ch'en Fu-liang are nowhere to be found in Korean writings.

References

Ch'oe Chae-sòk. 1972. "Chosòn sidae ui sangsok-je e kwanhan yon'gu" (Research on the inheritance system of the Chosòn period). *Yoksa hakpo* 53–54.

————. 1982. "Koryò sidae ui ch'injok chojik" (Kinship organization of the Koryò period). *Yoksa hakpo* 94–95.

Chong In-ji. 1955. *Koryò-sa*. Yonsei taehakkyo [Yonsei Univ.-Publisher] Seoul.

Chosen sotoku-fu. 1919. *Chosen kinsekibun soran* (Compilation of Korean Epigraphy). Seoul.

Deuchler, Martina. 1980. "Neo-Confucianism: The Impulse for Social Action in Early Yi Dynasty Korea." *The Journal of Korean Studies* 2.

Dardess, John W. 1973. *Conquerors and Confucians*. New York: Columbia University Press.

Duncan, John B. 1988. "The Koryò Origins of the Chosòn Dynasty: Kings, Aristocrats, and Confucianism." Ph.D. dissertation, University of Washington, Seattle.

————. 1989. "The Social Background to the Founding of the Chosòn Dynasty: Change or Continuity?" *The Journal of Korean Studies* 6.

Fox, Robin. 1967. *Kinship and Marriage*. Cambridge: Cambridge University Press.

Hatada, Takashi. 1972. *Chosen chusei shakai-shi no kenkyu* (Studies in the social history of medieval Korea). Tokyo: Hosei daigaku.

Ho Hùng-sik. 1977. "Kukpo Hojòk uro pon Koryò malgi ui sahoe kujo" (The structure of late Koryò society as seen through the National Treasure Family Register). *Han'guk-sa yon'gu* 16.

————. 1978. "Chosòn ch'o Sim Kyong-jong ui ch'usim-Ho wa ku punsok" (Analysis of the family register of Sim Kyong-jong of the early Chosòn dynasty). *Taegu sahak* 15–16.

————. 1980. *Koryò sahoe-sa yon'gu* (Studies in Koryò social history). Seoul: Ilcho-gak.

————. 1984. *Han'guk kùmsòk chonmun* (Complete Korean epigraphy). Seoul: Asea munhwa-sa.

Langlois, John D. 1981. "Political Thought in Chin-hua under Mongol Rule." In *China under Mongol Rule*, ed. John D. Langlois. Princeton: Princeton University Press.

Mun Ch'or-yong. 1982. "Yomal sinhung sadaebu dul ui sin yuhak suyong kwa ku t'ukching" (The acceptance of Neo-Confucianism by the newly rising Sadaebu of late Koryò and its features). *Han'guk munhwa* 3.

Pak Kyong-ja. 1974. "Koryò hyangni chedo ui songnip." (The establishment of the Koryò local official system). *Yoksa hakpo* 63.

Wrigley, C. Anthony. 1978. "Reflections on the History of the Family." In Rossi, A. S., Kagen, J., and Halevi, M. ed., *The Family*, ed. Rossi, Kagen, and Halevi. New York: W. W. Norton.

Yi Che-hyòn. 1959. *Yogòng p'aesol* (Scribblings of old man oak). *Taedong munhwa yon'gu-won*.

Yi Ki-baek. 1976. *Han'guk-sa sillon* (A new history of Korea). Seoul: Ilcho-gak.

Yi Kwang-gyu. 1977. *Han'guk kajok ui sa-jok yon'gu* (Historical studies of the Korean family). Seoul: Ilji-sa.

Yi Pyòng-do. 1961. *Han'guk-sa chungse-p'yon* (History of Korea—Medieval period). Chindan hakhoe ed. Seoul: Uryu munhwa-sa.

Yi Sang-baek. 1949. *Yijo kon'guk ui yon'gu: Yijo ui kon'guk kwa chonje kaehyok munje* (A study on the founding of the Chosòn dynasty: The founding of the Chosòn and the land reform problem). Seoul: Uryu munhwa-sa.

Yi Su-gòn. 1982. *Yongnam sarim-p'a ui hyòngsong* (The formation of the Yongnam sarim faction). Taegu: Yongnam taehakkyo.

————. 1984. *Han'guk chungse sahoe-sa yon'gu* (Studies in the social history of medieval Korea). Seoul: Ilcho-gak.

5

The Confucian Incursion into Vietnam

Nguyen Ngoc Huy

The Introduction of Confucianism into Vietnam: Its Impact Prior to the Fifteenth Century

The Vietnamese belong to the Southeast Asian group of nations. *"Ethnological and biological evidence as well as social and cultural indications shown strong affinities between the Vietnamese people and the peoples of the Indonesian and Thai racial families"* (Buttinger 1972, 22). It is known that by the seventh century B.C., some Viet tribes had founded a kingdom named Van Lang in the Red River delta and the northern part of present Vietnam. This kingdom was subsequently conquered by other Viet tribes from the northern part of present North Vietnam and the southern part of Chinese Guangxi Province. As a result of this conquest, a new kingdom, Au Lac, was formed in the last decade of the third century B.C.

Although both Van Lang and Au Lac were ruled by feudal lords, during this period Viet society was matriarchal. Legends related to the foundation of the Van Lang kingdom and its kings show that although the Viet royal family was then led by men, authority was transmitted by mothers to their eldest daughter: our first national heroines, the sisters Trung, descended from the Van Lang ruling family through their mother (*Lich su Viet Nam*, 1971, 1:80). In addition, the Viet people practiced levirate, a custom by which widows were required to marry their deceased husband's brother (Vu Van Mau 1970). Such a matriarchal system, with the eldest daughter's husband succeeding her father and thus ruling the country, was probably also in force in prehistoric China. Indeed, according to Chinese legends, Emperor Yao (r. 2356–2255 B.C.) abdicated in favor of Shun after marrying his two daughters to him, and when Shun's brother planned to assassinate him, he aimed at becoming the husband of his two sisters-in-law and thereby emperor (Legge 1960, 5.1.1, paras. 3 and 4, 343–44; 5.1.2, para. 3, 346–47).

By 180/179 B.C., Au Lac was annexed to the Nam Viet (Nan Yue) kingdom founded by a Qin general named Trieu Da (Zhao Tuo) who was formerly an official during the Chinese dynasty (221–207 B.C.). Nam Viet in turn was conquered by the Han (206 B.C.–A.D. 220) in 111 B.C. The Viet people remained under Chinese rule until A.D. 938. Confucianism was introduced into Vietnam during this millenary Chinese domination.

Initially the Chinese rulers did not impose their customs on the Viet people. The Trieu only appointed a civilian representative and a military officer to control the former Au Lac territory, while the administration of its population was entrusted to the Viet feudal lords (Vu Van Mau 1970, 1:79). After conquering the Nam Viet kingdom, the Han divided the former Au Lac territory into prefectures *(jun)* that were then divided into districts *(xian)* as in other parts of their empire. Each of these districts, however, corresponded to the territory of one Viet tribe, and the feudal lords were appointed as district chiefs (Dao Duy Anh 1964). Thus, during the first centuries of Chinese domination, the Viet people kept their primary customs and way of life. Confucianist principles were followed only by the Chinese living in Vietnam as officials, exiled people, or settlers and their descendants.

At the beginning of the Christian era, the Chinese instituted a policy of assimilation and tried to spread Confucianism among ethnic Vietnamese. Prefects Tich Quang (Xi Guang) and Nham Dien (Ren Yan) devoted themselves to teaching the Viet people elements of the Chinese morality based on Confucianism with particular attention to marriage rites. At first these officials attempted to entice the Vietnamese. For example, Nham Dien asked his clerks to contribute a part of their salaries to the costs of marriages for those natives who accepted the Chinese customs *(Dai Viet su ky toan thu* [hereafter TT] 1967–68, 1:89). This ingratiating policy did not provoke any resistance. But when To Dinh (Su Ding), a greedy and cruel prefect continued this process of assimilation, he met with fierce opposition from the Viet feudal lords. His vigorous repression against the protesters led to the revolt of the two sisters Trung (39–43). After defeating this insurrection, the Han no longer used the Viet feudal lords as chiefs of districts. Instead, they appointed Chinese civil servants to administer the entire Viet territory. From then on, the Chinese applied a constant and vigorous policy of assimilation in Vietnam.

As a result of this policy, Confucianism, and especially its rules concerning families, continued to spread in Viet society. Nevertheless, the matriarchal system persisted for centuries. Lady Trieu was followed by many people when she led an uprising against the Chinese government in 248. According to a report by Tiet Tong (Xue Zong), a prefect appointed by the Wu kingdom (221–280), several Viet people under his administration still practiced levirate

(Vu Van Mau). But beginning in the sixth century, revolts against the Chinese were led by men, and no longer by women. It seems that the Viet society by that time had been totally transformed into a patriarchy. Thus, Confucian morality, and its standards governing family conduct and interpersonal relationships was followed by the Viet people before the end of the Chinese domination. By then, the Viet family was then headed by a male who was permitted to have multiple wives. Furthermore, everyone had a family name, which was that of his or her father.

When Vietnam acquired independence in the tenth century, Confucianism was well rooted in a society that was entirely molded upon patriarchal principles. It was not, however, the most influential system of thought. Besides Confucianism, Taoism and Buddhism had also been introduced into Vietnam during the Chinese domination. Buddhism was brought first by Indian monks, then developed and reinforced by Chinese masters. Since its beliefs were well suited to the religious needs of the Vietnamese people, Buddhism was more influential than Confucianism and Taoism. Moreover, during the period of Chinese domination, Confucianist scholars of Vietnamese origin had been appointed as officials in other parts of China, and thus when Vietnam became independent, the most learned men were Buddhist monks. Inasmuch as they were versed in Chinese culture and did not participate in political struggles, these monks were respected and trusted by the Vietnamese rulers. They served as counselors to the Vietnamese court, especially in its relations with China. In addition, they played a significant role in education. Being open-minded and learned men, the Buddhist monks not only spread their religious beliefs, but also taught Confucianist philosophy to those who were destined to become civil servants for the administration.

The first generation of Vietnamese Confucianist scholars formed by Buddhist monks were, of course, devote Buddhists. But soon Confucianism had at its disposal enough learned men to expand without the help of Buddhist teachers. The result was that Confucian disciples played a more and more important role in the Vietnamese court. In addition, the Vietnamese rulers, although devoted Buddhists, also tried to extend the influence of Confucianism, which they considered necessary for their rule. For example, in 1070 Emperor Ly Thanh Tong built a Confucian temple in the capital that also served at the same time as a school, and the crown prince was ordered to go there for his studies (TT, 1:234). In 1075, Thanh Tong's successor Nhan Tong organized the first Confucianist examinations (TT, 1:236). This policy was followed by other rulers of the Ly (1009–1225) and Tran (1225–1400) dynasties.

As they became increasingly powerful, Confucianist scholars came to oppose Buddhism. Thus, in 1198 a Confucianist high dignitary, Dam Di Mong (twelfth–thirteenth centuries) was able to ask Emperor Ly Cao Tong to reduce the number of Buddhist monks and the sovereign probably followed his advice

(TT, 1:298). Buddhism regained its influence after the Tran replaced the Ly in 1225, but the new rulers continued to pay a great deal of respect to Confucianism. However, since the Tran early sovereigns always appointed one of their relatives as prime minister or commander-in-chief of the army, Confucianist scholars began to serve only in the lower ranks of the hierarchy. At a later date, however, they gradually gained more influence and expressed their hostility towards Buddhism.

In the official *Dai Viet su ky* (*Annals of Dai Viet,* 1272), historian Le Van Huu (1229–1322) often criticized the Ly emperors for being too influenced by Buddhist beliefs and teachings (TT, 1:191–92, 221, 262). In the middle of the fourteenth century, Confucianist scholars regarded one of their masters, Chu Van An (?–1370), as a paragon of Confucianist virtues. They praised and venerated him as a model and led new attacks against the Buddhists. In a stela built for the Buddhist temple Chieu Phuc in Bac Giang Province, Le Quat fourteenth century), an official of the Tran dynasty, wrote:

> Wherever there are human habitations, we can find Buddhist temples. They are rebuilt when abandoned, repaired when deteriorated. Their bell and drum towers occupy half of all the buildings in the country. Thus, Buddhism has no difficulty acquiring followers and is very respected. I have read books since my youth. My studies about the old and present times allow me to understand more or less the way of our Saint (Confucius). It educates people, yet is not unanimously accepted. I have traveled a lot to contemplate mountains and rivers, my feet have their prints in half of our country, yet I cannot find any trace of (Confucianist) schools or temples. Thus, I am very ashamed vis-à-vis Buddhist followers. (TT, 2:161).

If Le Quat showed more jealousy than hostility against Buddhism, his colleague Truong Han Sieu (?–1354) took a far more forceful position. Invited to prepare a text for the stele of Quan Nghiem Buddhist temple, also in Bac Giang Province, the latter wrote: "Superstitious beliefs must be banned while the Saint's way has to be restored" (TT, 2:14). In this text, superstitious beliefs refer to Buddhism, and the Saint's way to Confucianism. It was very unfair for a Confucianist scholar invited to compose a text for a Buddhist stela to take advantage of this opportunity and express such a hostile opinion about Buddhism. But this example shows the Confucianists' aggressive mood of the period.

At the same time, Confucianist scholars tried to convince the Tran emperors to adopt Chinese institutions, which were considered as more in line with Confucianist teachings. Emperor Tran Du Tong (r. 1341–69) followed their advice. But when his successor, Emperor Tran Nghe Tong (r. 1370–72), ascended the throne, he ordered the restoration of former Tran institutions:

Our forefathers, since the very beginning of the Dynasty, established their own system of law and did not follow the Song laws and institutions. Each of the Northern and Southern countries (China and Vietnam) is sovereign in its sphere and does not need to follow the other country's laws. In the Dai Tri reign (1358–1369), the pale-faced students who were consulted at the time, did not know the deep meaning of legislation: they abandoned the system of law bequeathed by our forefathers and adopted the Northern ways in the areas of clothes, music, institutions, and many other matters. (TT, 2:158)

Thus, until the end, the Tran kept their own institutions and did not blindly follow the Chinese ones.

Ho Qui Ly, who usurped the Tran throne and founded the Ho dynasty (1400–1407) proved to be an original Confucianist. He also opposed Buddhism: in 1396, as a minister for the Tran, he had asked the emperor to force Buddhist monks and Taoist priests under fifty years of age to be defrocked (TT, 2:198). Nevertheless Ho Qui Ly did not accept the Ming practice of elevating as exclusive the interpretations of Confucius's thoughts made by the Song scholars Cheng Hao (1032–1085), Cheng Yi (1033–1107), and especially Zhu Xi (1130–1200). For Ho Qui Ly, these Chinese scholars were well educated but untalented people who were not in touch with reality. Moreover, he thought that the person who ought be worshipped as the first Saint Teacher was the Duke of Zhou, architect of the Chinese feudal system established by the Zhou (1122–249 B.C.) and venerated as a model by Confucius himself; thus, Confucius had to be relegated to the second rank (TT, 2:194). In his preface to a translation into Vietnamese of the *Shi Jing (Book of Poetry)*, Ho Qui Ly discarded Chu Shi's explanations and set forth his own interpretations (TT, 2:199). He proposed establishing a Vietnamese brand of Confucianism different from that of the Chinese. Unfortunately for Vietnam, he was captured and brought to China when the Ming invaded Vietnam in 1407, and as a result his plans were not brought to fruition.

Thus, for centuries, Confucianism was rivaled by Buddhism and Taoism. But inasmuch as Buddhism and Taoism had no special teachings regarding the organization of the family, Confucianism had a primary role in this field. As a result, by the end of the thirteenth century, the Tran rulers had already attempted to promote the principles of Confucian familiar morality. In this concept it is reported that in 1295, one Le Thi Ta, upon hearing the death of her husband on a mission to the Yuan court, fasted for three days and then died. This was considered a model of loyalty toward her husband, a quality highly praised by Confucianists. To award her, Emperor Tran Anh Tong gave silver and silk to her descendants (TT, 2:74).

However, the Tran rulers did not apply all Confucianist teachings concerning the family. The most blatant violation of Confucianist morality was their decision to marry their close relatives. Indeed, because they had succeeded in usurping the Ly throne by maneuvering to have one of their daughters married to Emperor Ly Hue Tong (r. 1210–24), the Tran wanted to avoid similar occurrences by reserving the position of principal wife to a member of their own clan.

Thus, when the Ming conquered Vietnam in 1407, they found in the Vietnamese ways of life at that time "signs of barbarity and depravity." For them, the Vietnamese knew "neither rites nor righteousness" and their Confucian schools were "mean and vulgar." The Chinese were particularly shocked by the Vietnamese laxness "in their observance of mourning for their parents." A Chinese official then noted that when their father or mother died, the Vietnamese "only wore black [instead of white] clothing, and the local officials, students and clerks [continued their duties] instead of going into proper mourning." In short, although they had already adopted Confucianism before the Ming conquest of their country, the Vietnamese "social relationships did not match the Chinese ideals, and their religious beliefs were little better" (Whitmore 1977).

Confucianism in Vietnam from the Fifteenth to the Nineteenth Centuries and Its Impact on the Vietnamese Family

Having publicly declared that they were in Vietnam on a "civilizing mission," the Ming officials acted to control and transform what they considered strange Vietnamese modes of behavior "bureaucratically, legally, and academically." They forced the Vietnamese to adopt the Chinese style of clothing, and they changed cult practices by setting up their own local altars. Confucian temples were then built in every district (Whitmore 1977, 65, 67; TT, 2:250). At the same time, the Chinese moved to spread Chinese culture in Vietnam, especially Neo-Confucianism as officially defined by the Ming court. They established at least 69 medical, 54 astrological, and 126 Confucian schools (Whitmore 1977, 62, 68–69). The Ming court also sent to Vietnam newly edited classical Confucianist and other books.

Whatever the Ming intent might have been, the Vietnamese reproached them for betraying their promise to reestablish the Tran as rulers when they sent their army to Vietnam to fight the Ho. The heavy taxes and forced labor imposed upon the Vietnamese, as well as the hard repression against protesters caused more resentment and hatred for the Chinese and reinforced opposition movements that ultimately led to the independence for Vietnam.

The liberators of the country, Le Thai To (r. 1428–33) and his collaborators, especially Nguyen Trai (1380–1442)—who was himself a Confucianist—accepted the principle of an absolute imperial power as formulated by the Ming and did not oppose Neo-Confucianism. At the same time, by a natural reaction against the Ming domination, they rejected certain Ming institutions such as the Ming system of government and laws. Thus, the Le Code edited by Nguyen Trai was based not on the Ming but on the Tang and previous Vietnamese dynastic codes (Nguyen Ngoc Huy, Ta Van Tai, and Tran Van Liem, 1987). Under the first sovereigns of the Le dynasty (1428–1788), Vietnam was far from blindly following the Chinese model.

The efforts made by the Ming to spread New-Confucianism in Vietnam had a pronounced impact on the Vietnamese scholars. Emperor Le Thanh Tong (r. 1460–97) was a fervent disciple of this Chinese school. Out of respect for his grandfather and father, he did not abandon the Le Code to adopt the Ming Code. Thus, although Vietnam still maintained its originality vis-à-vis China, in many areas Le Thanh Tong strictly followed the Ming model. By successive modifications, he introduced the Ming system of government into Vietnam (TT, 3:193, 198, 239, 240–43; Phan Huy Chu, 1957). He also imposed Neo-Confucianist practices on the Vietnamese people. In 1469, he decided that only people who married according to exact Confucianist rites could be appointed as officials and, if they were already appointed, be promoted. The following year, he promulgated an edict to clarify rules concerning mourning. Rules for marriage were officially fixed in 1478 (TT, 3:226–27, 263). Le Thanh Tong also published a code of Confucianist morality including twenty-four articles and ordered the whole population to study them frequently and thoroughly. This code was promulgated again with commentaries by his son Le Hien Tong (r. 1497–1504) *(Kham Dinh Viet Su Thong Giam Cuoung Muc)*. As Le Thanh Tong's long reign was one of the most glorious in Vietnamese history, this emperor enjoyed a great deal of prestige. As a consequence, he succeeded in modeling Vietnamese society, and especially the Vietnamese family, according to Neo-Confucianist rules.

The Mac (1527–92) who usurped the Le throne in 1527 descended from Mac Dinh Chi, a great Confucianist scholar of the fourteenth century who enjoyed the prestigious title of Trang Nguyen (Zhuang Yuan, or first laureate of the national examination with the highest recognition in every copy). He was a high official of the Tran and was respected for his intelligence and integrity. The Mac family not only enjoyed great prestige, but had been devoted to Confucianism for a long time, and during the Ming domination had collaborated with the Chinese (Whitmore 1977, 64). With such a background, the Mac were naturally favorable to Neo-Confucianism and continued Le Thanh Tong's efforts to spread it in Vietnam.

After defeating the Mac, the restored Le (1593–1788) also officially applied Le Thanh Tong's policy and did not differ from this famous ancestor concerning the consolidation of Confucianist morality among the Vietnamese people. They continued to reward virtuous people who strictly followed the Confucian requirements concerning the family. Chaste widows, filial sons, and their descendants received emblems from the emperor and were sometimes exempted from corvee (TT, 3:114, 167, 177, 185).

But in the organization of the government, the presence of a Trinh lord holding the real power and treating the Le emperor only as a figurehead was a violation of Neo-Confucianism as a state ideology. Besides, while officially praising the kingly way *(wang dao)* in politics according to Neo-Confucianist teachings, the Trinh lords actually practiced hegemonic forms *(ba dao)* despised by the Neo-Confucianists. In the 1779 examinations, Lord Trinh Sam (r. 1767–82) ordered his officials not to proclaim as laureate a candidate who took a hegemonic position against the kingly way, but secretly invited him to be his adviser (Le Kim Ngan, 1974).

In South Vietnam, where the Nguyen lords officially recognized the Le emperor as their suzerain but in fact acted as independent rulers, Neo-Confucianism as state ideology was not treated better. Moreover, because they reigned over newly conquered territories where learned men were scarce, the Nguyen lords had to attract scholars into their country and were more tolerant than the Trinh lords about the personal status of these scholars. One of their most famous servants was Dao Duy Tu (eighteenth century) who descended from a family of actors and was not authorized to take examinations in North Vietnam because of his origin (Tran Van Giap 1971–72). On the whole, people in South Vietnam at that time were less deeply influenced by Confucianist practices than their brothers in North Vietnam.

The Tay Son (1788–1802) reigned for a short time over a divided and troubled Vietnam and exerted no great influence over Vietnamese society. However, when the Nguyen (1802–1945) reunified the country and imposed a new order, Confucianism received a new impetus. The rulers of this dynasty were more eager to follow the Chinese model than their predecessors. The legal code *Hoang Viet luat le* (Laws and Regulations of Imperial Viet) promulgated by Emperor Gia Long (r. 1802–19) was almost a copy of the Qing Code. Emperor Minh Mang (r. 1820–40) in his turn modeled his government after that of the Chinese court. He also promulgated ten articles of good conduct to be studied by the whole nation, in order to reinforce Confucianist morality (Woodside 1971).

With the Nguyen, Confucianism reached its highest influence in Vietnam. Yet, although the sovereigns of this dynasty tried to strictly follow the Chinese model, the Vietnamese people still maintained much of their uniqueness, and major differences existed. For example:

1. The Chinese family traditionally encompassed several generations living under one roof, and throughout the ages Chinese legislators had always tried to preserve the family's large size. Embodied in the legal codes of all dynasties, "being registered in a separate household or having separate property while the paternal grandparents or parents are still living" was considered as lack of filial piety—one of the ten heinous crimes (Tang Code, art. I, 6; Ming Code, art. I, 2; Qing Code, art. II). In contradistinction, the Vietnamese formed smaller families and had separate homes and properties while their parents were still alive. The Le legislators recognized this behavior as normal; in borrowing the provisions of the Tang Code article related to lack of filial piety, they eliminated the above sentence and replaced it with "disobeying one's grandparents or parents" (Le Code: Quoc Trieu Hinh Luat, art. 2). Breaking with Vietnamese tradition, the Nguyen followed the Chinese solution in their code (Philastre 1967); in practice, however, they were unable to implement its provisions relating to filial piety.

2. In Chinese society, women did not enjoy the same rights as men. Unlike their brothers, daughters could not inherit property from their parents. Divorced women and widows who remarried after their husband's death had no right to properties belonging to their former husband's family, even though they came from their own family or if they had contributed to their acquisition. They also had to return gifts received from their former husband's family during the ceremonies of engagement.[1] In contrast, although adopting the Confucian principle of male priority, the Vietnamese still granted women almost equal rights. Except for some restrictions concerning properties reserved for ancestor worship, daughters shared in the inheritance of parental properties on the same basis as their brothers. Divorced women and widows who remarried after their husband's death remained the owners of properties given to them by their own family; they were also entitled to half of properties acquired during their marriage (Le Code: Quoc Trieu Hinh Luat, arts 388, 374, 375, 376). Again in these matters, the Nguyen adopted the Chinese position (Philastre 1967, 1:369–70). But just as in the size and placement of the family, they were not able to actually implement it.

Thus despite a millennium of Chinese cultural influence, Confucianism did not entirely transform Vietnamese society, which, until the nineteenth century, still kept some of the old Viet customs and practices, especially about women's rights.

Confucianism in Vietnam from the Last Decades of the Nineteenth Century until the Present

After the French conquered Viet Nam (1861–67 for South Vietnam and 1884 for the remainder), Confucianism no longer served as the state ideology.

However, it still played the role of a moral code for the majority of the Vietnamese people. Until World War I, the Vietnamese family continued to be patterned upon Confucianist principles. Although Confucian scholars no longer enjoyed the great prestige of their predecessors, they were still respected by the population in general, and often served as advisers for the villagers for many social occasions, especially for marriages, funerals, and mourning.

In the 1920s, however, Westernized Vietnamese intellectuals began to criticize the traditional way of life. The movement gained strong momentum in the 1930s with the Tu Luc Van Doan (Self Reliance Pen Club), established a group of young and brilliant writers who wanted to reform and modernize Vietnamese society. Possessed of great talent, they ridiculed certain traditional behavior and fiercely attacked abuses committed by traditional leaders, especially in the villages. At the same time they criticized the old customs and social organizations as obstacles to progress and to a better life for the Vietnamese. Certain principles that had sustained traditional family morality were also under attack. Aspiring to more liberty for the individual, the reformers opposed the rule of total obedience to parents and elders in the family. They did not question the love and respect due to parents and elders, but they did ask for more autonomy for the children and younger members of the family, particularly in regard to issues that concerned them directly, such as the choice of a spouse. The new system of educational set up by the French fueled the movement and together they led to a slow but certain change in the Vietnamese people's mentality. Understandably, the conservatives feared that Confucianism might be totally abandoned by the Vietnamese. In his book about Confucianism, Tran Trong Kim compared it to an old and beautiful mansion that became ruined by lack of maintenance and was finally destroyed by a stormy wind (Tran Trong Kim 1930–33). Yet, in spite of this pessimistic view, the Vietnamese family was still strongly influenced by Confucianism until the end of World War II.

From 1945 on, Vietnam was deeply affected by political and social events. After the division of Vietnam in 1954, the Communists who controlled the North were committed to establishing a new society founded on a Marxist-Leninist base. They considered Confucianism as an ideology opposed to their aims and viewed the Confucianist scholars, who remained influential advisers of the Vietnamese, especially in the villages, as political rivals. As a result, they attempted to destroy all Confucianist traces in Vietnamese society. Most of the Confucian scholars living in the zones controlled by the Communists were arrested and jailed or sent to internment camps. Confucianism itself was depicted as a feudal system of thought that was to be replaced by a revolutionary ideology. To break the strong ties binding members of Vietnamese families that had been molded after Confucianist principles, the Communists encouraged betrayal among family members. They especially taught children to spy on their parents and report their acts and words back to the Communist authorities. They praised those who denounced their parents, who were then condemned by the Communist Party. During the 1955–56 agrarian reform in North Vietnam, Truong Chinh, then general secretary of the Party, served as an example of the struggle against the landowners by accusing his own father of being an exploiter of the people. Dr. Nguyen Khac Vien, presently the editor of publications in foreign languages for the Hanoi government, was trusted by the Party since, as a student in France, he had sent a letter to Vietnam praising the Party for having punished his father, Mr. Nguyen Khac Niem. The latter's crime was that of having served as an official of the Nguyen court and having owned some land in his village. He was arrested by the Communists in 1955 at the age of 68 and was beaten so severely during a session of the so-called popular tribunal, that he died from the blows he had received soon after he was brought to the camp where he was to serve a life sentence.

Over the years, the anti-Confucianist policy imposed by the Communists has completely changed the Vietnamese family structure. According to those who have contacts with relatives living in North Vietnam, people in their forties or older, that is, who received a traditional education when young, still maintain strong feelings vis-à-vis other members of their family. But younger people who have been entirely educated under the Communist system are not motivated by the same spirit.

In those areas controlled by the non-Communist side prior to 1975 (South Vietnam), the authorities did not carry out a policy systematically hostile to Confucianism. In fact, some were well disposed toward traditional education. But disruption of the old social frame due to war, which forced people to abandon their villages for urban areas, as well as the impact of new living conditions and broader contact with Western civilization also loosened traditional family ties. Children became more independent from their parents and the former strict obedience to the elders diminished. Nevertheless, affection and respect for parents and the elders still persisted. Close relatives still tried to help each other and it was not rare to see older siblings taking care of younger brothers or sisters at the expense of their own future. In dramatic contrast to the doctrine of filial piety, the Communists, following their conquest of South Vietnam in 1975, extended their policy of encouraging family members to spy on one another and to denounce them to the Communist authorities. This particularly applies to the children in regard to their parents and older siblings. There is no doubt that ultimately they will succeed in destroying the Confucian influence on the Vietnamese family, as they have in North Vietnam.

The majority of Vietnamese refugees who have left Vietnam since 1975, and who have settled in various countries of the free world, have been trying hard to help their relatives remaining in Vietnam. This is an indication that among non-Communist Vietnamese, ties between members of Vietnamese families influenced by Confucianism remain strong. But for Vietnamese families established abroad, problems have been arising with the younger members who have never been in Vietnam or who had left Vietnam before adulthood. These young people tend not to behave in a manner approved by their elders. Thus, ties among members of Vietnamese families established abroad may be expected to be loosened. As a result, unless Vietnam is liberated from Communist rule, there is no future for Confucianism among the Vietnamese people as a whole.

Note

1. See the substitutes following art. iv, 4 of the Ming Code and the corresponding article of the Qing Code.

References

Buttinger, Joseph. (1972). *A Dragon Defiant: A Short History of Vietnam*. New York: Praeger.

Dao Duy Anh. (1964). *Dat nuoc Viet Nam qua cac doi* (Vietnam through the Ages). Nha Xuat Ban Khoa Hoc Xa Hoi. Hanoi.

Dai Viet su ky toan thu (The Complete Book of the Historical Records of Dai Viet). (1967–68). [Herein abbreviated as TT] Translated from Chinese into Vietnamese by Cao Huy Giu. Nha Xuat Ban Khoa Hoc Xa Hoi. 4 vols. Hanoi.

Kham Dinh Viet su thong Giam cuong muc (The Text and Commentary of the Complete Mirror of Vietnamese History as Ordered by the Emerpor).

The Le Code: Quoc Trieu Hinh Luat, trans. by Nguyen Ngoc Huy. Ohio University Press, 1987.

Le Kim Ngan. (1974). *Che do chanh tri Viet Nam the ky XVII va XVIII* (Vietnamese Political Regimes in the 17th and 18th Centuries). Saigon.

Legge, James. (1960). *The Chinese Classics*, vol. 2: *The Works of Mencius*. Hong Kong: Hong Kong University Press.

Lich su Viet Nam (History of Vietnam). (1971). Nha Xuat Ban Khoa Hoc Xa Hoi, Hanoi.

Ming Code. Not published in English. Chinese characters only. Chinese publisher unknown.

Minh Mang chanth yeu (Minh Mang's Main Policies).

Nguyen Ngoc Huy, Ta Van Tai, and Tran Van Liem. (1987). *The Le Code: Law in Traditional Vietnam*. Athens: Ohio University Press.

Phan Huy Chu. (1957). *Lich trieu hien chuong loai chi* (Annals of the Laws and Institutions of Successive Dynasties), *Quan chuc chi* (Bureaucratic Section). Translated from the Chinese into Vietnamese by Cao Nai Quang. Saigon.

Philastre, P. L. F. (1967). *Le code annamite* (The Nguyen Code). Translated from the Chinese into French. 2nd ed. Taipei.

Qing Code. Translated from Chinese into English by Staunton.

Tang Code, translator Wallace Johnson, 1979, Princeton University Press.

Tran Trong Kim. (1930–33). *Nho Giao* (Confucianism).

Tran Van Giap. (1971–72). *Luoc truyen cac tac gia Viet Nam* (Summary Biographies of Vietnam Authors). 2 vols. Nha Xuat Ban Khoa Hoc Xa Hoi, Hanoi.

Vu Van Mau. (1970). *Co luat Viet Nam luoc khao* (Survey of Vietnamese Traditional Law). Saigon.

Whitmore, John K. (1977). "Chiao-chih and Neo-Confucianism: The Ming Attempt to Transform Vietnam." *Ming Studies*, Spring.

Woodside, Alexander Barton. (1971). *Vietnam and the Chinese Model*. Cambridge University Press.

6

A Japanese Legacy of Confucian Thought

George A. De Vos

Viewed historically, the previously manifest as well as presently lasting latent influences of Confucianism on the Japanese family trace back to religious-moral feelings that have been integrated into the experience of self in Japan, especially from the Tokugawa period on.[1]

An increasing awareness of Western science during the 1800s exacerbated a continuing tension in Japanese Confucian thought, as Craig put it, between virtue and knowledge (Craig 1965, 133ff.). As I shall discuss in my later chapter, there has been a continuing tension in modern Japan as elsewhere, considering morality as first principle, due to attempted internal psychological distinctions between *intentional causality* in divine and/or human will, and *mechanical causality* or "science" as a prior consideration in human thought.

Japanese Confucian thought harkens back to Sung dynasty Neo-Confucianism. Chu Hsi (1130–1200) was the most influential scholar who developed the tradition which was to become orthodox in Tokugawa Japan. While all was subordinate to a central principle, *li* (*ri* in Japanese), he also emphasized a rational approach to nature and the contemplation of the physical environment. Chu Hsi philosophy in some of its teaching can be interpreted as an empiricist's system—advocating empirical action in investigation and penetration of *ri*, or the gaining of knowledge in the investigation of things. By looking into things, there is penetration into a knowledge of *ri*.

But *ri* was to be better understood through the development of the individual mind, which was to be exercised in seriousness and reverence. Though some have therefore interpreted the system as advocating passive contemplation as the way to moral righteousness, others saw to it as an instigation to ethical action.

Some of the differences arising among Neo-Confucianism between Wang Yang-Ming (1492–1528) and orthodox followers of Chu Hsi were perhaps on the basis that Wang Yang-Ming put more emphasis on intuition and actualization through *doing* as a way of moving toward the realization of *ri*. Van Bremen (1984) has discussed how Yōmeigaku, as this school of Confucian thought is known, has been used in the past, and even recently by some dissidents and conservative activists such as Mishima, as an ideological ethical imperative to dissident political as well as social action.

Syncretism

When Confucian thought was fostered by the Tokugawa regime, it became influenced by Japanese cultural traditions. At the same time, Confucian influences interpenetrated both Buddhism and Shinto. For example, there were syncretic attempts to blend together Shinto concepts of *Kami* or divine force with *ri*. Hayashi Razan (1583–1657) sought to incorporate the Shinto Way of the Gods within the Confucian way of Chu Hsi by equating principle, *ri,* with the numinous[2] power of native deities, making the spiritual and temporal inseparable. The human, divine, and natural planes of existence were to be unified in man's behavior. Nevertheless, Razan remained basically a Confucian and saw *ri* as a central ordering principle still corresponding to the human mind (Nosco 1984, 171–72).

S. M. Yamashita 1984, 150 ff.) examining the discussions of Ōgyu (1666–1728) about his predecessor to Itō Jinsai (1627–1705) points up how he becomes more of a dualist than Chu Hsi. For Sorai there is a vitalist dimension to the cosmos which could not be completely known because there are limits to human intelligence. Sorai even posits that "heaven" (here vaguely intentionalized as divine will, or ghosts or spirits) are ultimately unknowable. The use of divination, manipulations related to Ying and Yang, and other practices that were aimed at correspondence with an ultimate unknowable were after all simply human belief learned from previous sages attempting to penetrate in this unknowable. Since heaven, the active forces of the cosmos, could not be known, one should concentrate on the refinement of the rites and ceremonial forms that can become better known.

Sorai discussed the process of refining original human nature by means of ceremonial forms—from original nature, *moto,* to culture, *bun* (an obvious precursor to the structuralist thought about nature and culture in anthropology). For example, in archery the original purpose of killing is transcended into the artistic refinements attendant upon the proper aesthetic use of a bow.

One "embodies" forms by proper practice, *okonai*. It is only by actually rehearsing and rehearsing classical etiquette or ritual and actually writing in classical styles that one truly *embodies* the ancient literary and ceremonial forms, and by so doing, refines one's nature, and achieves virtue (Yamashita 1984;

155). Sorai saw that ritual priority should be used to order one's mind. This ordering is virtue.

These discussions in Sorai are directly the line of thought to be found in Bushido, "the way of the warrior" or *samurai*. This code is usually attributed to Zen Buddhist influences. Such attributions to Buddhism ignore the essential Confucian concept of *virtue in ritual* as basic to all Japanese martial arts. I shall return in my subsequent chapter 9 to the psychodynamic implications of this Confucianist equation of ritual and virtue.

The inner relationship between Shinto, Buddhist, and Neo-Confucianist thought, whether in the Tokugawa period or later, has to be related to the use of all three religions to legitimatize the government. Buddhism as well as Shinto could be useful for stabilizing the Tokugawa regime. Some concept of social order is usually central to any legitimating religious system.

Scholars either indirectly or directly would not only borrow from other traditions' ideas that were in harmony with theirs but would also include the thinking of influential leaders that was directly derived from the other religious traditions. Whereas Neo-Confucianists, emphasizing the secular realm, would not well upon the ultimate link of the social order to a divine origin in the cosmos, Shinto could be used by them when some reference to origins was desired. Herman Ooms points up how Confucianists could use the work of Shinto scholars to legitimatize the Tokugawa state through reference to Shinto mythological origins (Ooms 1984).

Peter Nosco comments upon the mutually advantageous nature of the newly arrived Neo-Confucianist concepts with the Shinto theologies. Shinto theologies came to use to their advantage a Neo-Confucianist structure while at the same time Neo-Confucianist scholars would make use of Shinto concepts in furthering the spread of Neo-Confucianism (Nosco 1984, 11.) Buddhists were not to be left out. There were many justifiers of legitimacy within Buddhist scholarship that were used to deepen a sense of legitimacy and harmony for the Tokugawa regime (Tyler 1984).

Religion of course can be used by some in a contrary way as a means of political or social opposition or rebellion. The role of Uchimura Kanzo and nonchurch Christianity in Japan is well discussed by John Howes (1965). Uchimura was considered to have refused to bow to the Imperial Rescript On Education on the basis of his independent Christian belief system, which would not allow him to worship the rescript as a sacred document.

Intentionality versus Mechanical Causality: Confucian versus Western Scientific Explanations

From the time of Sakuma Shōzan (1811–64) onward, the distinction between science and ethics became an increasing problem to be directly and actively considered by the Confucianism of the late Tokugawa period. No such tension appeared in nineteenth-century Confucian thought in China (Craig 1965, 160). The essence of first principle in *ri* remained essentially an ethical, interactional causality. When first coming in contact with Western knowledge, science as it was conceived was principally considered as concerned with *ki*, a psychophysical, somewhat more mechanical concept, and not with the more ethical, *ri* (Craig 1965, 140 ff.). A common deprecatory view of Western thought, including science, was that it lacked any attention to the ethical. Without the cultivation of virtue man could not become truly human. It could be rationalized that it was all right to approach Western science as long as one saw that it was void of the ethical principles that ultimately must govern human behavior. Craig points out, however, that some began to suggest that perhaps Western science also was studying *ri*, but from a different standpoint. Some Confucianist scholars, such as Sakuma Shōzan saw that there would be a continual distinction to be made between the *ri* of ethics and the *ri* of science. He never wrote of *ri* without distinguishing between *butsuri*, the *ri* of things, and *dori*, the *ri* of virtue.

In my terms, there is an experiential distinction between moral intentionality and the mechanical causality found in nature. I shall in Chapter 17 briefly discuss this distinction from a developmental psychological perspective. I have written about this distinction elsewhere (De Vos and Suarez-Orosco 1987) in examining some of Piaget's discussion of precausal thought to be found in distinguishing religion and magic.

This split between ethics and the world of nature in late Tokugawa thought was especially apparent in the nationalist Ōgyu Sorai. Ethics became the issue. Its consideration was to be the defensive barrier against Western incursions. Superior Japanese ethics supposedly developed around the "ancient learning" found in Shinto scriptures. Reverence and other Japanese virtues were kept vital by the supposed unbroken continuity of Imperial Japan. The moral structure of Japanese society could help ward off corrosive foreign ethical systems, and at the same time allow for some adaptation of Western learning in technical or mechanical matters.

According to Yamagata Bantō (1748–1821) (cf. Craig 1965, 138ff.), and other Confucian scholars of the late Tokugawa period, *ri* in man is his inherent nature *sei*. Intellectual advance and ethical cultivation are the same. They are to be gained by ascetic discipline. But Bantō considered that meditation was only one approach to a realization of *ri*. Active, empirical inquiry was another. Active inquiry was a quasiscientific penetration into the laws of nature in order to comprehend *ri*.

Bantō saw scientific study of the innate order of the material world as a nonsubordinate approach to *ri*. Nevertheless, Bantō's heliocentric cosmology remains ultimately moral. The *ri* of nature and the *ri* of ethics were not independent of one another. As Craig paraphrases him, he found that Heaven's strange unfathomable nature to be both in man's heart and in the sun. Human duties proceed from the father in his social role. Creation of the firmament and earth come from the sun. The universe is ultimately one in *ri*. Nevertheless, Yamagata Bantō, of the late Tokugawa Period, was more materialist than the earlier Sorai. He said "There is no hell, no heaven, no self, only man and ten thousand things. In this world there are no gods, Buddhas, or ghosts, nor are there strange or miraculous things."

Nevertheless, *ri* for Bantō was still related to Chinese Yin and Yang, the set of opposites or juxtapositions in essence that organize the material world. His use of Chinese cosmology also referred to the five elements of earth, fire, water, metal, and wood. Chinese Confucianists of the time were also materialists in that they did not believe in any world of spirits, no existence beyond death, and no acting deities, certainly not acting to determine occurrences in the present world.

Bantō, as Craig points out (1965, 136ff.), remained a typical Confucian scholar in the tradition of Chu Hsi. He sought to demonstrate how the metaphysics of Confucianism with its concern with the ultimate principle, *ri,* has little time for the supernatural or other worldly concerns. Unlike a first cause in Christian thought this principle of *ri* was not directly deified. Japanese Confucianism, except when it was sometimes syncretized with Shinto, did not concern itself with origins or ultimate destiny. *Ri* remains an organizing principle, not an explanation of origins. Craig describes Bantō's use of *kokoro* (a term that intermingles concepts of mind, will, and heart) as a typical Japanese concept of a psychophysical force or substance which, in interaction with *ri,* is the essence of the material.

Prevailing Japanese thought of this period conformed to the Confucianist concept that *ri* can be grasped intuitively and that man's nature is good. Nevertheless, *kokoro* needs further cultivation by intellectual activity, ascetic self-denial, and discipline so that the *ri* can be free of the effects of crude desire. Bellah, in his volume on *Tokugawa Religion* (1957), has described very well this mode of thought and concepts of self-cultivation in the *chōnin,* or townsman, Ishida Baigan, founder of "Shingaku." There was continuous emphasis on self-discipline and self-development in Tolugawa religious thought among the townsmen culture as well as the samurai.

Present-day continuities of this emphasis on self-development and self-control remain central to childhood socialization in both home and school. This form of Confucian "Puritanism," while it teaches deferment of gratification, does not cause any sense of powerless. Some sense of control over events and a sense of power remains within the individual when he/she executes his or her social role. For a true Confucianist, the individual by controlling his own behavior has influence in the material world. Among Confucianists the doctrinal arguments are about how best to realize or cultivate *ri*, not about how to submit to fate.

The cultivation of *ri* is for purposes of proper action, not for any purposes of withdrawal from the world or withdrawal from one's social role. Rather, Confucianist suspect Buddhists of tendencies toward irresponsible withdrawal from allocated social obligations. They have been antagonistic to Taoists, whom they considered irrational and thereby not ultimately sufficiently self-disciplined.

Social Hierarchy in Traditional Confucian Thought

There is no doubt that Confucianism was used politically and socially as a conservative ideology concerning the state, the economic system, and gender relationships (see Deuchler 1977, 1980). What helped keep Confucian thought so socially conservative was that the patriarchal family society was seen as the embodiment of the natural order. In contrast, contemporary society came to be regarded by European philosophers of the Enlightenment as a distortion of natural order to be improved if possible.

Moreover, Confucian thought cannot be separated out from concepts of awe and reverence as inherent in social order. These sentiments are in one way or another to be cultivated so as to characterize age, gender, and social status relationships as sacred. Reverence is to be expressed toward some moral secular authority, but authority itself is sacred. The superior being in the well-ordered society is morally superior and thereby deserving of superior status.

The proper natural-social order depends upon the cultivation of the self, obedience in relation to father, deference to those older, service to the lord and, ultimately what is considered the awe felt before the mysterious, unfathomable Mandate of Heaven bestowed upon the particular head of the realm. It is this later mandate that in the Chinese understanding of Confucianism could see acts of replacement in dynasty, whereas in the Japanese reading of Confucianism, continuity was inviolate. The history of Japan was interpreted as an unending continuity of the imperial lineage, which later was to become so important in the ethnocentrism fostered by Tokugawa Shintō syncretized with Confucianism. This ethnocentrism and chauvinism was subsequently fostered or interpreted in such a way as to be able to conceive of Japanese virtues as central for a new world order.

The position of merchants and artisans as morally, as well as socially, below farmers was derived from Chinese Confucian thought that devalued money and the greed that inspired the acquisition of wealth. Confucianists considered successful agriculture basic to a well-ordered society. This orientation in viewing merchants as morally inferior also became an abiding concept of samurai Confucianism. In their writings, as in Jeffersonian democracy in the early United States, there was an emphasis on the agrarian basis of a just society. The monetary power acquired by merchants and traders was to remain suspect.

Korean Confucian thought among the Yangban was especially severe in its de-emphasis of trade and commerce. In Korea, for complex reasons, there was no internal development of trade comparable to that which appeared in Japan with the rise of a townsmen culture that eventually came to challenge the samurai grip on power.

Westerners, in their heritage of a class-stratified society historically, were deeply influenced by a mercantilist expansion into colonies. As a result they developed a type of social impersonality in social class and racist-caste relationships that was, to some degree, different from the sense of social hierarchy maintained within Eastern societies. Marxist thought about class consciousness and alienation derived from European mercantile capitalist models, past and present, does not directly apply (De Vos 1975).

Also one can improperly attribute to Asian cultures a complete lack of social mobility both past and present. There was in Chinese and Korean history the rise and fall of many specific families among the gentry. In Japan, while movement *between* social classes was indeed difficult, there was considerable mobility and rise and decrease of wealth *within* the classes of samurai, farmers, merchants, and artisans. There are not issues of particular concern here except to state that within family groups there could be continual hope for change of fortune and for seeking opportunity for family betterment through individual effort. Being tradition bound did not lessen hope or effort for advancement.

Although they were of inferior status within the Japanese class/caste system, merchants nevertheless sought respectability. There were attempts by those of merchant background (Baigan is a good example), to show that they too, could aspire to be good, proper Confucianists and should therefore not be unduly denigrated.

In this modern period trade and commerce have superseded agriculture. The legislative and administrative functions of government are no longer in the hands of samurai, yangban or gentry in modern Asian societies. They are more fully controlled by members of a newer business elite. One of the questions to ask, therefore, is how, and in what manner of modification in each cultural setting, the Confucian ethic and the high regard both for self-control and learning nevertheless has penetrated so pervasively among those both of rural-agricultural as well as of merchant origin. The concept of an administrative gentry or a samurai class has been replaced by those who to some degree have been indoctrinated at home and school with the principles that governed the governors.

Studies by Bellah and others within a Weberian sociological framework give us some clues as to how this has come about. Confucian thought pervaded all segments of society, even those living in poverty. A psychocultural approach helps understand how religious forces maintained the dignity of the family, and how these forces continue to operate in the preparatory socialization of children to avoid the permanent appearance of a perpetrated "culture of poverty" among the destitute or dispossessed. This family ethic became apparent to me in studying the social survival of the destitute Japanese rural migrants who came to the United States before 1924, and who encouraged the education of their children within a somewhat rejecting American society (Caudill and De Vos 1956).

What one has to look at ideologically and psychoculturally in this present period is how the economic competition fostered by the West has been accepted as a challenge by Asian families despite the fact that in the conservative agrarian-oriented Confucianist states of the past era the merchants were not seen as being able to attain higher virtue. The old Confucian elites are gone. In effect, in these post-Confucianist states, whether it be Japan, Taiwan, Singapore, or Korea, the merchant's competitive mentality has won out over a strict Confucianist ideology that would seek to preserve the ascendancy of the scholar in the social order. However, it should be noted that in his family life the merchant has been influenced through formal education and through family role behavior oriented by Confucianist principles. Ironically it is these principles of self-cultivation and the deferment of gratification that now puts the Confucian family unit, whether as part of a majority, or functioning as part of an ethnic minority, in good stead competitively in a world where the Western Protestant ethic no longer appears to govern the behavior of Western entrepreneurial endeavor.

Western economic competition was read as an early threat by some Japanese Confucianists who saw that proper heed should be paid to practical knowledge as well as ethical cultivation. For example, Craig (1965) quotes Bantō as saying, "All Europeans put profits first and their evil religion second." Bantō considered that the Confucianist could suffer from the same errors of concern with the supernatural as happened to devout Christians who became unworldly. Obviously most Christians were not that devout. For the proper Confucianist, Christianity was another set of erroneous doctrines designed to beguile the unwary. Craig quotes one Confucianist scholar, Sakoma, saying that "Christianity is Buddhism with hair on it."

One of the paradoxes of Confucianism historically is that in some instances it has lead to a lack of change and a lack of experimentation or integration of new modes of thought that became evident in the West. On the other hand, Confucianist rationalism itself could accept certain scientific discoveries of the West without any antagonism. And today it may be the Confucianist family that is providing East Asia a competitive edge over the West.

Confucian Influences on Formal Education During the Meiji Period

According to Dore (1965), between 40% and 50% of all Japanese boys and perhaps 15% of girls were already receiving formal education outside their homes by the time of the Meiji Restoration of 1868. Not only educated samurai but those with sufficient means among the merchants or wealthy farmers sought to provide education for their children. It must be noted that what was available was not a system of either free or compulsory education, but a voluntary system, often involving some sacrifice on the part of the parents to provide a much desired education for their children. The notion of individual self-improvement according to Dore (102) was widely diffused. The notion of national self-improvement espoused by Meiji reformers had common support when promulgated. By the late Tokugawa period, education was already established as a means to social mobility as well as a means of Confucianist self-development.

According to Dore (116ff.) there was also an explicit sanction in Confucian teaching espousing the exercise of political leadership, not as a means of gratifying a need for power but as a fulfillment of a social duty. There were explicit moral teachings to this effect in Confucianism that became part of everyone's primary training. In the Confucian tradition, politics was not to be the art of the possible, the choice of lesser evils, or the achievement of democratic compromise between conflicting interests. A good policy was one which could benefit everyone. Confucian government policy conflicts of interest lay between the producing ruled and consuming rulers. Enlightened government consisted in the kind of benevolence which would enable the existing rulers to enhance the general contentment for the benefit of all (118).

Loyalty toward superiors was to be cultivated. The loyalty was not simple obedience to commands, but the active anticipation of what would benefit one's superior. A truly developed loyal person, and there were many stories in the popular Confucian literature to exemplify heroic individuals dedicated to family or ruler, will seek out the ultimate benefit of the master rather than immediately gratifying any command. If need be, an individual may go against the superior's wishes when, in their considered loyal judgment, carrying out these immediate commands would be detrimental to their superior's ultimate benefit.

With the Meiji Restoration there was a spreading out into the total populace of Confucianist concepts brought about by the establishment of universal education based upon Confucianist concepts interpreted in a nationalist framework. This intensified the diffusion of the samurai ethic, not only through the merchants and townsmen, but also throughout the rural population. This diffusion has had a profound effect on Japanese family life which has extended to the contemporary period. One cannot understand Japanese family dynamics without some reference to these educational influences. The rigid four-class structure had been broken by the abolition of the samurai as a separate class. However, the universal education given to both boys and girls was directly based on samurai Neo-Confucianist loyalty. It espoused an age-graded sense of endurance with a continuing emphasis on hierarchy within family roles.

As a continuity it had been the samurai, especially the samurai women, who had deeply internalized the Confucian ethic. Note well that the conception of women's nature in the samurai class was one that stressed their capacity for self-control and their ability to maintain and enhance family honor. The entering bride was to be trained with necessary severity to this end by her mother-in-law and other elder women. This attitude toward women, while it emphasizes the subordination to men, also sees women as truly capable of self-control. This attitude is far different from the attitude toward women that marked some Western Judeo-Christian and Islamic traditions, especially in the Mediterranean area.

The Meiji Imperial Rescript on Education was an important document that explicitly made Confucian thought central to the moral education that was to guide National Polity. It was a sacred guide to be revered as laying down the religious tenets of social purpose for all Japanese. There is good evidence that the Japanese Confucianists who wrote the document drew heavily on the writings of the Korean Neo-Confucian scholar Yi T'oegye (Abe 1965, 1972).

It is not that the Japanese experienced no tension in being regulated by Confucianist principles. Confucianism was viewed as supporting the intellectual-moral side of the continuing conflict between social obligation, or *giri,* as opposed to a more spontaneous, emotional social feelings, *ninjo.* To attend to *giri* was to comply ritually with the anticipated and expected. It was a more formal adherence to moral expectations as opposed to the spontaneity of love and other sometimes socially disruptive human emotions. Confucianism is seen as more formal, "Chinese" in origin. Ninjo feelings were more untutored and native. Such dichotomies still exist in Japanese thought related to social status. For example, in Tokyo there is a differentiation between the lower status denizens of the old *shitamachi* merchant sections of Tolyo and the dwellers *yamanote,* the higher areas occupied by professional classes who are more reserved and do not as readily display their true emotions. From Tokugawa times those in government positions were to sit with propriety as an expression of their moral ascendancy, hence they were perceived as colder and more formal than the commoners. All through the Tokugawa period, the townsmen and rural folk both were seen as more lively and less stuffy than the samurai class. However, with the universal educational system in meiji, it was the samurai Neo-Confucianist precepts that set up the standard for the moral order.

What is going on in Japan presently is an attempted shift to some concept in educational policy, as in social goals generally, a search for happiness, *shiawase,* and a more spontaneous mode of existence. This has been a Western, individualist goal, leading to disturbing consequences. The Japanese are therefore very cognizant of the potential chaos that may result from suddenly unregulated behavior. Conservative Japanese are very concerned that their society may become chaotic rather than liberalized. There always has been careful attention to modes of potential rebellion in Japanese society. On the other hand, present liberal Japanese are very aware of how individuals are coerced into stifling conformity by group behavior. There is among many Japanese intellectuals today a wish to find a better type of formal training toward realizing a more individual sense of self without a loss of integrated social fabric. Liberal proponents are opposed by those who fear the consequences weakening the traditionally strong emphasis on social role inherented from Confucianist tradition.

In Meiji Japan, people such as Nakae Chomin sought to bring in liberal Western concepts of freedom and liberty. However, if closely examined, one can find that these supposedly Western adaptations by a Japanese thinker were actually related to certain tenets of Confucianism. Peter Nosco (1984, 22) suggests how Chomin's concepts of freedom and liberty were indebted to assumptions that can be traced ideologically all the way back to Mencius. Chomin's notion that freedom cannot be obtained without prior intense "cultivation" and "development" may seem odd to an intellectual historian familiar with the concept of freedom as it is used in the West. Freedom in a Confucianist context is something toward which humans may aspire which requires practice and *self-development,* rather than something acquired by wresting it free from others.

Japanese Confucian arguments (cf. Yamashita 1984, 155ff.) about moral cultivation (which ultimately were set forth in the Meiji Imperial Rescript On Education) are not too different from the later early-twentieth-century pedagogic arguments found in France and England as advanced by conservative collectivists (Fauconnet 1920). In discussing educational policies, some interpreted Durkheim's concepts (1947) of how society is constituted *prior to the individual* as necessitating moral teachings in the schools. Following this line of thought, to insure proper continuity, a society should inculcate moral teaching as central to school curriculum. Opposed to this line of thought have been liberal individualists whose concepts of human personality have seen a natural maturation possible without such deliberate moral guidance. Those more individualistic in their orientation, as was Piaget (1932) (whose theory we briefly discuss in chapter 17) would rely more on an education system fostering innate capacities in the developing child.[3] In chapter 17 I consider some psychological features of Japanese child development that owe much to the

Confucian heritage of Japan. In both cases, the child's mind is considered to spontaneously unfold conceptually with maturation toward forms of moral reciprocity and objectivity in thought, *given proper social encouragement,* rather than being rigidified behaviorally by indoctrination. There are similarities and differences in concepts of self-development arising out of the Confucian tradition compared with modern Western thought that need far more consideration and elaboration than we can give them here. We hope these issues will be given more heed in future comparative scholarship.

Notes

1. This introductory view of the Japanese Confucian tradition will only briefly refer to topics already well discussed by historians and social scientists much more competent to detail Japan's intellectual history (principally Maruyama Masao, 1952, 1974, who discussed at length the intellectual heritage of Confucian political ideology; see also Bellah 1957, Jansen 1965, Craig 1965, de Bary 1975, Najita and Scheiner 1978, Nosco 1984).

2. See Rudolf's Otto's definition of the numinous (1917).

3. As Western educational policy became more liberal, countries have sought to separate church and state. Religious training has been kept separate from secular education.

References

Abe, Y. (1965). *Nihon Shushigaku to Chosen* (Japanese Neo-Confucianism and Korea). Tokyo: University of Tokyo Press.

Abe, Y. (1972). "Nihon Jukyo no Hatten to Yi T'oegye" (The Development of Confucianism in Japan and Yi T'oegye). *Han,* 1.8: 3–27.

Bellah, R. (1957). *Tokugawa Religion.* New York: Free Press.

Caudill, W., and G. De Vos. (1956). "Achievement, Culture and Personality: The Case of Japanese-Americans." *American Anthropologist* 58:102–26.

Craig, A. (1965). "Science and Confucianism in Tokugawa Japan." In *Changing Japanese Attitudes toward Modernization,* ed. M. B. Jansen. Princeton, NJ: Princeton University Press.

de Bary, W. T. (1975). *The Unfolding of Neo-Confucianism.* New York: Columbia University Press.

De Vos, G. A. (1975). "Apprenticeship and Paternalism." In *Modern Japanese Organization and Decision Making,* ed. E. Vogel. Berkeley: University of California Press.

De Vos, G. A., and M. M. Suarez-Orosco. (1987). "Sacrifice and the Experience of Power." *Journal of Psychoanalytic Anthropology*. Vol. 10, no. 1, pp. 34–64.

Deuchler, M. (1977). "The Tradition: Women during the Yi Dynasty." *Virtues in Conflict: Tradition and the Korean Woman Today.* Seoul: Royal Asiatic Society.

———. (1980). "Neo-Confucianism: The Impulse for Social Action in Early Yi Korea." *Journal of Korean Studies* 2: 71–112.

Dore, R. P. (1965). "The Legacy of Tokugawa Education." In *Changing Japanese Attitudes towards Modernization,* ed. M. B. Jansen. Princeton, NJ: Princeton University Press.

Fauconnet, P. (1920). *La Résponsabilité: Étude de Sociologie.* Paris: Alcan.

Howes, J. F. (1965). "Japanese Christians and American Missionaries." In *Changing Japanese Attitudes toward Modernization,* ed. M. B. Jansen. Princeton, NJ: Princeton University Press.

Jansen, M. B., ed. (1965). *Changing Japanese Attitudes toward Modernization.* Princeton, Princeton University Press.

Maruyama, M. (1952). *Nihon Seiji Shisoshi Kenkyu.* (Research in the Political Ideology of Japan) Tokyo: University of Tokyo Press.

———. (1974). *Studies in the Intellectual History of Tokugawa Japan.* Princeton, NJ: Princeton University Press.

Najita, R. and I. Scheiner. (1978). *Japanese Thought in the Tokugawa Period.* Chicago: University of Chicago Press.

Nosco, P. (1984). *Confucianism and Tokugawa Culture.* Princeton, NJ: Princeton University Press.

Ooms, H. (1984). "Neo-Confucianism and the Formation of Early Tokugawa Ideology: Contours of A Problem." In *Confucianism and Tokugawa Culture,* ed. P. Nosco. Princeton, NJ: Princeton University Press.

Piaget, J. (1932). *The Moral Judgment of Children.* London: Routledge and Kegan Paul.

Tyler, R. (1984). "The Tokugawa Peace and Popular Religion: Suzuki Shosan, Kakugyo Tobutsu, and Jikigyo Miroku." In *Confucianism and Tokugawa Culture,* ed. P. Nosco. Princeton, NJ: Princeton University Press.

Van Breman, J. (1984). "The Moral Imperative and Leverage for Rebellion: An Anthropological Study of Wang Yang-ming Doctrine in Japan." Unpublished Ph.D. dissertation. University of California-Berkeley.

Yamashita, Samuel Hideo. (1984). "Nature and Artifice in the Writings of Ogyu Sorai (1666–1728)." In *Confucianism and Tokugawa Culture,* ed. P. Nosco. Princeton, NJ: Princeton University Press.

III

Hierarchy and Gender

7

Probing the "Three Bonds" and "Five Relationships" in Confucian Humanism

Wei-Ming Tu

In my essay "An Inquiry on the Five Relationships in Confucian Humanism," presented to the international seminar on *The Psycho-Cultural Dynamics of the Confucian Family: Past and Present* held in Yongpyong, Korea, September 1986 (Slote, 1986), I offer an ethicoreligious reading of the rationale of the "Five Relationships" *(wu-lun/wulun)* in the context of Confucian moral education. I examined these five primary human relationships in the perspective of Confucian self-cultivation as a communal act and attempted to show that "Confucians, by stressing the centrality of self-cultivation, do not undermine the corporate effort that is required for the family, the community, the state, and the world to become humane or fully human" (Slote, 190).

Indeed, the interchange between the self as an open system in a dynamic process of

> embodying: an ever-expanding network of human relationships, and society as a fiduciary community, constantly reenacting the ritual of actively participating in mutual exhortation, defines the Confucian project of self-realization in terms of personal and communal self-transcendence: "As the self overcomes egoism to become authentically human, the family must overcome nepotism to become authentically human. By analogy, the community must overcome parochialism, the state must overcome ethnocentrism and the world must overcome anthropocentrism to become authentically human. In light of Confucian inclusive humanism, the transformed self individually and corporately transcends egoism, nepotism, parochialism, ethnocentrism, and anthropocentrism for it to "form one body with Heaven, Earth and the myriad things." (Ibid.)

My purpose in presenting an inquiry on the Five Relationships from the perspective of self-cultivation philosophy is to show that, although the underlying structure of the Five Relationships suggests a strong concern for social ethics, the psychocultural roots that sustain the persuasive power of these relationships in Confucian moral education are deeply grounded in an "anthropocosmic" vision. Since this aspect of Confucian humanism is explored in my revised and enlarged edition of *Centrally and Commonality: An Essay on Confucian Religiousness* (1989), I intend to probe anew the problematic of the Five Relationships in terms of its implications for comparative cultural studies.

The Inner Logic of the Three Bonds

In the modern egalitarian and liberal perspective, the least defensible legacy of Confucian ethics is the so-called Three Bonds *(san-kang/sangang)* namely the authority of the ruler over the minister, the father over the son, and the husband over the wife. Chinese intellectuals' iconoclastic attacks on the Confucian establishment in the first decades of the twentieth century gave the impression that the rationale for the bonds was motivated by an authoritarian impulse to dominate the subservient, the young, and the female. Based on this perception, the Three Bonds have been depicted as three forms of bondage and Confucian ethics condemned as despotic, autocratic, patriarchal, gerontocratic, and male-chauvinistic.

Historically, the idea of the Three Bonds emerged in Confucian literature relatively late, almost four centuries after Mencius first advocated the virtues of the Five Relationships.[1] The concerted effort of the Han dynasty (206–220 B.C.) scholar-officials to transform Confucian ethics into a political ideology was instrumental in promoting the Three Bonds as an integral part of the core curriculum for moral education. Ironically, the first textual evidence of the idea occurs in the *Han fei tzu (Han fei zi)*, the Legalistic classic: "The minister serves the king, the son serves the father, and the wife serves the husband. If the three are followed, the world will be in peace; if the three are violated, the world will be in chaos."[2] Obviously, the Han ideologists, like the Legalists, were mainly concerned about the functional utility of the Three Bonds as mechanism of symbolic control for the primary purpose of social stability. The perception that regularizing these cardinal relationships helps maintain political order is at variance with the Confucian idea that basic dyadic relationships, private as well as public, are the foundation of a fiduciary community. However, the Three Bonds drastically altered the Mencian intention by relegating the spirit of mutuality to the background.

Obviously, the Three Bonds, based on dominance/subservience, underscore the hierarchical relationship as an inviolable principle for maintaining social order. The primary concern is not the well-being of the individual persons involved in these dyadic relationships, but the particular pattern of social stability which results from these rigidly prescribed rules of conduct. The centrality of the father-son relationship in providing the basic structure of justification for the Three Bonds has the advantage of giving added persuasive power to the political authority of the ruler and the husband. In a hierarchic and patriarchal society, it must seem convincing that the ruler or the husband, like the father, should be the interpreter, the executor, and the judge of the moral code, for he assumes full responsibility for the stability and harmony of society. Position and gender, like age, are conceived as natural patterns of the social landscape. If the inferior challenges the superior or the wife dominates the husband, which is analogous to the son defying the father, the moral fabric of society will be damaged. Once this line of reasoning (or, in our modern perspective, unreasoning) is accepted, the minister has no recourse but to demonstrate unquestioned loyalty as a defining characteristic of his being. Similarly, as the male-centered perspective becomes pervasive, position and age can both be subsumed under the category of gender: since the female under no circumstances should assume a dominating role, she must practice the art of "following"—as a daughter, she follows her father; as a wife, she follows her husband; and as a mother, she follows her son.[3] The value of obedience, specifically practiced by the son, the minister, and the wife looms large in the ideology of the Three Bonds. This politicization of Confucian ethics fundamentally restructures the Five Relationships, making them the "legalist" mechanism of symbolic control rather than the interpersonal base for the realization of the Mencian idea of a fiduciary community. I use the word "legalist" to describe the Three Bonds, both to note its apparent origin and to stress its coercive nature. However, the politicized Confucian implementation of the Three Bonds is much more demanding than their legalist origin and nature may suggest. When Han Fei Tzu pronounced that "if the minister serves the king, the son serves the father, and the wife serves the husband," then "the world will be in peace," he may have been simply making a descriptive statement concerning an ordered society in behavioral terms, but the politicized Confucian idea of the Three Bonds demands not only correct conduct, but right attitude, indeed orthodox belief. The logic of the Three Bonds seems distinctly Confucian in character. Of course the word "Confucian" here has taken on a new meaning. It is no longer the teachings of Confucius and his disciples who were politically powerless but spiritually influential proponents of the Way of the sage-kings. Rather, the Confucians who propounded the logic of the Three Bonds were prominent scholars of the Han court who, as shapers of an emerging political ideology defined in terms of Confucian categories, were invited by the emperor to reach a national consensus on the vital cosmological and ethical issues confronting the state. Needless to say, the ethics of the Three Bonds as an integral part of this politicized Confucian mechanism of symbolic control is a far cry from the Mencian idea of the Five Relationships.

The Mencian Idea of the "Five Relationships"

The reference to the Five Relationships in the *Book of Mencius* occurs in the context of an elaborate debate with a radical physiocrat who advocated that "[t]o earn his keep a good and wise ruler shares the work of tilling the land with his people" (*Mencius,* IIIA.4). Mencius, in arguing against the proposition that ruling the empire must be combined with the work of tilling the land, invokes the principle of the division of labor. Having established the claim that a hundred different crafts made by potters, blacksmiths, hatmakers, or weavers are necessary for society, Mencius advocates his famous thesis: "There are those who use their minds and there are those who use their muscles. The former govern; the latter are governed. Those who govern are supported by those who are governed" (*Mencius,* IIIA.4).[4] The thesis is predicated on the principle of mutuality, which specifies a pattern of interaction between two groups of people: those who are in the "service sector" and those who are in productivity. Mencius's initial response to the physiocratic challenge is that potters, blacksmiths, hatmakers, and weavers are, like farmers, all producers. He further states that those who are not directly involved in productivity but use their minds (the ruling minority) are vital to the well-being of the community.

For example, the sage-king Yao did not have the leisure to plough fields, for he was duty-bound to consider the security of the empire and the livelihood of the people his primary concerns. His success in restoring the human habitat after the flood resulted from his ability to appoint the right officers to share responsibility for bringing order to the empire and food to the people. Yet, although order and food provided the minimum condition for human survival, they were not enough for humans to flourish:

> Hou Chi [the minister in charge of agriculture] taught the people how to farm and grow the five kinds of grain. When these ripened, the people multiplied. This is the way of the common people: once they have a full belly and warm clothes on their back they degenerate to the level of animals if they are allowed to lead idle lives, without education or discipline. (*Mencius,* IIIA.4)

Human flourishing beyond the basic needs for physical comfort was the reason that the virtues of the Five Relationships were introduced. Thus, Mencius continues:

This gave the sage King further cause for concern, and so he appointed Hsieh as the Minister of Education whose duty was to teach the people human relationships: love between father and son, duty between ruler and subject, distinction between husband and wife, precedence of the old over the young, and faith between friends. (*Mencius*, IIIA.4)

The context in which Mencius introduced the Five Relationships suggests that the purpose of education is to combat idleness after a measure of economic affluence is secured. This helps us to understand that the virtues governing the relationships are prescriptive as well as demonstrative.

Father-Son

Love between father and son is intended to show that the proper relationship between them is mutual affection rather than one-way obedience; it also offers a "medicine" for those who fail to live up to the norm specified for such a relationship. Since affection between mother and son is more natural than that between father and son, love as a virtue can perform a compensatory function in harmonizing this transgenerational relationship. The ritual of exchanging sons for instruction for fear that formal education conducted at home by fathers might damage parental love was often practiced in traditional Confucian families. The Mencian advice is pertinent here:

> Kung-sun Ch'ou said, "Why does a gentleman not take on the teaching of his own sons?" "Because in the nature of things," said Mencius, "it will not work. A teacher necessarily resorts to correction, and if correction produces no effect, it will end by losing his temper. When this happens, father and son will hurt each other instead. 'You teach me by correcting me, but you yourself are not correct.' So father and son hurt each other, and it is bad that such a thing should happen. In antiquity people taught one another's sons. Father and son should demand goodness from each other. Not to do so will estrange them, and there is nothing more inauspicious than estrangement between father and son. (*Mencius*, IVA.18)

Ruler-Minister

Similarly, duty between ruler and subject is a response to the perceived danger of organizing this single most important political relationship in terms of profit motivation. The principle of duty *(i)*, or more appropriately righteousness, is sharply contrasted with profit *(li)*, for both moral and pragmatic reasons. Mencius observes that the main cause for conflict in the political arena is the abandonment of righteousness as the *raison d'être* for the ruling minority to enjoy privilege and status without involving themselves in productivity.

Their application of profit, as the defining characteristic of the rules of the game, in fact has made their legitimate claim to leadership suspect. As a result, their ability to govern is undermined and the public sphere over which they reign becomes privatized.

Mencius recommends the restoration of trust between ruler and subject as the precondition for reestablishing this particular proper relationship. Obviously, love between father and son and duty (or righteousness) between ruler and subject are not transferable, but the spirit of mutuality underlies both of them. In the case of the ruler-subject relationship, Mencius unequivocally states that the prince must earn the support of his ministers. Indeed, their attitude toward him depends upon how he treats them:

> If a prince treats his ministers as his hands and feet, they will treat him as their belly and heart. If he treats them as his horses and hounds, they will treat him as a mere fellow countryman. If he treats them as mud and weeds, they will treat him as an enemy. (*Mencius,* IVB.3)

Although love between father and son can serve as a standard of inspiration for duty between ruler and subject, the affection rooted in "flesh and blood" is radically different from the calling engendered by the division of labor in society, which not only recognizes the contribution of those who produce but also sanctifies the role of those who labor with their minds as leaders, governors, and servants of the public sphere. However, intent upon applying the virtues of the family as the microcosm of the world to the empire as a whole, Mencius insists:

> There is a common expression, "The Empire, the state, the family." The Empire has its basis in the state, the state in the family, and the family in one's own self. (*Mencius,* IVA.5)

What Mencius advocates here is the fundamental principle of extending the self to the family, the state, the world, and beyond. By implication, love between father and son is politically significant and duty between ruler and subject is recognizably a family ethic. This may have been the reason that in Confucian political culture love between father and son often serves as an analogy for duty between ruler and subject, even though the difference, as Mencius originally detects it, is enormous.

Husband-Wife

If age features prominently in the father-son relationship, gender is a defining characteristic of the husband-wife relationship. Although age and position are not irrelevant in the husband–wife relationship, they are subsumed under the category of "distinction" *(pieh/bie)*. It has often been assumed that, by stressing the importance of distinction in such a relationship, the Confucians deliberately undermine romantic love in the conjugal relationship. Quite a few scholars have noted that the value of duty looms so large in Confucian family ethics that the role of the wife must be preceded by that of the daughter-in-law. If children are involved, the role of the mother should also take precedence over that of the wife.

Nevertheless, the value of distinction that governs the husband-wife relationship is also based on a principle of mutuality. The underlying spirit is not dominance but division of labor. Occasionally, commentators cite the etymological origin of the word *ch'i* (*qi*, first tone, wife) as *ch'i* (*qi*, second tone, "equal") to support the view that the wife is the husband's equal. Although the idea that the wife, rather than the husband, should be the homemaker is being challenged nowadays, the division of labor between husband and wife, in a collaborative effort to raise a family, is still widely recognized as a necessity if not a virtue.

In a prescriptive sense, love and affection between a husband and wife are taken for granted. The instruction is to ask what precautionary measures are pertinent to such a relationship for the purpose of human flourishing. As the dangers of estrangement between father and son and profit between ruler and minister must be overcome to make their relationships mutually fruitful, the danger of excessive indulgence between husband and wife is a cause for concern. Conjugal intimacy may breed nepotism which may, in turn, lead to social irresponsibility if the interests of the nuclear family supersede concerns for other family members and the larger community.

Old-Young

"Precedence of the old over the young" governs more than sibling relationships. It underscores age as a factor in organizing human relationships. The word "precedence" *(hsu/xu)* also means order and sequence. Age is thus an ordering and sequencing principle. A distinctive feature of Confucian ethics is to accept seniority as a value in setting up social hierarchy. However, age alone does not automatically give one status. The unexamined assertion that Confucians respect the old loses much of its persuasive power in light of the Master's harsh words to an unmannerly old man (Yuan Jang) of his acquaintance: "In youth, not humble as befits a junior; in manhood, doing nothing worthy of being handed down. And merely to live on, getting older and older, is be a useless pest" *(Analects,* 14.46).[5]

The Confucian commitment to personal moral growth through self-effort justifies the condemnation of those who fail to realize their own potential. The aforementioned Yuan Jang (Yuan Rang) who prompted Confucius not only to use harsh words but to "hit him on the shank with his staff" (*Analects*, 14.46), seems to have consistently squandered his time and energy. However, to the Confucians, age normally embodies experience and wisdom and, therefore, commands respect. Mencius notes with pride the legacy bequeathed by Tseng Tzu (Zeng Zi), one of the most revered disciples of Confucius:

> There are three things which are acknowledged by the world to be exalted: rank, age, and virtue. At court, rank is supreme; in the village, age; but for assisting the world and ruling over the people, it is virtue. (*Mencius*, IIB.2)

Undoubtedly, in the Confucian order of things, virtue takes precedence over rank and age. However, as pragmatists and realists, the Confucians are acutely aware of the necessity of hierarchy in establishing stability and harmony in society. Tseng Tzu's strategy of using age and virtue in his confrontation with rank is characteristic of the Confucian approach to political power:

> How can a man, on the strength of the possession of one of these, treat the other two with arrogance? Hence a prince who is to achieve great things must have subjects he does not summon. If he wants to consult them, he goes to them. If he does not honor virtue and delight in the Way in such a manner, he is not worthy of being helped towards the achievements of great things. . . . Today there are many states, all equal in size and virtue, none being able to dominate the others. This is simply because the rulers are given to employing those they can teach rather than those from whom they can learn. (*Mencius*, IIB.2)

"Precedence of the old over the young" is thus a deliberate attempt to build an ethic on a biological reality. The reason that "filial piety" *(hsiao/xiao)* and brotherly love *(t'i/ti)* are considered roots *(pen/ben)* for realizing full humanity is partly due to the Confucian belief that moral self-cultivation begins with the recognition that biological bondage provides an authentic opportunity for personal realization. The duty-consciousness generated by the acknowledgment that we are beneficiaries of our parents and older siblings and that our well-being is inseparable from theirs is not one-way obedience. Rather, it is a response to a debt that one can never repay and an awareness that the willingness to assume responsibility for paying that debt is morally exhilarating. Of course, there is complexity in such an ethic. The legend of the sage-king Shun who had the misfortune of having a heartless father and a scheming half-brother amply illustrates the difficulty when the desired spirit of mutuality is absent (*Mencius*, VA.2). We need not unpack the whole legend here. Suffice it to say that the Confucians are aware of the ambiguity and paradox involved in assigning great value to generation and age in harmonizing interpersonally relationships at home.

Friend-Friend

Friendship, based on neither rank nor age, is the paradigmatic expression of the spirit of mutuality. Hierarchy may have been a dominant theme in Confucian ethics but even if it applies to the husband-wife relationship, it is certainly inapplicable to "faith between friends." The centrality of friendship in moral exhortation provides a basis for the teacher-disciple relationship, which, in turn, offers a model for Confucian self-understanding in reference to the ruler.

The case of Tseng Tzu, mentioned earlier, is instructive here. By claiming that both virtue and age were on his side, Tseng Tzu made it explicit to the king that he would not be summoned like an ordinary subject to the court; however if the king was willing to learn, he would give frank advice. Fully informed by this sense of dignity, independence, and autonomy, Mencius also conducted himself as a senior friend, a teacher to the kings he encountered. Thus, he confronted the ruler with his candid assessment of the lack of moral leadership in officialdom, embarrassed the ruler with his sharp criticism of the miserable state of affairs, and even startled the ruler with the likelihood of revolution. A trusted friend, in this sense, is a critic, a teacher, and a fellow traveler on the Way. Faith or trust (hsin/xin) between friends is sustained by a lasting commitment to mutual flourishing rather than by the temporary comfort of sharing food and drink. Consistent with Confucian ethics, a well-known Chinese proverb states that the "friendship" between shallow people is as sweet as honey, but friendship between profound persons is as plain as water.

The Psychocultural Dynamics of the Confucian Family

If we characterize the Confucian family in terms of the Three Bonds as they evolved into a highly politicized method of symbolic control, we must wonder why and how such an oppressive system, which totally undermines the weak, the young, and the female, has managed to survive for so long. On the other hand, if we naively believe that the Confucian family as it actually existed as a social unit throughout imperial China was the embodiment of the Mencian idea of mutuality, we must be perplexed by the wave after wave of iconoclastic attacks against traditional Chinese culture focusing on the Confucian family since the May Fourth movement. The psychocultural dynamics of the Confucian family lies in the complex interaction between the authoritarianism of the Three Bonds and the benevolence of the Five Relationships.

It may appear to be too simple, if not simple-minded, to characterize the Three Bonds as authoritarian and the Five Relationships as benevolent. Such a dichotomy seems to imply that while the Three Bonds as politicized Confucian ideology of control is detrimental to human flourishing, the Five Relationships informed by the Mencian idea of self-cultivation is not only compatible with, but also essential to personal growth. At a purely theoretical level, there is a measure of truth in this dichotomous thinking. After all, the institution of the Three Bonds was a deliberate attempt to utilize Confucian values for the maintenance of a specific social order. Mencius surely would not have approved the political act of converting the moral education of the Five Relationships to the ideological control of the Three Bonds. Surely, it is misleading to define the Mencian intent of the Five Relationships in terms of the logic of the Three Bonds, but a sophisticated understanding of the Three Bonds must also involve adequate appreciation of the Mencian conception of the Five Relationships. In other words, while we should not misinterpret the Five Relationships because of the social consequence of the Three Bonds, we must bear in mind that the Five Relationships served as an ideological background for the Three Bonds.

From our modernist point of view, the Three Bonds are callously exploitative, primarily based on power and domination, and hardly redeemable as family ethics. Paradoxically, however, the three principles (hierarchy, age, and gender) inherent in the bonds are fully recognized by the Confucians as constitutive of the human condition. To be sure, equality as a social ideal looms large in Confucian culture, but, contrary to Taoist relativism and Taoist universalism, Confucians accept the concrete living human being differentiated by hierarchy, age, and gender as an irreducible reality. This insistence that the person embedded in a given set of human relationships be taken as the point of departure in any ethical reflection makes the Confucians sensitive, susceptible, and vulnerable to the status quo. Even though this does not at all mean that the Confucians uncritically accept the existing power relationships, they are, as Max Weber has pointed out, prone to "adjustment to" rather than "transformation of" the world (Weber 1951). As a result, Confucian ethics is more likely than, for example, Protestant ethics to be politicized. Understandably, the family has been perceived by the Confucian state as a vitally important political unit.

The secularity of Confucian ethics in dealing with the mundane affairs of the world gives it a particular contour significantly different from those of the other major ethicoreligious traditions (e.g., Christianity, Islam, and Buddhism). The Confucian life orientation, being this-worldly, takes political authority seriously as an essential factor for the maintenance of social order. Confucians consider the respect for authority an important virtue, even though they are often highly critical of the existing power relationships. This is predicated on the Confucian emphasis on duty-consciousness, which is more demanding of the leadership (including the ruling minority and the cultural elite) than of the general populace. The rationale is that self-imposed discipline as a lifestyle of personal cultivation is a prerequisite for moral and political leadership. A clear manifestation of this lifestyle is the practice of frugality; the precarious livelihood of the farmer rather than the conspicuous consumption of the merchant serves as the basis for social ethics. It was not an accident that the Confucian intellectual considered the farmer, rather than the merchant, as the embodiment of the desired philosophy of life.

Historically the question of whether the traditional Chinese state was transformed, in symbol if not in reality, into an expanded family, or the family has become an instrument of the state, need not concern us here, but the characterization of the emperor as the "king-father" and local officials, such as the magistrates, as the "father-mother offices" seems to indicate that the Confucian attempt to give familial dimension to the political discourse was not inconsequential. An obvious result of this Confucianization (some might prefer ritualization) of Chinese politics has been to make the political arena inseparable from the ethical realm. What one does in the seemingly private confine of one's home becomes politically significant; moreover, a confirmed Confucian, whether in office or in retirement, views the affairs of the state equally as relevant and immediate as family affairs. Ethics that governs family relationships is automatically laden with far-reaching social and political implications. Although the pattern of domination underlying the Three Bonds has lost much of its persuasive power, the significance of hierarchy, age, and gender in family ethics remains important.

If we take a more differentiated view of authority as manifested in the Three Bonds, we notice that the ruler's authority over the minister is fundamentally different from the father's authority over the son. Since the principle that governs the ruler-minister relationship is righteousness, it is not only permissible but imperative that the minister remonstrate with the ruler for the well-being of the state. Indeed, the minister can choose to sever his relationship with the ruler by resigning, or to rectify the relationship by organizing a joint effort (often with the approval of the imperial clansmen) to have the ruler removed. The very fact that such incidents occurred in the Han dynasty when the Three Bonds reigned as supreme values indicates that the Confucian idea of justice was put into practice as a guiding principle for political action. The authority of the ruler over the minister informed by righteousness, far from being absolute is, at its best, a respect for hierarchy for the sake of political stability and bureaucratic efficiency.

The authority of the father over the son, on the other hand, is based on an irreversible biological lineage. The respect for age (normally a symbol for experience and wisdom) is characteristically Confucian, but as I have noted earlier, age itself does not necessarily command respect. The Confucian concern for human flourishing as a continuous process of self-realization impels the father as well as the son to engage in personal cultivation. The ideal father-son relationship is nourished by affection, but the son's cultivated sense of veneration serves as a basis for his tender care for the aging father. The fruitful mutuality between father and son is more frequently realized in the power of the adult son to provide for the dependent father than in the authority of the father to discipline the young son. Radically different from the ruler's authority over the minister, the father's authority is neither external nor contractual. It grows out of the son's increasing awareness of indebtedness. Indeed, despite well-established legal constraints in traditional China, the father's authority, like ritualized power, must be recognized, indeed actively acted upon, by the son to make it efficacious. The case of the sage-king Shun amply demonstrates that the authority of his undeserving father lies solely in Shun's unquestioned filial piety. If we fail to understand the voluntary participation of the son (I am tempted to say the power of the son) in maintaining the authority of the father, we cannot adequately grasp the grammar of action defining the father-son relationship.

The authority of the husband over the wife, which resulted from blatantly patriarchal conditioning, has no redeeming feature. Yet authority here means something different from either authority derived from status as in the ruler-minister relationship, or authority derived from age as in the father-son relationship. The husband-wife relationship is contractual and, therefore, not irrevocable. The Confucians acknowledge divorce as an unhappy eventuality in some marriages. There is no unworldly sanction against divorce. Confucius himself is said to have divorced (or separated from his wife three times). Rules for or against divorce are specific and based on social conventions designed to preserve family harmony.

It is not true that the Confucian wife is "owned" by the husband like a piece of property. The wife's status is not only determined by her husband's position but also by her own family's prominence. By implication, her ultimate fate is inevitably intertwined with the economic and political conditions of her children, both sons and daughters. While in the domestic arena, the husband's influence may also prevail, especially in extraordinary situations when vital decisions, such as the selection of tutors for sons' education, the wife usually wields actual power on a daily basis. We do not have to go to popular literature to confirm the fact that even though formally the husbands are always in control, the wives have numerous informal ways to do what they consider appropriate or, at least, to make their wishes known. With a strong emphasis on family harmony as a social value, indeed a political asset, the Confucian husband is well disposed to exercise the art of compromise in domestic affairs.

The Confucian wife is known for her forbearance, but her patient restraint is often a demonstration of inner strength. While her purposefulness may appear to be overtly and subtly manipulative, she has both power and legitimacy to ensure that her vision of the proper way to maintain the well-being of the family prevails; for the wife is not subservient to the husband, but is his equal.

In short, the Three Bonds, as they both reflect and shape the particular mentality characterized by despotic, gerontocratic, and patriarchal tendencies are not to be confused with the Five Relationships when they were applied. While the ideals governing the Five Relationships as Mencius conceived of them may have been realized only on rare occasions throughout Chinese history, they were actually put into practice in the formation of Confucian family ethics. However, the Three Bonds as they assumed canonical status in defining the modus operandi of the Confucian family, influenced the view of basic human relationships in traditional China. As long as the supremacy of the Three Bonds is primarily motivated by the political aim of social control, their contribution to human flourishing is at most a mixed blessing, if not outright negative. However, the psychocultural dynamics of the Confucian family lies neither in the authoritarianism of the Three Bonds nor in the benevolence of the Five Relationships but in the complex interaction of the two, namely the particular pattern of authority informed by hierarchy, age, and gender.

Prospects

The ills of the Confucian family as characterized by the authoritarianism of the Three Bonds have been thoroughly exposed by some of the most brilliant and influential minds in modern China. Pa Chin's (Ba Jin) novel, *The Family* (1958), representative of the intellectual mentality of the May Fourth generation, poignantly reminds us that the Confucian idea of "home," in the perspective of contemporary consciousness informed by Western liberal demo-cratic ideas, is actually a "prisonhouse" denying the basic rights of the indi-vidual and enslaving the creative energy of the young. Indeed, Confucian family ethics, as depicted by the indignant pen of Lu Hsun (Lu Xun) with telling effectiveness, is no more than "ritual teaching" *(li-chiao/lijiao)*, which instead of humanizing the world contains the subtle message of cannibalism, in his graphic phrase: "Eat people!" (Lu Hsun 1981). The slogan, "Down with Confucius and Sons!" is directed against the feudal past in general and the Confucian family in particular. Understandably many a social scientist has concluded that, both in theory and practice, the decline of the Confucian family is inevitable. For the first few decades of the twentieth century, the survivability of the Confucian family looked bleak. As recent as the 1970s, when the process of modernization was perceived as the linear progression and dissemination of Westernization, if not Americanization, the Confucian family was widely critiqued in academic circles as the single most important cultural factor inhibiting the development of the Sinitic world. The incompatibility of Confucian humanism in general and the Confucian family in particular with modernization was taken for granted.

The rhetorical situation drastically changed as the rise of Japan and subsequently the Four Dragons (South Korea, Taiwan, Hong Kong, and Singapore) as the most dynamic area of sustained economic growth since the Second World War demands a cultural as well as an institutional explanation. The need to reassess the Confucian role in East Asian modernity has become compelling. Peter Berger observes in an essay addressing the issue:

> For several years now the so-called post-Confucian hypothesis has enjoyed a certain vogue. It is essentially simple: both Japan and the newly industrialized countries of East Asia belong to the broad area of influence of Sinitic civilization, and there can be no doubt that Confucianism has been a very powerful force in all of them. The hypothesis that the key variable in explaining the economic performance of these countries is Confucian ethics—or post-Confucian ethics, in the sense that the moral values in question are now relatively detached from the Confucian tradition proper and have become more widely diffused. Historical evidence on the spread of Confucian education and ideology is very relevant to this hypothesis, but equally important is empirical research into the sway of Confucian-derived values in the lives or ordinary people, many whom have never read a Confucian classic and have little education, Confucian or other. Robert Bellah has coined the happy phrase "bourgeois Confucianism" to distinguish this from the "high" Confucianism of the Mandarin elite of traditional China. The work currently being done by S. G. Redding and his associates at the University of Hong Kong on the norms of Chinese entrepreneurs is informed by precisely this point of view. (Berger 1988, pg. 7)

Having outlined the "Confucian hypothesis," Berger offers his own opinion on the matter:

> I'm strongly inclined to believe that, as evidence continues to come in, this hypothesis will be supported. It is inconceivable to me that at least some of the Confucian-derived values intended by the hypothesis—a positive attitude to the affairs of this world, a sustained lifestyle of discipline and self-cultivation, respect for authority, frugality, and overriding concern for stable family life—should not be relevant to the work ethic and the overall social attitudes of the region. At the same time, I strongly suspect that Confucianism is by no means the only cultural and religious factor in play. Other factors will have to be explored. (Berger, 1988, pg. 7)

Consequently, the role of the Confucian family in making a positive contribution to the economic development and social stability of these dynamic areas in the Pacific Rim has gradually been recognized. The perennial issues engendered by the authoritarianism of the Three Bonds and the benevolence of the Five Relationships are still readily visible in East Asia. Both the corporate spirit of industrial East Asia and the feudal ghost of communist East Asia is infused with a strong dose of Confucian familism. The East Asian strength in maintaining social stability and the East Asian weakness in developing a full-fledged democracy are both intimately intertwined with Confucian ethics. The great subtlety in honoring age, and the blatant insensitivity in deprecating gender, equally reflect an East Asian mentality with deep Confucian roots. Families imbued with Confucian values are perhaps still the single most important social institution in imparting ways of learning to be human in East Asian societies. Whether or not we are witnessing the revitalization of the Confucian family, a sophisticated appreciation of East Asia culture past and present demands that we understand its psychocultural dynamics.[6]

Notes

1. In A.D. 75, an imperial conference was organized to settle some of the vital cosmological and ethical issues confronting the official ideology of the Han dynasty. It is in the record of that conference, commonly known as *Discussions in the White Tiger Hall (Po-hu t'ung/Bohutong)* that reference is made to the Three Bonds. See the chapter on "San-kan liu-chi/Sangang liuji" (Three Bonds and Six Principles) in *Po-hu t'ung,* chap. 29. For the precise reference, see no. 2 of the *Harvard-Yenching Institute Sinological Index Series (Index to Po Hu Tung),* authorized reprint (Taipei: Chinese Materials and Research Aids Service Center, 1966), 7/29/11a–b.

2. See the "Chung-hsiao/Zhong-xiao" (Loyalty and Filial Piety) chapter of the *Han fei tzu/Han fei zi.* For the precise reference, see *Han Fei Zi soyin* (Index to *Han fei tzu*), compiled by Zhou Zhongling, Shi Xiaoshi, and Xu Weiliang (Beijing: Zhonghua Book, 1982), chap. 51, p. 863.

3. This is clearly stated in the "Chia-ch'u/Jiaqu" (Marriage) chapter of the *Po-hu t'ung.* See *Po-hu t'ung,* the Pao-ching-t'ang ts'ung-shu/Baojingtang Congshu edition (Beijing: Shi-li/Zhili Book Co., 1923), chuan 9, chap. 40, pp. 1–11b.

4. Lau, 1:105. Lau uses "rule" and "ruled" rather than "govern" and "governed" in his translation.

5. For this translation, see *The Analects of Confucius,* translated by Arthur Waley (London: George Allen and Unwin, 1938; 192, 1988).

6. For a preliminary exploration of this issue, see Tu Wei-ming, "A Confucian Perspective on the Rise of Industrial East Asia," *Bulletin of the American Academy of Arts and Sciences,* 42.1 (October 1988): 32–50.

References

Berger, Peter. (1988). "An East Asian Developmental Model?" In *In Search of an East Asian Developmental Model,* ed. Peter Berger and Hsin-huang Michael Hsiao. New Brunswick, NJ: Transaction Books.

The Analects of Confucius. Translated by Arthur Waley. London: George Allen and Unwin, 1938; repr. New York: Random House, 1988.

Discussions in the White Tiger Hall (Po-hu t'ung/Bohutong). (1966). Harvard-Yenching Institute Sinological Index Series (Index to Po Hu Tung), no. 2. Taipei: Chinese Materials and Research Aids Service Center.

Lu Hsun (Lu Xun, 1881–1936). (1981). "A Madman's Diary." In *The Complete Stories of Lu Xun,* translated by Yang Xianyi and Gladys Yang. Bloomington: Indiana University Press; Beijing: Foreign Languages Press.

Mencius. Translated by D. C. Lau. Hong Kong: Chinese University Press, 1984.

Pa Chin/Ba Jin (Li Fei-kan/Li Feigan, 1905–). (1958). *The Family.* Translated by Sidney Shapiro. Peking: Foreign Languages Press.

Slote, Walter H., ed. (1986). *The Psycho-Cultural Dynamics of the Confucian Family: Past and Present.* Seoul, Korea: International Cultural Society of Korea.

Tu Wei-ming. (1988). "A Confucian Perspective on the Rise of Industrial East Asia." *Bulletin of the American Academy of Arts and Sciences* 42.1: 32–50.

———. (1989). *Centrality and Commonality: An Essay on Chung-yung,* see the revised and enlarged edition Centrality and Commonality: An Essay on Confucian Religiousness. Albany: State University of New York Press.

Weber, Max. (1951). *The Religion of China: Confucianism and Taoism.* Translated by Hans H. Gerth. Glencoe, IL: Free Press.

Zhou Zhongling, Shi Xiaoshi, and Xu Weiliang. (1982). *Han Fei Zi soyin (Index to Han Fei Tzu).* Beijing: Zhonghua Book Co.

8

The Orthodox Chinese Confucian Social Paradigm versus Vietnamese Individualism

Stephen B. Young

Vietnamese Variation on Chinese Orthodoxy

This chapter describes a Vietnamese psychocultural reality in the light of an orthodox Chinese model, often denominated as "Confucianism." However, as scholars in China and the West have long recognized, the label "Confucianism" loosely covers different aspects of the Chinese experience. There are the writings of Confucius himself. Second, there are the writings of a later generation still within the norms and expectations of feudal society and the Chou dynasty, reflected in the writings known as the *Book of Mencius,* the *Doctrine of the Mean,* and the *Great Learning.* Third, there is the government-promoted and imposed social code of orthodox personal behavior and mandarin administration that evolved under the Han dynasty. Fourth, there are the abstract moral and rationalistic teachings of scholars under the Sung and later dynasties known as Neo-Confucianism. This chapter uses as its model of Confucianism the orthodoxy established under the Han dynasty and shows how Vietnamese reality incorporated aspects of that orthodoxy into a different cultural matrix. To say that the Vietnamese are "Confucian" is to oversimplify their social and personal realities. Yet, significant parts of the Chinese Confucian orthodoxy were imported by the Vietnamese. Although dominated by China for almost a millennium and profoundly influenced in a multitude of ways, Vietnam has always maintained a unique identity of its own (see Huy, chapter 5).

Confucianism was introduced by China and was slowly adopted by the Vietnamese not only during the thousand years of Chinese administration, but also throughout subsequent centuries during which the Vietnamese elite borrowed from Chinese imperial practices. In particular, the Vietnamese incorporated Chinese constraints of fidelity to well-defined social roles. Idiosyncratic, individualized self-expression was subordinated to a stereotyped patterning that was considered appropriate for a society that maintained a fixed social status. Nevertheless, the Vietnamese never did fully conform to the Sinic model. For example, they preserved an individualism and a culturally powerful role for women (based upon traditional Vietnamese royal law), which was basically inconsistent with Chinese orthodoxy.

Paradigms of Propriety

The archetype for China's orthodox and highly structured approach to social intercourse was the aristocratic practice created by the kings and feudal lords of Shang and Chou China. The function and purpose of such ritualized behavior are best described in the *Odes,* the poems of Shang and Chou lords, and in the *Analects* of Confucius. The social theory originally propounded in the *Analects* by Confucius himself was the ordering of society into a hierarchy of superior and subordinate roles. Authority, prestige, and superiority were consigned (in theory) to those who demonstrated a trustworthy self-discipline. It was assumed that such persons were most likely to meet whatever expectations were set for their positions. Confucius told Duke Ching of Ch'i that there was government when: "Lords lord, ministers minister, fathers father and sons son" (Confucius 1960a, 12.11.2).

In the original Confucian scheme, one was to behave as one's role prescribed, not as one's nature, talent, or interests might determine. The standards of behavior for lords, ministers, fathers, and sons were in the public domain and easily accessible. The actions and expressions required from individuals were widely publicized so that conformity to expectations would not suffer from lack of knowledge. People were expected to learn how they were to act; therefore, lack of character, not ignorance, was felt to be the principal obstacle to proper conduct.

The public quality of the standards simplified the task of holding people accountable, therefore the judgment as to whether a lord was truly a lord was not hard to reach. Mencius provided a noted example of such critical assessment: he justified usurpation of the throne as valid when the incumbent ruler did not act as a true king. If the king did not conform to the established standards of kingly behavior, he lost any claim to kingly sway.

A review of passages from the *Analects* will sharpen our appreciation of original Confucian social theory. For example, self-serving assertion was disparaged: "He who acts with a constant view to his own advantage will be much murmured against" (Confucius 1960a, 4.12). Conformity to the preferences of superiors was highly valued: The Master said "If the son for three years does not alter from the ways of his father, he may be called filial" (Confucius 1960a, 4.20).

Propriety *(li)*, a core concept for Confucius, was demanded of all. It defined the correct, stylized behavior which was attached to social roles and forestalled the idiosyncrasies of individual expression. Confucius stated: "It is by the rules of propriety that the character is established" (Confucius 1960a, 8.8). He said, "Respectfulness, without the rules of propriety, becomes laborious bustle; carefulness, without the rules of propriety, becomes timidity; boldness, without the rules of propriety, becomes insubordination; straightforwardness, without the rules of propriety, becomes rudeness" (Confucius 1960a, 8.2). "To subdue oneself and return to propriety is perfect virtue" (Confucius 1960a, 12.1.1). "Look not at what is contrary to propriety; listen not to what is contrary to propriety; speak not what is contrary to propriety; make no movement which is contrary to propriety" (Confucius 1960a, 12.1.2). One who conformed would find perfect virtue, and "have no murmuring against [him] in the country and none in the family" (Confucius 1960a, 12.2).

Using status as a base, social roles could be specifically defined, and appropriate behavior could be more easily classified. An office or a capacity was thus defined for each role. Confucius believed that the first task in administering a state was to "rectify names." The status and duties of the people had to be made explicit before they could be expected to conform: "If names be not correct, language is not in accordance with the truth of things. If language be not in accordance with the truth of things, affairs cannot be carried on to success. When affairs cannot be carried on to success, proprieties and music will not flourish. When proprieties and music do not flourish, punishments will not be properly awarded. When punishments are not properly awarded, the people do not know how to move hand or foot" (Confucius 1960a, 13.3).

Correctness in interpersonal relationships was demanded. Confucius once commented, "Of all people, girls and servants are the most difficult to relate to. If you are familiar with them, they lose their humility. If you maintain a reserve towards them, they are discontented" (Confucius 1960a, 17.25). Thus social order depended on conformity to the code of named, formalized behavior, not individual self-determination. The Master said, "When a prince's personal conduct is correct, his government is effective without the issuing of orders. If his personal conduct is not correct, he may issue orders, but they will not be followed" (Confucius 1960a, 13.6).

Gradually within several generations, Confucius's original teachings were given a more abstract formulation. This was the second step in the development of China's Confucian orthodoxy. In the *Great Learning* text we read that the process of role conformity begins with discipline of one's thoughts. First, thought must be made sincere, then the heart can be rectified; with a rectified heart, the personality can be cultivated; with the personality cultivated, families can be regulated and, finally, then the state will be well ordered. The most difficult task was the initial challenge of making thoughts sincere. This effort demanded a watchfulness over one's self even when alone (Confucius 1960c, 358, 359, 366). The *Great Learning* further elaborates that regulating a family occurs when its members meet the duties of their respective stations. For example, the father should be simultaneously correct in his concurrent roles as father, son, husband, and brother (Confucius 1960c, 362, 372).

A companion text, the *Doctrine of the Mean,* adds to our understanding of Confucian role formalism: "The superior man does what is proper to the station in which he is; he does not desire to go beyond this. In a position of wealth and honor, he does what is proper to a position of wealth and honor. In a poor and low position, he does what is proper to a poor and how position" (Confucius 1960b, chap. 14).

Everyone was required to adhere to the responsibilities inherent in several of the five basic relationships: duties between sovereign and minister, between father and son, between husband and wife, between elder brother and younger, and between friend and friend. It is clear from this text that social distinctions were designed to create a hierarchy: "By means of the ceremonies of the ancestral temple, they distinguished the royal kindred according to their order of descent. By ordering the parties present according to their rank, they distinguished the more noble from the less. By the arrangement of the services, they made a distinction of talents and worth (Confucius 1960b, chap. 19).

The enduring Confucian approach, taking its genesis in the thought of Confucius himself, rested on an insight that a self could achieve integrity and autonomy without giving full indulgence to egocentric drives. This preferred kind of self was to find its purpose in living out a socialized role. Thus, an egoized self, an unsocialized self as it were, was to be restrained through conformity to the ways of Confucian propriety.

The promulgation of an official orthodoxy occurred under the Han dynasty when the Han emperors and their ministers perfected an imperial system of centralized, autocratic, bureaucratized, dynastic rule. With increasing sophistication, that pattern of governance survived in China until 1911. I define this imperial order as the formal system of traditional China. Part of the official orthodoxy sustained by the imperial hierarchy was a rigidified social code of propriety. The Han emperors established a canon of approved books of social thought and gradually recognized Confucius as the patron of their conformist social creed. In particular, they formulated the *Book of Rites (Li chi).* The *Hsiao ching,* or classic of filial piety, was also venerated. Neither book was written by Confucius or his students but both defined orthodox Chinese social practice.

The *Hsiao ching* expresses clearly a demanding conformity: "Filiality is the foundation of virtue and the root of civilization. Begun in the service of our parents and continued in the service of the prince, filiality is completed in the building up of our character" (Makra 1961, chap. 1). "He who loves his parents does not dare to hate others. He who reverences his parents does not dare to act contemptuously towards others" (Makra 1961, chap. 2). This submission of the egoized self to others was the *sine qua non* of the orthodox creed.

Further, the *Hsiao ching* promises contentment as a result of such submission: "There is nothing better than propriety for giving security to the rulers and keeping the people well governed. Propriety is essentially reverence. The son is happy when his father is reverenced; the younger brother is happy when his older brother is reverenced; the ministers are made happy when their prince is reverenced; all the people are happy when the one man [the ruler] is reverenced" (Makra 1961, chap. 12).

The *Li chi* collection of writings on propriety codified the conformity of the *Hsiao ching*. One book in this collection justified the use of ceremonial conformity as the principal method of social practice: "The rules of propriety serve as instruments to form men's characters, and they are therefore prepared on a great scale. Being so, the value of them is very high. They remove from a man all perversity, and increase what is beautiful in his nature. They make him correct, when employed in the ordering of himself; they ensure for him free course, when employed toward others. The superior man observes these rules of propriety so that all in a wider circle are harmonious with him, and those in his narrower circle have no dissatisfactions with him" (1885, book 8).

Part of orthodox Chinese social code was an unremitting, vigorous daily attention to others within the family. On rising, the son and his wife were enjoined to should dress according to the rules and then attend their parents (parents-in-law). With bated breath and gentle voice the children should ask if their parents' clothes were too warm or too cold, whether they were ill or pained or uncomfortable in any manner; and if so, they should proceed reverently to stroke and scratch the place. They should beg to be allowed to pour out water for their parents to wash. All this they were to do with an appearance of pleasure in order to make their parents feel at ease (1885, 10.1). Children should eat only after the parents have satisfied themselves. In the presence of the parents they should not sneeze, cough, yawn, spit, snivel, stretch themselves, stand on one foot, lean against anything, or look askance.

If a son should remonstrate with a parent when the parent was at fault and if as a result, the parent should become angry and displeased to the point of beating the son until blood flows, the son should not presume to be angry and resentful but be still more reverential and more filial. An unfilial son may be driven from the house by his parents and his wife sent away. If a son approves of his wife but his parents do not like her, he should divorce her. A son should not forget his parents in a single lifting up of his feet, nor in the utterance of a single word. "Not to disgrace his person and not to cause shame to his parents may be called filial duty" (1885, 26.2). In a filial son, there was no dissembling; what was bound up in his heart was manifested in his countenance. He was to continually examine himself to insure compliance with his parents' expectations. He was required to know what was in his heart and it was to be good.

The *Li chi* text is quite insistent that marriage and families were to have objectives other than personal happiness: "The ceremony of marriage was intended to be a bond of love between two surnames, with a view, in its retrospective character, to secure the services in the ancestral temple, and in its prospective character, to secure the continuance of the family line" (1885, book 41). Thus, being part of a family was a job to be executed with diligence and good faith. The *Li chi* further specified that in the household men should not speak of what belongs to domestic management, and women not of what belongs to the politics and society outside the home. Men and women should not hand vessels to one another, nor should they share the same mat in lying down.

The logic of such conformity as the prerequisite for enjoying social status also applied to positions other than the kingship. By such reckoning, what mattered most for a person in his or her relationships was not the free play of indulgent preferences but playing, or acting out, or being, a role. The Chinese notion for realizing in one's behavior such social requirements was *wei,* a verb connoting the fulfillment of a role.

The orthodox Chinese formula for social adjustment as created under the Han dynasty had various consequences. Success as a moral person could come not only through exemplary self-restraint, but also through posturing, by mechanistic, even hypocritical adherence to form. Conforming overtly to every jot and tittle of orthodox propriety did not guarantee actual elimination of the egoized self. External behavior was an imperfect guide to internal intentions, when having proper intentions was held out as the goal of system. Thus, the orthodoxy had a potential for alienating both those who saw through the hypocrisy it fostered and tolerated (they rebelled or sought refuge in Buddhism and Taoism) as well as those who succumbed to its heartless formalism (they became emotionally sterile, petty, and rigid). Role responsibility was a code of duty which imprisoned individual uniqueness and self-expression within the confines of proper behavior. Mannered, fussy etiquette was the degenerate consequence of orthodoxy's social code.

Confucius, as portrayed in the *Analects,* seemed aware of these negative consequences of role conformity, of living through acts of self-conscious *wei.* He did not value as an end complete suppression of the self by social norms. Rather, he held out a more ideal state of sublime ego–awareness where the self willingly embraced the role and found a transcendence of mind in such submission so that the self no longer perceived an alienation from its culture and yet still possessed a liveliness and alertness. A lively self-surrendering to discipline would produce a trustworthy person, one fit for leadership.

By counterexample, the first Taoists taught release from the torments of role conformity with the doctrine of *wu wei,* "nonaction," or not consciously striving to meet the terms and conditions ascribed to a social role. These philosophical Taoists advocated a spontaneous evolution of the self in complete congruence with natural ways, of living by impulse and through unmediated responses to conditions without the mental exertions demanded by the *Great Learning* text. In imperial China, philosophical Taoism never exerted an influence equivalent to orthodox thought derived from Confucian teachings. From the Han dynasty on, government authority was used to enforce Confucian norms, not Taoist freedoms.

As early as the Han dynasty, the penal laws of the Chinese imperial system enforced the social orthodoxy prescribed in the above works (Ch'u 1965). Unfortunately, the oldest extant text of a penal law code dates from A.D. 737, reflecting provisions as revised in 653 C.E. by the T'ang court. The T'ang dynasty, like the Han before it, followed a brief father and son imperial succession where the father had unified all China under one central administration but the son had then lost the throne. Succeeding such an ephemeral dynasty, the T'ang political elite set out to replicate the norms and institutions of the imperial system as developed under the Han, a system which had kept the ruling clan in power for 400 years. The T'ang penal code therefore incorporated principles of law previously used under the Han to consolidate an imperial order.

Article 6 of the T'ang Code lists the ten most heinous crimes (Johnson 1979). A review of several of these provisions illustrates how strenuously the governing imperial bureaucracy of China attempted to enforce conventional social role conformity. As the *Hsiao ching* had argued, conformist individual morality created conditions promoting stable government. The T'ang rulers endorsed this.

Several heinous crimes directly threatened the dynasty itself such as the act of plotting rebellion, sedition, or treason. But equally serious was contumacy such as the beating or the plotting of the death or the killing of paternal grandparents or parents, senior relatives, or a husband. The fact that it was not contumacy for a husband to kill his wife, reflected the different roles assigned to men and women in the approved patrilineal descent family system.

The seventh heinous crime was lack of filial piety. This included accusing or cursing one's parents or paternal grandparents. This section also punished a child who moved into a separate household or had separate goods while parents or paternal grandparents were still living. The state thus enforced the power of parents over their children far beyond the age of psychosocial maturity for the children. The subcommentary to this section of the T'ang Code says: "While the paternal grandparents or parents are alive, the sons and grandchildren must put no limit on supporting them. When going out, sons and grandsons state where they are going, and when returning, report to their parents without following their own wishes" (Johnson 1979, 75). The subcommentary cites the *Li chi* as authority for these rules.

The article on heinous crimes also insisted on mourning for one's parents and paternal grandparents and punished laxity. Under the heinous crime of unrighteousness, a wife was compelled to mourn for her husband and not be lax in such observances. On hearing of his death, the wife must cry out and grieve. The heinous crime of discord included the wrong of beating or making an accusation to the court about one's husband or of close or older relatives.

Chinese Orthodoxy in Vietnam

The orthodox conformist social ethic came to Vietnam at the hands of Chinese overlords. Before the Chinese occupation (which began in 221 B.C.), the Vietnamese followed matriarchal family patterns. The Chinese introduced their patrilineal ideal and their ceremony of marriage as the taking of a woman into a patrilineage to bear heirs for that descent system. A consequence of this colonial imposition was the revolt of the Trung sisters against Chinese rule in A.D. 39. The uprising was unsuccessful but it is most relevant to note the leadership given by women, daughters of Viet chiefs who, under the old matriarchal rules, would have enjoyed the power and prestige which the Chinese then gave to their husbands and sons.

The revolt failed; Chinese sovereignty over the Vietnamese lasted for nine more centuries. Under Chinese tutelage, the Vietnamese slowly adopted the Chinese social orthodoxy as part of the imperial order of political regulation. In particular, the Vietnamese incorporated into their way of life the orthodox role for men. This office in the sequence of its personal responsibilities, consisted first of a man's assignment as a son, second as a father, and third as a husband.

The noted Vietnamese scholar Nguyen Binh Khiem wrote this poem in the sixteenth century.

> Since your were born a man
> why don't you read and learn?
> Hugging game fowls, you rush to cock fights
> Lured by hound bells, you go on hunts.
> At night you prowl behind some wench.
> By day you dally with a ball.
> You shun your teacher, your school friends
> You treat your books like mortal foes
> When my own son so carries on,
> What hope does it hold out for me?
> Oh well! I'll down a cup of wine
> to soothe the grief that never ends. (Thong 1979, 37)

Nguyen Trai, the fifteenth-century adapter of orthodox learning, warned of sensual involvement.

> Lust is your foe—beware a woman's charms.
> The world has seen the wreck of many homes.
> Why sap your spirit and impair your soul?
> One solemn task a married man performs
> To sire some heirs and save the family line. (Thong 1979, 95)

And yet the soul of Vietnamese individualism fretted in the Confucian straightjacket and peeped out from time to time. Nguyen Thien Tung wrote:

> Accept your lot and live your life, fish moth.
> "It's just a station, gratitude" they say.
> You don't belong with flowers and orioles.
> Lean on your tablet, view the hills—that's joy. (Thong 1979, 49)

These orthodox views on the role of men are still held by many Vietnamese. Given the nature of the patrilineal family, the ideal of filial piety says that being a good husband and father constitutes the acceptable way for an adult man to be a good son to his parents. Filial piety therefore implies both that a male never fully grows up and that the interests and well-being of the family take precedence over the needs and desires of individuals (see Slote, chapter 16).

The responsibility of a man is to bring honor and status to the family. In this way he makes his ancestors proud and gives an example for his descendants. In theory, honor and status derived from a man's *duc* or virtuous charisma. The consequences of one's vitality survive death so that the more honor and status achieved in this life, the more powerful spirit the man can bequeath to succeeding generations after his death. And his descendants will have good reason to worship and revere such a potent ancestral spirit more than they would an ordinary one. Achievement during life to establish *duc* becomes the central mechanism continuing the sequence of filial piety from generation to generation. As a poem of moral instruction says, "achieving a reputation brings good fortune from Heaven for 10,000 generations" (*Gia huan ca,* line 561).

Thus the task of man lies outside the family in the competitive arenas of society and politics. His lot is to make a career which brings *duc* to himself and, in consequence, recognized social status to his family. Therefore, as a boy, his role is to study and prepare himself for the highest possible career. The objective in a career is not self-satisfaction in one's own daily work but gaining title and preeminence; whether it is or is not fulfilling work is not of consequence. A family gains less benefit from an industrious, honest but unambitious son; only high rank brings home the benefits desired from a man's career. The *Gia huan ca* poem contains a section advising wives to encourage their husbands to become officials, saying that "from then till now women depend on the bounty created by their husbands; glory makes up for the times of no meat and thin gruel; for Heaven's bounty and public achievement to arrive, husbands should be mandarins so their wives can be ladies."

Commensurate with a man's status outside the home, is the formal authority he has within the family. The man, as father, officiates at family worship rites. As long as he lives, his wife and children must obey. His is the right to physically discipline the children by beating them with a rod. As a father, a man is not expected to show love or affection for his children. He is the stern and distant master. He should not become involved with his children by responding to their individual emotional needs. However, he is expected to set an example of right conduct for them. He is a model for emulation, not a confessor or confidant. There is a Vietnamese saying that "If you love your children, beat them; if you hate them, give them sweets to eat."

If a man's role is outside the family, then a woman's place is very much within it. Wives and mothers are called *noi tuong*—or "generals of the within." The ideal woman therefore mobilizes the family's resources to support the man's career. If he needs money to ingratiate himself with a superior or to pay for printing his personal literary magazine, it is often her responsibility to provide it. Her fate is to serve. As the *Gia huan ca* says, "the word 'follow' describes the fate of a woman." Or as in another line—"When young, obey your father; when married, your husband; and when old, your son."

The *Gia huan ca* advises Vietnamese children to follow the orthodoxy:

Regarding parents
> Father's relatives and mother's relatives are the same,
> Don't favor one side over the other.
> In the pain and aggravation of raising us, our parents have
> accumulated merit thick and wide;
> We must persevere in being filial night and day.
> Because affection arises, they frequently reprimand,
> Wanting us to correct our faults and become better people.
> Carefully and circumspectly,
> Record in your heart and soul parental words which are worthy of
> being engraved therein.
> Don't be either heavy or frivolous with your words;
> Don't let your body show your anger, or let your face show your
> feelings.
> If you have money, offer
> Good food and rich soup no less than your siblings;
> If you have nothing, rest easy

For how can the elders be angry with you then?
Whenever some rule is violated,
You should be beaten out of the front door and made to enter from
    the back.
When parents are feverish or chill, we must serve their needs tenderly,
Look to every aspect of their food and medicine.
Frequently visit and inquire of them,
When they are well, our hearts will be peaceful.
The task of being filial demands dedication to its requirements,
In want or in riches manage as is best under the circumstances.
Do not compete or be divisive,
It brings disorder to the village and the nation and you will be laughed
    at afterwards.

Vietnamese Limitations on Orthodoxy

Victory of the Chinese pattern, however, was far from total. First, the Vietnamese have preserved a resolute individualism that, in particular, influences their politics. Second, they have insisted upon a compromise on power within the family blending patrilineal authority with matriarchy.

Individualism

Every Vietnamese carries within a longing for those months of earliest childhood when love was unconditional, when the baby was accepted without question before the strictures of orthodox social roles came into play. Even while conforming to the orthodoxy, Vietnamese intensely seek something more satisfying than performance of duties. This drive for acceptance, for recognition, makes them uniformly very hardworking and extremely charming as they probe others seeking attention and centrality in any relationship.

We may note that most Vietnamese achievements have resulted from the exercise of individual prowess—the skills and talents of intellectuals, poets, solo musicians, composers, master craftsmen, farmers working their own fields, or lonely military heroes.

Individualism in Vietnam is conceptualized not through the validation of power in the self but rather through a scheme of fatalism. Each individual has a unique destiny, a fortune, called *so*. Each individual is thus autonomous, but not necessarily powerful. Power rests with the dispositive dictators of destiny, not with the individual to any meaningful degree. Each person is born to a destiny, produced in a vague fashion by past karma generated by the self and by immediate paternal and maternal ancestors.

Because fate implies autonomy, belief in destiny has long infused the Vietnamese community with a sense of its own independence. In 1076, a Vietnamese general, facing an invading army from Champa allied with a Chinese expeditionary force, gave his men courage with the following poem:

> In the rivers and mountains of the southern nation [Vietnam],
> The southern king holds sway.
> This elemental destiny has been fixed in Heaven's book.
> What possible cause do these marauders have to invade?
> The spectacle of their complete defeat will come to pass. (Thong 1979, 3)

Not only did the Vietnamese have a legitimate right to rule the southern kingdom, but the power moving the pen of Heaven stood behind that right. Invasion of Vietnam, no matter how massive, was stupid and resistance to foreign conquest was both appropriate and certain of victory. The power to prevail, it is important to note, came from Heaven, not from the will of the Vietnamese soldiers assembled to do battle.

Yet if destiny were no longer to smile on the Vietnamese, then invasion would triumph and resistance would be stupid. In the mid-nineteenth century as the French moved to conquer Vietnam, the Tu-Du emperor in Hue acquiesced in inevitable defeat. He wrote:

> The enemy's embarkations are swift as the breath of the wind and their artillery mighty as the stroke of thunder. Do you really wish to confront such power with a pack of cowardly soldiers? It would be like mounting an elephant's head or caressing a tiger's tail. How would we differ from a swarm of flies dancing over the grass or from a host of locusts kicking a carriage? With what you presently have, do you really expect to dissolve the enemy's rifles into air or to chase his battleships into hell? (Lam 1967, 4)

Implicit in the Vietnamese notion of individual destiny *(so)* is rugged individualism of a Darwinian nature. A fate peculiar to each individual dominates that person's life. It prevails over social norms; it intrudes into family relationships; it makes or breaks friendships. This partially is why Vietnamese are most reluctant to adopt children. It is like buying a pig in a poke: you don't know what you are getting and if it's bad, there is nothing you can do about it then. Innate individual character, so dispositive of communal realities, rests within each person separately. Society is the sum total of individual accretions; individuals do not take their purpose and their coherence from the social order but from fate itself. The orthodoxy in Vietnam, therefore, is only a covering for reality. Its capacity to provide order is intermittent.

Professions of social solidarity or family loyalty should be taken at face value only in Vietnam. Just underneath the surface of conformity are the tuggings and tensions of highly self-conscious individuals. Vietnamese children are so bright and alert because from birth they have been treated as if they are someone unique and special in the sense of having their own destiny.

Vietnamese believe that destiny is driven by the energized substance of the cosmos, *khi* (Ch. *ch'i*). *Khi* crests and eddies in predictable rhythms of moving *am* (Ch. *yin*) and *duong* (Ch. *yang*). The interaction of the self with *am* and *duong* can be contemplated through three methods of appraisal: reading horoscopes, geomancy, and physiognomy. Horoscopes, by charting the trends of *am* and *duong* proper to each year in the endlessly repeating sixty-year cycles of time, permit predictions of auspicious and inauspicious periods in one's life. Contrasting one's personal confluence of *am* and *duong* with those of others permits predictions of who will augment one's good fortune and who will work one ill. Through such calculation one gains the power of foreknowledge, but not a power to change destiny in significant ways. One can control one's associations where possible and wait for better days to start important personal projects. Yet all one's best precautions may still be overtaken by a contrary destiny.

In Vietnamese as well as Chinese astrology, life and the universe are manifestations of endless cycles of changing *am* and *duong*. Each moment of time has its *am* and *duong* propensities. Two cycles are said to repeat themselves over time. One is a cycle of ten numbers running from one to ten and then repeating. The second is another cycle of twelve animals—the rat, the ox, the tiger, the cat, the dragon, the snake, the horse, the goat, the monkey, the rooster, the dog, and the pig. Each animal sign represents its own combination of *am* and *duong*. The pairing of the same number with the same animal occurs as the two cycles mesh each sixty years. The changing combination of number and animal gives each year its own character within that sixty year cycle. Matching the known *am* and *duong* character of an individual given by his or her birth year against the different propensities of the coming years will indicate which years will either facilitate or frustrate the individual's activities (Lau).

Aside from numbers and time, *am* and *duong* produce the material world. This is done through the interaction of the Five Elements—water, fire, wood, metal, and soil. Each of the Five Elements has its own unique proportion of *am* and *duong*. The Five Elements produce changes in the material world through separate cycles of procreation and destruction. In the generative cycle, soil turns to metal, which becomes water, which next generates wood, which produces fire, which leads again to soil. In the destructive cycle, soil fades into water, which succumbs to fire, which passes away in favor of metal, which decomposes to wood, which decays to soil. Water is considered completely *am* and fire is completely *duong*. The three other elements are a combination of both energy modes.

In casting a horoscope, the first calculation is to fix the personality in terms of the Five Elements—the year, month, day, and hour of one's birth and the month and day of one's conception (using a rule of nine lunar months between conception and birth). Each of these times has the *am* and *duong* balance of one of the Five Elements. The best fortune is to have all Five Elements represented among those six moments. If one or more of the Five Elements are missing, the person should prominently wear clothing of the color corresponding to the missing element to improve his or her fortune. In locating a harmonious spouse for a child, someone born in a year linked to the same element as corresponds to the birth year of the child is to be avoided, except if the element for both is soil, for two soils combine to make a mountain.

In each great cycle of sixty years there are only a fixed number of hourly birthdates, a total of about 518,400. Clearly many people must have the same horoscopes, yet their fates remain unique. *Am* and *duong* move in other arenas—the earth and one's physical constitution—to produce individual destinies. Other techniques are available to estimate the movements of *am* and *duong* not captured by astrology.

Geomancy reads the composition of *am* and *duong* in the earth. In this way auspicious and inauspicious sites may be located for houses, work environments, and graves. Living close to an accumulation of *khi* energy in the ground which complements one's astrological allotment can bring increased abilities to be successful. Some places may contain enough power to offset the drift of troubled times. A person has more choice over where to live, work, and be buried than over the moment of birth. Geomancy gives people some control over their fortunes. Geomancers who describe the contours of earthly *am* and *duong* are in great demand and command a high price for their services.

Nguyen van Thieu strongly believed in the efficacy of geomancy. Once there had been a statue in Saigon's Chien Si circle which had been destroyed during the war. Chien Si circle was believed to be the resting place of a dragon's tail, with other prominent boulevards and government buildings making up the rest of the beast. With the statue gone, nothing held the tail down so it flailed this way and that and caused turmoil in Saigon politics. As president, Thieu had a new statue built to keep the tail motionless and insisted that the statue be surrounded with a pond and fountain to keep the tail cool. We may scoff, but Thieu lasted in power the longest of all South Vietnamese leaders.

About 1956 Thieu relocated his grandfather's grave in the family village of Tri Thuy near the city of Phan Rang. After that, his fortunes began to rise. But in 1975, after he ordered South Vietnamese troops to abandon the central highlands without a fight, furious soldiers on retreat went out of their way to seek out Tri Thuy, locate the grave, and smash the bones of Thieu's grandfather.

When this news was brought to Thieu in his presidential palace, he turned ashen and collapsed. He lost his capacity to lead, and within weeks he resigned.

In 1010 when Ly Thai To founded Vietnam's Ly dynasty, he assembled the geomancers of the realm and bade them find the most auspicious site for a capital city. While moving down the Red River, the king then saw a dragon leave the water and enter the Heavens. He checked with geomancers who confirmed that that area was most favorable. The city of Hanoi was therefore founded and called Thanh Long or "citadel of the dragon." Saigon, on the other hand, was built by the French between the Vietnamese settlement of Gia Dinh and the Chinese market of Cholon. Either Gia Dinh or Cholon has better geomancy than Saigon. Thus the fall of French power, based as it was in Saigon, was inevitable. Similarly, the American-supported nationalist regimes in South Vietnam had an Achilles heel in the location of their capital city. It is perhaps no accident that, after unification of the country under their rule, the Vietnamese Communist leadership kept their capital in the more auspicious city of Hanoi.

In 1248, Tran Thu Do, the patriarch of the Tran family who had just placed his nephew on the throne of Vietnam in order to found the Tran dynasty, dispatched geomancers to every corner of the kingdom. Their mission was to locate each site upon which a potential king could be born or on which someone would be buried with the effect that his descendants might become kings. When the sites were found, Tran Thu Do ordered them altered, effaced, or destroyed in order to protect his dynasty's hold on supreme temporal power. This historian who recorded this added a comment of his own:

> Since the beginning of Time those mountains and rivers have stood. As Heaven turns in its cycle, superior men appear; everything is in accordance with fate (so). Even if you do believe that the method of such manipulation can alter natural forces, what can you do once the superior man appears as scheduled to prevent his dynasty? (Dia Viet su ky toan thu, 2:28).

To confirm the historian's point of view, Tran Thu Do's effort proved bootless. The Tran dynasty foundered of its own accord. The next dynasty was founded by Le Loi, who had been born in one of the sites defaced on Tran Thu Do's orders 200 years previously.

Under the principles of geomancy, the khi energy in the earth flows from duong concentrations to am concentrations. What is high belongs to duong; what is low to am. Mountains and hills are duong; the greater the height the more powerful the duong energy. Rivers and streams are am; the wider the more bountiful the am energy. The presence of energy is called a dragon—long. It has am characteristics when stable. The flow of energy is called thuy or water. With motive power, it has duong characteristics. Yet a mountain being stationary also partakes of a dragon nature and so, am. If a flow, thuy, runs out of its source from left to right, it has *duong* characteristics; it runs from right to left, it has an *am* nature.

Geomancy examines four features of the earth: *long* or the presence of energy; *sa* or the vertical rise and fall of the terrain; *thuy* or water or energy flow; and a *huyet* or a gathering point of both *am* and *duong* energy. To have *sa* or terrain there must be a difference in height of at least 3 cm. Without *sa* there can be no *thuy* or flow. Without flow there can be no *huyet*, just separate concentrations of *am* and *duong* in high and low places. Finding a *huyet* with *sinh khi* or generative energy is the apex of geomancy's achievement.

A *huyet* is from 300 to 1,000 square meters in area. It is distinguished by seven interrelated features. First is a form in the terrain *(huyet chong)*. Second is a point of entrance where the energy flows in *(nhap thu mach)*. Third are boundaries on the right and left *(noi cuc sa)*. Fourth is the flat space where the energy congregates *(minh duong)*. Fifth, is a high point of earth in front of the flat focal point *(an)*. Sixth is an exit for energy to flow out *(thuy khau)*. Seventh is a clear compass orientation of the entire formation. In the center of the huyet can be found a *thai cuc vong,* a circle wherein *am* and *duong* undulate (Trung 1971; Skinner 1982).

The third precise way to measure the energy believed to cause changes in the fortune of any individual is to study the shape of the person's face (Khau 1967; Mau 1986). Physiognomy interprets the features of one's face just as geomancy does the surface of the earth. The face is a map to character and destiny. Physiognomy does not contain a power to change either, but it reveals much about a person. Thus by reading the faces of others, one gains intimate knowledge about them, knowledge which can be put to work on one's behalf. Insincere, greedy, hypocritical people can be avoided; loyal people can be sought out as friends and associates. Another person's character may be beyond one's power to change, but because it can be known, calculations of maneuver and intrigue regarding that person can bring one advantage in interpersonal relations.

Vietnamese physiognomy is called *tuong so,* or the destiny of one's appearance. The notion is that the energy imparted to us in our conception is both unique and fixed within us. Our allotment limits our opportunities in life just as wealth sets bounds on our lifestyle.

Tuong so reads the face as geomancy seeks out the flow of *am* and *duong* in the earth. Every face has five mountains *(ngu nhac)* and four rivers *(tu doc)*. The five mountains are the forehead, the nose, the chin, and the two cheeks. The four rivers are the ears, the eyes, the mouth, and the nose. The nose, being both mountain and river, partakes of *am* and *duong* and so is the single most important feature of the face.

The Five Elements are also reflected in the shape of the face as well. A square face is considered as metal, a thin face is matched with wood, a fat, short face is linked to water, a face broad at the forehead and narrowing at the chin is tied to fire, and one with large, domineering features is linked to soil. Further, on each face the forehead is tied to fire, the nose to soil, the mouth to water, the right ear to wood, and the left ear to metal.

When a newborn infant is first seen, its features are scrutinized. Vietnamese remember with perfect clarity the minute features of relatives and people they have not seen for years, features an American would hardly notice, much less remember.

However, the most important aspect of *tuong so* is not the individual parts examined separately but the degree to which the face as a whole has balance and proportion. A nose should not be too large for the mouth or the eyes. A high forehead should be balanced by large ears. A thin lip or bony cheeks can detract from an otherwise auspicious *tuong*. The more balance and proportion to one's face, the more vital is one's inner energy and the better is one's fate. Now a face, such as Abraham Lincoln's or Eleanor Roosevelt's, would perhaps strike us as homely or unattractive, but such a face is still balanced and proportional and constitutes a successful *tuong*. Such a face, though irregular, displays vigor and command, indicating the presence of cosmic power and an opportunity to manipulate destiny in one's favor.

Neither horoscopes, geomancy, or *tuong so* alone can independently give us a complete preview of our destiny. Each form of calculation has its own truth and the changes in our lives mandated by fate can only be estimated by analysis of all three. A good *tuong* can be undercut by an internally tense horoscope. An auspicious horoscope can come to naught because of an ancestor's poorly located grave. But when the energies of Heaven, earth, and man fall into alignment, then there is harmony, prosperity, and the ripe fullness of a bountiful life.

When his or her fate is auspicious, a Vietnamese is said to possess *phuc duc* or "merit-virtue." In reflecting on recent years the turmoil and tragedy in Vietnam, the influential South Vietnamese general, Do Mau, ended his auto-biography by analyzing the *phuc duc* of the Vietnamese people in his generation and the role of destiny in creating that poor fortune (Mau 1986, 1024). Vietnamese assess more than their own lives according to *phuc duc* and the tendencies of cosmic fortunes.

As discussed by Slote in chapter 16, *phuc duc* provides Vietnamese with an explanation of fate and fortune, removing both from the realm of arbitrary and unjust whimsy. Briefly, *phuc duc* is a karma, earned both by an individual in previous incarnations and, most importantly, by male and female progenitors, especially the female. Good *phuc duc* will determine that one is born with auspicious astrology, geomancy, and *tuong so*. From this perspective, the three occult sciences which permit prognostication reflect the manifestations of *phuc duc* earned by selfless deeds in the past.

The scheme of destiny places individuals in isolation, driven by forces beyond their control. People cannot be assumed to be reliable, for they may not have the ability to control what they do. A defensive wariness is the best stance for interpersonal relations among Vietnamese. There is little that bonds one Vietnamese to another. All political movements and religions are split into factions and rival tendencies. Loyalties, where they exist, run to those individuals who provide a basis for trust or opportunities for one's self-advancement, not to institutions. Further, individuals cannot pass their leadership on to sons or loyal subordinates. Followers develop limited solidarity.

Ironically, the Vietnamese disposition to believe strongly in individual destiny reinforces adherence to a conformist social ethic. If individuals are perceived to be driven by the beyond, then their conformity to social codes is a necessary means of placing them under some control. Conformity to role engenders the trust necessary for social intercourse. Role conformity is used to measure, not another's motivation, but his or her tractability. For this reason, the orthodoxy of role conformity has a place in Vietnamese culture.

Conformity and individualism coexist in perpetual tension. Society demands conformity; destiny provokes individualism. This conflict most often leads to a grudging external conformity to the obligations of role and private lamentations over the vagaries of a cruel fate. Such insincere conformity frequently fails when the opportunity arises to evade role responsibilities. If the conforming performance is secretly reluctant, then tomorrow may bring deviance, defiance, and failure of orthodoxy. Thus, for Vietnamese, orthodox behavior today is no guarantee of reliable behavior tomorrow. Vietnamese know how each person should perform in a given role, but they are neither surprised nor disappointed when a burst of selfish individualism prevents another from conforming as desired. The surprise comes when someone consistently and without obvious repression of the self meets the responsibilities of a social role. Such a person quickly becomes known for having character.

In addition, the submission of self necessary for the orthodoxy to function contains a power to shape destiny. By being selfless, a Vietnamese can acquire *duc* or virtuous élan. That quality, the end product of self-generated restraint, both attracts friends and followers. *Duc* brings high position as one is found to be reliable and trustworthy. *Duc* also produces a favorable karma, which results in improved *phuc duc*.

Female Empowerment

The Vietnamese made adjustments to the institution of patrilineal marriage which the Chinese imposed on them. The Chinese patriarchy gave too much power to the male in his roles as father and husband for Vietnamese tastes. As a counterweight, Vietnamese norms gave the woman in her role as wife and mother considerable control over the family. The overt, external social power of the man was offset by a covert, internal, emotional dynamic which gave the woman influence in the home that was rarely questioned. In common parlance, the wife is the *noi tuong* or the minister of the within. Thus, the approved role for women in the home was given special meaning by Vietnamese, with social powers not permitted to women under the orthodoxy in China.

Imperial Chinese orthodoxy does not justify this Vietnamese feminism. To provide conceptual coherence for powerful women within the Vietnamese cultural context, the scheme of fatalism proved generous. The quality of one's fortune is ascribed primarily to the virtues of one's grandmother, mother, or wife. The important poem, *Gia huan ca,* simply said: *phuc duc tai mau,* "Merit virtue is caused by the maternal." Deserving women of good conduct bring felicity to their descendants. Tragedy, poverty, and other incidents of bad fortune can be blamed on one's wife, mother, or grandmother. Women thus have power, awesome power for the Vietnamese; they can create destiny.

According to the *Gia huan ca,* and as preached for centuries in every Vietnamese home, the first responsibility of a woman is to produce a male heir. Then she is to conserve and increase the family's wealth. She must be frugal and thrifty. She must be dedicated to the family. No self-indulgence is permitted. Clothes must be modest. A woman's posture must be demure, her voice soft, and above all, she must be chaste.

Such a well-behaved daughter, according to the poem, will bring peace to her parents' hearts and renown to her family forever and ever. No hot fire can tempt her once her disposition becomes fixed and tempered. If she is tempted by the promises of sweet words of the butterflies and the bees (men), the word of her transgressions will reach the authorities and crushing shame will weigh down her family. Self-discipline and dedication are expected from the worthy woman.

The two watchwords for a woman to learn while growing up are *kheo* and *khan*. *Kheo* is skill with the hands at household tasks; *khan* is cleverness at being proper and correct in family etiquette. The four virtues for women are *dung, cong, ngon,* and *hanh*. *Dung* is appearance, which should be neat and attractive. *Cong* is industry, which should be precise and careful. *Ngan* is speech, which should be submissive and respectful. *Hanh* is character, which should be upright, filial, devoted, and trustworthy.

A woman must also put up with her husband's weaknesses and shortcomings, his drinking, gambling, and his mistresses. She must not be jealous of his minor wives. She must not take objection to his words so that she can maintain harmony in the household. But the *Gia huan ca* reminds women that sweet, wise words can change a husband's ways. A wife must be gracious to her husband's friends. Then she must instruct the children to be selfless and compassionate. A woman must watch her own selfish instincts, for she must repress them to build up *phuc duc* for the family.

Next the poem lists a few specific rules of good behavior for women:

Don't go out in the dark without a light
Only talk when spoken to
Be economical but not stingy
Receive guests with open generosity
Don't be fickle; be consistent
Don't force too low a price when buying; don't charge too much
    when selling
Don't steal from the poor
Don't lie
If you are rich, don't boast or be haughty; if poor don't complain for
    your time will come. No family is rich or poor for more than
    three generations.
Don't charge high interest as a lender of money; don't push borrowers
    to the wall.
Pay your debts
Don't worship money, be cool about it
Don't gossip, the less said the better
Go straight home from the market
Keep the house tidy from sunrise to sunset; be clean even if you are
    poor
If you lose something, blame Heaven; don't spread doubt on others,
    for one lost item leads to ten doubts but one doubt leads to ten
    sinful wrongs.
Always cook enough; keep pickled vegetables on hand, learn to sew
    well with small stitches.
Remain grateful to the ancestors; don't be absent from worship
    ceremonies; present clean incense and offerings; be poised; join in
    the worship meal, eat heartily, don't be standoffish.

Other choice words of advice sprinkled in the poem are:

Your words must be agreeable and sweet; listen to your husband to
    maintain harmony,
Obedience is the word for a woman.
Don't be jealous of minor wives, that's vulgar.
Control your annoyance when your husband's friends drop by; don't
    take out your anger by shouting at your children

There we see the image of the virtuous Vietnamese woman, one with
the power to earn *phuc duc*. Given their responsibility for the family's welfare,
Vietnamese women seek and most always are readily given control over the
money and property that is in the husband's name. The woman's power of the
purse acts as a check on the husband's legal advantages and social prominence.

Outside the family, the husband precedes his wife and dominates conversation. He will sit at the head, be served first, participate in politics, fight the wars, and go on to higher education. When the husband completes his studies with distinction and receives government patronage, the family gains gentry status, emoluments, and economic opportunity. The wife takes quiet satisfaction knowing that her efforts produced such felicity. A paradigm of the successful couple has the wife working laboriously to support a young family while her husband studies for the mandarin examinations, or in modern Vietnam, at graduate school to become a professional. Society correctly ascribes to the wife considerable *phuc duc*. The husband can thank his mother for having enough *phuc duc* to have brought about such a fortunate marriage for him.

It is assumed by Vietnamese that prosperous families are blessed with a woman of *phuc duc,* either in this or a previous generation. As a consequence, many Vietnamese women will seek the external circumstances of wealth and ease to prove to others that they have admirable moral qualities. Poverty or other ill fortune explicitly rebukes a woman in the family. The tragic death of a child raises a question of whether the birth mother, the paternal grandmother, or maternal grandmother was most responsible for the death because of her deficient *phuc duc*.

In selecting a wife for her son, a Vietnamese mother will guess at the young woman's ability to generate *phuc duc* for the patrilineage in addition to checking her capacity for receiving good fortune from *am* and *duong*. A family known for its *phuc duc* and good luck has no trouble marrying out its daughters.

A woman has another important role, inherent in her position of wife, which is as daughter-in-law to her husband's mother. As such she moves into her mother-in-law's house and serves the needs of her husband's family. It is acceptable for the husband's mother to be cross, unpleasant, cutting, and condescending toward the daughter-in-law. The husband's mother has full power over the household and the daughter-in-law's role is to meekly and even happily obey. The fact that she is a wife and mother in her own right gives her no claim to consideration from her husband's mother.

The relationship between a Vietnamese wife and her mother-in-law is fraught with unusual animosity and rivalry. Both women seek control of the man who is husband to one and son to the other. The mother's need to claim paramount authority arises from the risk to her *phuc duc* posed by the daughter-in-law. The mother as principal accumulator of *phuc duc* is still responsible for the fortunes of her son and his children. Accordingly, she wants to minimize any danger to herself and her descendants which might arise from her daughter-in-law's inability to accumulate *phuc duc* in her own right. But the younger woman also wants credit and accompanying social status for all good fortune which comes her husband's way. The daughter-in-law seeks her autonomy, and is predisposed to belittle the mother's qualities. Getting less credit for *phuc duc* if the mother-in-law's excellence is emphasized will reduce the wife's claim to the benefits of gratitude which she should receive from her husband and children. In this way, gaining *phuc duc* gives the wife power that the orthodox social code does not provide.

If conflict between husband and wife is brought to public notice, orthodoxy demands that all genuflect before the norms of patriarchal superiority. Few courts will enforce a woman's power within the family. Nor will her mother-in-law in the normal case support her against her husband. Other means must be found to give a married Vietnamese woman the power she knows is her due but which is not openly and simply given to her by the orthodox code of family role responsibilities. Often a wife turns to emotional manipulation of her husband. Temper tantrums, running away to her family, going on strike, withholding sex and cooking are the principal power levers in domestic Vietnamese politics. Another strategy of the wife is to put the husband in an embarrassing position vis-à-vis his relatives or the public. To preserve face, meaning his role in public, he invariably gives his wife the covert power she seeks. A deal is struck: he has power in public; she has power in private. His power is sanctified by the orthodoxy; hers by *phuc duc*. The two powers rest in an uneasy balance.

The husband has emotional weapons of his own. He may take a mistress to show his wife that he does not need her. Many marriages break up over such philandering. The husband may threaten to gamble away the family's wealth. The woman thereby loses both the substance of control and her reputation for *phuc duc*. In facing marriage, women fear most a man who will philander or gamble—which many Vietnamese men do.

In my observation, many Vietnamese marriages are fragile vessels sailing fitfully on stormy seas. Very frequently, the husband does not believe himself capable of standing up to his wife's fierce emotions, leaving him vulnerable in the private struggle between them. He can find power and resulting reassurance in the realms of religion, politics, or social involvement, but only by acquiring followers and influence. Thus, many Vietnamese men are domineering prime ministers in waiting, reluctant to cooperate with others, ever seeking to be a leader in their own right. A wife, on the other hand, also needs the reassurance that actual power brings, so she seeks as much as practical leverage she can get. The more *phuc duc* she displays, the more power she can claim. As a result of this competition, many marriages are diplomatic alliances, in which social form is preserved. But privately, out of the public gaze, each spouse goes a separate way. The power of women in Vietnam reinforces the presence of individualism in social interactions.

Conclusion: The Cost of Orthodoxy

The presence of orthodox insistence on role conformity in the Vietnamese cultural context immediately runs into conflict with the Vietnamese preference for individualism as legitimated by destiny. The culture has no easy way to resolve the conflict; both orthodoxy and opposition to orthodoxy make their claims on individuals. Each point of view has its spokespersons within the social structure and each has its means of influence. But following one's preferences may, on occasion, be excessive and in conflict with one's duties.

This conflict over the value of one's individuality frequently begets insecurity regarding one's dignity and power. Fate may give each Vietnamese uniqueness at birth, but thereafter part of their culture is after them to fit in with the orthodoxy. The individual self is not valued unless it demonstrates powers of self-restraint, and so becomes trustworthy. But Vietnamese individualism tugs against such limits on thought and action. Maintaining strong self-esteem under such conditions is a challenge. Many find the struggle to do so fatiguing.

Insecurity of self is exacerbated by another consequence of orthodoxy as well. To the extent Vietnamese adopt the orthodox point-of-view, they should be validated by others, not for what they are as unique psychosocial expressions of will and value, laughter and tears, but for their adherence to the punctilios of role responsibility. The inner self, the self of intimate personal cognizance, is not recognized as being worthy. Far from it, the inner self, a source of individualism and ego-assertion, threatens the person's ability to conform. The self therefore contains danger and should be disparaged, belittled, placed under control, the better for the person to meet the requirements of role.

It is a matter of relevant interest that, in Vietnam, high prestige attaches to those who display selflessness. The most admired political leaders are those without wealth who sacrifice material well-being for a cause. Similarly, those who retire from positions of pomp and circumstance may increase their circle of influence by such abnegation. Celibate, abstemious monks and priests have considerable influence in Vietnamese politics. There the extinction of self becomes the highest virtue—a complete selflessness. The Buddhist monks who, in 1963, committed suicide in protest against Ngo Dinh Diem's government combined the act of ultimate ego extinction with powerful political expression.

Suicide is also a culturally accepted resolution for inner personal turmoil. The person with little faith in his or her worth commits suicide.

Self-indulgent, aggressive, swaggering military officers of the classic warlord variety are the antithesis of admirable leaders for Vietnamese. Vice Air Marshall Nguyen Cao Ky and General Nguyen van Thieu were not widely popular or respected leaders of South Vietnam. They drew their ability to govern from the formation of self-interested alliances with a multitude of parties, sects, and factions. Perhaps Ho Chi Minh's studied pose of selfless rectitude best approximated the Vietnamese ideal, generating his almost mystical appeal to many Vietnamese, even among those who despised Communist tyranny.

The tension of self-assertion grinding against role responsibility begins early for the Vietnamese. This tension gives rise to lowered self-esteem. Education into the orthodoxy starts at age two when the child first learns to say "No." Mothers who for months have indulged a child's every whim will turn with sudden anger on a toddler who shows public contrariness. The role of the child is to obey, not to question the orders of a parent or grandparent. The good child, the valued child, is the child which is *hoan,* "compliant," or who is *le phep,* "decorously behaved." Out of the family's hearing or sight a child may continue to enjoy freedom and assertiveness among peers in the yard or around the compound. When guests arrive, the child is called in to bow and demonstrate quiet politeness for a short while. Then the child, having performed as expected, is dismissed to return to play freely. The space beyond parental sight and hearing is a free space, beyond the demands or propriety.

Mothers in particular have little patience with children who assert themselves. The reasons for discipline are frequently not explained to the child; no compromise is tolerated by the mother as the interaction rapidly becomes a zero-sum confrontation between rival authority figures—child and mother. By framing the situation in those terms, mothers escalate conflict to the point where they must prevail at all costs over the wishes of their children. With the stakes raised so high, the mother must exercise powerful means to ensure her victory. She withdraws her love and support—refusing, for example, to feed an angry child. Or saying before the family "Do this and Mommy will love you," an affirmation of conditional rather than unconditional love. Convincingly, the point is communicated that the mother's affection and approval rest exclusively on the child's conformity, not on the child's integrity as a person. Role responsibility is rewarded while inner drives are ignored.

Such behavior in mothers is most understandable. They rely for their status and authority not on their role in the orthodox family but on family members' individually acknowledging the mother's power. When young children say "No," they cut to the center of their mothers' vulnerability and provoke fear in her. The mother cannot trust the young child to exercise sensitive self-control and thereby confirm her status. Instead, with cunning and keen instinct, she pushes the child into conformity.

Not being trusted by the mother, the young child learns that he or she is not trustworthy and may lack self-control. The value of the child's self comes into doubt and lowered self-esteem undergirds the child's personality from then on. Such children mature to seek their self-esteem not in themselves, but in external roles and positions.

The orthodoxy endlessly regenerates itself through this mechanism. Producing low self-esteem in children, it generates a need for external, formal social roles to provide a substitute for inner self-worth. Even while conforming, Vietnamese desperately seek something more satisfying than fulfillment of duties. This drive for acceptance, for recognition, makes them uniformly very hardworking and extremely charming as they probe others, seeking attention and centrality in any relationship.

Such isolated, autonomous success seems incongruous as the result of an orthodoxy which seeks to coordinate different actors in a larger, cohesive drama—each person playing a separate role designed both to rely upon and to support others. But the unexpected result in Vietnam, where orthodoxy not only clones itself anew with each generation but also breeds a profound sense of individual alienation and disaffection, shows how loosely the orthodoxy fits in the Vietnamese context.

References

Ch'u, T.-T. (1965). *Law and Society in Traditional China*. Taiwan: Rainbow Bridge.

Confucius. (1960a). *Analects*. In *The Confucian Classics*. Hong Kong: Hong Kong University Press.

Confucius. (1960b). *Doctrine of the Mean*. In *The Confucian Classics*. Hong Kong: Hong Kong University Press.

Confucius. (1960c). *Great Learning*. In *The Confucian Classics*. Hong Kong: Hong Kong University Press.

Gia huan ca. Saigon: Translated by Stephen B. Young.

Johnson, W. (1979). *The T'ang Code*. Princeton, NJ: Princeton University Press.

Khau, T. and D. Thue. (1967). *Tuong phap tinh hoa*. Saigon: Mac Lam.

Lam, T. B. (1967). *Patterns of Vietnamese Response to Foreign Interventions, 1858–1900*. New Haven, CT: Yale University Press.

Lau, T. (1979). *The Handbook of Chinese Horoscopes*. New York: Harper & Row.

Li chi. (1885). *The Sacred Books of the East,* ed. M. Müller. Oxford: Clarendon Press.

Makra, M. L. (1961). *The Hsiao Chin*. New York: St. John's University Press.

Mau, D. (1986). *Vietnam: Mau lua que Huoung toi*. Fresno, CA: Author.

Skinner, S. (1982). *The Living Earth Manual of Feng Shui*. London: Routledge and Kegan Paul.

Thong, H. S. (1979). *The Heritage of Vietnamese Poetry*. New Haven, CT: Yale University Press.

Trung, C. (1971). *Dia Ly Ta Ao*. Houston: Xuan Thu.

9

Psychocultural Features of Ancestor Worship in Modern Korean Society

Dawnhee Yim

Introduction: The Functional Utility of Ritual

Filial piety and rituals for ancestors has continued to draw a great deal of attention from modern Korean intellectuals. There seems to be a general consensus that filial piety, at least in the form of respect for parents' wishes and care of elderly parents, is certainly beneficial for Korean society. On the negative side, the large expenditures of money and human effort which ancestral rituals entail are commonly regarded as their major faults. Shamanistic beliefs about ancestral hostility and shamanistic rituals for the dead are especially regarded with opprobrium, not only because of their expense but also because they are regarded as useless "superstitions." Even among those intellectuals who treasure Korean traditions, shamanism is more often defended for its artistic merits rather than for its practical consequences.

There are two purposes to this chapter. The first is to question the adequacy of these usual evaluations of filial piety and traditional Korean beliefs and practices involving ancestral spirits, particularly in light of contemporary changes. I shall not argue that filial piety is essentially harmful. Nor will I assert that traditional beliefs and ritual practices are primarily beneficial. These are value judgments and are best made after one has attained a fuller understanding of the consequences of ancestor-rites. My goal is to contribute to that understanding. I shall try to show how Korean child-rearing practices, mutual dependency between successive generations, acceptance of filial piety as a moral axiom, and performance of ancestral rituals are psychologically related. More specifically, I shall try to show how the sacrifices demanded by formal ancestral rituals and shamanistic rites for the dead help to alleviate psychological difficulties engendered by filial piety, even in modern Korean society. In

formulating my analysis, I have drawn heavily from the anthropological litera-
ture on ancestor worship in China and sub-Saharan Africa (Fortes 1959, 1961;
Goody 1962; Freedman 1966, 147–53; 1967, 95; Ahern 1973, 191–219), but
I have adapted the theoretical insights gained from these writings to our
Korean data.[1]

Much else could be said about the functional consequences of filial piety
and ancestor worship in Korea: the promotion of extended kin group *(tangnae,*
munjung, sijok)[2] solidarity, the advancement of claims to high social status, the
extension of deferences to persons outside the immediate family *(kajok),* and
so on. In the present chapter, however, I shall limit my analysis to parent-child
relationships. A full discussion of the social and psychological functions of
ancestor-worship traditions and their consequences would require at least an
entire monograph.

Ancestors, Women, and the Korean Family

A second related contention of this chapter is the psychological inter-
relatedness of formal Confucian ancestor worship carried out by males on the
one hand, and shamanic practices that are principally initiated by women, on
the other. Students of Korean society have long recognized its sexual division
of religious life. One of the first to point this out was the Japanese scholar
Akiba Takashi (1933, 1957). He used the term "dual social organization" to
designate a fundamental bifurcation of Korean society into two contrasting
arenas: Confucianism, observed by males and comprising its elite culture, and
shamanism, followed by females and constituting its vernacular culture. Akiba
regarded shamanism as the older of the two, but he also recognized that both
these traditions continue to influence Korean life. Many Korean folklorists
(e.g., Chang Chugün 1973, 238; Lee Du-Hyun 1984, 146–47; and Yu Tongsik
1975, 254–55) subsequently adopted similar views of Korean society.

Recently, scholars with more of a social-anthropological orientation have
further explored this male-Confucianism/female-shamanism dichotomy in Korea.
Ch'oe Kilsöng (1982, 91–125), for example, contrasts Confucian rituals based
on "blood" (agnatic) ties with shamanistic rituals based on territorial affiliation.
Laurel Kendall, in her work on Korean shamanism (1985), while arguing that
neither women nor shamanism are peripheral to Korean society, nevertheless
accepts the fundamental sexual division of ritual labor observed by others. The
Janellis (1982, 148–76) also compare and contrast Confucian-style ancestor
rites with shamanistic rites for ancestors.

The second purpose of this chapter is to demonstrate how the Confucian and shamanistic styles of ritual activity performed by men and women in
Korean households originated in their respective family experiences.

Some Psychological Consequences of Filial Piety

Throughout the known history of Korean society, no other moral axiom seems to have been as important as filial piety (cf. Yi Hui-dok 1973). Although evidence indicates that its significance declines with increasing urbanization, the same evidence (Chung Bom Mo et al. 1972, 474–75; Moon Hyun-Sang et al. 1973, 47–48) provides some useful statistics. The 986 married women of Seoul who were sampled gave strong support for the traditions of filial piety. Although well over half these women were under thirty-five years of age, two-thirds of the Seoul sample felt that children's support of aged parents was always necessary. Another 28 percent thought that the necessity of such support depended on the circumstances of the situation. Only 6 percent voiced the opinion that children's support of aged parents was unnecessary.

The social benefits of filial piety cannot be gainsaid. Most prominent among these are the *enhancement of the care of elderly parents and the promotion of mutual help and cooperation* between generations. But the social benefits of filial piety are not free; they are paid for with psychological anxieties.

First of all, the ideal of filial piety demands a great deal of the offspring, especially eldest sons. Care of the elderly is a difficult and onerous burden. And because adult offspring genuinely accept the demands of filial piety as a moral obligation, they feel responsible for living up to its very high expectations. In other words, the responsibilities of filial piety are not merely external, imposed only by parents and other members of society. More importantly, these obligations are internalized, become part of the superego, and are accepted as right and proper. As a result of this internalization, adult offspring feel *a sense of guilt* whenever they cannot fulfill their moral responsibilities. Educational psychologist Kim Chae-ün[3] has made a similar observation about the consequences of children internalizing the high expectations:

> However, a problem arises because parents expect an excessively high degree of filial piety: offspring have feelings of guilt whenever they cannot live up to their parents expectations in actuality. These feelings of guilt apparently originate in the superego formed by authority figures (i.e. the father, and also the mother). (1974, 58)

A second psychological difficulty engendered by the morality of filial piety is *the suppression of hostile feelings* toward parents. Eldest sons in particular inevitably chafe under the authority of elderly parents, especially as the latter approach senility. The transmission of effective household headship from fathers to sons is a major point of conflict, for fathers are often as reluctant to surrender their control as their sons are eager to obtain it. One of my rural

Korean acquaintances confided to me that other people actually envied him because his three sons had been born relatively late in his life. This was a fortunate circumstance, he explained, because he would not have to surrender control of his household until he was really old and genuinely needed someone to care for him. Although a father formally retains the title of "household head" *(hoju)* until his death, and although the current Korean civil code upholds his authority over household affairs until his death (Bae Kyung Sook 1973, 64–67, 69, 137), fathers can rarely maintain actual control of their households in advanced old age.[4] This seems to have been true before Korea's recent industrialization as well as today. As Lee Kwang Kyu (1975, 81) observed, transfer of authority within a Korean household was traditionally marked by a shift in living arrangements; the retiring couple or surviving spouse would move into poorer or less spacious rooms when they surrendered control of their household to the succeeding generation.

A certain amount of conflict between elderly parents and their adult offspring is probably characteristic of all human societies. Such conflict is intensified, however, by the co-residence of successive generations of married couples who share a common budget. Psychological difficulties arise in Korea not so much because of the conflict itself but rather because the morality of filial piety demands its suppression. Not only must sons refrain from any overt act of hostility toward parents, but even thoughts of such hostility are morally condemnable and therefore suppressed (Slote, chapter 2). Psychiatrist Hahn Dongse (1972) cites suppressed hostility toward superiors, especially parents, as a major cause of emotional disturbances among Korean men.

Korean children, especially eldest sons, are thus confronted by conflicting feelings. Although they find the task of caring for elderly parents an onerous burden, they accept this responsibility as a moral obligation. They cannot admit openly, perhaps not even to themselves, that they would like to be rid of their parents; but the desire must inevitably arise. It may well account for the popularity of the Koryŏjang story, a narrative which centers on an allegedly old custom of carting off and burying parents when they became elderly.[5]

The morality of filial piety exacerbates normal guilt toward parents and tensions between successive generations, but it does not affect men and women equally. Primary responsibility for the care and support of elderly parents falls on sons, especially eldest sons, and it is they who are continually subject to the moral demands of elderly parents. Daughters may be praised for acts of filial piety, but they do not bear the same responsibilities as their brothers, especially after marriage. Daughters-in-law are ideally responsible for the care and welfare of their husband's parents, but in reality they too are not subject to the same moral obligations as their husbands. Conflict between parents-in-law and daughters-in-law is more openly tolerated. It is often the subject of humorous treatment in Koreans oral literature. Because overt conflict between a woman and her husband's parents does not evoke the same moral condemnation and social disapproval as conflict between a son and his parents, the former can be dealt with more freely. There are no funny stories or proverbs about a son's hostility toward his parents, for such a conflict is viewed as far more serious and reprehensible. Thus, filial piety does not provoke the same intense guilt feelings in women as it does in men, and women need not repress as strongly as their husbands feelings of hostility toward the senior generation of their household.

Psychological Difficulties Evident in Ancestor Worship

Thus far I have argued primarily on theoretical grounds that filial piety engenders emotional difficulties. I have suggested that offspring internalize the morality of filial piety and then feel guilty whenever they cannot live up to its demands. Very likely, feelings of guilt toward deceased parents result not only from such failures, but also from feelings of hostility toward parents during their lifetimes. Even if offspring do not commit overt acts of hostility, they still may be culpable for mere thoughts of hostility toward deceased parents. I shall now examine some of the beliefs and practices surrounding ancestors for evidence of such guilt feelings and other emotional problems engendered by filial piety.

The Korean mourning costume, worn openly until outlawed by the Ritual Simplification Law of the mid-1970s, is particularly instructive. The costume of a chief mourner is said to resemble the clothing of a criminal, for he is thought to be guilty for the death of a parent. Had he provided his parents with better care, they might well have lived longer. Of course, not everyone who wears this costume may personally feel guilt, but the costume itself and its traditional explanation do express the generally accepted idea that sons do not adequately carry out their obligations of filial piety and that they are partly responsible for their parents' death. No matter how hard a son tries, he inevitably falls short of the impossible ideals of filial piety.

The image of ancestral spirits as elderly and weak parents suggests that the most difficult period of the parent–child relationship occurs during its final years. Apparently this period generates the greatest emotional anxieties among the junior generation and they project these anxieties into their beliefs about the afterlife. From a Korean perspective, it may seem only natural that dead parents would be imagined to retain the same physiological features which they had at death. But a study of ancestor worship in a Taiwanese community (Ahern 1973) affords a striking contrast. There, dead parents were thought of as active and middle-aged, even if they had died in advanced old age. In that Taiwanese community, maintains the anthropologist who studied it (Ahern

1973, 213–19), the early years of the parent-child relationship are made especially difficult by harsh child-training practices. She concludes that children's
anxieties engendered during this period are later projected into their images
of ancestral spirits. Hence, they visualized ancestors in much the same way as
a young child sees his parents.

Other evidence of emotional difficulties in the parent-child relationship
can be found in beliefs about ancestral affliction. Ancestors are sometimes thought
to inflict sickness or other misfortune on descendants (1) when formal ancestral
rituals *chesa* are omitted, (2) when these rites are performed with some slight
imperfection, such as letting a hair fall into the food offering, (3) when graves
are uncomfortable, or (4) when ancestors simply want a shamanistic ritual *kut*.
The latter three motivations for affliction are particularly revealing, for they show
how easily and inadvertently ancestors may be provoked to afflict their descendants. Such folk beliefs suggest that offspring are apprehensive about the dead,
for they often have no way of knowing in advance that a particular act will anger
an ancestor. In other words, dead parents seem as cantankerous as living elders,
and their demands are often just as arbitrary. These beliefs show that the living
are apprehensive about satisfying the expectations of deceased parents, just as
they are apprehensive about fulfilling the expectations of living parents. Because
the junior generations have feelings of guilt for deficiencies in their treatment
of parents and for the feelings of hostility engendered in them when the latter
were alive, offspring suspect that their dead parents are resentful and easily
provoked to punish them. When minor misfortune occurs, therefore, offspring
may surmise that it was caused by ancestral intervention.

Filial Piety and Child Rearing

If filial piety exacerbates emotional difficulties in the relationship between
parents and children, one may wonder why it has remained such a basic value
until modern times. Perhaps the prestige and influence of formally sanctioned
Confucianism is partly responsible. But filial piety is too fundamental and too
thoroughly internalized to have been the product of mere encouragement by
political leaders or intellectual persuasion. The widespread appeal of filial piety
as a moral axiom must also result from deeper and more personal motivation.

I suggest that a major cause for the popularity of filial piety in Korea
is to be found in child-rearing practices. The warm and indulgent treatment
of infants in Korean society is readily apparent and openly recognized by all.
The following lines of a Korean funeral chant, which I obtained from
Twisöngdwi, a village in Kyonggi-do, provide articulate expression of how
parents are thought to treat infants:[6]

When my parents raised me
What efforts they made.
Parents live in a wet place
To lay their baby in a dry place.
With food as well, they first test it
Eating the bitter themselves
And feeding the sweet to their baby.
On the hot days of May and June
They worry of mosquitoes and bedbugs [biting their babies];
Though tired they cannot sleep
With both hands they hold a fan
And chase away all kinds of worries
They carry me on their back
And spare no effort.
Silver baby, golden baby [think the parents]
Treasure baby from the deepest mountains.
On the water, sun and moon baby [?]
Patriotic baby for the nation
A baby with filial piety for his parents
A baby affectionate toward his family and kin
Could we buy you even with gold?
Could we buy you even with silver?
The extreme love which we feel for you
How can we express?
When one thinks of his indebtedness to his parents
Isn't it bigger than the greatest mountain?
Who would deny this?

As the Korean funeral chant shows, offspring are indebted to parents for the love and sacrifices of the latter during their earliest years. The care and support of elderly parents is a repayment, though inevitably inadequate, of this indebtedness. Reciprocity between parents and children is further fostered by childhood training after infancy. As Kim Chae-ün (1974, 54–58) observes, Korean children are not encouraged to be independent of their parents. Instead, parents view children as extensions of themselves and inculcate children with a spirit of mutual dependency between successive generations. Just as young children are dependent on their middle-aged parents, so parents, later in life, dependent on their middle-aged children. The contrast with American society is particularly striking. Not only do American parents encourage their children to be independent and self-reliant in their earliest years, but parents are also extremely loathe to become dependent on their adult offspring in old age. It seems evident that Korean child-rearing practices produce children to whom the idea of filial piety is far more appealing.

Psychological Functions of Ancestor Worship

A major psychological benefit of rituals for deceased parents is the alleviation of guilt. As chapter 10 of the *Hyo Kyŏng* states, sacrifices to deceased parents are another form of filial piety. Thus, rituals for ancestors prolong beyond death the parent-child relationship and obligations toward elderly parents. Through these rituals, it is possible to do what one should have done, or more than he could have done, for parents during their lifetimes. From this viewpoint, the more extravagant the ritual and the more lavish the offerings, the greater the psychological benefit.

Many of the Korean ancestor-worship traditions evince an attempt to keep parents alive, so to speak, even after they have died. In other words, the living deliberately attempt to prolong their relationship with parents even after death occurs. In Kyŏnggi Province, and elsewhere in Korea, descendants construct a spirit throne *sangch'ŏng* where the spirit of the deceased is said to "reside" *kyesinda* for the duration of the mourning period. Villagers in Twisŏngdwi, where I collected the funeral song quoted above, explained to me that an ancestor is treated just like a living person as long as he or she is enshrined in this spirit throne. For example, portions of the family's daily meals are presented before the ancestor's tablet and/or photograph. Guests who visit the house may be brought to bow before the spirit throne, just as they would be led to greet a living elder. A small package of food is often prepared to be placed on a spirit throne after a major social celebration in the village, just as such packages are sometimes prepared for living elders who could not attend the event themselves.

The attempt to recreate the living presence of a parent can also be seen in the timing of death-anniversary rituals *(kijesa)*. Many households in Twisŏngdwi perform these rites just before midnight, on the day preceding the actual death anniversary. Informants justified this practice by explaining that the rituals should be offered on the anniversary of a day on which the ancestor had been alive *(san nal)* rather than exactly on the day of death. After all, argued one informant, dead people do not eat.

By prolonging the parent-child relationship beyond death, ancestor-worship traditions help to alleviate guilt in two ways. Not only do they make it possible for children to compensate parents for inadequacies (real or imagined) in the care and treatment which they received in their final years; but they also help alleviate guilt in a more subtle manner. If, as the Koryŏjang legend suggests, children have a suppressed desire to be rid of elderly parents in order to be relieved of the onerous burden of feeding and caring for them, children may well feel guilty for such thoughts after the death of their parents. Because ancestor worship is an obligatory part of filial piety, however, adult offspring can feel their parents' death did not really relieve them of their responsibilities, and thus that they had no reason to wish for their parents' demise.

In addition to formal rituals of ancestor worship *chesa,* shamanistic rituals for the dead provide another means of alleviating guilt for inadequacies in the care of elderly patients. Such rituals also entail large sacrifices, supposedly for the benefit of ancestors in the otherworld *(chosung).* And the needs of ancestors are very much the same as the needs of living parents: food, clothing, money, and so on. Here again, the living appear to deal with their anxieties about the care of elderly parents through supernatural beliefs about the welfare of ancestral spirits.

Ancestral Malevolence and the Protection of the Family

The following discussion contrasts two types of rituals offered in Korean households on behalf of ancestors. These differences can be explained by showing how these dissimilarities reflect the contrasting experiences, perspectives, sources of power, benefits, and interests that arise from men's and women's respective social positions within the family.

Confucian Ancestor Rites and Shamanistic Seances

Although several types of Confucian ancestor rites are found in Korea, the most frequently offered rites can be divided into two broad categories: domestic and lineage. At the former, individual ancestors within four generations are commemorated on their death anniversaries[7] and on major holidays at the households of their respective primogeniture descendants (eldest son's eldest son's eldest son, etc.). At the latter, ancestors who are beyond four generations are commemorated at their gravesites, usually in the fall of the year.

Shamanism too includes several different types of rites for a whole pantheon of supernatural beings, including gods, ghosts, and ancestors.[8] Designed to feed, entertain, and otherwise please these supernaturals, the shamanistic rites *(kut)* usually take several hours to perform and entail large food offerings, singing, and dancing. A typical shamanistic rite consists of twelve segments, each of which is directed toward a different deity or category of supernatural beings. The segment which is aimed at the ancestors consists of a seance in addition to the other usual activities.

Previous comparisons of Confucianism and shamanism have attempted to develop generalizations from the entire assortment of rites found in both these ritual systems. Such comparisons offered a useful first step for understanding the differences between the two systems, but they do not permit a particularly fine-grained analysis. It is a controlled or more narrowly focused comparison that I will attempt here. Specifically, I will contrast domestic Confucian ancestor rites with shamanistic seances because both deal with ancestors of the household and are thereby more directly comparable. I will discuss in turn the following characteristics of these two rites: images and personalities of ancestors, identities of ancestors, identities and roles of ritual participants, and ritual styles.

The scope of my analysis is also limited geographically, not so much by choice as by necessity. Its data are taken primarily from Kyönggi Province, located in the central-eastern part of the Korean peninsula. Although an abundant literature on Korean shamanism amply covers most of the Korean peninsula, field investigations by social anthropologists focusing on rites for ancestors are sparse, the two major studies (Kendall 1985; Janelli and Janelli 1982) both having been conducted in Kyönggi Province.[9]

Images and Personalities of Ancestors

Ancestors at Confucian rites are benevolent. These rites are performed in order to repay the debt that descendants incurred from parents and other forebears: ancestors raised these descendants in addition to giving them life, property, and social status.[10] Ancestor's have every reason to wish for and promote their descendants' well-being, just as parents do everything they can for their children's welfare. The formal ritual prayer *ch'uk* which is usually addressed to parents on their deathday rites reminds offspring of this obligation (Janelli and Janelli 1982, 96).

Ancestors at shamanistic seances, on the other hand, are regarded as selfish or malevolent. The reason for performing shamanistic rituals is to placate disgruntled supernaturals who have sent misfortune to the household. When a family faces a serious misfortune, the senior woman of the house may visit a shaman to find out its cause and be told that one or more ancestors are responsible. Ancestors who suffer discomfort or who are dissatisfied with their care and treatment may send misfortune to their family in order to get attention or relief. The Janellis list fourteen different cases of such misfortune caused by ancestors (Janelli and Janelli 1982, 156–60). Kendall (e.g., 1985, 149, 151, 156) also illustrates several cases:

> A woman's inflamed leg was caused by her father-in-law's first wife because the dead woman's ancestor rites were denied by the father-in-law's second spouse.

> Mrs. Im's son's taxi accident was attributed to an ancestor who was unhappy about his grave.

A young man's constant headaches were caused by his cousin who had drowned while unmarried.

In view of the characteristics attributed to ancestors by Confucianism and shamanism respectively, it is hardly surprising to learn that ancestors at Confucian rites are welcomed figures while ancestors at shamanistic seances are not. Whereas ancestors at the former rites are involved through prayer and other ritual procedures, at ancestor seances they come on their own initiative and may be urged away with "Take your travel money and go" (Kendall 1985, 144). Moreover, a fixed schedule prescribes the dates for formal rites, but shamanistic seances follow no calendar.[11] Instead, seances are held when ancestors have sent misfortune: people offer shamanistic seances to mollify these ancestors, relieve their anger, ease their discomforts, and urge them to stop visiting their kin. Unlike the Confucian ancestor rites, therefore, shamanistic rites are compelled by actions of the ancestors.

Another important difference between ancestors in these ritual domains involves their degree of activity. Ancestors at Confucian rites are depicted as quiet and passive: they eat, are bowed to by descendants, and leave. In general, they are depicted as old parents who are feeble and in need of support. Ancestors at shamanistic seances, by contrast, are neither feeble nor weak. Instead, they are depicted as active, strong, and talkative. They come voluntarily, speak loudly, complain of their discomfort, weep, scold their descendants, and make demands. This salient divergence between the Confucian and shamanistic personalities of ancestors has already been observed:

> Ancestor worship idealizes ancestors. At ancestor rites, the dead conform to the perfect image of retired elders: although benevolently inclined, they have neither strong personalities nor great power. They passively await the offerings on which their welfare depends and accept them as expressions of indebtedness proffered at the initiative of their offspring. According to a metaphor common in literary sources, forebears are the roots of a tree and descendants are its leaves and branches. Each automatically nourishes the other. Even the food offered at ancestor rites is later eaten by participants. Shamanism, by contrast, portrays ancestors as self-interested, afflicting their kin to enhance their own comfort or satisfy their desires. Ancestors demand costly sacrifices purely for their own welfare. A family that sponsors a kut [shamanistic rite] does not even consume its food offerings after the rite. In sum, ancestor worship idealizes ancestors and their mutual dependency on their closest living kin. In shamanism, ancestors are threatening, and their dependency on their closest relatives channels their acts of affliction toward them. This dual personality of ancestors has been noted in other Korean villages as well. (Dix 1979, 69–71; see also Janelli and Janelli 1982, 166)

Identities of Ancestors

Whereas the ancestors commemorated at Confucian rites are limited to the household head's agnatic forebears within four generations[12] and their legitimate spouses, ancestors at shamanistic seances are drawn from a much wider range of relatives. These "ancestors" include the household head's collateral agnatic kin, cognatic kin, in-laws, and kin who belong to the same or a junior generation.

Ancestors who receive formal rites may be limited to a narrower genealogical scope but they are drawn from a deeper generational range. The four generations of ancestors commemorated at the former may or may not be personally remembered by those who offer their rites: parents and paternal grandparents are usually known to descendants, but less often are great-grandparents, much less great-great-grandparents. At shamanistic seances, by contrast, the ancestors who are more than a few generations removed from their present descendants do not appear. It is understandable that only ancestors who are personally remembered speak to the living at shamanistic seances. Descendants need some knowledge about an ancestor's life history in order to interact with him or her.

Another difference between the identities of ancestors at shamanistic and Confucian rites is that those who participate at the former are not limited to any prescribed number. Whereas each Confucian rite is offered for a specific ancestor or pair of ancestors,[13] informants say all the ancestors come when a shamanistic rite is offered. Moreover, informants do not agree as to how many ancestors or which ancestors may speak at any given seance. In Twisŏngdwi, the village where we did research, participants at one shamanistic seance could not agree on how many place settings (i.e., pairs of chopsticks and wine cups) to set out on the food offering table (Janelli and Janelli 1979, 86–87). At formal ancestor rites, there is never such confusion about the number of ancestors being commemorated.

Ancestors at formal Confucian rites and those at seances typically had different life histories and now exist in different states. Ancestors at the former rites are generally those who enjoyed a good life: they married, produced sons, and died of old age in the bosom of their families. They now receive offerings regularly and have no particular discomforts. More prominent at seances are ancestors who do not attain an ideal life or who are now unhappy or uncomfortable. They may have died unmarried and without descendants and are thereby denied regular food offerings. They may have died unexpectedly through such accidents as drowning, shooting, or suicide, and thereby cannot enter the other world. Or they may have enjoyed a good life but are now uncomfortable due to a poor grave site, hungry because of the omission of an ancestor rite, or simply eager for the attention, entertainment, and treats which will be offered them at a shamanistic rite.

Ancestors who are thought to have sent the misfortune which promoted the shamanistic rite usually make a dramatic appearance at the seance, and they too are typically the ancestors who suffered ill fate during their lives. In the village of Twisöngdwi, two cases of misfortune were caused by an ancestor who had been shot. An additional case of misfortune was caused by an unmarried bachelor. Kendall (1985, 156) also illustrated a misfortune caused by a drowned bachelor and another caused by a woman who died in childbirth.

The ancestors who appear at shamanistic seances have various degrees of activity. The most active ancestors are those who died in tragic circumstances, for these unfortunates carry their grudges into the afterlife and are a constant source of misfortune to related households. Ancestors who have specific grievances, by contrast, are not, although they may send misfortune because of an act of neglect or other offense committed by their descendants. Uncomfortable gravesites are a popular cause of such action, for a grave is considered to be an ancestor's shelter and therefore requires proper care to ensure the ancestor's comfort. Among fourteen cases of misfortune in Twisöngdwi, four were caused by gravesites; and Kendall (1985, 149) also cites two such cases. In addition to graves, omission or careless performance of ancestor rites are often causes of misfortune. There was one such case in Twisöngdwi, and two more instances occurred in Laurel Kendall's village (1985: 149). Finally, the ancestors' selfishness is yet another cause of misfortune. Without any fault on the part of descendants, ancestors sometimes send misfortune just because they want to be treated to a shamanistic rite. Four cases of misfortune in Twisöngdwi were attributed to such selfishness on the part of ancestors.

The real-world experiences which form the basis of beliefs about ancestral affliction are not hard to identify. As we have seen, there are three reasons why ancestors send misfortune: *an ancestor's unfortunate state, a descendant's fault,* or *an ancestor's selfishness.* In each case, an analogous phenomenon can be found in the world of the living. First, the unfortunate status of an ancestor may bring misfortunes to their family just as a miserable person in the world of the living becomes a burden to their living kin. Second, ancestors are like living parents. They punish children whenever children do not behave as they are supposed to. Third, living parents too are sometimes selfish. No matter how hard descendants try to please them, parents may demand more. Likewise, ancestors too may cause discomfort even without any fault on the part of descendants.

Identities and Roles of Ritual Participants

The participants at formal ancestors rites differ from those at seances in three ways. Whereas men perform the formal rites, women perform the shamanic rituals. Whereas the participants at the former are agnates of the ancestors they commemorate, participants at shamanic rites are non-agnates (i.e., daughters-in-law, other in-laws, neighbors, and shamans). And whereas junior brothers are dependent on their elder brothers for formal ancestor rites, the households of junior sons independently sponsor shamanistic rites. At formal ancestor rites, the eldest brother almost always occupies the role of *cheju* (the sponsor and chief ritual officiate at a Confucian ancestor rite), but at a shamanistic rite the wife of a younger brother occupies the comparable role of *kyeju* (the house-wife of the household which employs the shaman's services; Yi Huisung 1982, 220)[14] when her household sponsors a shamanistic rite.

Ritual Styles

Ritual styles at the two types of rites for ancestors differ in at least three ways. The first entails their respective degrees of flexibility. Formal ancestor rites are carried out according to a set of explicit rules but ancestor seances are not. The rules for the former—which entail preparing and presenting food, bowing, and offering wine—are widely available in printed manuals, known beforehand, and carefully followed. Therefore, there is little flexibility or variation in ritual procedures from one ancestor rite to the next. The procedures at seances, on the other hand, exhibit greater diversity. At shamanistic seances the ritual procedures are less planned and more ad-hoc. No two seances are identical because the number of ancestors who speak, the nature of their communications, and the responses of the living participants vary, for example, as noted above, the disagreement at one seance about the number and identities of ancestors for whom place settings should be set. Participants may also disagree about other ritual procedures or about which ancestor is speaking at any given moment (Janelli and Janelli 1979, 88).

The quantity of communication between the living and the dead also differs at these two rituals. Formal ancestor rites involve no verbal interaction between descendants and ancestors, except for the formal address *ch'uk* presented to the commemorated forebears. Seances, however, include diverse and lively forms of verbal exchange. Ancestors alternately cry, complain, scold, and console descendants; the living apologize, ask forgiveness, and plead for good fortune. They may also bicker with the dead (Kendall 1985, 144). Women of neighboring households also join in, siding with descendants and complaining to the ancestors. When a sick man's dead parents spoke at a seance, these women of neighboring households demanded of the ancestors, "Why have you made your own son sick? Please, make him well" (Kendall 1985, 7).

A third difference between the two rituals can be seen in the noise level of each. Formal ancestor rites are performed in a quiet and subdued manner. There is not a sound from the ancestors and very little from their descendants, except for the recitation of the formal address. Seances are much noisier. They include singing, dancing, talking, crying, shouting, and even quarreling.

Sources of Ritual Diversity

The dissimilarities between Confucian rites and ancestor seances can be largely explained by the differences between the social experiences of men and women in Korean society. As we noted above, the formal rites are performed by men for their agnatic forebears whereas shamanistic ancestor seances are performed by women primarily for their in-laws. The duality of ritual forms allows each gender to express its own relationships with the family members who later become the objects of the two rites.

Images and Personalities of Ancestors

The images and personalities of ancestors at the two rites appear to be determined by benefits received from, or burdens inflicted by, the dead who receive these rituals. Men received the gift of life from, were raised by, and inherited the property of their agnatic forebears. Women, on the other hand, occupy a very different position vis-à-vis the ancestors with whom they communicate at seances. A woman is born and raised in one family, but upon marriage she moves into that of her husband. She then has to deal with his relatives for the rest of her life; and her position in her husband's family is at the bottom of the family hierarchy. As one Seoul woman—herself a young daughter-in-law, humorously told me, "the position of a daughter-in-law is the lowest. Only the family dog is lower than she is." Although that statement may be somewhat of an exaggeration, it coincides with the fact that a daughter-in-law has to call her husband's young siblings *Tŏryonnim* ("Mister") and *Agassi* ("Miss"), the same terms used by servants toward their master's children. And not only is the daughter-in-law's position low; her life is also very difficult. "The life of a daughter-in-law *sijip sari* is an often used metaphor for describing hardships experienced while under someone else's authority and subject to their direction and interference" (Yi Hüisŭng 1982, 2181). Moreover, her in-laws, both younger and older than herself, place many demands on her labor but give few benefits in return. Given the nature of her relationship with these in-laws, it is hardly surprising that she forms an image of her husband's ancestors as selfish and malevolent. Although men welcome their ancestors at the Confucian rites, therefore, women have little reason to welcome them at seances.

The different degrees of dynamism attributed to ancestors by men and women, on the one hand, are derived not from the benefits or burdens they receive but from the manner of their transmission. A man's inheritance from his parents is nearly automatic in the sense that the senior generation exhibits little discretion in the transmission of its property. Although the precise proportion of shares allocated to each son may vary according to a particular family's economic circumstances, cases of parents who do not transmit their farmland to their sons are unknown. Similarly, the bestowal of social status in a society where such status is ascribed by heredity does not entail a conscious, deliberate decision. For women, by contrast, the amount of hardship inflicted by their in-laws displays a much wider range of variation and greater scope for willful choice. Thus women view ancestors as more active than do their husbands.

Identities of the Ancestors and Ritual Participants

Men and women possess different goals, concepts of the family, and sources of power. Men emphasize the mutual dependency of successive generations and cooperation between brothers. For them, parents and siblings as well as wives and children are important family members. Moreover, a man's power and influence over family affairs largely derive from his parents, who gave him property and were more likely to have sided with him rather than his wife in the event of a dispute. From such facts of family life derive the mutual dependency and cooperation of the Korean family acknowledged by many ethnographers and psychologists (e.g., Brandt 1971, 138, 172–76; Dix 1977, 195–201; Hahn Dongse 1972; Harvey and Chung 1980, 148; Kim Chaeün 1974, 54–60). Indeed, the following perception of the Chinese family offers a good description of Korean men's perceptions of their own families:

> A major Chinese cultural postulate is father-son identification and continuity of generations. The father automatically bequeathed his wealth to his sons and was duty bound to see all his children married and well placed. In turn, sons were responsible for the pleasure and welfare of parents in life and after death. Socially, the mutual sharing of their statuses was even more automatic. . . . The father's prestige determine[d] the son's social position when the son [was] young; the order [was] reversed when the son [came] of age. . . . Because of such manifestations of the Chinese premise of father-son identification, I concluded that Chinese did not have to fear harm by the spirits of their ancestors. The mutual bond between them was culturally defined as too automatic to leave room for such harm. (Hsu 1979, 527)

Women, on the other hand, view the family in a more independent and competitive light. To a woman, a husband and children are the most important family members. They comprise what could be termed the "Korean uterine family."[15] Parents-in-law, husband's siblings, and other in-laws are of far less concern to her. Moreover, the source of her power and influence over family matters, which increase with time, owes its existence primarily to her children, especially her sons, rather than her parents-in-law. The husband's power may be initially high, thanks to his parents, but it gradually declines; a woman's power increases over the years thanks to the support she receives from her adult sons, with whom she has established a strong and affectionate bond. Whenever her in-laws request her help, therefore, she is more likely than her husband to view their solicitations as a competing demand on the wealth, labor, or other limited resources which she would rather use to satisfy the needs of her uterine family.[16] If her husband's parent or brother is ill and requires funds for medical treatment, for example, the housewife is likely to be less willing than her husband to make that expenditure.

Mutual dependency and cooperation are clearly evident in Confucian ancestor rites. Ancestors are dependent on their descendants for the food offerings provided on these occasions; and these offerings are explicitly viewed as repayments for the care and nurturance received from parents when the offspring were dependent on them. We also noted that a younger son cannot offer their own ancestor rites but is ritually dependent on their eldest brother instead. Cooperation between brothers and more distant agnates, moreover, is manifested in the composition of the group which offers Confucian rites. Agnatic first cousins, for example, often reciprocate by participating in rites for each other's fathers.

Ancestor seances, on the other hand, reflect a woman's view of her uterine family as an independent entity in competition with other families. Its independence is reflected in the fact that any household, whether that of an eldest or junior son, may sponsor a shamanistic rite. Competition between uterine families is obliquely evident in that the ancestors who speak at seances are often those who inflicted the greatest burden on the sponsoring housewife's uterine family. Her husband's siblings, if they are perpetually sick or poor, for example, place continual demands on that family; so do dead relatives who died in unfortunate circumstances. Deceased parents-in-law, to cite another example, often repeat the very demands which they made while alive. Living parents-in-law may complain about the food which their daughter-in-law prepared for them or the comfort of their room. Ancestors send misfortune because an ancestor rite is omitted, its food offering is unclean, or their grave is uncomfortable. The misfortune itself is analogous to living parents-in-law scolding a daughter-in-law.

Although a daughter-in-law may feel that she does her best to serve her parents-in-law, the demands of elderly parents-in-law seem endless. The image of selfish ancestors who send misfortune in order to have a shamanistic rite, even without any fault on the part of descendants, are evidently modeled upon this experience.

Ritual Style

The rigidity or flexibility of the performance styles at the two rituals reflects the different modes of interaction between a son and his father, on the one hand, and a woman and her in-laws, on the other. The interaction between fathers and sons is reflected in Confucian ancestor rites. Ordinarily, there is little communication between an adult son and his father, and their interaction is very formal. Similarly, ancestor ritual procedures are quiet, highly structured, and not relaxed:

> Even during adolescence, a son's relationship with his father is stiff and formal. In public at least, fathers remain aloof from their adolescent and grown-up sons. Sons in turn are expected to defer to their father's wishes and respect his authority. We never saw a mature son talk back to or disagree publicly with his father. Thus adolescent and adult sons are rarely at ease in their father's presence. Even mature sons may not smoke in front of their fathers, and if they drink wine, they must turn away as if to make their drinking less obvious. (Janelli and Janelli 1982, 47)

The ritual style of shamanic rites, on the other hand, is modeled upon the interaction of a woman and her husband's relatives. This interaction is far less formal than that of her husband and his father, and overt conflict with them is more common. Whereas conflict between fathers and sons seldom is expressed openly, antagonism between a woman and her in-laws is widely recognized in scholarly publications (e.g., Lee Kwang-Kyu 1981; Pak Pujin 1981) as well as in Korean oral literature. One proverb, for example, states: "After wishing that mother-in-law would die, one thinks of her [i.e., misses her labor] when pouring water over the barley and husking it" (*Shiömöni chugörago haettöni, poribanga mul puönok'o saenggak nanda*) (Hanguk Minsokhakhoe 1972, 231–32).

The quantity of communication between the living and the dead at the two types of rituals also reflects differences between how men address their fathers and women converse with their in-laws. Communication between a father and his son is rare; they seldom sit together and chat. One eldest son with whom we had been talking got up and departed as soon as his elderly father appeared at our door. He excused himself simply by stating that he had to leave now that his father had come. On another occasion, when the father had accompanied us to a village meeting, another lineage member politely asked him to leave so his son could attend (Janelli and Janelli 1982, 48). A daughter-in-law and mother-in-law interact more informally and in a greater variety of ways. Like ancestors at a seance, mothers-in-law order, scold, complain, and console their daughters-in-law, and the latter obey, apologize, and ask forgiveness. Also, a daughter-in-law expresses her resentment of her in-laws to her friends and neighbors. Her friends are usually sympathetic and side with her. Similar behavior was observed at a seance by Laurel Kendall:

The manshin [shaman] is possessed by Grandmother Chon's mother-in-law and father-in-law.

> The neighbor women demand of the ancestors, "Why have you made your own son sick? Please make him well."

> "Will he live past ninety, then?" Grandmother Chon asks the manifestation of her mother-in-law.

> "Ninety, that's too long," says the ancestor. There is laughter.

> "Past eighty, then?" (Kendall 1985, 7)

Conclusions: Ancestor-Rite Traditions and Contemporary Social Change

Korean family life exhibits both harmony and conflict, cooperation and competition, dependency and independence. Men experience more of the former and women more of the latter, although neither gender is oblivious to the social phenomena which predominate in the minds of others. We have tried to present each in sharp contrast to the other, but men and women do not live in entirely different social worlds, and thus they do not have completely different views of the Korean family. Brothers occasionally argue about property division, and the wives of brothers are often each other's allies. Men too are aware of the existence of conflict, competition, and independence, just as women are cognizant of their opposites. Therefore, women support Confucian ancestor rites to the extent of preparing the necessary food offerings, and men support shamanistic rites by granting the financial resources that they require. But these are minor concessions to the fundamental disparities between their respective social experiences; and consequently the sexual division of ritual life remains an important characteristic of Korean society.

Korean residence patterns (elderly parents living with their eldest son), parents' regarding children as extensions of themselves and the acceptance of mutual dependency between generations, the appeal of filial piety, beliefs about the afterlife, and traditional rituals for ancestors are all psychologically interrelated. They are interconnected, like industrialization and pollution, such that it is difficult to enjoy the benefits of one without suffering the discomforts of the other. However beneficial the norm of filial piety may be for the Korean social system, it may exacerbate an individual's emotional difficulties. Traditional rituals for ancestors are one means of dealing with these difficulties.

Because the present generation of middle-aged Koreans were raised very much along traditional lines, they still find filial piety and traditional rituals appealing. But as major changes occur in residence patterns, transmissions or property, and the autonomy of adult offspring, traditional rituals for ancestors may well lose the appeal which they now enjoy. Although I cannot provide a systematic comparison of past and present, my casual observations suggest that major "changes" are now taking place. In talking with middle-class Seoul women, I found generally that those in their sixties readily gave all their property to their sons. They fully expected to live with their eldest sons and receive their care and support. Women in their fifties, however, might give most of their property to their sons; but these women tended to keep some of their property for their own use. They disliked having constantly to ask for money whenever it was needed. Moreover, these women thought that living with their eldest son would be an ideal but not a necessary arrangement. Women in their forties, by contrast, said they did not intend to surrender all their property until their death. Finally, women in their thirties seemed to feel that providing children with a college education would be an adequate fulfillment of their parental role.

As the above comments show, parents now distinguish between their own economic welfare and that of their offspring, and they are less willing to sacrifice everything for the succeeding generation. If my observations are indicative of changes occurring throughout Korea, then filial piety is very likely losing its preeminent place in Korean morality. Future generations of children will no longer feel the same sense of indebtedness to parents, nor the same degree of responsibility for their welfare, nor the same sense of guilt for any inadequacies in their care and support. As a result, ancestor-worship traditions as well are likely to lose some of the psychological value which they now have.

Notes

1. My data were obtained primarily from fieldwork in Kyonggi-do, P'yongt'aek-kun, Chinwi-myon, Kagong-ni—Hubuk, also known as Twisŏngdwi. The village was undergoing rapid industrialization between my first visit in 1973–74 and my subsequent fieldwork four years later. I am deeply indebted to the villagers for their generous hospitality and kind assistance with our research. The second period of my fieldwork was undertaken between December 1977 and August 1978.

2. Korean words have been romanized according to the McCune-Reischauer system. Names of individuals have been similarly romanized, except when citing authors who have used a different spelling in their publications. In all cases, surnames of Korean authors are given before their personal names.

3. I am indebted to Clark Sorenson for calling my attention to Kim Chae-ŭn's work.

4. There is some measure of regional variation, however. According to Lee Kwang-Kyu (1975, 80), fathers in the southwestern part of Korea (primarily the Chölla provinces) do not surrender household headship during their own lifetimes.

5. Choi In-hak (1979, 292) cites eleven versions of this tale that have been collected in Korea.

6. This text was kindly recited for me by Mr. Kwön Chang-sik, a thirty-seven-year-old resident of the village.

7. Throughout most of Korea, ancestors and their spouses are commemorated together. Thus each ancestor is the object of an ancestor rite on his or her spouse's death anniversary also.

8. These categories are similar to those found in China (Jordan 1972; A. Wolf 1974), but the contents of each is somewhat different from those found in China. The Korean deities, for example, are not organized into a supernatural bureaucracy, and there is very little communication between them (Yim Suk-jay 1970, 87–88).

9. Though located in the same geographical region, the respective villages on which these two works are based are socially diverse. The village studied by the Janellis was dominated by a lineage whose members were descended from Chosön dynasty government officeholders. Kendall conducted her research in a village which was not dominated by any one lineage and whose residents were closer to the lower end of the traditional Korean social scale.

These differences in turn are reflected in the data obtained from each research site. Seances in the non-lineage village, for example, manifested a higher proportion of deceased persons who were not agnatically related to the head of the household sponsoring the rite.

10. Social status is popularly thought to have been hereditary in premodern Korea.

11. Although it is often said that a shamanistic ritual should be offered by each household every three years, while conducting field work in Twisöngdwi I did not observe any rites that followed this routine. Each of the shamanistic rituals I witnessed had been provoked by misfortune.

12. Some etiquette manuals describe procedures for death-day rites on behalf of collateral agnates who presumably have no descendants of their own. However, I know of no actual instances of their observance. Such collateral agnates are often commemorated at holiday rites, but informants regard these as ancillary to the rites offered to agnatic forebears on these days.

13. Three ancestors are commemorated together if a male ancestor had two consecutive legitimate spouses.

14. Yim Suk-jay (1971, 178) maintains that the proper term for this role is *kiju*.

15. By its inclusion of the husband, this Korean group differs from the Chinese "uterine family" described by Margery Wolf (1972).

16. Griffin Dix originally made this point in a paper presented at the annual meeting of the Association for Asian Studies in Washington, D.C., in 1980.

References

Ahern, E. A. (1973). *The Cult of the Dead in a Chinese Village.* Palo Alto, CA: Stanford University Press.

Akiba, T. (1933). "Mura matsuri no niju soshiki" (The Dual Organization of Village Rituals). *Choson minsok* [Korean Folklore] 2: 5–10.

———. (1957). "A Study on Korean Folkways." *Folklore Studies* 16: 1–106.

Bae, K. S. (1974). *Women and the Law in Korea.* Seoul: Korean League of Women Voters.

Brandt, V. S. R. (1971). *A Korean Village: Between Farm and Sea.* Cambridge, MA: Harvard University Press.

Chang, C. (1973). *Kankoku no mingan shinko* (Folk Religion of Korea). Tokyo: Kinkasa.

Ch'oe, K. (1982). "Musok e issoso 'chip' kwa 'yosong' " (Women and the Household in Shamanism). In *Han'guk musok ui chonghapchok koch'al* (A Comprehensive Study of Korean Shamanism), ed. K. Inhoe et al. Seoul: National Cultural Research Institute, Korea University.

Choi, I. (1979). *A Type Index of Korean Folktales.* Seoul: Myong Ji University Publishing.

Chung, B. M. (1972). *Psychological Perspectives: Family Planning in Korea.* Seoul: Hollym Corporation.

Dix, G. (1977). "The East Asian Country of Propriety: Confucians in a Korean Village." Ph.D. dissertation, University of California at San Diego.

———. (1979). "How to Do Things with Ritual: The Logic of Ancestor Worship and Other Offerings in Rural Korea." In *Studies on Korea in Transition,* ed. D. R. McCann, J. Middleton, and E. J. Shultz. Honolulu: Center for Korean Studies, University of Hawaii.

Fortes, M. (1959). *Oedipus and Job in West African Religion.* Cambridge: Cambridge University Press.

———. (1961). "Pietas in Ancestor Worship." *Journal of the Royal Anthropological Institute* 91: 166–91.

Freedman, M. (1966). *Chinese Lineage and Society: Fukien and Kwangtung.* London: Athlone Press.

———. (1967). "Ancestor Worship: Two Facets of the Chinese Case." In *Social Organization: Essays Presented to Raymond Firth,* ed. M. Freedman. Chicago: Aldine.

Goody, J. (1962). *Death, Property, and the Ancestors: A Study of the Mortuary Customs in LoDagaa of West Africa*. Palo Alto, CA: Stanford University Press.

Hahn, D. (1972). "Maturity in Korea and America." In *Transcultural Research in Mental Health*, ed. W. T. Lebra. Honolulu: University of Hawaii Press.

Han'guk, Minsokhakhoe F. S. (1972). *Han'guk soktam chip* [A Collection of Korean Proverbs]. Seoul: Somundang.

Harvey, Y. K., and S. Chung. (1980). "The Koreans." In *People and Cultures of Hawaii: A Psychocultural Profile*, ed. J. F. J. McDermott, W. Tseng, and T. W. Maretzki. Honolulu: University of Hawaii Press.

Hsu, F. L. K. (1979). "The Cultural Problem of the Cultural Anthropologist." *American Anthropologist* 81: 517–32.

Janelli, R. L., and D. Y. Janelli. (1979). "The Functional Value of Ignorance at a Korean Seance." *Asian Folklore Studies* 38.1: 81–90.

———. (1982). *Ancestor Worship and Korean Society*. Palo Alto, CA: Stanford University Press.

Jordan, D. K. (1972). *Gods, Ghosts, and Ancestors: The Folk Religion of a Taiwanese Village*. Berkeley and Los Angeles: University of California Press.

Kendall, L. (1985). *Shamans, Housewives, and Other Restless Spirits: Women in Korean Ritual Life*. Honolulu: University of Hawaii Press.

Kim, C. (1974). *Han'guk kajok ui simni: Kajok kwan'gye mit chiptan songgyok* (The Psychology of the Korean Family: Family Relations and Group Personality). Seoul: Hagyonsa.

Kim, S. (1975). *Hyangduga, Songjoga*. Seoul: Chongum-sa.

Lee, K. (1975). *Kinship Systems in Korea*. New Haven, CT: Human Relations Area File.

———. (1981). *Han'guk kajok ui simni munje* (The Psychological Problems of the Korean Family). Seoul: Ilchisa.

Moon, H. (1973). *Fertility and Family Planning: An Interim Report on the 1971 Fertility-Abortion Survey*. Seoul: Korean Institute for Family Planning.

Pak, P. (1981). "Han'guk nongch'on kajok ui kobu kwan'gye" (The Mother-in-Law–Daughter-in-Law Relationship in the Korean Farm Family). *Han'guk munhwa illyuhak* [Korean Cultural Anthropology] 13: 87–118.

Wolf, A. P. (1974). "Gods, Ghosts, and Ancestors." In *Religion and Ritual in Chinese Society*, ed. A. P. Wolf. Palo Alto, CA: Stanford University Press.

Wolf, M. (1972). *Women and the Family in Rural Taiwan*. Palo Alto, CA: Stanford University Press.

Yi, H., ed. (1973). "Developpement de la notion de piété filiale on Corée." *Revue de Corée* 5.2: 5–23.

————. (1982). *Kugo taesajon* (Unabridged Korean Dictionary), rev. ed. Seoul: Minjungsorim.

Yim, S. (1970). "Han'guk musok sosol, I" (An Introduction to Korean Shamanism, Part I). *Asea yosong yon'gu* [The Journal of Asian Women] 9: 73–90.

Yu, T. (1965). *Han'guk mugyo ui yoksa wa kujo* (The History and Structure of Korean Shamanism). Seoul: Yonsei University Press.

10

Male Dominance and Mother Power:
The Two Sides of Confucian Patriarchy in Korea

Haejoang Cho

The assessment of women's status in any Confucian society is a highly complex issue, and perhaps nowhere more so than in Korea. Depending on the researcher's position and personal inclination, totally conflicting evaluations can be made. Generally, Korean society has been described as an extreme form of patriarchy, especially during the Yi dynasty. Women had no public positions and were forced to be passive and obedient to men, who were structurally central. However, there is another view, now being propagated through the mass media and supported by rather conservative scholars, asserting that Korean women are so powerful and liberated compared to their Western sisters that there is no need for any women's liberation movement. They further claim that of the three East Asian countries, Korean women are the most powerful. Their argument is based on the observation that surnames were not changed upon marriage and that, unlike China or Japan, "sexist" customs such as foot-binding or decorative wives were not to be found. They also emphasize that Korean women have extensive economic power since they have separate incomes and manage all household finances.

In fact, a contradictory image of women is now a common theme in ethnographic accounts of East Asia. Tanaka (1981, 229), in discussing "maternal authority" in Japan, distinguishes moral from jural authority. She emphasizes that a jurally dependent status in and outside the household does not necessarily imply that Japanese women fail to exert strong moral authority. Tanaka maintains that the mother's moral authority has been highly respected in Japan because mothers have been regarded as becoming the very embodiment of the family ethos, and forming the basis of one's existence. Wolf (1972) also attempts to explain this apparent contradiction by introducing the concept "uterine family." Chinese mothers have secured their position and exercised their power within a patriarchal family system by creating focal families of their own through emotional ties of loyalty, thus binding their children to them and excluding the father.

Kendall and Peterson (1983) in the introduction of their co-edited book, *Korean Women: View from the Inner Room,* urged us to reconsider the Confucian idealization of the passive and sequestered women of traditional Korea. Drawing on early writings by missionaries, travelers, and anthropologists, they provided materials disproving this stereotyped image (Kendall and Peterson, 1983, 13). For example, Jones (1896, 223) wrote that "woman has exercised in Korean national and private life a degree of influence out of all proportion to her theoretical position in society." Gale (1898, 49) recalled how he was cross-examined by "a number of clarion-voiced females." He wrote: "One able-bodied Amazon, smoking a long pipe, pushed to the front, saying: 'I'm going to have a look at him—wouldn't they want to see me if I were in his country.'" He further generalized: "If the truth were told—we would know that the little woman in that enclosure is by no means the cypher he [the husband] pretends her to be; but that she is really mate and skipper of the entire institution, and that no man was ever more thoroughly under petticoat government that this—Korean gentleman (1898, 189)." DAllet (1954, 123) described Korean women as "violent and insubordinate, [they] sow division and ruin in their households, fight with their mother-in-law, take revenge on their husband by making his life unbearable, and continually provoke scenes of wrath and scandal." Underwood (1905, 222–23) portrayed female power more positively by saying, "[a woman of her acquaintance] was the real man in resourcefulness, energy, and ability to manage. . . . Many a Korean woman does that, however, and they are quite used to it."

In this chapter, I tackle this apparent contradiction of how a seemingly powerless position could be powerful, by examining the case of traditional Korean women. A theoretical frame of opposing public versus domestic status has been adopted as the major conceptual scheme for evaluating women during the Yi dynasty. Rosaldo and Lamphere (1974, 17–18) attempt to explain the universal asymmetry in cultural evaluation of the sexes by proposing a structural model that relates recurrent aspects of psychological, cultural, and social organization to an opposition between the domestic orientation of women and the extradomestic or "public" orientation of men. The dichotomy of public and domestic implies that although women may exercise a great deal of informal "power," the "authority" of men over women appears to be almost a human universal. A further observation is that women's status is higher in those societies where in the evaluation of status the family plays an important social function, that is, where the domestic realm itself becomes a locus of social, economic, and political power.

There are three levels of social reality to be considered in discussing women's role and status: economic roles, ideological background, and social organization. As for the first, one must note that the economic organization of traditional Korean families necessarily influenced both the ideological and psychocultural dimensions of family life. Some basic inferences about the economic functions of the family can and should be drawn prior to any other considerations. Economic production during the Yi dynasty depended on family-based labor-intensive agriculture. Most of the land was, in theory, controlled either by the state or the major clan lineages (Choi 1983; Chong 1984). Private property rights were recognized but from the middle of the dynasty they were exclusively transmitted through the patrilineal family line (Peterson 1983, 42–43; Choi 1979). The family was the basic unit of economic production and consumption. Family self-sufficiency relied for its existence on the labor of all the family members; both men and women had to cooperate for the family to survive (see Lee, chapter 13). Various studies on women's status in the agrarian societies of both the East and the West reveal that women under such social conditions played an important role both in economic production and in management, and thereby gained a "certain rough and ready equality" (Hamilton 1978, 46; Friedl 1975; Boserup 1970). However, with the rise of industrialization and a capitalistic economy, women's economic dependency upon their husbands increased. Zaretsky (1973, 263–71), in his book *Capitalism, the Family and Personal Life,* argues that the capitalist society is the first in human history to socialize production on a large scale, resulting in a split of socialized forms of commodity production and private labor. As capitalistic societies emphasize labor in the public sector of economic growth, domestic labor is undervalued and the family becomes isolated from the major sociopolitical process. Subsequently, male supremacy is institutionalized in the form of extrafamilial economic production, in sharp contrast with precapitalist societies where male supremacy was defined largely in ideological and political terms.

Second, in order to understand the ideological foundation of gender relations during the Yi dynasty, we need to understand the political history of Korea. The Yi dynasty was established by a new class of Confucian scholar-officials who legitimized their ascendancy by spreading Confucianism throughout all social segments. They expelled previously powerful Buddhist elites, and monopolized political power solely on the basis of Confucian teachings (Cha 1984). Deuchler (1980) has also shown that the founders of the Yi dynasty adopted Neo-Confucianism not merely as a philosophy of reform, but as the basis for completely rebuilding the polity. Although there were other religious and ideological influences emanating from shamanism and Buddhism, only Confucianism was publically recognized. Regardless of this, the majority of the people could not afford to approximate the practices or ideological purity as advocated by the elite. For example, they were economically unable to confine their women. However, in the absence of empirical studies, one cannot assume that the lower classes had developed their own distinctive culture as many young scholars and students have begun to claim.

Third, various aspects of Korean hierarchical social organization, that is, "the prestige system," are critical for understanding gender relations (Ortner and Whitehead 1981, 3). A precapitalist society constitutes a quite different social order from a capitalist one. Zaretsky finds examples from ancient Greece where political participation was the activity that distinguished men's "human" life from the "animalistic existence of women and slaves." In medieval Europe, surplus appropriated from peasant families supported institutionalized religion and the aristocracy, which together defined the purpose and meaning of the entire society: both women and the peasant class were equally oppressed and defined as "ignorant." As the prestige system always has a powerful interaction with the gender system, mere facts, such as women's contribution to the economy or exclusion from public positions, must not be interpreted as a direct index of women's status. Women's status in the most precapitalist, hierarchical societies may be understood properly by examining the political system, the lineage organization, and their dynamic interaction.

Kinship organization in particular defines the most important structural relationships between men and women in precapitalistic societies. Ortner (1981, 386), in her study of Polynesia, asserts that the marriage ties in Polynesia are weak. Most non-Western societies with a short history of industrialization show weaker ties between husband and wife, in contrast with stronger ties between parent and child or between siblings. Since kinship encompasses marriage ties in these societies, the "highly culturally assigned status of women as kin—encompasses their lower status as wives, and produces an overall cultural respect, or at least lack of disrespect, for women in general" (Ortner 1981, 394). In Polynesia, sisters receive greater respect than wives, and women in general are regarded more as sisters than as wives. A similar argument can be made in the case of Yi dynasty mothers, whose maternal role was of extreme importance in determining the overall status of women. Although mother power cannot be equated with women's power, understanding the sociocultural aspect of mother power is crucial to assessing women's status. Korean society might be an ideal case for studying the relationship between mother power and woman power and the mechanism by which a rigid male dominant system can be maintained alongside overwhelming mother power.

These three levels just noted are closely interrelated, but they also have their own autonomous mechanisms of transformation. Therefore, they need to be examined as separate systems employing both evolutionary and symbolic analyses. Particular importance should be given to the method of actor-centered analysis in which the focus is on ways in which an actor's perceptions of the world is shaped. The concept of the "actor" is central in that "meaning does not inhere in symbols but must be invested in symbols and interpreted from symbols by acting social beings" (Ortner and Whitehead 1981, 5). Gender conceptions, like any other social construct, can be viewed as "functioning aspects of a socio-cultural system through which actors manipulate, interpret, legitimize and reproduce the patterns . . . that order their social world" (Collier and Rosaldo 1981, 311). Maintaining a balance between socioeconomic structure and psychocultural structure can only be achieved by examining reality from both actor-centered and system-centered perspectives.

Various data are utilized in the following section for purposes of analysis—initially through published research, historical documents, and novels, followed by data from my own research, obtained through interviews and participant observation among modern women as well as from women from rural aristocratic lineages (Cho 1981a, 1981b, 1984).

Women, Confucianism, and Confucianization

Women's life during the Yi dynasty will by examined through the analysis of Confucian philosophy, values, and norms, following which a historical analysis will be attempted by examining the Confucianization process. The framework of the discussion is presented in table 1.

Table 10.1
Dimensions of Female Status in the Late Yi Dynasty

	Suppressing Female Autonomy	Encouraging Mother Power
Economic Condition (labor-intensive agriculture)	Patrilineal descent and inheritance Strict sex-role prescription	Family-centered subsistence economy Strict sex-role prescription
Ideological Ground (Confucianism)	Hierarchical cosmic order of the heaven (male) and the earth (female) Sex-differentiation and segregation	Complementarity emphasized by the yin-yang principle Family-oriented social order Values such as respect for the aged and filial piety
Sociocultural System (1) Polity characterized by a power balance between the monarch, the bureaucracy, and the local gentry (2) Supreme importance of lineage membership	Exclusiveness of lineage organization (chulga-waein) Importance of women's behavior for reputation of husband's family and lineage (e.g., severe restriction on women's behavior and prohibition of remarriage)	Importance of mother's consanguine identity (e.g., women's keeping of their natal surnames) Social acknowledgment of women's contribution to the welfare of the family (e.g., good manager, chǒngbu, yǒlyǒ, hyobu)

Confucianism: Ideology of Male-Supremacy and Harmony

Although ideology does not determine the course of history, it definitely does constrain it. Yi dynasty policy set out to construct an ideal Confucian society. Confucianism served as the major source of gender definition and symbolization. *Namnyŏ-yubyŏl* (sex-difference) and *namjon-yŏbi* (honored men, abased women) were two major principles governing the interactions between the sexes. The concept of *namnyŏ-yubyŏl* served as the basis of the social arrangement assigning men (*sarang* and *bakat,* meaning the outer space) and women (*an,* meaning the inner space) domain, that is, the public versus domestic opposition (see Lee, chapter 13). *Namjon-yŏbi* states explicitly that the two domains are hierarchically ordered. Y. O. Park (1985), in her analysis of Confucian texts such as *Shu-ching, Shih-shing, Lun-yu, Meng-tzu, I-Ching,* and *Li-chi,* illustrates how the idea of male supremacy is found in almost all of these Confucian texts, although there may be some differences in emphasis and degree. For example, the *I-Ching* describes women as the earth who must follow men. Men are the heavens, high and destined to lead. Heaven is strong with the principle of "one" while the earth is low and soft with the principle of "many." *Samjong-jido* (A woman must follow three men in her lifetime: her father, her husband, and finally her eldest son), *chilgŏ-jiak* (the seven codes for expelling a woman from her husband's home), and the rigid segregation between the sexes after the age of seven as stated in *Li-chi* were the basic rules for guiding women's life. I found that most of the old women of *yangban* families whom I interviewed had thoroughly internalized this idea of the differential status between men and women. To the question, "Why are men superior to women? Aren't both the earth and the heaven indispensable?" one woman responded: "The earth cannot step on heaven, can it?" She also explained that chastity was required only of women because the earth cannot have two heavens.

There are, however, aspects of Confucianism that support women's rights. These are related to familialism and the yin-yang dynamics regulating human relations. As mentioned above, Confucianism clearly differentiates between the public and domestic domain. But it also specifies that a man cannot attain public virtue unless he internalizes domestic virtue first: "Susin chega chiguk pyŏngchŏnha," "A man can be a true public leader only after he cultivates himself and regulates his family in harmony." This implies that domestic virtues are fundamental and are inclusive of public ones. This emphasis on family-centered social order seems to have worked toward elevating women's status. Women, through their maternal identity and role, could receive considerable respect not only in the family but also in the society. In fact, the wives of high public officials of the Yi dynasty were endowed with public formal titles (Chong 1973).

Filial piety was upheld as the ultimate value in Confucianism, at least in Koreanized Confucianism. When the value of filial piety was in conflict with that of loyalty to the king, priority was given to filial piety. Public officials, for example, were expected to return to their villages to perform the three-year mourning rituals for their parents, even if that meant giving up their public positions. Filial piety extended to both sexes nondiscriminatingly. As mothers were highly regarded and rewarded, a woman's life goal, naturally, was to produce successful sons.

The following folktale tells us how proud and free a woman can be once she accomplishes this life goal. There was a renowned scholar and prime-minister who lived during the middle of the Yi dynasty. One day, he was having a social gathering with his fellow officials. He heard someone urinating in a chamberpot in the next room. Very embarrassed, he dashed into the room and found that it was his mother. His mother said with a calm voice: "It was the hole that delivered the famous prime-minister that did it. Should it be refrained from doing anything?" (Park 1972, 3–158). We cannot tell clearly what the main message of this story was to the social actors; it might have been just a fictional catharsis for oppressed women, or it might have been a story reflecting the reality of the overwhelming power of mothers at that time. At any rate, we can deduce from the story that the elderly mother was, indeed, a very powerful symbol. Producing sons was the most important duty for women. It was also the major means for women to achieve social status and power. A woman who did not have a son was considered a nonperson. By having a son, a woman finally became significant. In fact, an agrarian economy and the Confucian value system both contributed to making the Yi dynasty a strong family-oriented society. Under these social conditions, mothers were assigned a high social status despite the extreme sexist bias inherent in Confucianism.

The principle of yin and yang and the emphasis on the harmonious social order seem to offer another basis for women to maintain some degree of power and self-respect. Interdependence between the sexes and women's complementary roles were highly idealized. Separated from the men, women would have their own religious beliefs (shamanism and other folk beliefs) and social activities. Kendall (1985, 177), in her study of Korean shamanism, presents a comprehensive description of how shamanistic rites reflect women's interests. Furthermore, she asserts that Korean women in their religious roles deal with broader family and community concerns as compared with the religious roles of women in Chinese society. From Chinese ethnography, Kendall also notes that Chinese women were symbolically coded as relatively more unique and profane. This difference between Korean and Chinese women's participation in rituals seems to indicate that there was a stricter division between the women's and men's domain in Korea, and that Korean women were viewed as less threatening to familial harmony than Chinese women. In fact, there was a strict division in emphasis between shamanism and Confucianism, as there was in daily life. Shamanism dealt basically with explanations and remedies for unfortunate events in a person's life; Confucianism offered a model of social order. Confucian scholars seemed to recognize this complementarity; they implicitly allowed women to perform the shamanistic rites despite their atheistic orientation.

On the other hand, women, by having their own living quarters and forming social groups among themselves, were not directly dominated by men. They developed their own hierarchy of authority and their own reward system. Young women were dominated by their mothers-in-law, but they could also find support systems and reference groups within the women's world. They could develop a separate value system of their own, which provided them with a sense of personal worth.

However, the women's subculture functioned ultimately within the patriarchal framework. Shamanism, as the religion of the "domestic" sphere, could not offer any alternative model for a new social order. The women's group itself was mainly organized through women married into their husbands' lineage. The value of women, recognized and reinforced within this reference group, was ultimately measured by how faithfully they performed the assigned roles as wives, mothers, and daughters-in-law.

Confucianization: Tightened Lineage Organization and Strengthened Mother Power

Adopting Confucian principles to govern the people, and using the ideology to gain political power, ("moralizing politics" and "politicizing Confucianism" to use Tu Wei-ming's expression [1984, 90, 105]), are two different issues. In the early part of the dynasty Confucianism was a philosophy of government, and as such it was somewhat flexible, incorporating room for change. Nevertheless, it was gradually dogmatized as Confucian rationalizations became the major source and means of obtaining power during severe periods of political strife. In the process, Confucius was almost deified and Korean society became extremely rigid (Par 1981; Cho 1986).

M. Peterson (1983, 42–43) divides the Yi dynasty into four stages: (1) the period of initiation at the end of the fourteenth century, (2) the period of implementation of a completely Confucian government during the fifteenth century, (3) the beginning of arguments about changing the social order during the sixteenth century, and (4) the period of broad Confucianization into local levels during the seventeenth century and beyond. What is noteworthy here is that the sixteenth century was a period that saw a fundamental transformation of the social order. This was accomplished not through institutional reform but through the widespread implementation and acceptance of Confucian practice at the normative level. At the same time, lineage organizations were tightened in order to protect the status quo (Kawashima 1979; Kim 1983). The obsession with ritual formality and dogmatic ideological imposition on the one hand, and the great emphasis on consanguinity on the other, became the major characteristics of Koreanized Confucianism. The supreme importance of the consanguine principle is reflected in the practice of women keeping their father's family name even after marriage.

The Confucian mode of conduct defining women's status was confined to the *yangban* class during the early part of the dynasty, and did not restrict all women's conduct as it did in the later years. Detailed historical analyses have shown that women had many more legal rights in the areas of inheritance and adoption in the early dynasty compared with the latter part of the dynasty (Wagner 1983; Peterson 1983). It was in the fifteenth century that the strict prohibition of remarriage of widows was legalized. This policy was supposedly brought into being in order to realize the Confucian familial ideal of serving only one husband in a life time. However, a study has indicated that it was primarily established in order to limit the rapidly increasing number of candidates for the state examination. Moreover, the conduct of widows in ones' lineage served as a major index for grading the prestige of lineages and as an excuse for eliminating political rivals (Lee 1985, 40–41).

The major agent of full-scale Confucianization was the group of retired or purged public officials and their descendants, who established and maintained their power base in the rural areas. As the vitality of the newly established loyal leadership waned, members of the excessively aggrandized ruling class began to compete as groups and individuals for limited resources in the form of land and power. In the absence of a clearly defined set of objective criteria for classifying ruling status, descendants of *yangban* had to struggle to maintain their dominant position in their own localities. This was accomplished by emphasizing their role as Confucian teachers and consolidating their power through alliances with other *yangban* lineages and local governors. Especially through marriage alliances and networks maintained by participants in Sowon (the memorial halls established to honor distinguished Confucian scholars), prominent *yangban* lineages formed major power blocks. However, such an alliance did not provide a secure and permanent basis for maintaining power and privilege. The social prestige of *yangban* lineages, from the well-established to those newly emerged, were constantly assessed and reassessed according to numerous criteria. The ranking of *yangban* became a relative and intersubjective matter largely determined by the following factors: the fame of their ancestors as nationally known scholars and statesmen, the purity of their bloodline, the ritual propriety of all their lineage members, and the socioeconomic resources the present lineage members had accumulated (Cho 1982). In this process, hereditary lineages became a more effective means of social control than the direct imposition of state authority. Thus, *chokbo* (the written records of the family tree) were highly regarded. Compared with the Chinese examination system, the Korean system of state examinations was more restrictive, prohibiting sons of concubines from even applying to take the examination (Song 1981, 213–16). This indicates that familial origin became more critical in Korea than in China. In this context, the mother's family background began to exert greater importance, and women came to have distinct social identity and value.

As the society depended for its social control on Confucian ideology and lineage organization, filial piety was increasingly reinforced. An individual's conduct was judged in terms of this ultimate value, which in turn determined the status of the family and the lineage to which she or he belonged. Exercising filial piety literally became the ultimate life-goal for a person, regardless of sex or status. When a woman lived up to the ideal of the virtuous daughter and wife, she was rewarded by the state as *hyoyŏ* (filial daughter) or *yŏlyŏ* (faithful wife). A man was rewarded by the state as *hyoja* (filial son) and *chunsin* (faithful subject). By producing a *yŏlyŏ* or *hyoja,* the family could get tax exemptions or even raise their class status. We can easily guess that many accomplishment-minded women strived to be *yŏlyŏ* or at least worked to receive forms of respect by thoroughly conforming to the Confucian values and norms. A Confucian scholar in the eighteenth century proudly reported that Korean women's faithfulness to their husbands was so sincere that Chinese women could not compete with them (Lee 1985, 49–51).

It must be emphasized again that a woman's accomplishments served only her husband's family. Daughters were regarded as *chulga-woein* (out-group). As rivalry and competition among the lineage intensified, daughters were pushed further away from their natal families.

The following tale handed down by an aristocratic family tells why "married out" daughters had to be avoided. The family had produced a great scholar in the middle of the dynasty, and around the same period, one of their daughters also produced a famous scholar-official. She delivered the child at her natal house. A famous geomancer told the family that the house site was predetermined to produce three great men, which implied that there was only one more to come. In order to prevent a son of their daughter from taking away the *ki* (spirit) of the house site, the family established a rule prohibiting their daughters from delivering babies in this house. As the story reveals, the daughters were considered out-group members, if not enemies. Young women, sometimes facing inhuman treatment from their husbands' families, could hardly find any place to turn. As the society was tightly organized under the principle of patrilineality and people were anxious to protect the interests of their family and patrilineage, little protection was offered to women by their natal families. Under such conditions, women had only one choice: they had to endure and survive within their husbands' families, and accomplish their objectives through and for their sons.

The following tale deals with the ambivalent position of women caught between two kin groups by presenting the case of a woman who was faithful to her husband's family by outsmarting her natal family. In the scheme of folk religion, women cater to ghosts and ancestors from their natal and affinial homes, and sometimes even from their mothers' natal homes. Akiba was so impressed by the number of powerful gods acquired through women that he mistakenly described the tradition as "matrilineal" (Kendall 1985). From women's perspective, women's emotional association with the *chinjŏng* in their natal homes, has been strong throughout history. A wife of a poor *sŏnbi* (a generic term for a scholar who was preparing for the state examination and who was expected to be concerned only with public virtue) attended her grandfathers' funeral. That night she happened to overhear her father and a geomancer discussing a burial site over a hill. The geomancer told her father that the site seemed to be in an excellent location that would surely guarantee the prosperity of the family. However, he added that an on-the-spot survey was required in order to make certain that the place was not too wet. The daughter, being covetous of the site, climbed the hill and walked back and forth pouring water on it all through the night. The next morning her father and the geomancer were disappointed to find that the spot was wet, and they had to find a new burial site. After the funeral, the daughter asked her father to give the deserted burial site to her, to which he readily agreed. Later, she buried her husband (or her father-in-law, depending on the version) there, and her husband's family became prosperous. She produced many sons who became high public officials, and her descendants were abundant. Widely known, this story served the function of indoctrinating women to be loyal to their husband's families instead of to their natal families. As the story emphasizes, it is the position of mother with which a woman must identify. By focusing on their sons' and descendants' success, women can be effectively persuaded to direct themselves to their husband's family and lineage.

Women, as wives of scholarly men or of men imitating the scholarly lifestyle who were supposed to be indifferent to such "minor" issues as daily life activities, had to take on the burden of managing what were often poor households as efficiently and resourcefully as possible. The old women of aristocratic families whom I interviewed recalled that they were prepared to marry poor *sŏnbi*. The life of a poor *sŏnbi's* wife was described as being very much like that of a faithful *sŏnbi* in a declining state (Chong 1985, 67). On one tombstone inscription, a poor *sŏnbi's* wife was praised because she could "suspend the decline and prevent the breakdown of the family, managing an impoverished household, making three meals a day, preparing the ancestral rites, and making family gatherings happy and comfortable." It ends with "whose spirit will be nobler than hers!" Women also took great pride in being *chŏngbu,* the daughters-in-law of the main family. A *chŏngbu* whom I interviewed said that it was truly a challenging job. She learned in her childhood how to manage a poor household, never letting others notice that she was hungry. In order to be a successful and respectable *chŏngbu,* she said that one had to be practical, hardworking, and skillful in managing economic and human resources. She must also be strong and firm just like a *yŏjangbu,* a woman commander. In fact *yŏjangbu* is a distinctive female image cherished by Korean women and portrayed by novelists even now (Choi 1983; Park 1979; Kim 1982). Most aristocratic lineages which I have studied (about ten in number) had one or two role models of this type. Typically, *yŏjangbu* had several sons, all of whom passed the state examinations. They had the ability to forecast the future, and managed the family estate with great energy. The image was further elaborated with descriptions of physical characteristics, usually ugly faces, strongly built asexual bodies, and vigorous activities such as horseback riding.

Similar images were also cherished among commoners. A wise and hardworking daughter-in-law who revived the declining family is one of the most frequently recurring folk figures. Through her determination, intelligence, and diligence, a woman can make her inadequate husband a great man or accumulate wealth for her family. In both cases, the heroine shares the personality characteristics of independence and strong will power. Shimchong and Baridegi (or Pyong-gang-Kongju) are stories basically portraying the same personality traits: a daughter overcoming tremendous hardships by herself and finally bringing happiness to the whole family. It is important to note here that women's lives were basically similar regardless of their class. As supporters of their "noble" husbands, women had to lead lives of hard work. A folk song describes the reality as follows: "Will there be any difference in a woman's hardship, whether she is rich or poor? Our husbands know little of daily living, but are concerned only with their tasteful appearance."

In contrast to men, to whom power was assigned, women of the Yi dynasty had to achieve power and authority through their own efforts. Except for being state officials, men's status was more or less defined in a world circumscribed by kinship and community, leaving little room for them to accomplish on their own. But a woman basically had to strive throughout her entire life, not only for her own survival but also for her family's. Once a wife internalized Confucian patriarchal values, it was permissible, even desirable, for her to exhibit what Korean society considered as a legitimate form of self-interest because the end product was inextricably linked to her husband's family's well-being. This life pattern produced practical and aggressive women in contrast to idle and formalistic men. Korean women, who moved from being powerless daughters-in-law to becoming powerful mothers-in-law, and who survived rough and troubled histories as the stronghold of the family, naturally developed a sense of power and fortitude. This sense of power, as the major supporters of the family, made women even more aggressive about maximizing their own self-interest, which were, at least in appearance, predominantly familial.

Mother Power, Familism, and Social Change

I have tried to show in the above discussion that these were two sides of Confucian patriarchy in the late Yi dynasty: extreme suppression of women on the one hand and extreme idealization of motherhood and the encouragement of the mother's accomplishment on the other hand. In Confucian texts, we find both fundamental sexism based on the principle of agnation and an emphasis on the complementary relationship of the sexes. At the organizational level, heavy emphasis on the family lineage functioned to exclude women, particularly daughters and wives, but at the same time accommodated them as daughters-in-law and mothers. The strict spatial and role division between the sexes had both positive and negative effects on women's lives. Women were empowered by their activities as economic producers and household managers as a counterbalance to their husbands, who ideally were like sŏnbi. However, it should not be overlooked here that economic power was relatively insignificant in comparison with political and ideological power at that time.

What does all this tell us ultimately about women's status? How can mother power be assessed in its function of maintaining and creating social change? In order to answer these questions, we need to probe further into two aspects: the nature of mother power and the social conditions under which mother power has been institutionalized. First of all, it is essential to remember that it was only mothers and legitimized wives who could exercise power and authority in the late Yi dynasty. The society guaranteed tremendous rewards for mothers' devotion, ignoring any other type of women's faithfulness, such as in their roles as sisters or wives. Daughters and concubines had no institutionalized power at all. Although daughter's noninstitutionalized power is acknowledged in folk tales such as Shimchŏng and Baridegi, it only actually occurs when she undertakes the nurturing role of a mother substitute.

As Wolf (1972, 3) pointed out in her studies of the Chinese family, it was through extreme emphasis on motherhood that a male ideology that excluded women made its accommodation with reality. Guisso (1982) presents a similar interpretation of this by saying that in traditional China, a women's liberation movement could not be brought into being because the age factor exceeded the gender factor; old mothers were free from the restrictions imposed upon young women and they received the highest respect and care at the final stage of their lives. In fact, legitimizing mother power might be the way of accommodating women under the male-dominated social system. Compared with wife power, which can be found mostly in the Western countries, or sister power in Polynesian societies, mother power may be the most secure source of power for women under the patriarchal system. Mothers, whose ultimate concern lay in their sons' well-being, were made pillars of the establishment and this worked to reduce any feeling of what one might call class solidarity among women as the oppressed group.

Moreover, mother power basically stays at the personal level and has a conservative tendency. Mothers are able to defer their gratification so much longer than wives or sisters that they, although feeling discontented, tend to hold on and endure with a vague hope in the future for their children. Of course, women with institutionalized mother power can be much more independent psychologically from their husbands than those women equipped with wife power. However, they have much more difficulty in achieving independence from their sons and establishing their identity as autonomous individuals. This conservatism stemmed from the symbiotic nature of mother/son relationships, and the heavy emphasis on the identity of women as mothers is, in fact, the major stumbling block in the women's rights movement in Korea today. It is not motherly to feel oppressed; it is even less so to complain about one's own hardships and to protest for one's own rights. Young women hesitate to join the women's movement, feeling that they are not yet fully grown persons until they get married and become mothers.

An important aspect of matrifocality may be that the more central women become in maintaining their families, the more peripheral and alienated men become from their families. Men, insisting on the ideology of male supremacy and, following the image of *sonbi,* have consistently kept their distance from family members and pretended to be aloof from daily life activities. In this way Korean men seem to have relegated their power and authority to women. Most Korean men now are quite confused about their familial and social responsibilities. Although they still may be recognized and serve as the head of the family by their wives, in actuality they may not be the de facto family heads. Consistent with this argument, literary critics have recently begun to note that a distinctive characteristic of Korean novels is the absence of the father figure (Choi 1987). When Korean feminists search for proper ways to realize gender equality in Korea, they may have to seriously consider this psychocultural dimension of Korean society that has been sustained by powerful mothers and their dependent sons and husbands.

Here we may raise the question of the relationship between mother power and the nature of society: under what conditions does mother power become a socially important force? As described above, mother power has been fully activated and has influenced the social process in a direct and pervasive way in Korea. Matrifocal tendencies seem to have been intensified through the modern period characterized by distorted modernization and foreign domination. During early modernization, inhuman legal practices, such as the prohibition of remarriage and concubinage, were banned and the education of women was urged by new elites. But familial ideology and cultural obsession with consanguinal ties remained largely the same. During the Japanese colonial era, many families were pulled apart. A great number of men left home due to emigration, the independence movements, and voluntary and involuntary labor, and women had to assume heavier responsibilities as family heads in the absence of male family members. Furthermore, the Korean War, again, separated many men from their homes, reinforcing matrifocalization. Under these social conditions where family survival itself was at stake, women quite naturally assumed the crucial male roles, and their aggressiveness was accepted, even encouraged. During the period of rapid industrialization, mothers had to be busy on behalf of the "status-reproduction" of the family (Papaneck 1985). Throughout a hundred years of modernization, the ideology of family continuity has waned, and the family has nuclearized, at least in form. But familism, which contains little possibility of transcending the biological circle, persists. The mother-son relationship still predominates over the conjugal one and the conflict between mother-in-law and daughter-in-law remains the major source of social conflict.

Now we can go back to the Rosaldo and Lamphere (1974) proposition that women's role and status are central where the family has important social functions, that is, where the domestic sphere itself is more powerful. As discussed above, family-centered production and Confucian ideology have characterized traditional Korea as a "family state." The long-lasting sociopolitical instability since the latter part of the Yi dynasty, and subsequent foreign domination, reinforced family-centeredness. In this historical process, exclusive familism has become the core value, leaving little room for a more general public organization and ideology.

It must be remembered here that familism has been one major way to organize societies. However, it was usually found in smaller and simpler societies. In those societies, the opposition between the domestic and public sphere was not clearly drawn, and even where it did exist the activities in the public domain were relatively insignificant when it came to social survival. Korean society can be classified definitely as a society that makes a very clear distinction between the public and domestic domains. We also know that industrialization is a social process marked by sudden expansion of the public domain. How can we then explain the existence of strong familism in a complex and industrialized society? We can easily guess that when a society is struggling for bare survival, offering little protection to its members, people try to survive on their own as tightly consolidated family units. The persistent existence of extreme family-centered values and matrifocality throughout the modern history of Korea may then be interpreted as an indication of the relative weakness of the politics of the public sphere. The survival strategy of Korean society for the last several centuries, including during recent modernization, seems to have been based on the self-help principle of the blood-related kinship unit rather than expanding the public sphere.

The majority of Korean people still agree with the old expression, "There is nothing but family (blood) that a person can trust" (Lee 1984). People distrust any kind of social group or institutions such as the company, the school, the nation, or even the voluntary association. Nepotism is still a major social problem. This tendency of exclusive and egocentric familism seems to have been strengthened rather than weakened through the recent rapid industrialization. Women as "housewives," whose only concerns were confined to family welfare and who have not been exposed to the public "work" world of men, have guarded familial values most faithfully and transmitted them to their children. Unlike the middle-class housewives in Western societies or in Japan, Korean women have little interest in charitable roles or community welfare programs (Tinker 1980, 4). They invest their time solely in immediate familial interests, such as visiting schoolteachers to give "envelopes" of money to solicit the upgrading of their children's scores or engaging in informal businesses in the area of real estate or *kye* (rotating credit associations) to improve family finances. Children rely heavily on their mothers' effort in helping them pass school entrance examinations and in the selection of marriage partners.

Mother domination is reflected in the attitude of activists in recent student movements on campus. The effect of one's behavior on one's mother can be a source of severe psychological guilt for some activist students. As a result, some hesitated to join in the movement because of the anticipated reaction of their mothers. As soon as a student is arrested for organizing or participating in a demonstration, he is usually informed that his mother was shocked and fainted. An attempt is usually made by the prosecutor, or his teachers and relatives, to persuade him to swear that he will not involve himself in the movement any longer for his mother's sake. Potential or actual illness can be used as a mode of psychological control, as is true in Japan. On the other hand, there are some committed activist students who wish to believe that their mothers will join in the antigovernment movement once they find that their sons have been sentenced. This may be a dynamic part of mother power. However, the number of "converting" mothers does not seem to be significant.

What kind of mechanisms still enable exclusive familism to persist? I do not attempt here to offer an answer to the question. But I do want to introduce another characteristic of Korean society, that is, the dual structure of formal and informal spheres. Informal manipulation in the public domain has a direct relationship with the persistence of familism and kin networks in the family domain. In fact, the behavioral distinction between the public and domestic domains is made only at the formal level; both men and women faithfully perform expected roles in public. At the informal level, however, it can be blurred; family considerations and the mother attitudes in particular can interfere with decisions and policies. I am not arguing that it is the personality of "aggressive" mothers who are ultimately responsible for backstage manipulation and for maintaining familistic values. The structure itself is responsible. What I am suggesting here is that any kind of fundamental social change cannot take place unless this dual structure, "public and domestic," is undermined. Mother power is in effect institutionalized in the Confucian heritage as practiced in Korea.

Mother power, familism, and the "overdependence" between men and women, which are largely the unintended product of Confucian patriarchy, have been contributing significantly to the continuation of an extremely conservative social system. Some studies (Kim 1983; Cho 1986) have shown how Korean familism and close kin ties came to be utilized successfully in early industrialization. Success was facilitated by psychosocial functions such as the pooling of the familial economic resources and energies and by providing emotional support for individual members during the period of crisis. They have also suggested that traditional values would soon be a liability rather than a strength in making the family more rational, human. Releasing the society from rigid familism would be one of the major tasks of modernization. Redefining the spousal roles of men and women would make the mother role less powerful. Women, both younger and older, should be encouraged to be more independent, less focused on their sons, and better integrated into activities within the public domain, while men need to be encouraged to take more responsibility at home, as well as at the workplace. When Korean women give up their "mother power," we may expect great changes in Korean society. In social theory, explicit studies of how Korean mother power works would focus attention on it and perhaps instigate momentum for change. Only after we discover the other "domestic" side of formal Confucianism will we be able to write a more holistic Korean social history.

Note

I am indebted to Drs. Laurel Kendall and Elaine Kim for providing valuable comments on this paper.

References

Boserup, E. (1970). *Women's Role in Economic Development*. New York: St. Martin's.

Cha, Sŏng-whan. (1984). "Ideological Change and Social Stratification during the Transitional Period from the Koryo to the Yi Dynasty." *Sahoehak Yongu* (Sociological Studies) 1. Seoul: Deyong-sa.

Cho, Hae-joang. (1981a). "A Comparative Study of Marital Power between Employed Wives and Housewives." *Hanguk Sahaehak* (Korean Sociology) 15.

———. (1981b). Continuity and Change in Korean Women's Lives." *Asea Yosong Yongu* (The Journal of Asian Women) 21. Seoul: Sukmyong Women's University.

———. (1982). "Hyangchon-ui Kwonryokjipdan-ul Tonghaeso bon Hanguk Chontongsahea (Organizational Principles of Local Elite Groups in Traditional Korea). Seoul: Korean Social Science Research Council.

———. (1984). "The Republic of Korea: Those Left Behind." *Women in the Village and Men in the Town*. Paris: Unesco.

———. (1986). "The Transformation of the Korean Patriarchy." *Hanguk Yosonghak* (Korean Women's Studies) 2. Seoul: Hanguk Yosonghakhoe.

———. (1986). "Male Dominance and Mother Power: The Two Sides of Confucian Patriarchy in Korea." In *The Psycho-Cultural Dynamics of the Confucian Family: Past and Present*, ed. Walter H. Slote. Seoul: International Cultural Society of Korea.

Choi, Jae Hyŏn. (1983). "Hanguk Chŏnjabonju-ŭi Saengsanyangsik-ŭi Kaenyŏmkyujŏng Munje" (A Theoretical Discussion of the Mode of Production during the Yi Dynasty). *Hanguk Sahoe-ui Chontong-gwa Byonhwa*. Seoul: Bommunsa. (Tradition and Change in Korean Society)

Choi, Jae Suk. (1979). "Choson Sidae-ui Chokbo-wa Dongjokjojik" (Yi Dynasty Genealogies and Clan Structure). *Yoksahakbo* [Journal of History] 1981.

Choi, Myŏng Hi. (1983). *Honbul* (The Light of the Soul). Seoul: Donga-ilbo-sa.

Choi, Won Sik. (1987). "Yŏsŏngjuŭi-wa Abojibujae-ŭi Munhak ŭi Uimi" (Feminism and the Meaning of Fatherlessness in Literature). *Yosong, Haebang-ui Munhak*. Seoul: Pryongmin, (The Literature of Women's Liberation) sa. [Publisher].

Chŏng, Sŭng Mo. (1984). "Dongjok Chiyŏngongdongche-wa Chosŏn Chŏngtongsahoe Kujo (Lineage Mode of Production and Korean Social Structure). *Taedong Kojŏn Yŏngu* 1. Seoul.

Chŏng, Yo Sŏp. (1973). "Women's Social Status during the Yi Dynasty." *Asea Yŏsŏng Yŏngu* (Journal of Asian Women) 12. Seoul: Sukmyŏng Women's University.

Chŏng, Yang Wan. (1985). "The Image of Korean Women: Based on an Analysis of Traditional Norms. *Hanguk Yŏsŏng-ŭi Chŏntong-sang* (The Traditional Image of Korean Women). Seoul: Minum-sa. [Book]

Collier, Jane and Michele Z. Rosaldo. (1981). "Politics and Gender in Simple Societies." *Sexual Meanings,* ed. S. Ortner and H. Whitehead. Cambridge: Cambridge University Press.

D'Allet, C. (1954). *Traditional Korea.* New Haven, CT: Human Relations Area Files. (Originally published in French in 1874)

Deuchler, M. (1980). "Neo-Confucianism: The Impulse for Social Action in Early Yi Korea." *Journal of Korean Studies* 2.

Friedl, E. (1975). *Women and Men: An Anthropologist's View.* New York: Holt, Rinehart, and Winston.

Gale, J. S. (1989). *Korean Sketches.* New York: Fleming H. Revell.

Guisso, R. W. (1982). "Thunder over the Lake: The Five Classics and the Perception of Women in Early China." *Women in China,* ed. R. W. Guisso and S. Johannesen. New York: Philo Press.

Hamilton, Roberta. (1978). *The Liberation of Women: A Study in Patriarchy and Capitalism.* London: George Allen and Unwin.

Jone, G. H. (1896). "The Status of Women in Korea." *Korea Repository* 3.

Kawashima, F. (1979). "The Role and the Structure of the Local Gentry Association in Mid-Yi Dynasty in Korea: A Preliminary Study of Changnyong Hyangan, 1600–1838." 1st International Conference on Korean Studies, Academy of Korean Studies, Seoul.

Kendall, Laurel. (1985). *Shamans, Housewives, and Other Restless Spirits: Women in Korean Ritual Life.* Honolulu: University of Hawaii Press.

Kendall, Laurel and Mark Peterson. (1983). "Introduction." *Korean Women: View from the Inner Room,* ed. L. Kendall and M. Peterson. New Haven, CT: Little Rock.

Kim Ju Hi. (1983). "Hanguk Chontongsahoe-ae-issossoui Ichajipdan-ui Songgyok" (The Characteristics of Secondary Groups in Traditional Korea). *Hanguk Munwhainryuhak* 15.

Kim Kyong Dong. (1983). "Hanguk-ŭi Sahoe Byŏndong" (Social Change in Korea). In *Kyongje Songjang-gwa Sahoe Byŏndong* (Economic Growth and Social Change). Seoul: Hanul.

Kim Chŏng Han. (1982). "Surado." *Kim Chŏng Han Sosŏlsŏnjip* (Selected Novels of Kim Chŏng Han). Seoul: Changjakkwa Bipyŏng.

Lee Kwang Kyu. (1975). "Women's Status in the East Asian Patriarchal Family." In *Hanguk Kajok-ŭi Kujo Bunsŏk* (The Structural Analysis of the Korean Family). Seoul: Ilji-sa.

Lee Ok Kyŏng. (1985). "Chosŏn Shidae Chŏngjŏl Ideology-ŭi Hyŏngsŏng Kiban-gwa Chŏngch'ak Bangshik-ae-kwanhan Yŏngu" (A Study on Formational Conditioning and Reinforcing Mechanism of Chŏngjŏl Ideology of the Yi Dynasty). M.A. thesis, Ewah Women's University.

Lee Yŏng In. (1984). "Hanguk Toshi Kajok-ŭi Kajokjuŭi" (Familism in an Urbanized Korea). M.A. thesis, Yonsei University.

Ortner, Sherry. (1981). "Gender and Sexuality in Hierarchical Societies: The Case of Polynesia and Some Comparative Implications." In *Sexual Meanings.* Cambridge: Cambridge University Press.

Ortner, Sherry and Harriet Whitehead. (1981). "Introduction: Accounting for Sexual Meanings." In *Sexual Meanings.* Cambridge: Cambridge University Press.

Papaneck, H. (1985). "Family Status—Production Work: Women's Contribution to Class Differentiation and Social Mobility." Paper presented at the Conference on Women and the Household, International Union of Anthropological and Ethnological Sciences, New Delhi.

Park Kyŏng Lee. (1979). *T'oji* (The Land). Seoul: Chisik Sanŏpsa.

Park Yong-ok. (1985). "Re-examination of the Confucian View of Women in Korea." *Hanguk Yŏsŏnghak* (Korean Women's Studies) 1. Seoul: Iwu-sa.

Park, Y. J. (1972). *Hanguk-ŭi Chŏnsŏl* (The Legends of Korea). Seoul: Hanguk Munwha Tosŏ.

Park, Yong Sin. (1983). "Hanguk Sahoe Baljŏnron Sŏsŏl" (An Introduction to the Development Theory of Korean Society." *Hanguksahoe Ŏdiro Kagoinna?* (Where Is Korean Society Heading?). Seoul: Hyŏndaesahoe Yŏnguso.

Peterson, Mark. (1983). "Women without Sons: A Measure of Social Change in Yi Dynasty Korea." In *Korean Women: View from the Inner Room,* ed. Laurel Kendall and Mark Peterson. New Haven, CT: Little Rock.

Rosaldo, M. Z. and L. Lamphere. (1974). "Introduction." *Women, Culture, and Society.* Stanford, CA: Stanford University Press.

Song, Jun-ho. (1981). A Comparative Study of State Examination Systems: China and Korea. Kwagŏ. Seoul: Iljogak.

Tanaka, M. (1981). "Maternal Authority in the Japanese Family." In *Religion and Family in East Asia,* ed. G. DeVos and T. Sofue. Osaka: National Museum of Ethnology.

Tinker, I. (1980). "Toward Equity for Women in Korea's Developmental Plans." A report prepared for the World Bank. UNDP Korea Project ROK 78 002, Washington, D.C.

Tu Wei-ming. (1984). *Confucian Ethics Today: A Singapore Challenge.* Singapore: Federal Publications.

Underwood, L. H. (1905). *With Tommy Tompkins in Korea.* New York: Fleming H. Revell.

Wagner, Edward. (1983). "Two Early Genealogies and Korean Women's Status in Early Yi Dynasty in Korea." In *Korean Women: View from the Inner Room,* ed. L. Kendall and M. Peterson. New Haven, CT: Little Rock.

Wolf, Margery. (1972). *Women and the Family in Rural Taiwan*. Stanford, CA: Stanford University Press.

Zaretsky, Eli. (1973). *Capitalism, the Family, and Personal Life*. New York: Harper & Row.

11

Confucian Gender Role and
Personal Fulfillment for Japanese Women

Takie Sugiyama Lebra

The Japanese version of Confucianism, or more correctly of Neo-Confucianism—which was developed, systematized, and institutionalized during the Tokugawa era (1603–1867), and subjected to sociopolitical change thereafter—managed in one form or another to survive the revolutionary Westernization of the subsequent "modern" period. Today Confucianism is dismissed and sometimes ridiculed as hopelessly antiquated, destined to soon vanish from the memory of the oldest generation. Whether this dismissal is warranted or not is open to question, and the use of the past tense in the following discussion should not be taken necessarily as exclusive of the present situation.

The primary human relation from the Confucian point of view is that of parent and child, most significantly, father and son, tied by filial piety. Let the parent-child relation, therefore, be called the Confucian bond. This chapter,[1] however, takes up another, secondary relation, the relation of man and woman as it is interlocked with the Confucian bond. Specifically, I will focus on women and attempt to recapture their way of life bound to what I regard as the Confucian gender ideology, as far as one can infer from oral autobiographies given in interviews. Life histories have been collected over the years since 1976 (Lebra 1984) and include materials on women from different classes—lower class, middle class, through the upper-class prewar aristocracy—both rural and urban.[2] For the present purpose, the sample of informants used will be drawn more from the prewar generation than from younger individuals. This includes the generation of the "Confucian sandwich" (Plath 1975). The oldest informant, now deceased, was born in 1888, and the oldest age at interview was 91. Some attention will be paid to class differences insofar as particular statements apply more to one class than to another.

My principal objective is to delve into the psychological problems faced by women that arise from the constraint of Confucian norms, their strategies in coping with them, and possible ways of attaining personal fulfillment. I could well reverse this objective by asking how they failed to cope with problems or to achieve fulfillment. It will be shown, however, that success and failure are complementary to and thus informative of each other. Equally informative of a Confucian type of fulfillment are non-Confucian alternatives, which I shall therefore touch upon at the end.

Womanhood and the *Ie* in Confucian Structure

The main characteristic of the Confucian gender ideology in my view is its *structural* emphasis on the roles and statuses of men and women as an integral part of the overall social order, which in turn is embedded in the law of the universe. Man and woman are supposed to relate to each other through the complementary rights and obligations attached to their structurally assigned roles and statuses. The relations are to be structurally mediated rather than direct and immediate, and thereby protected from the impulses and whims of individuals. This structural bias may reflect the Tokugawa regime's political use of Confucianism to maximize the stability and predictability of human relations after centuries of civil warfare.

Confucian *structure* may be thus placed at the opposite pole from *personhood,* or to put it another way, personhood in Confucianism characteristically involves discipline or role discipline, not the entirety of a person including his or her emotions and impulses. Structure in this sense comes close to what Turner (1969) meant by the same term although for him it was merely a heuristic point of departure to elaborate on its opposite, *liminality.*

Confucian structuralism in this sense seems particularly important in governing gender relations. To my mind the following principles are involved for gender roles and womanhood: dichotomy in role spheres, gender hierarchy, and sexual distance.

Dichotomy in Role Spheres

Women's foremost role should be that of *good wife and wise mother,* and her role sphere should be domestic, "inside," and backstage, clearly set apart from the male sphere, which is public, "outside," and on stage. If a woman participates in the male sphere, she is obliged to do so only as a surrogate for her husband, son, or other male kin, or invisibly from the backstage. The Confucian woman, then, is a prime example of "the Other" devoid of subjectivity (de Beauvoir 1972). Through this dichotomy, woman and man are expected to enjoy harmony as yin and yang based upon role interdependence.

Gender Hierarchy

Man is placed above woman, just as the heaven is above the earth, and the head above the body. This status asymmetry involving female inferiority, subordination, and vulnerability ties in with jural patricentricity in property ownership, household headship, and succession. Japanese Confucianism assimilated the Chinese idioms of such gender hierarchy as "the seven rationales for divorcing the wife" (including jealousy and loquaciousness), and woman's "three obediences" (first to her father, then to her husband when married, and last to her son when widowed). These were understood not necessarily literally but at least symbolically to impress male superiority and dominance.

Sexual Distance

Confucianism separates man and woman at a young age, as young as seven. The rule of segregation ought to be adhered to until marriage, which necessitates matchmaking for marriage by a third person(s) who defines the expected "roles" of husband and wife for the candidates in advance. Even after marriage open intimacy is prohibited, since marriage means the incorporation of the incoming spouse into the receiving household, more than a dyadic union of man and woman as sexual partners. Filial piety to parents and parents-in-law precedes spousal compatibility. To compensate for the sexual distance of the married couple, the husband, but not the wife, has the prerogative of extramarital sexual access and concubinage.

Underlying the above gender ideology is the integrity of the *ie,* household, which was a basic jural unit in the prewar civil code. At this point we should remind ourselves that Japanese Confucianism became closely interlocked with the institution of *ie* so that one was inconceivable without the other. The concept of *ie* has been overworked in Japanese anthropology and sociology, leaving us little to explore. However, for the purpose of the present chapter, I would like to point out two attributes of *ie:* spatial and temporal. First, the *ie* refers to a spatial unit—physical, social, and symbolic—to which all the co-residents "belong." A person not only belongs to and stays in a *ie,* but may "depart" from one *ie* and "enter" another *ie.* This spatial image of *ie,* while the *ie* itself is no longer recognized as a legal unit, is retained even now in the form of the *koseki* or house register. The *koseki* is an official, cumulative record of a household cycle regarding the "entries" and "departures" of family members through birth, death, marriage, adoption, and divorce. Unlike the American birth certificate or marriage license, which is carried by an individual, this is a collective documentary unit to which all the members of the family "belong." Under the postwar civil code, each new couple is entitled to a newly "created" *koseki* of its own, instead of entering the preexisting parental *koseki,* a change that reflects the legally sanctioned nuclear-family ideal. But at the same time, the couple is, in legal terminology, to "enter" their new *koseki*.

Second, interlaced with this spatial dimension of the *ie* is its temporal one. The *ie* exists not only here and now but is an entity durable over generations (Pelzel 1970). Viewed this way, the *ie* includes not only the living generation but ancestors who are dead and descendants yet to be born. Genealogy is a sacred symbol of *ie* continuity, and ancestor worship is an essential rite. Equally important is succession, and this is where the Japanese system differs from its Chinese and Korean counterparts. Succession is strictly unigenitural usually in favor of the eldest son but not excluding the options of succession by a younger son, daughter, brother, other kin, or nonkin.

The family with daughters but no sons would expect one of the daughters, usually the eldest, to stay as heiress or "*ie*-daughter" and to marry an adopted husband who "enters" her *ie*. Historically, male primogeniture was a relatively recent outcome among commoners of the Meiji Restoration that assimilated features of the upper-class succession rule. Gender-blind primogeniture had been a more widespread pattern (Suenari 1972). Ironically, the "successful" birth control of present-day Japan, causing male successors to be in short supply, seems to be contributing to a reversion to the option of succession by a daughter along with uxorilocal residence.

The imperative of succession required a marriage arranger to take precautions not to match two succors, heir and heiress. For the same reason and bound by the belief in female inferiority, a woman's worth was reduced to that of a "womb-loaner" to nurture a male seed. A wife's status, therefore, remained precarious until she proved fertile.

The spatial and temporal dimensions together placed the *ie* above and beyond individual members of a family, even beyond kinship itself. An individual was insignificant or irrelevant apart from his/her membership in the *ie* and his/her contribution to the perpetuation and enhancement of the *ie*. It was this transcendental status of the *ie* that characterized Japanese family ideology. As for the class variable, upper classes were (and are) more likely than lower classes to carry the full weight of *ie* as a transcendental ideational entity.

In the modern era from Meiji through Taisho (1868–1926) there were heroic movements to emancipate women from the structural constraint of the *ie* and Confucianism. But they were eventually swallowed by the aggressive nationalism of Showa (post-1926) centered around the emperor. Women were reeducated into being good wives and wise mothers not only for their own families but for the country (Hirota 1982; Igeta 1982; Nagahara 1982). Prewar women thus embodied a patriotic version of Confucian womanhood.

How was this structural constraint taken, accepted, or rejected by women? And how could they achieve their personal fulfillment under the circumstances? By fulfillment I mean the emotionally charged attainment of one's long-range goals or expectations. A sense of fulfillment may be double-focused. On the one hand, fulfillment may be self-focused, involving one's achievement, accomplishment, mastery, autonomy, self-respect, and the like. On the other, it may be relation-focused in that fulfillment is derived from the awareness of interdependence, support, solidarity, intimacy, love, and so forth. These two foci, granted that they may well become indistinguishable, should be kept in mind in the following analysis as a frame of reference.

The Structured Life Course and Emotional Loads

Listening to the life histories of Japanese and American women, I was struck with a cultural difference in recalling what agents steered their life courses. American women tended to recall and understand their past as a sequence of their own decisions and commitments, locating themselves at the center of each experience and relegating other people to the periphery or oblivion. Frustrating to me was the paucity of information on the society surrounding the individual. The whole life history was presented as more or less self-programmed. This does not mean that the American autobiography had held a clear notion of her life goal and adhered to it throughout. On the contrary, her life course impressed me as surprisingly precarious and hazardous, interrupted by indecision, bewilderment, drifting, and procrastination. This kind of randomness I regard as a proof (or price?) rather than a disproof of self-direction.

By contrast, a Japanese woman would typically underscore the absence of options and portray her life course as steered, sometimes forcibly, by someone else or by a surrounding group. This characteristic is best illustrated by the way in which a young woman faced her major life transition, marriage. Since premarital social segregation ruled out a woman's direct encounter with prospective mates, arranged marriage was a general rule. Even when a man and woman happened to meet without an introducer and fell in love, the proper thing for them was to call on or wait for a mediator to take action. To illustrate: when her male colleague confessed his love, a schoolteacher told him to desist, but recontact her through a proper channel.

The *miai* (an arranged meeting for introduction of the two prospective spouses) took place as a matter of course in most cases of arranged marriage. That the personal choice and emotions of a bridal candidate were not salient would be best demonstrated occasionally by the marriage of strangers that was *not* preceded by a *miai*. Some highly respectable families seemed to scorn it as too fashionable and kept their daughters blind to the appearance of their future husbands until the very day of their wedding. A woman, thus married, rationalized this by saying that she knew marriage had nothing to do with a woman's choice. (In such cases, the bridegroom also was blind, but there is evidence that grooms had opportunities to glimpse their future brides in a sort of socially contrived one-way mirror or at least to look at their pictures.) Such cases were the exception rather than the norm, but it was more common among upper-class women for whom status-matching of the two *ie* was the major consideration. Among the latter, I also found a few cases of child betrothal, another indication of total disregard of the principal's will and choice.

Marriage proposals were accepted for reasons that were extraneous to the candidate's emotions toward her husband-to-be as a person. Among the often mentioned reasons were: a debt of loyalty to the matchmaker (parent, brother,[3] uncle, other kin, employer, boss, etc.) or trust in his/her judgment; fear of offending the proposing family by rejection; the urgency of the woman to marry somebody because of her age or because her younger siblings were lining up awaiting their turn; the wish to prove her femininity (or desirability?); acceptability of the occupational status of the husband-to-be or his family. A remarkable example illustrating extraneous motives was that of a local leader of the National Defence Women's Association, a divorcee, inflamed with wartime patriotism, she agreed to remarry a widower fifteen years her senior because his daughter had just become a war widow.

It is clear that the bridal candidate's personal likes and dislikes were irrelevant to spouse selection. Arrangements were already going on, informants recalled, without any prior consulting with the candidate, so that they often found themselves already "given" away to another *ie* when first learning about what was going on. Whether this was what really happened in each instance may be questioned, but the point is that my autobiographers tended to stress the absence of any concern with personal feelings or active suppression of their subjective preferences and choices by others responsible for decisions at this most critical time of life. Interestingly, even a successful "love marriage" was in some instances described as a product of the uninvited interference by some third person or vague "surrounding" that had "trapped" the woman into a match.

With her life course seemingly programmed in advance, the Japanese woman did not have much time for random distraction. Usually, after school graduation, she would be trained in domestic skills or bridal arts[4] in anticipation of becoming "a good wife and wise mother," prepared to receive and accept a marriage proposal. On the surface, this might look like the life course of a *role robot*. Indeed, there were women who did not question the authority of their parents or other senior persons to determine their destinies, who fitted their given roles without feeling any discrepancy between their obligations and personhood. "I thought that's they way things are;" "I never thought I was not free." We find this kind of perfect match between culture and personality more in upper- than lower-class women.

But true role robots were exceptional or perhaps nonexistent. Even those who sounded like robots would betray, in an in-depth interview, an inner self which was not entirely encased by role propriety. One informant as an heiress to an *ie* was prepared to accept "anybody" who would be kind enough to move in as an adopted husband, and did marry such a "proper man." It turned out, however, that there was another man whom she could not wipe out of her mind though she knew they could not marry since he, too, was to succeed as heir. At age 77, this woman was still obsessed with this unconsummated romance, unable to stop talking about it. No such intensity of feeling was to be detected about her actual husband who had died the previous year after fifty years of peaceful marriage.

Emotional loads thus seem to accumulate through the structured life course, which is quite understandable within our common sense knowledge of human nature. In addition, it should be remembered that the tradition of Japanese culture has extolled pure emotions and sensitive feelings located in the "heart" of the individual and immune to structural control. This heart-focus is traceable back to the prehistoric, and certainly pre-Confucian oral tradition as articulated in the Kojiki and Nihongi (Pelzel 1974). Romantic love, particularly illicit love, as an expression of pure or true heart has long been an essential ingredient of literary tradition. Motoori Norinaga (1730–1801), the most notable leader of the nationalist school that arose in reaction to the resurgence of Confucianism, found the truly *Japanese* spirit in poetic sentiment, pure emotions, heart, romantic feeling, or even illicit love, which would be revealed only if unencumbered by Confucian rigidity or any other alien influence (Yoshikawa 1969). If Japanese Confucianism is of a masculine nature (as exemplified by samurai warriors), Japanese nativism, as espoused by Motoori, comes to embrace femininity as its central quality.

While having internalized Confucian ideology sometimes to the point of performing as a role robot, women could not remain unaffected by the tradition of heart-centered romanticism, and their internal discontent seemed to seek surface from time to time.

Most women complied, resigning themselves to parental decisions, but some remained resentful, resisted, or even overtly rebelled, only to relent later. It is no wonder, then, that the narratives of Japanese women were highlighted with dramatic episodes of conflict between the inner self and external role demands. (Again, class differences should be noted: such dramatization is more characteristic of lower- or middle-class women than of upper-class autobiographers.) Not infrequently the narratives were given in tears. Paradoxical as it may sound, the structured life course binding Japanese women seems more conflict-ridden, dramatic, and eventful than that of the self-directed life course described by American women.

Unless one was an heiress within one's family, a sense of marital transition was sharpened by a woman's departure from her own *ie* and entry into an unfamiliar household. After this transition, internal conflict reached a peak. Most of my Confucian-trained informants, knowing that their primary obligations were to their in-laws, tried to do their best to become accepted, especially by mothers-in-law. The latter, however, were found voracious in making demands upon new brides. The jealous mother-in-law continued to mother her son, and subtly or unsubtly interfered with the growth of intimacy between the newlyweds. The continuing triad of mother–son–daughter-in-law was stressful enough, but what made it more insufferable occasionally was a further alliance of a mother-in-law and a sister-in-law.[5]

More serious in the long run than in-law problems was the husband-wife discord. The intensity of in-law stress would lessen if the husband were firm in support of his wife, but it was more likely that rules of conjugal distance mixed with the husband's filial guilt and unresolved attachment toward his mother kept the couple apart. In-law conflict contributed to marital estrangement as the husband began to stay away from home in avoidance of getting caught in the middle.

With or without an in-law in co-residence, the most common complaint of wives was about the emotional reticence of their husbands. The well-known silence of the Japanese husband may be attributed to an overcommitment to his occupational career, leaving no energy left for conjugal conversation, and this is certainly true with "company men" of today, whether they are Confucian or not. Compounded with this was the traditional denigration of talkativeness. Especially embarrassing for a man was to express loving emotions to his wife. So, "in our entire married life, my husband has spoken not a single tender word to me." The wife would deeply appreciate a word of acknowledgment from her husband for whatever she did, but he would say nothing, no comment on the flavor of a dish she had cooked. An informant gave a detailed account of how a little gift delivered to someone in return for a small favor she had received was enthusiastically accepted and profusely thanked for. "I have never been so happy," she exclaimed, "in my fifty-five years of marriage." Her husband was a perfect provider preoccupied with his profession, making no fuss about his wife's home management, but was not inclined at all to engage in any conversation with her.

It may be unfair to attribute all this uncommunicativeness of the husband to Confucianism. More responsible may be Japaneseness, and in fact the wives labeled their mute husbands "a typical Japanese male." It is safe, however, to assume that the Confucian gender ideology—dichotomy, hierarchy, and distance—significantly contributed to the husband's aloofness or reluctance to express conjugal love. It may be also unjustifiable to blame conjugal coolness on the husband alone. As De Vos (1974, 128) observes, "on the deepest level probably many Japanese wives do not 'give' themselves completely to their husbands because the marriage has been forced on them." What cannot be denied is that emotional overloads are inherent in many a highly structured marriage.

Not that there was no affection. An initially loveless cohabitation, some informants confessed, gradually grew into a conjugal attachment of sorts, as expected of an arranged marriage. Nevertheless this attachment did not necessarily lead to emotional consummation, as revealed by several informants whose marital life was peaceful but lacked the excitement of sexual love: "I want to know what love is like"; "Ending a life without knowing love at all [as in my case] is truly abnormal, isn't it?"

Most painful in a conjugal life, informants concurred, was the husband's infidelity. The husband, emotionally as deprived as the wife, would frequently find an outlet in an extramarital liaison, and this was unbearable enough to drive his wife to contemplate or attempt suicide.[6] Just like alcoholic addiction, womanizing for some husbands was an "incurable disease," repeated over and over after promises of reform. Even at her husband's deathbed, such a wife might remain resentful and punitive.

Still, divorce did not seem a viable alternative for a number of reasons. Women had to leave children behind with the "househead" to whom they belonged. Even when custody would be obtained, there would be worries about the future social plight of fatherless children. The honor of the wife's natal family could be besmirched. There was even fear of starvation, so complete could the ostracism of a divorcee be. The only strategy available was "endurance," a practice cultivated since childhood as a feminine virtue. Under the circumstances, endurance might even take the form of aggressive masochism, as inferred from such expressions as "I persevered quietly, gritting my teeth inwardly." As a defensive strategy, the wife might become totally detached from her unfaithful spouse, cease to be jealous, and go as far as to encourage his *affaire d'amour*.

A woman, if inordinately frustrated with her husband for his marital profligacy, inadequacy as a provider, uncommunicativeness, or any other reason, might try, as did some of my informants, to regain her autonomy by stripping herself of feminine identity and presenting herself as "more like a man." No self-denigration was involved in this sexually reversed self-image since the same women were firm believers in male superiority.

In addition to these self-focused strategies, relational strategies were called for to sustain emotional equilibrium. Most likely, a woman retained or revived her bond with natal kin, with her mother in particular as long as she lived. Such ties between mother and married daughter are being prolonged and intensified today in the urban middle class (Perry 1976) and more openly displayed. (And this daughter–mother alliance is to reproduce the in-law conflict,

conflict between this team and the daughter/sister-in-law.) The prewar-generation woman, bound by her obligatory sense of exclusively belonging to her husband's *ie,* maintained her natal bonds in a more clandestine manner. Her elder brother, too, might provide her psychological support or present himself as a buffer between his kid sister and her husband or in-laws.

More indispensable for the woman's mental health was, of course, the presence of her child. As the aloofness of the Japanese husband is culturally typical, so is the Japanese mother's devotion. Unlike husband-wife intimacy, mother-child bonding is culturally sanctioned and revered. The wife's attachment to her child may be a compensatory reaction to her conjugal frustrations, but it, in turn, is likely to escalate marital estrangement. It is as if the emotional energy unexpended upon a spouse must be released upon a child or, conversely, energy being overspent on a child diminishes spousal love. This "principle of equivalence" of psychic energy (Jung, cited in Maddi 1972, 80) or what Nadel (1951, 316) calls the law of "uneven levels of mental energy" does not always hold true for the wife-husband-child triad (note, for example, the popular saying that the child cements a marriage). But as far as I could observe, and not surprisingly, there seemed to be a correlation between the woman's intensity or compulsion in her child care, and her frustrations with or indifference to her husband. A self-reflective informant admitted that her overinvolvement as a mother of two children was a selfish compensation for her discontent as a wife.

The mother-child intimacy involved the prolonged breast-feeding, co-sleeping, and co-bathing, and, as observed by Caudill and Weinstein (1974), communication through physical contact more than verbal exchange. The mother tended to feel her child to be a part of herself *(bunshin)* and typically to develop a sense of double-identity in which the child's identity was fused into her own. When the child grew into school age, the mother's devotion intensified as a helper for the child's academic success. Even though the label *kyoiku-mama* is attached to contemporary mothers who thoughtlessly would drive their children for educational achievements in response to the postwar democratization in educational opportunities, I find among my Confucian-generation informants quite a few who labeled themselves "incipient *kyoiku-mama.*" One of them sat in her son's class, much to the teacher's embarrassment, so that she would be able to tutor him with homework. (In those days there was no *juku,* the commercially run facility to supplement regular school training, which, today, is proliferating primarily to train examination candidates.) It is evident that these women enjoyed an incomparably stronger sense of vicarious achievement through their children's school performance than through their husbands' career success. It is equally clear that the woman ultimately reinforced the Confucian bond at the expense of the conjugal bond. To be noted here is the primacy of the mother-child (not necessarily limited to mother-son) bond over father-son bond. The patricentricity of Confucian ideology seems to be psychologically channeled into matricentricity. Moreover it is not filial but maternal piety that generates the matricentric version of Confucian bond.

Fulfillment in Retrospect

The life history does not end here, but continues further to disclose something else. I came to realize that a typical informant would divide her life history into two parts so that her experience of frustrations, hardship, and endurance as described so far should pertain to the earlier half only. When her recollection reached into her prime or where she stood now, her perspective was turned around. She now became aware that her earlier suffering was necessary for later gratifications and fulfillment. Probably this retrospective turnabout may account for the possible exaggeration by some autobiographers of stress and conflict they had gone through earlier.

The middle-aged housewife would witness her once domineering, incorrigible mother-in-law, if she was still alive, no longer standing in her way but, instead, transformed into a dependent child calling her "Mom," and "obeying" her; if senile, she would recognize and trust nobody but her daughter-in-law, her blood daughter and former ally having faded out of her memory; if dead, she would reemerge as a deified benefactor and mentor who had trained her so well. Nursing the long-living in-law was a burden, but the middle-aged daughter-in-law would take this opportunity to present herself as a role model for the younger generation, *her* daughter-in-law in particular.

Nor did conjugal perseverance prove totally futile. As the children achieved their independence, the wife realized the need of rebuilding her conjugal solidarity. By this time the husband who had been womanizing, gambling, drinking, violent, or otherwise abusive, was likely reformed. Having been obsessed with his occupational career, the husband now would see its ceiling, and turn around to redeem his guilt as a neglectful spouse. The woman who had thought of divorce many times was now glad that she had persevered. Even where marriage was broken irreparably and the wife welcomed widowhood, marital endurance meant something positive. It appeared as if many years of co-suffering in marriage were taken, in retrospect, as a form of accomplishment, and commiseration as a form of togetherness. (One is often told that marriage is not for pleasure or joy but to share suffering and perseverance.)

Something else is possible for a middle-aged couple. The wife, with years of experience as a mother, may come to settle into a maternal role in relation to her husband. My informants did not hesitate to liken their husbands to their eldest, and most unruly sons, and to characterize the behavior of their husbands in terms of childlike *amae*. *Amae* seemed to offer a culturally acceptable style for expressing conjugal love without threatening male dignity. In fact, *amae* in the Japanese context could be an expression of both love and male dominance.[7] It seems that the strained conjugal relationship could regain an optimal state of congeniality by converting wife and husband into mother and son, the blocked communication channel being reopened by a free flow of *amae* emotions. In other words, the woman in her prime could be a mother for all, for her aged in-laws and husband as well as her real children.[8]

However successful in the strategy of such role conversion, the wife would not take her husband for more than a substitute child. The most important source of gratification and fulfillment for a woman at a later as well as an earlier stage was her real children. The woman's fulfillment was intertwined with her son's passage of a competitive college entrance examination, his promising career in a large corporation, and with her daughter's marriage to say, an electronic engineer. With no planned parenthood, she had many children, all of whom she was proud of having brought into full adulthood, allowing each to establish his/her *ie*. Her pride might extend to the school performance of her grandchildren. All these were achievements of none other than the mother herself, just as a child's underachievement broke the mother's heart as her own failure. It was she who had made such investments in the children's future with her own labor.

If these were the mother's self-focused accomplishment, however vicarious, she was fulfilled relationally also. Her grown-up children would not forget her hardship, sacrifice, and perseverance, which were for their sake; they would feel thankful and willing to repay her in filial piety. The mother might overhear her eldest son and successor telling his wife to be nice to the old lady "because she had suffered so." She would refuse to anticipate the day when she had to come under the care of her children, above all, her daughter-in-law, but most of my informants were comfortably sure that their children would be available if and when necessary.

The interviewer came to realize that the term *filial piety* was being used with two totally different meanings. An informant would look smug when talking about her adult children's *oyakoko,* but resentful when discussing her husband's *oyakoko*. The latter is a sort of euphemism for the husband's lack of consideration for the wife. The woman was a beneficiary of one *oyakoko,* and victim of the other *oyakoko*.

The earlier suffering would thus be reevaluated as a prologue to a later fulfillment, the earlier endurance as a worthy investment which was to yield profits. Having undergone this kind of lifelong investment and payoff, older women emphasized the importance of having a hard life while young.

The Confucian gender ideology and the transcendental status of the *ie,* which had been overwhelming sources of stress and deprivation for a bride, would begin to show a brighter side some decades later as she acquired domestic expertise. If a woman was role-bound, this constraint might generate a reward: role-obligations went hand in hand with role prerogatives. The home-bound Japanese woman, while economically dependent upon her husband, was obliged *and* privileged to manage domestic affairs single-handedly. A woman engaging in real estate transactions without consulting her husband was not uncommon. Role monopoly or immunity of the Japanese housewife as a byproduct of the clear-cut role dichotomy amounted to the kind of power, mastery, and autonomy which her American sister would envy (see Vogel 1978 in this regard). The earlier struggle could now be reappraised as a necessary apprenticeship toward a matriarchical license, and the *ie* would become a sanctuary for its mistress. When her mother-in-law became incapacitated, an informant in her forties said to herself, "Here comes my kingdom at long last!"

Furthermore, the woman master of the house, when aged, would feel closer to the ancestors of the house, not her own but her husband's, as she had been *the* caretaker for the household shrine, and would anticipate "joining" them. Her final fulfillment would derive from the assurance that she was the key link between the forebears and descendants of the *ie,* not just loaning her womb but now handing down the *ie* tradition learned from her mother-in-law to her daughter-in-law. The Confucian life cycle thus came to complete itself.

Adjustment to Structural Instability

The foregoing is admittedly an oversimplified picture. Although most of my old informants described their life paths roughly in this manner, no one's life was in fact structured quite so neatly. First of all, the lifelong role investment is a risky business in that, like any other business, it is liable to bankruptcy. The husband may continue to play around without a sign of remorse against everybody's prediction, until he stops breathing. The risk is doubled and tripled if investment is made in one's children, in view of the unprecedented social and cultural changes taking place in present-day Japan. The heavily invested child may turn out to be a loser, a delinquent, or an ingrate. Popular "home-drama" series on TV which used to depict a spiteful mother-in-law, now focuses more on a heartless and greedy son and his wife who abandon his aged parents after swiping their savings. The life cycle of the older generation is unlikely to be repeated by younger generations. Hence the phenom-enon of a sandwiched generation losing to both the ascending and descending generations. My informants, though not victims of this sort, told me about their neighbors and friends as such victims; they were keenly aware of media-carried signals and warnings about the breakdown or reversal of the generational hierarchy.

The structural or Confucian programming of a life course, thus becoming dubious, must be supplemented by something closer to self-direction. Role investment should be shorter-ranged or more self-focused; the need of perseverance must be weighed against its cost; divorce should count as a feasible alternative to the risk of enduring a miserable marriage too long; life should be regarded as reversible; a woman should have options to live outside the domestic confinement including options for singlehood. In other words, non-Confucian alternatives should be legitimized.

Indeed, Japanese women today are trying to redirect their lives toward a greater self-reliance. The steady increase of postparental women employed as part-timers, in face of social critics' charges against working mothers as responsible for the delinquency, school violence, and mental disorders of contemporary children, would be inconceivable without taking into account the women's enjoyment of economic autonomy (even though they tend to justify their work in other terms). Further, an old woman's self-discipline to maintain good health hopefully until the very moment of sudden death indicates her concern for physical autonomy that does not need the nursing care of relatives. The housewife's involvement with studies and hobbies is a way of attaining emotional self-sufficiency. Interviews further revealed a special religious discipline which some women had undergone in order to achieve this-worldly Buddhahood, the purpose of which was to avoid relying upon their offspring for their postmortem salvation. They would not reject ancestor rites to be conducted for them by their descendants willingly, but not as a matter of burdensome obligation (Lebra 1979, 1984).

If the generational hierarchy is unstable or even reversed, intergenerational co-residence ceases to be an ideal for the older generation as well. Ambivalence to the idea of sharing residence with one's son and his wife is further compounded by the sharp rise in life expectancy, which protracts the period of two or three adult generations living under one roof. Some of my informants confessed that they would rather enjoy their "privacy" than feel constrained in the presence of younger co-residents. The general tendency was either to postpone such joint residence until the mother became widowed or ill, or to resort to a new architectural design for the dwelling which would enable the two generations to live together while protecting each other's privacy.

Self-reliance, freedom, and privacy require a reallocation of time and energy to one's own work, study, play, ritual, and health care. The woman's workload as a caretaker for the family must be reduced accordingly. Not surprisingly, the Japanese mother, while she claims that her purpose of life lies in her children, still welcomes being relieved of maternal chores when her children have grown up. She may extend her maternal love to her grandchildren, but to repeat caretaking for them is contrary to her desire. Also at some point of life she would like to relinquish her wifely chores as an all-around caretaker for her husband as well, despite the maternal nurturance and childish dependency that may be curative of conjugal strain at a certain stage of the marriage. Widowhood often turns out, therefore, to be embarrassingly blissful even for a happily married wife, and remarriage is viewed as a foolish repetition of servitude.

If the Confucian life cycle is thus challenged, so is the Confucian gender ideology. Without bringing out the latest feminist movement in this connection, I should say a word on women's nondomestic careers, namely full-time, lifelong professional careers. Career women are not products of women's liberation in the 1970s but rooted in a longer history even in Japan. Change has taken place only in terms of the widened repertoire of such careers. Among my older informants there were career women, though none called themselves by that fancy name, for example, a kindergarten teacher, a hairdresser, a culinary specialist, a midwife, a pharmacist, and the like. Everyone of them was more eager to talk about their professional experience than anything else, and stressed her life would not have been so fulfilling without her profession. They assumed a double career, professional and domestic, which they admitted was difficult to adhere to, but in retrospect they found their life paths most satisfactory and would not trade them for any other alternative. (In some cases the double career involved two women, the career woman and her mother, the latter being in charge of domestic chores on behalf of her professional daughter. This arrangement could be made most naturally in uxorilocal marriage with an adopted husband, and probably this explains why uxorilocally married career women looked happiest and considered themselves luckiest.) The greatest pleasure seemed to derive from their performances for the benefit of the public clientele, appreciations expressed by the latter, and professional reputations thus built up. Ideologically conservative, these women's life reviews demonstrate that the most profound fulfillment for both men and women calls for an involvement in public roles.

Conclusion

Is Confucianism dead? Is there any Confucian legacy which is viable in contemporary Japan? I think Confucianism is dying if it is taken as a set of precepts governing particular human relations such as parent and child, husband and wife, and so on. The Confucian legacy continues to influence the Japanese way of life, I believe, as an abstract, generalized ideology applicable to a wide variety of human relations. A great majority of Japanese remain Confucian, I speculate, in the sense that they perceive a life course as a cycle with a beginning and an end. Aware of this trajectory of life, they believe life has to be built up from its very beginning in order to enjoy fulfillment toward its final stage. They seem to take it for granted that strenuous effort and hardship as well as deferment of gratification at the earlier life stage is a necessary investment for a later payoff, that there will be no reward without sacrifice, that there will be no success without trying. This long-range perspective of life seems even to be intensifying in view of the increasingly longer and greater expenditure of the child's energy and family resources for educational achievement.

Enmeshed with this life view is the suppression of self-interest as a motive for action, which may be also partially attributable to the Confucian legacy. The Japanese in general, while strongly concerned with themselves, shy away from outright selfishness or egoism. When in fact egoistically motivated, they are compelled to justify their action in altruistic terms since the pursuit of self-interest has not been culturally sanctioned. The content of altruism (altruism for whom, and in what way, for instance) has changed and probably become non-Confucian, but the suppression of self-interest is persisting as a cultural style of self-presentation or in the form of intolerance of some other person who has acted selfishly. For Japanese one's self is either what is to be intermingled in empathy with another's self or what is to be internally contained and disciplined.

The Confucian gender ideology, together with the *ie,* is becoming outmoded, but the above heritage of Confucianism cannot help affecting the woman's life as well. The longer the life stage of preparation and investment for later fulfillment extends, that is, the more the period of childhood is lengthened, the greater will be the portion of a woman's life to be taken up for motherhood. And motherhood is an embodiment of selflessness. The possible result is a strengthened bond of mother and child, as foreshadowed by the phenomenon of *mazakon,* mother complex, which young women today, after marrying by their own choice, are distressed to see in their well-educated, career-promising husbands. One might speculate whether this trend will delay the death of the Confucian gender ideology or exacerbate the emotional stress for young women that we have described as inherent in Confucianism.

Notes

1. This paper was prepared while I was on sabbatical and a recipient of a Japan Studies Endowment Award, for which I wish to thank the University of Hawaii.

2. Fieldwork has been conducted four times since 1976 for different purposes under the support of the National Science Foundation, the Japan Society for the Promotion of Science, the Social Science Research Council, and the Japan Foundation. Their generosity is gratefully acknowledged.

3. In my sample, the elder brother's authority over younger sisters was striking, sometimes superseding the father's, particularly in the matter of spouse selection. The emotional ties between brother and sister were also noted.

4. The life interval between school graduation and marriage varied widely by classes: for upper- and middle-class daughters this was a time for learning bridal arts from house-calling tutors or at bridal schools; lower-class girls often became live-in maids with urban higher-class families, and while working, expected to learn good manners and domestic skills.

5. There was class difference in this regard in that the upper-class bride experienced much less hardship with her in-laws if she did at all. Many reasons are conceivable but to mention a few: because of the availability of servants, the bridal duty did not include labor; contact with parents-in-law was no more than ritual, with servants as communication mediators; mother-in-law's jealousy was weaker or nonexistent due to the emotional distance between mother and son (again it was a nurse-maid, not the mother, who actually reared the son). Furthermore, succession did not mean co-residence of two generations as automatically as in other classes: neolocal residence by a successor son and his wife was more common in the upper class.

6. Even the pre-Confucian elevation of heterosexual emotions, as cited above in association with Motoori Norinaga, seems sexually more asymmetric than might be expected. *The Tale of Genji,* for instance, which is often cited as a classical example of unhampered sexual emotionalism, reveals that free, multiple, illicit access to the opposite sex was enjoyed by men. Their wives and mistresses suffered tremendous agony, depressions, and, in some cases, psychogenic death imputed to a rival woman's witchcraft.

7. Salamon (1975) demonstrated that "male chauvinism" could be combined with conjugal love through the cultural means of *amae.* The age group she was referring to was younger than mine, but her point nonetheless is instructive.

8. I think that in Japan mother and child are the "dominant dyad," to borrow Hsu's (1971) phrase, in a generalized or figurative sense, covering a variety of relations including those between men. The boss and his subordinate in a modern company, for example, are more like mother and child than father and son in that the former is responsible for "bringing up" the latter. It seems that trustful intimacy is best built up in the mother-child configuration irrespective of gender. In this sense, I propose Japanese "paternalism" to be renamed "maternalism." And, of course, the other side of maternalism is filialism, if we may coin a word. Among Americans such intimacy seems to call for a sexual pair.

References

Caudill, William and Helen Weinstein. (1974). "Maternal Care and Infant Behavior in Japan and America." In *Japanese Culture and Behavior: Selected Readings,* ed. T. S. Lebra and W. P. Lebra. Honolulu: University of Hawaii Press. Reprinted in the 1986 revised edition.

de Beauvoir, Simone. (1972). *The Second Sex*. London: Penguin.

De Vos, George. (1974). The relation of guilt toward parents to achievement and arranged marriage among the Japanese. In *Japanese Culture and Behavior: Selected Readings* (See Caudill above for reference). Also reprinted in the 1986 revised edition.

Hirota, Masaki. (1982). "Bunmei kaika to josei kaiho-ron" (Westernization and Women's Liberation). In *Nihon josei-shi* (The History of Japanese Women), vol. 4, ed. Josei Sogo Kenkyukai. Tokyo: University of Tokyo Press.

Hsu, Francis L. K. (1971). "A Hypothesis on Kinship and Culture." In *Kinship and Culture*, ed. F. L. K. Hsu. Chicago: Aldine.

Igeta, Ryoji. (1982). "Meiji minpo to josei no kenri" (The Meiji Civil Code and Women's Rights). In *Nihon Josei-shi*, vol. 4. (See Hirota above for full reference.)

Lebra, Takie Sugiyama. (1979). "The Dilemma and Strategies of Aging among Contemporary Japanese Women." *Ethnology* 18: 337–53.

———. (1984). *Japanese Women: Constraint and Fulfillment*. Honolulu: University of Hawaii Press.

Maddi, Salvatore R. (1972). *Personality Theories: A Comparative Analysis* (rev. ed.). Homewood, IL: Dorsey Press.

Nadel, S. F. (1951). *The Foundations of Social Anthropology*. London: Cohen & West.

Nagahara, Kazuko. (1982). "Ryosai kenbo-shugi kyoiku ni okeru ie to shokugyo" (The Ie and Jobs in the Educational Policy in Favor of the Good Wife and Wise Mother). In *Nihon Josei-shi*, vol. 4. (See Hirota above for full reference.)

Pelzel, John C. (1970). "Japanese Kinship: A Comparison." In *Family and Kinship in Chinese Society*, ed. M. Freedman. Stanford, CA: Stanford University Press.

———. (1974). "Human Nature in the Japanese Myths." In *Japanese Culture and Behavior: Selected Readings*. (See Caudill above for full reference.) Reprinted in the 1986 revised edition.

Perry, Linda L. (1976). "Mothers, Wives, and Daughters in Osaka: Autonomy, Alliance and Professionalism." Ph.D. dissertation, University of Pittsburgh.

Plath, David W. (1975). The Last Confucian Sandwich: Becoming Middle Aged. In *Adult Episodes in Japan,* ed. D. W. Plath. Leiden: E. J. Brill.

Salamon, Sonya. (1975). " 'Male Chauvinism' as a Manifestation of Love in Marriage." In *Adult Episodes in Japan,* ed. D. W. Plath. Leiden: E. J. Brillo. Also reprinted in *Japanese Culture and Behavior: Selected Readings* (rev. ed., 1986), ed. T. S. Lebra and W. P. Lebra. Honolulu: University of Hawaii Press.

Suenari, Michio. (1972). "First Child Inheritance in Japan." *Ethnology* 11: 122–26.

Turner, Victor W. (1969). *The Ritual Process: Structure and Anti-Structure*. Chicago: Aldine.

Vogel, Suzanne H. (1987). "Professional Housewife: The Career of Urban Middle-Class Japanese Women." *The Japan Interpreter* 12: 16–43.

Yoshikawa, Kojiro. (1969). "Motoori Norinaga no shiso" (Motoori Norinaga's Ideas). In *Motoori Norinaga Shu* (Collected Works of Motoori Norinaga), ed. K. Yoshikawa. Tokyo: Chikuma Shobo.

IV

Contemporary Exigencies

12

Confucianism and the Chinese Family in Singapore: Continuities and Changes

Eddie C. Y. Kuo

Confucianism and the Chinese Family

As other chapters of this volume have already indicated, Confucianism forms the core of Chinese culture and the foundation of Chinese social organization. Fundamental to the ethics of Confucianism is its emphasis on the five canonical human relations, namely, sovereign-subordinate, father-son, brother-brother, husband-wife, and friend-friend. The whole system of Confucian ethics and Confucian social order can be said to be based on the family institution, which still provides the cornerstone of social organization in China. A search of relevant literature reveals that the following elements are essential as the underlying core values of the family and family relations within the Confucian system:

- Filial piety, both in terms of the respect shown to the parent, and the care, material as well as non-material, provided to the parent.
- Ancestor worship, which extends filial piety to include deceased ancestors, a "caring" for the parent (and his forefathers) in the other world.
- Family continuity (which subsumes the value of son-preference), patrilineally organized, with the primary concern that the family name shall continue and deceased ancestors shall receive offerings from living descendants.
- An extended kinship network, and extension of the core father-son axis, which forms a system of mutual help and mutual support.

It should be noted that all the above are based on filial piety, with patrilineal organization as its central value (Hsu 1968). Extended upward, patrilineage emphasizes ancestor worship, and extended downward, family continuity. Laterally, the family relations are extended to cover kin of various types, implying different sets of rights and obligations. The ideal form of the family is therefore a large extended family with five generations of family members living under the same roof, with a patriarch on top of the pyramid to take total charge. Even if family members are not living under the same roof, the kinship network extends beyond the physical boundaries of the immediate family/household. The rights and obligations among such relatives remain unchanged. In traditional China, therefore, the family is a social organization based on the principles of ascription and particularism. The values of the Confucian family fit into the functional needs of the traditional agricultural society. How have they fared among the modern Chinese who are the children of previous waves of immigrants to Singapore?

The Family and Early Chinese Immigrants

Confucianism is a dominant living philosophy that has permeated Chinese society for centuries. The values of Confucianism have been transmitted from generation to generation, not only through formal education and indoctrination, but, probably more effectively, through the "little traditions" of folklore and folk religious practices. In this sense, most Chinese can be said to some extent to be Confucian.

Early Chinese immigrants to Southeast Asia were no exception. In fact, it is evident that their thinking and behavior were deeply influenced and guided by Confucian ethical imperatives. This is clearly demonstrable from their history of migration.

First, early Chinese immigrants relied on support from kin at home for pooling resources to make the trip to the South Seas possible. Such financial and moral support from kin could be taken for granted, since members of the extended kinship system, following expected Confucian ethics, should assist each other in time of need. Such support would be reciprocated in due time. At the place of migration, the new immigrants further relied on those relatives (or "pseudo-relatives") who had arrived earlier for assistance in settling down. Such assistance often came in the forms of lodging and job placement.

Second, soon after an immigrant was settled with a job that provided some meager income, one of the first things he would do is send a remittance back to the folks at home. Such monetary contributions were expected to continue as long as the immigrant still had immediate family back at home. The amount remitted depended on the financial ability of the immigrant. There was a common belief that one had such economic obligations toward other family members and toward the place of his origin in general. There is no doubt that the more money a person could send, the more honor he would bring to himself and the family.

Third, for many successful overseas Chinese, an important part of their retirement plan was to return to China "to enjoy the rest of one's life in peace." Some who could not make it back would arrange to have their coffins delivered to China after death, so that their souls could receive proper offerings from their descendants.

From the above, it is evident that early Chinese immigrants continued to identify themselves with the family and their natal community back in China. The demonstration of filial piety and ancestor worship was directed toward the parents (and other relatives) and the ancestral hall. Such Confucian values of family orientation were among the important forces that bound the overseas Chinese to their kin in the homeland for decades, until the mid-twentieth century.

Living in a foreign land, early immigrants were unable to form their own "complete" family unit and fulfill the ideals of the Confucian family for two major demographic reasons. First, early immigrants tended to be young able-bodied males. There were simply not enough young females around for the number of young males who wanted to form families of their own.

Second, early immigrants were geographically highly mobile, moving frequently between homeland and place of new settlement. Since many still identified closely with their community of origin, it was an established pattern for many of the young "sojourners" to return "home" to make marriages, arranged by elders, with girls whom they had never before met. After a short "home visit," the young men, often unaccompanied by their newly-wed wives, once again ventured to the land of opportunity overseas to continue to seek their fortune. As such the new family, when initially formed, was more likely to be located in China rather than overseas. Only after several years and a few home visits were men considered to be sufficiently settled to plan the relocation of the family. And only the more successful ones could afford to bring their wives (and by then, often children) in order to establish their families overseas.

However, as more immigrants arrived and settled, and as the Chinese population began to grow and stabilize, new overseas Chinese communities prospered. Naturally new marriages were contracted locally and new families formed. These developments reflected the beginning of the trend of indigenization. Some forms of adaptation of the traditional Chinese family to a new immigrant environment can be noted.

One significant modification of the traditional system was the rise of the wife's status relative to that of her husband. Freedman (1957, 225–26) accounts for this change by noting that in the new immigrant community, a wedding no longer involved "uprooting" the wife from her own home community and placing her in her husband's, which was often totally alien to her and where she felt overwhelmed and powerless. In addition, in the immigrant environment the tendency toward individual family led the household, instead of the clan, to become the functional unit of the community.

Closely related to the changed status of the wife was a concomitant ascendance in the status of maternal relatives. Kinship relations and exchanges displayed increasing "bilaterality."

Further, the term "relatives" *(chin jen)* was expanded to include all those who had the same surname or were from the same village of origin. This tendency stemmed from the need to gather the resources of the small community together in order to survive in a strange and sometimes hostile environment. The same functional need also led to the development of Chinese voluntary associations such as clan and district-based associations, which to a great extent replaced the functions played by lineages in China (see Freedman 1960).

Finally, there was an erosion in the traditional kinship system as its complex rights and obligations were no longer observed in their original forms. This was partly because early immigrants tended to be of peasant background and were less knowledgeable about the details of the kinship system. The second and third generation immigrants were even less conversant with the details of such fine kin distinctions. The distinction between *tong* (patrilineal cousins) and *biao* (all other cousins), which is of primary importance in the traditional kinship system, is often ignored among contemporary Chinese in Singapore today.

From the above, it is clear that the traditional Confucian family system could not be maintained in its ideal form and had to adapt to a new social environment as Chinese immigrants began to settle in the new land.

Social Change in Contemporary Singapore

Singapore society went through a crucial phase of transformation in the 1950s. Politically, the anticolonial struggle was gaining strength, and Singapore eventually achieved self-government in 1959. Economically, the society was struggling to move toward industrialization from a preindustrial and underdeveloped economic structure. Sociologically, as a result of the war, the society had experienced serious problems of social disorganization, and was in the 1950s in the process of reorganization.

For the Chinese population in Singapore, the 1950s also represented a significant period of transition. The isolation of China since 1949 forced the overseas Chinese, in Singapore as elsewhere, to wean themselves from the "motherland" and to seek a new identity of their own and an identification with their adoptive land, which was now an independent state. Concurrently, the demographic trend also played a role in this process of indigenization. The sex ratio of the Chinese population in Singapore was by the 1950s more balanced, and the accumulated generations of Chinese permitted the development and formation of an extended kinship network in the now settled Chinese community. The Chinese in Singapore started to look inward rather than outward for their kinship ties and were ready to develop a family system modeled on the ideals of Confucianism. This potential development, however, was thwarted by the emergent social forces of industrialization, urbanization, and a series of social policies which were not totally compatible with Confucian values. The family institution had to deal with such new social forces, which generally meant further curtailment of Confucian family values.

Foremost among the social trends that affect the family institution in contemporary Singapore are urbanization, public housing, industrialization, family planning, population control, mass education, and the promotion of English.

Urbanization and Urban Renewal

The rapid population growth since the 1950s and the successful urban renewal programs in the 1960s and 1970s transformed Singapore into a highly urbanized society. This is true not only in the sense that most people in Singapore now live in densely populated new towns, but also in that urbanism has become a way of life. Urban renewal programs broke up older communities and dispersed their residents into new communities. This, made possible by the successful public housing scheme, has somewhat weakened the extended family structure. However, given the small geographical size of Singapore, such relocation did not mean severe curtailment of kinship contact and exchanges, and a new form of modified extended kinship network has emerged, as we shall discuss in more detail later.

Public Housing Policies

Confronted with the problem of serious housing shortages in the 1950s, the government set up the Housing and Development Board (HDB) in 1960, which was responsible for building low-cost flats for the needy population. The success story of HDB is by now well known (see Yeh 1975; Wong and Yeh 1985). Singapore's public housing policy has not only provided decent living conditions for the population but also effectively transformed the social and physical environment of Singapore. At present, more than 85 percent of the population live in HDB flats. As the housing units built under HDB plans were designed mainly for small families, and as the housing policies in the early years were such that they also tended to encourage the setting up of nuclear family units, it is commonly believed the housing policies of the 1960s and 1970s are at least partly responsible for the emergence of the nuclear family system in urban Singapore. The significant social implications of the public housing policies are well recognized. In recent years, the HDB has adjusted its policies to strengthen family ties. More of this will be discussed later.

Industrialization and Economic Development

Singapore launched its first industrialization programs in the early 1960s and within two decades reached a level of economic development which earned Singapore the status as one of the newly industrialized countries (NICs). The success in industrialization and economic development has brought with it the values of individualism, utilitarianism, and achievement-orientation. The functional importance of the large extended family to its members has declined, and the role relations among family members are undergoing realignment. Especially significant is the changing status of women in the family and the society. While in 1960 females formed only 12.6 percent of the total labor force, in 1980, the proportion has increased to 34.5 percent. Female labor force participation outside of the home has resulted in changes in the role and status of wife/mother as well as in the practices of child rearing and socialization. These new developments have disturbed the traditional power hierarchy and role relationships within the family and have not been conducive to the retention of Confucian values.

Family Planning and Population Policies

Singapore is a densely populated island-state, and the government gave priority to family planning programs in the 1960s and 1970s in order to reduce the fertility rate of the young republic. After twenty years of successful family planning campaigns, the fertility rate has declined from 3.6% in 1960 to 1.6% in 1984. To promote such programs, the government had to attack those traditional values which were incompatible, substituting the concept of the small family as the primary model. Of particular consequence among such debunked traditional standards were: preference for a large family, preference for sons, and dependence on children for old age care. It is obvious that many of these traditional values are essential to the Confucian family institution.

Mass Education and the Promotion of English

As part of nation-building efforts, the Singapore government has actively promoted public education, making educational opportunities available to all school-age children. Furthermore, English has been promoted as the dominant language for the multilingual population, both in schools and in society at large. Education invariably brings to the younger generation of Singaporeans new knowledge, new values, and a new perspective often unknown or unappreciated by the old. This has tended to make the young increasingly independent from their parents, leading to a decline in the authority of traditions. The promotion of English further facilitates the intrusion and acceptance of Western ideas, some of which weaken traditional values. Again, those in authority are aware of the situation and have implemented certain policies, bilingual education being one of them, to counter such trends. In recent years, moral education has been particularly emphasized. Especially relevant is the now well-known introduction of Confucian ethics as one of the options for compulsory religion courses for Secondary Three and Four students in Singapore, with the explicit aim of strengthening family ties in a rapidly modernizing society.

Confucianism and the Family in Singapore Today

From the above discussion, it is clear that in Singapore the traditional Confucian family values have been confronted with certain social forces associated with industrialization and modernization. The Chinese family, which still draws fundamental values of Confucian ethics from various sources, has to adapt to the reality of a new urban-industrial state. The crucial question is then, to what extent are the traditional Confucian values still retained under such circumstances? Or, more appropriately, in what forms has the Chinese family adapted to the new urban industrial system? We will make use of relevant empirical data to evaluate the following essential aspects of Confucian family values in Singapore today: (1) filial piety, (2) son preference, (3) ancestor worship, (4) family continuity, and (5) kinship network.

Filial Piety

The concept of filial piety, as defined in the Confucian tradition, is very difficult to operationalize for sociological research. If it is defined as absolute submissiveness and obedience of the child to the parent, there is no doubt that parental authority in the family has been seriously curtailed in an urban-industrial society like Singapore. On the other hand, if the emphasis is on love and affection shown by the child to the parent, then it may be safe to suggest that children today feel more free to express their love and affection (rather than just deference and reverence) to their parents. Many children, when asked about their views on the classical examples of the twenty-four "filial models," disapprove of the foolishness of some of these "models." Yet this need not mean that they care for and love their parents less today than children in the traditional society. They simply are different in their perception and demonstration of filiality.

One fundamental element of filial piety is of course the physical care of the aged parent, or so-called filial nurturance (see Jordan, chapter 4). (Some Confucian scholars argue that this is a rather insignificant aspect of Confucianism, but that view will not be taken up here.) We do have some empirical survey data showing that the great majority of people in Singapore consider that it is the natural duty of children to look after their aged parents.

In a 1983 survey of a national sample of 3,000 married women (Ministry of Social Affairs 1984), 93 percent of the respondents agreed that children had the responsibility to support their aged parent, and 84 percent believed that employed children should give part of their income to their parents. On the question of whether aged parents should be sent to a home for the aged, 89 percent of the sample disagreed strongly. Such are some of the indications of the national sentiment about the responsibility of the child to care for their aged parent, at least as far as the attitudes of married women are concerned.

Yet, when it comes to their evaluation of the present younger generation, as many as 78% of the sample deplored that the young today were not as filial to the elders as the respondents themselves. Even so, the majority (55%) of them still believe that their own children will support them when they are old, while another 35% cautiously replied "It depends."

Son Preference

In the traditional Chinese family system, sons are accorded special status. They continue the family name and conduct the rituals of ancestor worship ("to continue the incense smoke"). At the same time, the sons are expected, more so than the daughters, to be responsible for the support of the parents when the latter become dependent. Family planning workers in China would painfully testify to the strength of son preference among the Chinese. Yet in Singapore, as we have discussed earlier, the family planning authority has quite effectively propagated the idea that daughters are just as desirable (or undesirable, depending on one's perspective) as are sons.

Two sets of comparative data are available for an assessment of the level of son preference in Singapore. One is the Value of Children Survey (Chen, Kuo, and Chung 1982), the other is the Ethnicity and Fertility Survey (Kuo and Chiew 1985). The findings of the two Singapore surveys have been incorporated into a comparative analysis by Arnold and Kuo (1983) and Wong and Ng (1985), respectively.

Arnold and Kuo (1983) compared son-preference data from eight areas and concluded that the level of son-preference in Singapore is lower than comparable samples in Taiwan, South Korea, Thailand, and Turkey, but stronger than those in the United States, the Philippines, and Indonesia. Furthermore, the comparative analysis made by Wong and Ng (1985) reveals that the Chinese in Singapore show a rather balanced view on gender preference and are weaker in son-preference measurement than the urban Chinese in Malaysia, Thailand, the Philippines, and Indonesia. We may conclude that son preference as a traditional Confucian value is less strongly adhered to in Singapore than in areas more strongly influenced by Confucianism, such as Taiwan and Korea. Compared to the Chinese in other Southeast Asian cities, the Singaporean Chinese are also less traditional.

Ancestor Worship

According to Freedman, there are two functional components relating to the practice of ancestor worship in Chinese society (1957, 148). One relates to the collective rites which function to strengthen lineage solidarity; the other component relates to the function of memorialism. In Singapore, the collective rites traditionally performed at the lineage ancestral halls are only of marginal significance, as only a few lineages have their own ancestral halls established in Singapore. Although some clan associations do conduct annual Spring and Autumn rites at lineage ancestral halls, such rites usually involve a small number of association officials and prominent personalities of the clan. In such rites, the function of collective solidarity extends beyond that of the kinship and lineage.

The practice of ancestor worship in Singapore centers at home. Based on his fieldwork in the 1950s, Freedman (1957) reported that Chinese families here did not usually put up the wooden ancestral tablets at home. This according to Freedman, was because "the houses in which people live in the Nanyang are not genuine homes. Such houses are not . . . the milieux for the continuance, generation after generation, of the kinship line" (1957, 213). In place of wooden tablets, some houses put up pieces of red paper with names of deceased parents and their ascendants, sometimes accompanied with small photos. Such a piece of red paper, usually framed, is called *kong-ma-pai* (grandfather and grandmother tablet) and is placed beside the idols or pictures of family gods on the family altar. Regular offerings are made and incense sticks are burned at the altar, presumably to both family gods and ancestors.

Here we observe the other essential element of ancestor worship, that is, memorialism. Freedman observed that Singapore was the "field par excellence for the flourishing of memorialism" (1957, 219). As the *kong-ma-pai* displays only the names of the ancestors of the immediate past generations (usually not more than two), the symbolic meaning of commemoration is especially prominent.

In this connection, it is interesting to note a rather peculiar form of ancestor memorialism in Singapore today. Chinese newspapers regularly display "messages," paid for by the primary kin, in commemoration of the anniversary of the death of their deceased spouse, father, or sibling, who died one, two, or even thirty or forty years ago. On one average day on September 27, 1986, not less than four such messages were found on a single page of a local Chinese newspaper. Interestingly, such messages are usually "addressed" to the deceased, hence clearly reflecting the nature of memorialism of such newspaper displays. This appears to be a unique form of ancestor memorialism in Singapore and Malaysia (and perhaps other Chinese communities in Southeast Asia).

The housing situation in the 1950s when Freedman did his fieldwork in Singapore was quite different from that of today, when 85 percent of the population live in flats. Traditional family altars are not exactly compatible with the modern flat design and modern furniture which is popularly used today. Inasmuch as the design of HDB flats is typically asymmetrical, the traditional practice of having the family altar facing the main entrance has to be modified. It is understandable thus some young couples may find it "inconvenient" to have such family altars in their modern flats. More importantly, there has been an increase in the number of Chinese claiming to be of Christian faith and concomitantly a corresponding decrease of traditional Chinese religious practitioners in the past decades, as revealed by the census statistics. Thus the number of families who practice ancestor worship at home has, as expected, declined. This is supported by the findings of a small-scale survey of 400 young mothers, of whom 81 percent reported that ancestor worship was practiced by their own parents. But only 46 percent of the respondents said that they did so themselves (Tsoi and Kok 1984). A similar trend was reported regarding the ritual observation of the Ching Ming (Grave Sweeping) Festival. While 85 percent of the respondents reported that this was observed by their own parents while they were young, only 35 percent of the respondents stated that they did so themselves.

Based on the above observations it can be concluded that, as far as ancestor worship is concerned, the religious element seems to have been abased, while the commemoration component, which is more akin to the value of filial piety, continues in Singapore.

Extended Family Structure

As pointed out earlier, the majority of married women disapproved of sending aged parents to a home for the aged. It is therefore important to determine the prevalent pattern of living arrangements when a grown child forms his own family and when the parent becomes old and dependent. For the latter situation, a national survey of the aged (Ministry of Social Affairs 1983) reveals that, of the 5,538 aged persons (55 years and older) in the sample, 88% were living with their relatives, 8% with nonrelatives, and only 5% were living alone. (Many of those living alone were first generation immigrants who did not have relatives in Singapore at all.) The general pattern is that an aged parent is expected to live with one of his or her grown children.

This, however, does not mean that young Singaporeans do not aspire to form their own households independent of their parents after marriage. A study of 1,000 youths (Saw and Wong 1981, 42) reveals that there is a high degree of variability in attitude about whether a couple should set up an independent household immediately upon marriage. The answers were: 37.6% agree, 31.4% disagree, and 30.8% saying "It depends." If forming an extended family can be said to be an ideal of the Confucian family, what we find from the above statistics is that the younger generation is divided in its view on this matter. However, the Chinese youths in the sample, compared with those of the Malays and Indians, appear to be more "Confucian," that is, more likely to object to setting up independent households. At the same time, they also seem to be more confused. As statistics show (table 12.1), these younger Chinese had the highest percentage of disapproval for setting up independent households after marriage. They also show the highest percentage giving inconclusive ("others") answers.

As far as living arrangements in Singapore are concerned, there appear to be stages of joining and separating throughout the family life cycle. Many newlyweds stay with the husband's parents (a smaller percentage with the wife's parents) for a while, simply because many of them cannot afford to have a flat of their own until they are financially better established. The young couple stay with the parents until they have obtained an HDB flat after a

Table 12.1
Percentage Agreement toward Forming an Independent
Household Immediately after Marriage

Ethnicity	Agree	Disagree	Others
Chinese	31.6%	34.9%	33.5%
Malay	57.0%	21.5%	21.5%
Indian	40.2%	27.6%	32.2%

Source: Saw and Wong 1981, 42.

period of waiting, or until the wife is pregnant and the parental home becomes too crowded with the coming of the third generation. (We also notice that the pregnancy and the obtaining of the flat are often synchronized.) The young couple then move out and form a separate household. Yet the relations between the married children and their parents generally remain very close. The functional exchanges in the forms of meal preparation (and sharing), baby sitting and care, and joint recreational activities, continue to be frequent and regular, and indeed institutionalized. (More on this type of modified extended family contact will be discussed later.) When the parents are retired, reaching the late stage of their life cycle, or almost certainly when one of the parents has passed away, it is a common practice for the parent(s) to join and live with one of the married children. Hence, a three-generation family may be formed when the parent becomes elderly. It is significant that, while there seems to be a preference for (or expectation of) living with a son, cases of those living with a daughter appear to be on the increase.

The predominant family form in Singapore is the nuclear family. This does not necessarily mean the large extended family has broken down. Nor is there any evidence that the pattern of the family structure observed in Singapore today is a departure from that of traditional China. Many anthropologists and sociologists have argued that the large extended family might have been an ideal rather than reality in traditional China (see Lang 1946; Freedman 1958; Levy 1968; Cohen 1975; and Wolf 1982). In fact, I have earlier estimated that between 60 and 65 percent of the households in Singapore today are of nuclear family form. This ranks Singapore as a city less dominated by this family form than other contemporary Chinese cities, such as Tianjin, Beijing, Hong Kong, or Taipei (Kuo 1985).

Kinship Network

The formation of nuclear families independent of the parental home does not diminish the importance of the contact and exchange between the parents and married children. Married children living away from the parental home continue to maintain frequent and intimate contact with parents and are aided in this by the small geographical size and the convenience of communication and transportation in this island-state. Since most young men and women are working, young couples often "return" to the parental home almost daily to have dinner together, prepared by the mother (mother-in-law). After children are born, grandparents again become ideal caregivers. In many cases, the baby stays with grandparents regularly, only to be taken "home" by parents on the weekend.

In a 1975 exploratory study (n = 168 couples) on kin contact in urban Singapore, Wong and Kuo (1979) found that kin identified as most intimate were invariably primary kin, that is, parents, children, and siblings. As many as 20 percent of the sample reported that they met their close relatives daily; another 40 percent, at least once a week. Ho (1982) confirmed these findings in a later study of visiting patterns between married children and parents.

In a recent national survey of married women (Ministry of Social Affairs 1984), 37% of the respondents replied that they visited their relatives "very often," and another 34% did so "sometimes." Moreover, the survey reveals that as many as 53% of the sample have relatives living "nearby." As for the rest who did not have relatives living nearby, 80% of them indicated that they "wished" they did. Also, the National Senior Citizen survey, quoted earlier, indicated that, among those who had children living apart from them, 13.7% received daily visits and another 46% received weekly visits from their children (Ministry of Social Affairs 1983, 48).

In this connection, it may be of interest to note that the HDB has in recent years implemented several policies to encourage the primary kin to live together or at least to live nearby in order to strengthen family ties (see Chong, Tham, and Shium 1985, 252–57). Of these policies, two are most important. The first is called "Multi-Tier Family Housing Scheme," which gives priority to joint applications involving married children and parents. The policy, implemented in 1982, was reported to be only of moderate success. The other is called "Joint Balloting Scheme," which is to allow joint balloting for applicants who are related to each other (such as parent and child, or siblings), so that such related families can live next door to each other or at least in the same block or neighboring blocks. This scheme was first implemented in 1978 and is reported to be quite successful. This is another indication that the modified extended family arrangement (also called the confederated form), instead of the extended three-tier type, may be the ideal form in an urban-industrial society. As Litwak puts it, such a family form has "all the virtue of the nuclear family, with much in the way of resources" (1970, 388).

This is clearly attested to by an in-depth study conducted by HDB in 1982 on a small sample of joint balloting cases with families of two generations living next door to each other. The researchers found that the elderly members of these families, living close to their children, enjoyed not only financial support but also emotional and psychological stability. On their part, they contributed to childcare while the younger parents continued to pursue their careers. Moreover, as there were more members in the joint household, daily domestic work was shared by more persons. These are advantages commonly attributed to extended families. Yet as the two generations did not live in the same housing unit, "these advantages were enjoyed without crowding and serious family conflicts because each family could retire to the privacy of their own flats" (Chong, Tham, and Shium 1985, 253–54).

Conclusion

Certain aspects of Confucian family values appear to be incompatible with industrialization. In an industrial society, achievement is recognized far more than ascription and birth. Consequently, the family is no longer a status-conferer and has less to offer an individual in exchange for his submission. The value structure of the Confucian family institution is more likely to lead to nepotism, since recognition and preferential treatment rely on kinship ties rather than on considerations of performance and competence. Nepotism, as we know, is not compatible with a modern bureaucratic structure.

Similarly, industrialization and urbanization are incompatible with the maintenance of Confucian family traditions. Geographical and social mobility tend to weaken kinship ties. The new economic structure also creates jobs for women and the young. The patriarchal power structure of the Confucian family is often challenged. The family role relationships are becoming symmetrical and reciprocal and are moving away from being authoritarian and obligatory. The particularistic nature of the kinship-oriented social organization has to give way to the universalistic nature of modern industrial society and the nation-state. Under such circumstances, the traditional Confucian family has to adapt to the emergent social forces in an urban-industrial social system.

In this chapter, we have observed that Confucian family traditions have made some adaptations in contemporary Singapore. We can find both continuities and changes in the family institution as Singapore undergoes social transformation. As such, this is a testing time for traditional values, as only those which are compatible with modern society will survive to form part of the ongoing stock of traditions.

Of the fundamental Confucian ethics, we find the value of filial piety still strongly held among the Chinese of Singapore. The concept, however, has apparently been given new interpretations, and its forms of expression and demonstration have also changed. The obligation to support the aged parent remains one traditional value strongly adhered to in Singapore and sanctioned by the community.

Many sociologists and anthropologists now believe that the large extended family was never more than an ideal in China and that the nuclear type has been dominant in number. In Singapore, we have observed that, for the general public, the large extended family has ceased to be even an ideal form although it is now officially encouraged and indeed supported by policies in public housing and taxation. The preferred arrangement appears to be of the confederate type with married children (and siblings) living separately but maintaining regular functional contact with parents (and siblings). This form of urban kinship network is particularly prevalent in Singapore partly due to the convenience in communication and transportation and partly due to the conscious policy design of the public housing authority. This is apparently a very successful form of adaption to retain traditional kinship ties and functional exchanges in an urban-industrial environment. An aged dependent parent, however, is expected to live with one of his or her children.

The values of son preference and family continuity seem to have been seriously weakened as a result of the success of the national family planning program in Singapore. Such value changes are consistent with the shift from a patriarchal family system to one that is now characterized by egalitarianism and companionship. As daughters are now valued and treated (relatively) equally to sons, they begin to share with their brothers the duty of contributing to the welfare and care of the parents. This pattern also reflects the trend in kinship relations, which increasingly show more features of bilaterality. While the nuclear family form predominates, contacts and exchanges among kin continue to perform important functions in modern Singapore. One major form of adaptation identified in this respect is that the kinship contact and exchange now imply a stronger element of voluntarism, with the possible exception of the obligatory duties to the parents. People in modern urban-industrial society constantly encounter secondary relations and are in need of emotional support from the primary group. Other than the nuclear family, which serves the important functions of tension reduction and emotional support, kinship relations also provide a basis for selectively building up such primary contacts. The voluntary nature makes kinship ties in modern industrial society similar to those of friendship, yet kinship relations appear to be more secure, as they usually are in other societies.

Finally, the practice of ancestor worship has also gone through some modifications. There has been a decline in the function of collective lineage solidarity, while the memorialism element of ancestor worship is still retained. On the other hand, the religious dimension of ancestor worship has apparently been weakened, but ancestor worship as a form of commemoration seems to be in common practice.

In the above discussion of the Singapore experience, we find that, paradoxically, tradition does play a role in cultural change. In the process of social change, traditional elements do not remain static, but are often adapted to the new social conditions and given new interpretations and new forms of expression and demonstration. Cultural change, therefore, implies cultural continuities.

In our analysis of the family institution in contemporary Singapore, we find that some elements of Confucianism are retained and in fact have to some extent become compatible with the urban-industrial system. At the same time, the urban-industrial social order in Singapore is also subject to the influence of Confucianism. Culture is seen here as a dynamic organism, and tradition and modernity should eventually find a balance to reach a synthesis.

In this connection, it is not entirely irrelevant to discuss Singapore's present policy to reintroduce Confucian ethics in the school curriculum. I call this a "reintroduction" because I believe the values represented by the Confucian teaching have long been a part of the traditional values shared by most Chinese as well as a part of the "hidden" curriculum in the Chinese educational system. The design of the Confucian ethics course indeed involves a reinterpretation of such values in an urban-industrial society. The mission of the scholar consultants who have been invited to help to design the course is tantamount to designing a new moral order from a rich but partly obsolete tradition. This new moral order must be made compatible with the workings of a modern society, and conducive to the attainment of its objectives.

This is a great experiment being unfolded before us. It is too early to project the outcome of the experiment. What should be borne in mind is that, as in other cases of social planning, the real success will come only when people, the Chinese at least, in Singapore make Confucian ethics a part of their thinking, their values, and their life, rather than a mere additional subject in school. The real test therefore rests within the family. Eventually, whether the reinterpreted moral system will take root in this urban-industrial society and become a part of the "new tradition" will depend on the cultural and structural compatibility between such selectively reinterpreted Confucian ethics and the rest of the social and cultural system. Confucian ethics simply cannot survive in isolation, totally irrelevant to the experience in real life. In the end, what needs to be designed is not merely a moral order, but also a new order of complementarity between family, economy, polity, and culture. A new synthesis, hopefully, will emerge, representing a fusion of tradition and modernity.

References

Arnold, Fred and Eddie C. Y. Kuo. (1984). "The Value of Daughters and Sons: A Study of the Gender Preferences of Parents." *Journal of Comparative Family Studies* 15.2: 229–318.

Chen, Peter, Eddie C. Y. Kuo, and Betty Chung. (1982). *Dilemma of Parenthood: A Study of the Value of Children in Singapore.* Hong Kong: Maruzen Asia.

Chong, Kim Chang, Tham Yew Fang and Shium Soon Kong. (1985). "Housing Schemes: Policies and Procedures." In *Housing a Nation,* ed. Wong and Yeh.

Cohen, Myron. (1976). *House United House Divided.* (New York: Columbia University Press).

Freedman, Maurice. (1957). *Chinese Family and Marriage in Singapore.* Colonial Research Studies, no. 20. London: Colonial Office.

Freedman, Maurice. (1960). "Immigrants and Associations: Chinese in Nineteenth-Century Singapore." *Comparative Studies in Society and History* 3.1: 25–48.

Ho, Kong Chong. (1982). "Networks of Interpersonal Relations: A Comparative Study of Friendship, Kinship, and Neighbourhood Relations." Unpublished master's thesis, National University of Singapore.

Hsu, Francis L. K. (1968). Chinese Kinship and Chinese Behavior. In *China's Heritage and the Communist Political System,* ed. Ping-ti Ho and Tang Tsou. Chicago: University of Chicago Press.

Kuo, Eddie C.Y. (1985). "Familism and Social Change: The Case of the Chinese Family in Singapore" (In Chinese). Paper presented at the Second International Conference on "Modernization and Chinese Culture," November 4–8, 1985, Hong Kong.

Kuo, Eddie C. Y. and Seen Kong Chiew. (1984). *Ethnicity and Fertility in Singapore.* Singapore: Institute of Southeast Asian Studies.

Kuo, Eddie C.Y. and Aline K. Wong, eds. (1979). *The Contemporary Family in Singapore.* Singapore: Singapore University Press.

Lang, Olga. (1946). *Chinese Family and Society.* New Haven, CT: Yale University Press.

Levy, Marion. (1949). *The Family Revolution in Modern China.* Cambridge, MA: Harvard University Press.

Litwak, Eugene. (1970). "Technological Innovation and Ideal Forms of Family Structure in an Industrial Democratic Society." In *Families in East and West,* ed. Reuben Hill and Rene König. Paris: Mouton.

Ministry of Social Affairs, Singapore. (1983). *Report on the National Survey of Senior Citizens.* Singapore: Author.

Ministry of Social Affairs, Singapore. (1984). *Report on National Survey of Married Women: Their Role in the Family and Society.* Singapore: Author.

Saw, Swee Hock and Aline K. Wong. (1981). *Youths in Singapore.* Singapore: Singapore University Press.

Tsoi, W. F. and L. P. Kok. (1984). "Chinese Culture and Child Rearing Practice." Paper presented at the Conference on "Child Socialization and Mental Health: The Case of Chinese Culture," August 6–15, 1984, Honolulu, Hawaii.

Wong, Aline K. and Eddie C.Y. Kuo. (1979). "Urban Kinship Network in Singapore." In *The Contemporary Family in Singapore,* ed. Kuo and Wong.

Wong, Aline K. and Shui Meng Ng. (1985). *Ethnicity and Fertility in Southeast Asia: A Comparative Analysis.* Singapore: Institute of Southeast Asian Studies.

Wong, Aline K. and Stephen H. K. Yeh, eds. (1985). *Housing a Nation: 25 Years of Public Housing in Singapore.* Singapore: Maruzen Asia.

Yeh, Stephen H. K., ed. (1975). *Public Housing in Singapore: A Multi-Disciplinary Study.* Singapore: Singapore University Press.

13

Confucian Tradition in the Contemporary Korean Family

Kwang Kyu Lee

When the Chosön or Yi dynasty (1593–1910) adopted Neo-Confucianism as the state religion of Korea, it became more than a political ideology. It became the moral philosophy that ruled the basic principles of education, and a family religion which emphasized ancestor worship.

From the beginning of the dynasty, Confucian philosophy was made the standard through which the upper class monopolized the bureaucratic world; one learned the classics of Confucianism in order to pass state examinations and receive promotion up the bureaucratic ladder. Official life became an important aspect of Confucian practice. During the subsequent 500-year history of the dynasty, Confucianism penetrated into the life of the middle class and set lineage practices even among the lower classes. It can therefore be said that Korea became a paradigm of East Asian Confucianism.

During the last several decades, Korea has undergone a remarkably rapid social change due to accelerated processes of industrialization and modernization. Korea is fast becoming a modern nation. Although this is particularly observable in metropolitan centers, it is increasingly evident in rural areas. Thus one rarely sees traditional houses with straw roofs, and traditional household utensils are now only used as ornaments or decorations.

Modern modes of behavior, which exist side by side with remaining traditions, have produced variations in the behavior of Koreans. In a modern commercial company, for example, the relationship between employers and employees still relies on a traditional vertical relationship between authority and subordinate. However, in rural communities members of the younger generation do not use the traditional honorific form of speech directed toward elders that once was required and was maintained by severe social sanctions. These mixtures of traditional and modern modes of behavior reflect conflicts at the level of ideology and values as well.

In the early phases of recent modernization, traditional Confucianism was criticized as a hindrance and obstruction to change. Since Confucianism emphasizes the vertical structure of relationships, especially the obedience of younger to elder and the subordination of inferiors to the authority of superiors, it was considered authoritarian and opposed to the horizontal structure of a democratic society. Rather than being congenial to a democratic emphasis on individual freedom and equality, Confucianism was considered to manifest several social disfunctional aspects, such as unconditional obedience and nepotism in political and economic networking.

However, some now argue that aspects of Confucian behavior and attitudes have actually contributed to modernization, such as inducing a high-achievement motivation, a high valuation placed on education, a nonconfrontational approach for the sake of the group, and personal sacrifice for the prosperity of the family. Personal integrity in social relationships and an attendant atmosphere of trust has been connected with past Confucian scholars who valued honest poverty rather than immoral compromise. The spirit of the Confucian scholar was symbolized by four plants: pine, bamboo, orchid, and chrysanthemum representing devotion, honor, chastity, and honesty. This spirit could be labeled "Confucian puritanism." Just as the Christian ethics of Protestant puritanism formed the backbone of the development of capitalistic society in the West according to Weber, it can be argued that some form of "Confucian puritanism" provides the basic ethics of modernization in Korea, as well as the other countries of East Asia.

In looking into the essence of this "Confucian puritanism" and its function in modernization, I have selected the family as my unit of analysis. According to Confucian teaching, the family is the basic unit of society. Filial piety is in its final form connected with loyalty to the state. The family unit carries out the social education of children, initially by performing family rituals in a *proper* way. The family remains the locus wherein moral philosophy is to be practiced in daily behavior. In a word, Confucianism is a family-oriented religion, philosophy, and social ideology governing behavior from birth to death.

This contention will become apparent as I deal first with the traditional family in the past, its development and characteristics. I then examine changing aspects of the family in modern society with special emphasis on modern family life in an urban setting. Finally I shall interpret various attitudes and behavior of contemporary Koreans as manifestations of "Confucian puritanism."

The Traditional Family

Confucianism was first adopted by the elite of the three kingdoms of Korea in the fifth century A.D. All three states established schools for Confucian education, and the teachings of Confucius became the main focus of state examinations for officials in the government. Confucianism became the basis for moral thought and ethics among the elite from among whom government officials were drawn during the Three Kingdoms period and the subsequent Koryo dynasty. Confucian thought was emulated by the other classes of society as well, but, major social values and norms adopted by the general population during these epochs were based more on Buddhism and the teachings of Buddhist monks.

During the Chosön or Yi dynasty, from A.D. 1600 to 1910, Confucian teachings became increasingly emphasized as the major principles upon which the nation was based, and as the accepted state religion. To better promote Confucianist control, Buddhist influences were actively suppressed as a continuing policy of the state. The Yi dynasty fully embraced the Neo-Confucianism of Chu-tze, (Chu Hsi) of Sung dynasty China.

Emphasizing family solidarity and lineage, premodern agriculturally based Confucianism supported the family as the basic unit of production and consumption. Since production in agriculture depended totally on the manpower of the family, parents wanted to have many children. To afford survival a family had to supply and manufacture all its material needs, including food, shelter, and clothing.

Merchants and artisans were ranked below farmers in status hierarchy. In all families however, lineage was to be honored. The family was the most important place for the young to learn proper attitudes and prescribed behavior. Even among poor Korean farmers, as part of their inheritance, children were taught honorific language and obedience to elders from early childhood. As they grew there was much more to be learned. Thus the son was taught to use the highest honorific terminology in addressing his father, to never stand higher than his father, to enter a room after his father, and never smoke or drink in front of him. There was a saying that father is a stern parent and mother is benevolent. The basic relationship was between father and son and it established the standard for all other relationships among family members. "Filial piety" stressed the repayment by offspring for parental love, upbringing, and training.

There were many ways in which a son embodied filial piety. Supporting old parents with good food and warm clothes was a primary duty. Providing comfort and ease of mind was even more important than material benefits. Keeping one's own body in good health and clean was an expression of filial piety because the body is a gift from parents. Becoming an honorable man demonstrated filial piety because it promoted family honor. There was no limit to fulfilling filial obligation. "Parental benevolences are deeper than any sea and higher than any mountain."

Ideally, filial piety promoted friendly relationships among siblings, it enforced solidarity among all family members, and it demanded the sacrifice of oneself for the family unit. For a man, "filial piety" was connected with loyalty to lord and state. For a woman, it was connected with being a wise mother and good wife.

As the focal point of family life the Korean father had three major rights and obligations: representing the family in society, supervising family members, and controlling family property. The first son not only had the right but the obligation to perform ancestor worship. The traditional Korean family was a typical patriarchy.

The family in the past was characterized by a strict division of labor and the separation of roles between men and women. In the social sense of rights and obligations, women occupied a subordinated position. Nevertheless, it was she who controlled the consumption and the allocation of resources within the family and household. For example, the buildings and farm land belonged to the family head, but the housewife managed the keys for the rice box and storage rooms. Generally, the "inside" of the house was within the jurisdiction of the housewife and the "outside" was the responsibility of the male family head. Therefore, the husband was called the "outside master" while the wife was called the "inside master." This division of jurisdiction was also symbolized by the assignment of space in the home. A Korean rural house still usually has two separate buildings, one considered "inside" and one "outside." The "inside" building is occupied by the wife, and the husband lives in the "outside" building. The traditional house shape often is some variant of the form of two "L"s surrounding a courtyard.

In the traditional family there were important rules based on established principles which governed the relationship between family members: first, the hierarchy of elder over younger, and second, segregation by sex. This has also been the basic order of the larger society in most of its traditional functions and ceremonies.

Confucianism during the Yi dynasty emphasized the proper performance of rites of passage as prescribed in the book *Four Rites* by Chu-tze. These rites dealt with initiations, marriages, funerals, and ancestral ceremonies. Previous to the Yi dynasty rites of passage usually had different characteristics based on locality and were slightly different for each family in accord with individual family tradition. However, the Yi administrators stringently emphasized the rites of passage prescribed by Chu-tze, and locals who did not follow the exact procedures as defined in the book were punished according to state law. Since such rites were to be carried out within the family, the family was considered the center for Confucian learning. Rites of passage for both sexes explicitly drew attention to Confucian ethical practices in accord with interpersonal role expectations and moral philosophy. Attendance at initiation ceremonies and other rites were considered sources of education and moral cultivation for the people.

Among the four rites, ritual service honoring ancestors was considered the most important. One had to perform three different kinds of ancestral ritual—one on commemoration day, another on holidays, and a third in front of the ancestors' graves once a year. Ritual procedure was precisely specified; for example there was a fixed order for different dishes on the table, food was presented in a fixed place, and one was supposed to perform the rites at a fixed time and in the proper manner as set forth by the ritual book.

In *yangban* or upper-class households, there was a shrine to the ancestors behind the main building. The ancestral tablets of four generations were kept therein by the eldest son who was the direct lineage descendant. The poor kept their tablets on a shelf in a room. The direct lineal male descendant performed the ritual services for his ancestors on commemoration day at midnight. Ancestor worship was not only a simple ritual of commemoration, but also a belief in ancestor spirits who protected their offspring, rewarding them for the proper performance of the services. In effect, ancestors became family gods who assured the prosperity and continuity of the family.

In the Korean family system there are two different types of families formed with the marriage of the sons. The main family, continued by the eldest son, has a higher social status than the branch families, formed by younger brothers. Performance of ritual services is one of the most important rights and privileges possessed by the direct lineal descendant, the first-born. The second-born and younger sons leave the parents' house after marriage to establish their branch families. The eldest son and his wife must live with the parents, taking care of them as they grow older and performing the ritual services for the ancestors who dwell in the family shrine. Above all, the house of the main family is kept as the dwelling of the ancestors and the place of ritual performance.

There are no ancestors in the branch family until the death of the first generation. The head of the branch family, however, has an obligation to continue to participate in the ritual service of the ancestors held in the main family's house. Although the branch family maintains a household that is economically and socially independent from the main family, it is connected to the main family through the ritual service of the ancestors, which makes for a form of moral dependency. This kind of dependent relationship is maintained until the descendants are three generations removed from the initial family head. The division of these patrilineal relatives is called the "small lineage" or *so-jong* and this division is marked by the extension of kinship terminology and mourning obligations. When the families of the small lineage live together in a communal neighborhood there develops the atmosphere of a large family, helping and influencing each other. This is the reason why the term "extended family" is applied in such situations though such arrangements often consist of a stem family and several surrounding nuclear families.

Beyond the fourth generation, the ritual service for ancestors was performed only once a year at the graveyard. To perpetuate this ritual service, kinsmen established lineage organizations, *mun-jung*. One lineage could organize many lineage organizations depending on their economic capacities, the locality, and the number of prominent ancestors who could be honored as important persons.

One lineage could also have many sublineages. The most important concern of a lineage organization was its communal property, which included farm land for ritual services, a graveyard with stone monuments, and a ritual shrine. The lineage organization usually brought together a general assembly serving as a legislative body headed by a selected individual acting in an executive capacity for the organization. Besides this head, in each instance there was the direct lineal descendant who actually performed the ritual service at the grave.

The most important social organization during the entire Yi dynasty was the local lineage organization and its concern with ancestor worship. In this sense, ancestor worship in traditional Korean society was not only a religion but a series of major social activities giving rhythm to the calendar year. The lineage organization was an extension of the cyclical activities of the basic family units.

For economic as well as religious reasons, married brothers tended to live together in the same vicinity. They inherited the common property of the father and the neighborhood was composed of brothers or patrilineal cousins. Such arrangements easily developed into a village composed of one lineage. Even when not a lineage village, the typical village in the traditional society had the characteristics of a lineage community because several generations lived together. Neighbors helped each other in order to maintain harmony and solidarity. In the case of large family affairs such as marriages and funerals, the villagers came together periodically to help one another. Under these circumstances, even though each family had separate stem families or was a simple conjugal family, they lived as an extended family which took on the crucial additional function of supervising individual moral and ethical behavior.

Characteristics of the Modern Family

Korea has undergone tremendous change within the last few decades. Looking only at political events, after liberation from Japanese colonial rule in 1945 it has suffered the Korean War and three *coup d'états* within three decades.

The three-year-long war between South and North Korea in the early 1950s destroyed whatever industry existed throughout the peninsula. The result of the Korean War was not only the destruction of production and widespread famine, but also the deepening of antagonism between South and North and abrupt changes in values and ideology. The former concept of four social classes with *yangban* at the top disappeared, and much of the authority of elders, including that of the family head, weakened during the years of difficulty and upheaval.

In the South these changes were further exacerbated by the rapid industrialization of the 1960s. Under the motto of "rehabilitation for the country," the government undertook an ambitious economic development plan. Heavy industries were established in urban areas, and new urban and industrial centers were founded. The most direct impact of industrialization was the great migration from rural to urban centers. The population ratio of urban to rural areas was 3:7 immediately after World War II; within forty years, according to the census of 1983, the ratio of urban to rural became 7:3. The ratio is still increasing year by year.

After completing military service young men did not want to go back to a monotonous life in the countryside, instead they sought jobs in the cities. More recently, students from rural areas seek jobs in urban areas after finishing their schooling. Young women, instead of becoming farm brides, also began to emigrate to the cities where they can find employment. As a result of the exodus of younger people, there are now virtually no families in rural areas who do not have a departed member; indeed there are almost no families in which all members live together. Today the most typical family is composed of the older grandparents, mother, and younger children. Although sons who left home and succeeded in business invite their parents to live with them, the older parents are rarely able to adjust to urban life and instead return to the countryside, where they have their friends, their own business, or their land. Until the elderly couple is in ill health, they live independently. Only when one of them dies, does the remaining parent go to the son's house to live.

As a result of this migratory pattern, there are virtually no farm hands left in rural areas, and as a result the older people must work even longer and harder in the fields than in earlier times, even though new technologies for rice cultivation have been developed, and new types of farm machines are now widely used. Inasmuch as the younger generations are better educated and earn more money than their elders, many traditional practices have lost their meaning. As a result, the older people have been unable to maintain their prestige and authority. The communal ethics of older days have faded, and even in the rural areas the lineage organization of the traditional society has lost its base of support.

Even greater changes have occurred within urban families. Most have migrated from diverse rural regions. The heterogeneity of the population and the general short history of the expanding urban neighborhoods make it difficult to form integrated or interacting urban communities. Even though there are large compounds of apartments and houses, there are no true networks forming in present-day urban culture which would regulate community life and provide the supervision necessary to guide the activities of young people. Those young who migrate to the cities are away from the moral supervision of their parents and their relatives in the country. They are also too busy with their own activities to maintain intimate contact with any of their relatives who might live in the same city.

One of the most important changes in urban family life is the limited physical space found in apartments and houses. Unlike rural homes, there is no "authority space" for the family head, nor is there a separate room for the wife. Given those conditions, it is extremely difficult to recreate the traditional way of living and its rules of propriety. As a result, the typical family in the city is conjugal. Even the older people in urban areas tend not to live with their married sons because of the difficulty in maintaining social etiquette with daughters-in-law within a restricted living space. The daughter-in-law would feel even more constrained by the need to maintain deferences with no place to remove herself. The urban family, therefore, tends to become a nuclear family. Only when one parent has died does the son bring the surviving parent into his home and form a stem family.

There is a clear trend in the urban family toward a decline in size. People in urban areas are mainly white-collar or blue-collar workers. Limited incomes, the long period of offspring dependency, and the high costs of education discourage large families. Also the government encourages family planning, thus resulting in fewer children.

Another characteristic of the urban family is its isolation from neighbors. Even though the houses in urban settings are located very close together, people remain isolated from each other. Urban families tend to be far more mobile than rural families because of changes in type and place of employment. Also, people in cities have little time to make contact with their neighbors. The result is that urban families have many physical neighbors, but very few social neighbors.

These characteristic tendencies of new families—namely, declining size, increase in nuclear families, and the isolation of the family—are a new phenomenon not only found in urban areas but, with increased frequency, in rural communities as well. In the country it is now common to find a large house occupied by only one or two older persons. Until the 1970s, families with one or two inhabitants were very rare (i.e., 5 percent of total households in a village). Today, roughly 15 percent of rural households are composed of one or two persons. The community in rural areas has thus lost its traditional atmosphere, its *Gemeinschaft* feeling.

The New Family Lifestyle

Not only has the outward form of the family undergone great changes during modernization, but so too has the covert domestic side of family life. In urban areas, the husband dedicates himself primarily to his work. As the breadwinner, he spends most of his time and energy outside the house. Even after official working hours, he must join gatherings of his colleagues to maintain harmonious and close relationships with them. He leaves home early in the morning and comes back late at night. He has little time to fulfill his role as family head, and he cannot carry out his role as husband and father. The result is a "fatherless" complex. There is no recourse but for the housewife to take over the role of family head. She must participate in community meetings and deal with administrative offices, banks, and schools, in addition to being responsible for the maintenance of the household. She must take care of every small emergency in the household. She manages the property and makes the daily decisions. As a result, the children come to depend almost entirely on the mother.

In the past, the father was called the "solemn" parent and the mother, the "benevolent" parent. But children tend to experience just the opposite today. The mother is no longer seen as a benevolent parent. The care of the children includes supervision, education, and even punishment. The father has virtually no time to spend with his children. When he does have an opportunity, he no longer disciplines them as he did in the past, but just plays with them. Above all, the father in the urban family has lost his position of authority except when it is useful for the mother to call upon him symbolically to back up her wishes.

In the past, there were unquestioned traditional ways to raise children, but today young mothers with modern education do not wish to keep to the traditional ways of the past, and yet have formed no coherent idea of the "modern" approach. Children in the modern world are growing up in a society which is very different from that of the past. What is to be done? It can be readily observed that there are two extremely different types of parental approaches: one type is characterized by overprotection of the child, and the other by excessive permissiveness. In the former case, middle-class mothers with a high level of education devote themselves exclusively to their children. They are given the best food and clothes from early childhood onward. They are sent to expensive kindergartens and in addition to the local schools, they are sent to private supplementary schools for music, painting, and gymnastics. At times such a mother intervenes in school activities or problems and even intrudes into the selection of friends. In such cases, the children are, in effect, the focus of their mothers' personal ambitions, and many children do fulfill the

mother's expectations. Indeed, some are made neurotic by the pressures exerted upon them. Conversely, parents who give children too much freedom are
mainly to be found among poorer families. These mothers tend to have little
education and because they must work long hours, they have little time to
devote to their children. Children in such cases must learn for themselves.
Often they tend to grow up in an intellectually impoverished home environment, one not conducive to higher education or occupational advancement.
Under these circumstances, children's reactions differ. Some develop good
work habits and become productive; others frequently develop behavioral
problems.

One of the interesting characteristics of the modern Korean family,
urban as well as rural, is the great emphasis placed on education. There are
no differences in this respect between the poor and rich. Education is considered a ready means of social mobility and serves as the ladder for promotion in the workplace. In rural areas, parents may even sell part of their rice
fields to pay for the education of their children, although they fully understand when a child has finished college, he will not return to the farm or
his parents' house. Nevertheless, if possible, parents try to send all their
children to college. When the economic conditions of the family are such
that it is impossible to send all, the eldest son is sent to college. The other
sons are sent through middle school while daughters finish primary school.
This pattern reflects the traditional inheritance pattern and the division of
property practiced in the past, favoring the eldest son, and all sons at the
expense of daughters.

Competition for college and the enthusiasm for education are even
greater in urban areas. The worst period of education for both students and
parents is the so called "third grade," the last year of senior high school. In
preparing for final examinations, especially during the senior year, the student
sleeps only a few hours and studies day and night. In fact, the routine of the
entire family is changed. Family members wake up early in the morning for
him and keep quiet when he is at home. Table manners are also changed, and
he is given the best food. At night, the mother sits by him, waking him up
when he falls asleep. His anxiety, discontent, and uneasiness about the future
are called "symptoms of the third grade of high school." Not only the student
but the entire family suffers from these symptoms. Above all, this period
disrupts ordinary family relationships. The student tends to become cantankerous
and demanding, and the father and mother both suffer from their overconcern.

Through modernization, daily domestic family life has changed more
drastically than the family's outward form. The role of housewife has been
broadened to include virtually all the responsibilities of daily life. Thus the
modern family has become a matrifocal family, whereas the family of the past
was more patrifocal. The married couple's relation to elders and to children has

also changed; the modern family tends to be a more children-oriented family instead of the parent-oriented family of the past.

Continuities in the Confucian Tradition

In contrast to the rapid and profound physical changes in the family wrought by modernization and the urban patterns of urban residency just examined, Koreans have retained a number of traditional social norms and values which, in effect, give the family a strong Confucian flavor. For instance, when one examines family life closely, one can still find an intimate hierarchical relationship between parents and offspring, despite the separation of living arrangements. A first-born son living in the same city as his parents will still carry warm soup to them. And when the father or mother dies, the remaining parent almost always comes to live with the son.

In an emotional sense, living apart may result in a stronger rather than a weaker relationship between parent and child. Offspring in the cities send money or gifts to their parents and visit them several times a year especially during birthdays or holidays. Parents who farm send the products of their fields to their children in the cities, and they clearly enjoy visiting their offspring, especially if they live in different parts of the country. Perhaps what is weakened is the exercise of formal authority but not the *emotional dependency* based on a sense of nurturance.

Family structure, then, in Korea has not faded away, but it has been extended geographically. In this respect, the modern family is called a "modified stem family," as opposed to the traditional "classical stem family." In the classical stem family, three or four generations live together under the authority of a household head. In the modified family, parents and offspring live separately while keeping intimate contact with each other.

Another aspect of the modified family is its composition. In the traditional family, only the first-born son had the obligation to live with the parents. Now, parents live with their favorite son or even with a married daughter. Nevertheless, whether the family takes this form or another, it preserves a very important principle, the continuity of the patrilineal family.

Social values dictate that the family should not only continue, but prosper. The prosperity of the patrilineal family was the second principle in the past, and it is now more strongly effectively achieved by the modern family. *Education not land* is now considered the main means for climbing the social ladder. As mentioned earlier, parents even sacrifice their property interests for the education of their offspring. And the modern Confucian ethic is for sons and daughters to work hard to assure the prosperity of the family.

An interesting phenomenon in the urban family is the performance of the ritual services for the ancestors. Young couples do not perform the ritual services when they are in rental houses in poor condition, but once they have their own house, they do. They cannot prepare the ritual table in the proper way and cannot perform the rituals in the formalized traditional fashion, but they perform them with more enthusiasm. The main reason offered for performing the rituals are the social, emotional, and educational functions of the rituals, not the exercise of authority or the propitiation of ancestors to gain their assistance and to avoid their sanctions. In urban areas, there are few opportunities for siblings to get together. Commemoration days for parents and grandparents are good occasions for a party. Through the ritual service, offsprings show respect to their parents. During the meal after the service, the father will explain the past behavior of their ancestors to inspire moral behavior in their offspring.

As time passes, the contemporary marriage ceremony has become even more extravagant than in previous times and it serves to enhance the status of both families. The marriage ceremony is usually held in as expensive a ceremonial hall as can be afforded, with the bride and groom wearing exquisite clothes. However, to an outside observer, the exchange of presents between guests and hosts can give the impression of being an ostentatious display of new wealth somewhat resembling that of a Pacific Northwest Indian potlatch. Aware of the impropriety, the government has passed laws toning down excessive display at marriage rituals. Yet the public laws have not curtailed the informal exchange of presents between the families of the bride and groom. Besides being responsible for the new residence of the wedded couple, the groom's family is expected to give many presents to the bride. Over and above buying family utensils for the new couple, the bride's family in turn is expected to spend a great deal for presents for the groom and his family and relatives. Like the potlatch, competition in the cost of presents exchanged can be used to enhance "face."

Social status is also important in funeral ceremonies for parents and the decoration of their graves. In the past, grave decoration was dictated by the rank of the deceased person. But there is no limit now; the only restraining factor is money. The newly rich decorate the graves of their parents like those of nobility.

Another new and interesting phenomenon in the cities is the formation of urban lineage organizations. In the past, the lineage organization, *mun-jung,* was limited in size and covered one subprovince or county and was located mainly in rural areas. The new lineage organization, *chong-ch'in-hoe,* is located in metropolitan areas with nationwide branches. Every organization holds a general assembly once a year, either in spring or autumn. At these meetings, hundreds of representatives from different parts of the country come together. The most important function of such general assemblies is to demonstrate the solidarity of the lineage to the outside.

The development of most of these new lineage organizations follows a standard pattern. In the first stage, they publish newsletters usually four times a year. In the second stage, they establish a scholarship foundation for the education of their kinsmen. In the third stage, they build an impressive monument to honor the founder of the lineage or a famous and nationally known ancestor; in the fourth stage, the lineages publish a new style of genealogy. Because earlier genealogies were written only with Chinese characters, the younger generation cannot read them. Many genealogies are now translated into modern phonetic Korean. In recent years, they have even begun to make highly expensive video recordings of genealogies.

There are both differences and similarities between the old type of lineage organization, *mun-jung,* and the new type, *chong-ch'in-hoe.* The former was small in membership and located mainly in rural areas; the latter has a large membership and is located mainly in urban areas. The old type was concerned mainly with ritual services for ancestors; the new with the protection and welfare of kinsmen. Both are organized, however, to maintain solidarity among lineage members and to assure mutual prosperity. Through their actions, the members enhance the lineage's image to outside observers and they identify themselves through the lineage with their ancestors. In a word, the same functions of lineage solidarity and prosperity are being enhanced despite the different context offered by a modern rather than a traditional society.

Conclusion

Confucianism is a highly developed philosophy which prescribes basic rules for personal behavior. In the past it provided the moral principles which guided traditional family life as well as providing religious rituals which maintained and strengthened family ties. From the viewpoint of the family member, Confucianism combined ethics, philosophy, and religion. The traditional Confucian family was ruled by two important principles: regulating social hierarchical order by distinguishing (1) age and (2) gender differences. These principles extended into the wider society in traditional times. Families performed ritual services in the proper manner to educate the children and to identify themselves with their ancestors. Moral responsibility was further embodied in the patrilineal kinsmen who formed small lineages having the characteristics of large extended families.

Modernization and industrialization have produced great changes in the Korean family environment. From a sociological point of view, these have resulted in smaller family size, a conjugal family form, and isolation of the family from neighbors in urban areas. Great changes can be seen also in the family structure. The instrumental authority role carried out by the family head in the past has been taken over in large part by the mother in daily family life. The father's authority and privileges were unconditional in the past, but are now seen as his reward for being a good provider. And the filial duty and obligation of children to their father has changed to a more interactive or expressive relationship involving compromise. In a word, the family has moved from a more vertical structure dependent on formal authority toward concerns with nurture and care; and toward more horizontal interaction between husband and wife, to more wife-dominated situations. It has moved from a family centered on parents and property to one that is focused on child education.

Even though there are major changes in family structure, there are also continuities between traditional and modern society. The common thread has been the assurance of solidarity and prosperity in maintaining the family. From a male-dominated and father-oriented structure, it has become matrifocal and child-oriented one that is attempting to preserve the integrity and continuity of the family in a competitive, changing social world.

One of the main reasons for such structural change in the modern Korean family is the role of education. Parents sacrifice their immediate interests for the future welfare of their children and dedicate themselves to seeing that their children's future is assured by being well educated. Education is considered essential to the maintenance of status or upward social mobility. Parents now value their children's education before inherited property. In the past, the opportunity for education was limited to the upper class. Extending it to all has unleashed a tremendous force in Korean society. The ideal person in traditional Confucian society used education for social mobility. He learned all the classic Confucian teachings, passed the state examination, became a high official, practiced Confucian teachings, and enlightened the people. Now, however, the high value placed on education for the child translates into a higher level of family material prosperity in the next generation. Confucian values derived from a landed gentry are now inherited by a commercial-industrial class-oriented society.

The high value of education and a strong achievement motivation are directed toward the prosperity of the family and establishing or maintaining a good family reputation—values which reflect the old Confucian tradition in new forms. As with the *yangban* in the past, young people today think of their moral responsibility to the family name. Holding family honor high is a very important aspect of Confucian puritanism. In the past, people sacrificed themselves for the reputation of their families and gained a sense of personal identity by worshipping their ancestors. But in modern Korean society, people dedicate themselves to the reputation of their families and identify themselves through the success of their offspring. In short, a major shift from the past to present is that the former society had an ancestor orientation with no sense of change and the latter a future orientation in a consciously ever changing technologically oriented modern state.

Even though it was the state doctrine for all during the Yi dynasty, Confucianism was monopolized by the upper-class land-owning *yangban*. But in modern Korean society, it has become the ethic of all people. In this way, Korean society is undergoing a "yangbanization" process. Whether it was lowly or high in the past, every family and lineage now tries to achieve a higher status. And as every lineage attempts to achieve the status of *yangban* in the future, Confucian puritanism continues as an enduring philosophy for most Koreans.

References

Brandt, Vincent S. (1972). *Korean Village: Between Farm and Sea.* Cambridge, MA: Harvard University Press.

Choe, Hong-Kee. (1979). "Change in Family and Kinship System in Rural Korea." *Proceedings of the Seventh International Symposium,* 67–111. National Academy of Sciences, Seoul.

Chun, Kyung-soo. (1984). *Reciprocity and Korean Society: An Ethnography of Hasami.* Seoul: SNU Press.

Crane, R. S. (1969). *Korean Patterns.* Seoul: Hallym Corporation.

Eikemeier, Dieter. (1980). *Documents from Chjangjwa-ri: A Further Approach to the Analysis of Korean Villages.* Wiesbaden, Germany: Otto Harrassowitz.

Hough, W. "Korean Clan Organization." (1899). *American Anthropologist* 1.1: 150–54.

Janelli, Roger. (1973). "Anthropology, Folklore, and Korean Ancestor Worship." *Korean Cultural Anthropology* 6: 175–90.

———. (1978). "Lineage Organization and Social Differentiation in Korea." *Man* 13: 272–89.

Janelli, Roger and Dawnhee Yim. (1982). *Ancestor Worship and Korean Society.* Stanford, CA: Stanford University Press.

———. (1983). "Ownership Rights to Lineage Property in Rural Korea." *Korean Cultural Anthropology,* 15: 281–94.

Kendall, L. and M. Peterson, eds. (1983). *Korean Women: View from the Inner Room.* New Haven, CT: East Rock Press.

Kim, C. I. Eugene, ed. (1968). *Aspects of Social Change in Korea.* Kalamazoo, Michigan: Korean Research and Publishing.

Lee, Chang-soo, ed. (1981). *Modernization of Korea and the Impact of the West.* Los Angeles: East Asian Studies Center.

Lee, Kwang-Kyu. (1972). "The Korean Family in a Changing Society." *East Asian Cultural Studies*, 11.4: 28–43. Tokyo University Press, Tokyo, Japan.

————. (1975). *Kinship System in Korea*, 2 vols. New Haven, CT: Human Relations Area Files, Inc. (HRA Flex Books AAI-002). Yale University Press, New Haven.

————. (1983). "Korean Family System: A Comparison with China and Japan." *Proceedings of the Conference on Sino-Korean-Japanese Cultural Relation*, 601–20. Institute of Ethnology, Taipei, Taiwan.

————. (1984). "The Concept of Ancestors and Ancestor Worship in Korea." *Asian Folklore Studies*, 43.2: 199–214. Nanzan University, Nagoya, Japan.

————. (1984). "Family and Religion in Traditional and Contemporary Korea." In *Religion and Family in East Asia*, ed. George De Vos and Takao Sofue, 185–199. National Museum of Ethnology, Osaka, Japan.

————. (1985). "Changing Aspects of Rural Family in Korea." In *Family and Community Change in East Asia*, ed. K. Aoi, K. Morioka, and J. Suginohara, 158–90. Japanese Sociological Association, Tokyo.

Lee, Kwang-Kyu and George De Vos. (1981). "An Inquiry about Possible Dilemmas of Authority of Postcolonial Korean Modernization." In *Modernization of Korea and the Impact of the West*, ed. Lee Chang-soo, 150–72. University of Southern California—Los Angeles Press.

Lee, Yo-chai. (1968). "The Changing Family in Korea." *Journal of Social Sciences and Humanities*, 29: 87–99.

Lee, Man-gap. (1970). "Consanguineous Group and Its Function in the Korean Community." In *Families in East and West*, ed. R. Hill, 338–47. Mouton, Paris.

Mattielli, Sandra, ed. (1977). *Virtues in Conflict: Tradition and the Korean Woman Today*. Seoul: Royal Asiatic Society.

McCann, David R., J. Middleton, and E. J. Shultz, eds. (1979). *Studies on Korea in Transition*. Honolulu: Center for Korean Studies.

Mills, John. (1958). *Ethno-Sociological Reports of Three Korean Villages*. San Francisco: UN Command Office of the Economic Coordinator for Korea.

Moon, Seung-Gyu. (1974). "Ancestor Worship in Korea: Tradition and Transition." *Journal of Comparative Family Studies* 5: 71–87.

Osgood, Cornelius. (1951). *The Koreans and their Culture*. New York: Ronald Press.

Pak, Ki-Hyuk and Sidney D. Gamble. (1975). *The Changing Korean Village*. Seoul: Shinhung Press.

Pearson, Richard J., ed. (1971). *International Conference on Traditional Korean Culture and Society*. Honolulu: Center for Korean Studies.

Yang, Key and Gregory Henderson. (1958). "An Outline History of Korean Confucianism." *Journal of Asian Studies* 43: 81–101, 259–76.

V

Psychocultural Continuities

14

Filial Piety in Taiwanese Popular Thought

David K. Jordan

Filial piety is the root of virtue and the basis of philosophy.

—*The Classic of Filial Piety*

Filial Piety

"Filiality or filial piety *(shiaw)* is the guiding value permeating all aspects of Chinese society." That, whatever it means, is the opinion most generally elicited in Taiwan from Chinese of all walks of life whenever the question of values comes under discussion.[1] This chapter is a tentative consideration of some of the psychological implications of Chinese filial piety, based on observations in the course of a total of about four years of fieldwork and residence in Taiwan, and an examination of various Taiwanese publications aiming to inculcate filial piety or discussing the necessity of doing so.[2] In Taiwan official circles, filiality is often described in a matrix with other virtues. People speak, for example, of "the eight virtues" *(ba der)* (universally remembered in the order in which they occur as names of parallel main streets in Taipei: Loyalty, Filiality, Benevolence, Love, Sincerity, Righteousness, Harmony, and Tranquility).[3] But there is no doubt, at least for traditional Chinese, that filiality is supreme among all these virtues.

Filiality, whether in pre-Communist mainland China or in contemporary Taiwan, is a focal concern and not only in discussions of child rearing. It is central in all thinking about moral human behavior. "Of the hundred excellent things, filial piety is first," says a proverb; "Filiality must be pursued with all one's might," says an old school textbook; and "In Chinese society, being unfilial to one's parents is the thing most despised," writes a native Christian missionary (Wu Shyh-fang 1984, 18). In the course of another study, Daniel Overmyer and I had occasion to review texts used or created by modern sectarian societies in Taiwan. Often such texts include passages like the following (all here quoted from Jordan and Overmyer 1986):

> [E]ven [such Buddhist terms as] purity and Nirvana really arise from filial piety. Without filial piety, how could one obtain the fruits of Buddhahood? Thus, even the great monk of the western region, the Buddha Śakyamuni, was also totally filial toward his parents. (p. 56, revelation attributed to the Maitreya Buddha[4])

> Filial sons and daughters enjoy Heaven; disobedient sons and daughters return to Purgatory. I warn you now: do not trifle with the kindness of your parents! (p. 62, revelation attributed to a sect patriarch[5])

> What does filial piety mean? It means obedience *(shùn [shuenn])*, that is, obeying one's parents. Wherever one looks in the world, filial piety is at the beginning of things; it is the first principle of all conduct. For people to lack filial piety is like a stream having no source, and thus being sure to dry up. (p. 69, from a 1973 revelation attributed to the god Guan Gong)

But such themes are found not only in old proverbs and sectarian revelations. They emerge from newspaper editorials, PTA meetings, university symposia, and village catcalls. The nearly universal Chinese view, in other words, is that concern with filial piety is a most, or more likely *the* most conspicuous feature of the Chinese moral system, and hence at the center of Chinese behavior and ideals. The importance attributed to filiality by Chinese creates its importance for an analytical understanding of Chinese culture. This chapter explores filial piety as it has been explained to me by informants in the course of various fieldwork periods in Taiwan and suggests some tentative conclusions about recent incipient changes in how filial piety is conceived.

Filial Obedience

The most salient feature of filial piety is the subordination of the will and welfare of each individual to the will and welfare of his or her real or classificatory parents. Psychiatrists Tzeng Wen-hsing and Hsu Jing (1972, 28) write:

> The virtue of filial piety, as understood by the Chinese, consists of several qualities, including unquestioning obedience to the parents and concern for and understanding of their needs and wishes with the intention of pleasing and comforting them. This relationship which begins between the child and his own parents is eventually extended to his relations with all authority.

Filial piety is quintessentially described as the subordination of a son to his father, but filial piety should also characterize the emotions of a son toward his mother, of a daughter toward her parents, and of a daughter-in-law toward her husband's parents. Stepmothers should be objects of filial attention as much as natural mothers.[6] Filial feelings should also be experienced and filial behavior exhibited toward grandparents, great grandparents, and all higher lineal ancestors, living or dead. For a woman, filiality is focused on her husband's lineal ascendants, but not entirely removed from her own.[7]

If the behavior and attitudes of children to parents are clearly defined, so are the behavior and attitudes reciprocated by the parents to the children. Parents are described as being preferentially "stern and dignified" (yan) in the case of an ideal father, "gentle and compassionate" (tsyr) in the case of an ideal mother. These sensitivities and associated behaviors are considered to be inherent characteristics of a person acting in the status of parent or child, however; the failure of a mother to be "gentle and compassionate" in no way diminishes a child's obligation to be filial, and a wayward child's lack of filiality does not mean that a virtuous parent will not still exhibit sternness or compassion.

Francis Hsu speaks of the "filial obligation," which he describes this way (Hsu 1970, 78f.):

> [T]heir most important cultural ideal [was] that support of the parents came before all other obligations and that this obligation must be fulfilled even at the expense of the children.

> Economic support is not, however, the only way in which Chinese children are obligated to their parents. The son not only has to follow the Confucian dictum that "parents are always right," but at all times and in all circumstances he must try to satisfy their wishes and look after their safety. If the parents are indisposed, the son should spare no trouble in obtaining a cure for them. Formerly, if a parent was sentenced to prison, the son might arrange to take that parent's place. If the parents were displeased with their daughter-in-law, the good son did not hesitate to think about divorce. In the service of the elders, no effort was too extraordinary or too great. In addition to parents the elders in question could be a man's stepmother or a woman's parents-in-law.

It is not quite the case that Confucianism maintains that "parents are always right." Classical Chinese thought elaborates the notion of filiality by the additional term "remonstrance" (jiann or jiannjeng). Remonstrance refers to the duty of a child (or any jural subordinate) to attempt to dissuade his parent (or any jural superior) from a patently impractical or immoral course of action. Thus, it is reasoned, filiality is not mere obedience, but exhibits a broader and more genuine concern with the parent's welfare than mere obedience would suggest. Having remonstrated, the model son or daughter in the end must obey the will of a determined parent. This obligation is sanctioned by an oft-cited passage in the Confucian *Analects* (4.18):

> When serving parents, a son may remonstrate with them mildly, but if he sees that they are determined, he is even more respectful and does not resist them, doing the painful work without complaint.[8]

As a practical matter, remonstrance is of course a daily occurrence in family life. In popular thinking about filial piety, however, remonstrance is rarely considered. What parents seek from their children is obedience, not remonstrance; and what moral heroes are heroes about is obeying, not remonstrating.

Filial Nurturance

Beyond obedience to parental will is sustenance of parental welfare. The two are terminologically distinguished, for *shiawshuenn* is a stative and transitive verb meaning "to show filial obedience [to]."[9] In contrast, nurturing a parent is *yanq*. It is in the nature of things that obedience dominates when the filial child is indeed a child, while nurturance dominates when the filial child is an adult, with the parent aging and increasingly dependent. Still, both obedience and nurturance are part of the picture all along. In popular thinking, nurturance offered to a parent is thought of almost exactly as is the nurturance offered to a child. (Mandarin-speaking purists pronounce the same graph *yeang* when it refers to nurturing a child or animal, but pronounce it *yanq* when the nurturance is offered to an aged parent. Few speakers seem to observe the distinction in practice, suggesting that the difference is not particularly salient.[10])

Nurturance is most importantly symbolized by (1) feeding, (2) carrying, or (3) attending to the bodily processes of the nurtured individual, whether child or adult. (Less often, entertaining the baby or parent and educating the small child, are also described.) These same forms are also found in the care of helpless children by parents (although not exclusively by parents). Moreover, the element of reciprocity is involved in adult children "payin' for their raisin' " by administering to helpless elderly parents.[11]

Feeding

Chinese informants, speaking of nurturant aspects of being filial, inevitably stress provision for the feeding of elderly people. In some cases, stories and anecdotes recounted to illustrate the concept center on offering aging parents especially desirable food. In popular tales, the oral motif can take on a greater intensity when the nurturance of parents is concerned than when nurturing children is at issue (although in practice the difference is probably not as great). In popular stories, the oral symbol is often medicine which must be prepared for an elderly parent, and many a moral tale focuses on medicine made with items that are difficult or impossible for the filial child to obtain. This forces the exemplary filial child to extravagant self-sacrifice in quest of the rare ingredients. Many times the ingredients are not in fact part of the Chinese pharmacopeia, and it is the self-sacrifice involved in obtaining them that seems to give them their efficacity. One of my informants recounted how her childhood death in an earlier incarnation (revealed to her in a local temple) had come about because she was exposed to chilling winter weather during an improbable quest for a kind of grass to heal her ill mother. A common account of the earthly life of the goddess Guan'in tells of her sacrificing her hands and eyes so that they can be made into medicine for her disagreeable but ailing father (this enjoyed popularity as a poignant movie in the 1960s).

Self-Sacrifice

The extent of sacrifice is effectively limited only by the death of the child. Stories abound throughout China of people cutting off their own flesh for literal cannibalization by parents. Francis Hsu provides an example (1970, 79):

> In the district histories and genealogical records to be found in every part of the country are many individual biographies of local notables. After a cursory reading of about fifty of them, I obtained at least five instances in which men and women were said to have sliced flesh from their arms to be boiled in the medicine pot of one or another of their parents. One man did this twice during one of his father's illnesses. Because the elder's condition remained serious, the filial son decided to take a more drastic course of action. He cut out a piece of what he thought was his "liver" instead. Both he and his father died shortly afterward.

Filial Piety as Duty and as Emotion

Filial piety is simultaneously (and ambiguously) both a mental state and a behavioral code, and the behavioral code is (also simultaneously and also ambiguously) both a set of actions and a system of values underlying those actions. Thus we find that for Chinese informants filial piety may be defined in three quite separate ways: (1) Informants describe filiality as *action* directed toward a parent and exhibiting submission and nurturance. (2) Informants often experience filiality as an *emotion* of love toward a parent that is understood to differ from other sorts of attachment. (Filial piety as emotion is particularly vivid in the context of funerals, which provide strong cultural support for this interpretation of a mourning child's affect.) (3) Informants attempt to instill filiality in children as part of a *system of values,* which must be self-consciously cultivated. Some informants ("traditionalists"), see that system as cosmologically inevitable; others ("modernists," by contrast) appear to see it as a convention of a distinctively Chinese cultural tradition, and therefore in the end arbitrary rather than inevitable.[12] I shall return to this theme at the end, but turn briefly now to some of the countless traditional supports that have traditionally worked together to represent filial piety to all members of society but particularly to growing children as the moral basis of society. These representations still function today in Taiwan.

Education for Filial Piety

Since filial piety centers on self-sacrifice at the individual level, it is reflected in the education of children by conscious efforts to inculcate in the child (1) a strong sense of the inherent desirability of self-subordination (and a glimpse of the sanctions a group can exert against nonconformists) and (2) an exalted estimate of the inherent significance of the parents and their surrogates. Associated with this is a strong emphasis upon the cosmic inevitability of all of this. China's filial heroes rank with her military ones,[13] and both are self-consciously presented as especially appropriate models for children. This ideological education proceeds on a variety of fronts from earliest childhood, and is reinforced by constant explicit reference throughout an individual's life to filiality and the behaviors associated with filiality.

In traditional Chinese formal education, two texts in particular were devoted specifically to the instruction of children in the ways of filiality: the *Classic of Filial Piety (Shiaw Jing),* and the *Twenty-Four Filial Exemplars (Ellshyrsyh Shiaw).* The *Classic of Filial Piety* has been part of the Confucian canon since the Tang dynasty (618–906). The text itself probably dates from before the Hann dynasty (206 B.C.–A.D. 209), although the exact date and author are unknown.[14] The *Twenty-Four Filial Exemplars,* by Guo Jiu-jinq of the Yuan dynasty (1260–1368), is a much humbler text about twenty-four filial children from Guo's own era back to the time of the legendary Emperor Shuenn (traditionally 2255–2207 B.C.), a culture hero singled out by Confucius himself as a prime exemplar of the filially virtuous sovereign. By no means part of the Confucian canon, the work's clumsy prose and curious stories are something of an embarrassment to many Chinese intellectuals, and apparently have been so for some centuries, but they enjoy continued wide circulation among ordinary folk. The collection was to serve as a model for children of all stations to encourage them in filial behavior. In later years other authors produced similar collections,[15] and "Twenty-Four Filial Exemplars" thus gradually evolved from a specific literary work to a literary genre, including numerous examples in modern Taiwan (Jordan 1986).[16]

Beyond these two influential and widely distributed works specifically devoted to filial piety, there are countless references to it in other children's books, both traditional (such as the works that were used in teaching elementary reading) and modern (in edifying works with names like "a hundred good children" [Su 1978]). Moreover, adult texts, like the sectarian revelations mentioned at the beginning of this chapter, provide ideological reinforcement of filial piety themes.

Explicit education for filiality also takes folkloric form in proverbs, theatrical performances, and songs. The moral heroes noted for filial devotion are celebrated graphically on temple murals and (as a late-breaking fashion in Taiwan in the 1980s) on ceramic tile decorations for graves. The symbolism and ritual associated with weddings and funerals stresses filial obligations, as do quintessentially the numerous individual and collective rites to ancestors. In rural areas particularly, divination conducted through a spirit medium in times of family crisis often results in the attribution of family problems to unresolved structural problems in the family genealogy, which in turn links back to the same tired issues of the individual's obligation to his family and particularly to his generational superiors in it.

The traditional and modern cultural supports for filial piety in the form of explicit and implied injunctions are therefore overwhelming. We turn now to what it feels like to follow them.

Filial Piety and Frustration

In his excellent sketch of Chinese modal personality, Richard Solomon (1971) explores the psychodynamics of a much overdetermined Chinese "desire to find pleasure and security by being cared for by others" (p. 40), partly engendered by "considerable anxiety about disobeying . . . [parental] instructions" (p. 52). Part of "growing up," Solomon argues, involves learning to curb this passive dependency and to structure its expression into culturally acceptable channels, preferably at as little psychic cost as possible. This is true of most people, Chinese or not, of course. But Solomon sees it as particularly central to the operation of filial piety as the Chinese practice it. The explicit ethic of filial piety, in other words, is the cultural form in which Chinese structure the expression of this psychological synamic. However, Solomon also suggests that this may be more acute among Chinese, for reasons linked to childhood experience and to culturally shared interpretations of that experience. In view of Solomon's discussion, it is easy to see why Chinese parents should find filial piety comfortable, but the same considerations should make it particularly uncomfortable to be a filial child, however much well-socialized adults may deny that this is so.[17]

What reduces the psychic cost? Without attempting here to develop a full-blown theory of Chinese personality (and therefore without aspiring to answer that question completely), I suggest that two associated behaviors and beliefs seem to be directed in part toward mitigating that potential discomfort: identification of the individual with the parent, and identification of the individual with the family as a whole.

Identification with the Parent

If we accept Solomon's view that Chinese adults find "pleasure and security by being cared for by others," we must imagine it may be even more painful to provide this nurturance to those very individuals who were formerly the source of it.[18] One way in which this pain may be mitigated for Chinese informants is the tendency to identify with parents. By this I do not refer to "identification with the aggressor" (although there may be an element of that). I mean instead that in some contexts cultural sanction is granted to blurring the boundaries between a child and his parent.[19] One way this is done is by stressing that the child can occupy the same status with respect to his children that his parents occupy with respect to him, that he himself is in other words, at least potentially a parent even as he is a child.[20]

Chinese informants are quite explicit about a kind of continuity, if not exactly reciprocity, implicit in filial subordination. The concern with obedience and nurturance makes filial piety a guide for behavior (and for the experience of emotion) regardless of the absolute ages of parent and child, and as such it is easy to see the parent whom one serves today as the self who is served tomorrow. Psychological interdependence of parent and child, with strong cultural approval, has been remarked on by some observers as standing in contrast to Euro-American concern with the development of "autonomy" as a crucial feature of maturity. Yet psychological cross-identification seems to me also to be a prime psychological resource for an individual embedded in a cultural system that exalts highly asymmetrical filial piety.

Chinese informants stress filial piety as related to the statuses more than to the personalities of their parents. A child honors its father because he is a father, whether or not he is by any other criterion a worthy person. The duties and benefits of filial piety, like the manipulation and benefits of geomancy, are unrelated to personality. Depersonalization of the obligation may be related merely to the abstraction inherent in its being a self-consciously held general cultural value. Then again, it may be harmonic with an individual's sense of participation on both sides of the arrangement so that, in a sense, it is cognitively irrelevant exactly who it is that is making sacrifices for whom.

Being an Adult

Identification with the parent occurs as well in a slightly different sense. The cultural obligation to care for parents is incumbent on children of all ages, but as a practical matter, the actual act of caring for a parent in a significant way is primarily a sign of adult competence. Becoming ever more a provider of nurturance rather than a consumer of it is therefore part of growing up and achieving an identity as an adult. Particularly for adolescents, this may be a significant compensation for the self-sacrifice that filiality requires.[21]

Being a Martyr

Closely linked to the notion of filial nurturance as an adult activity is the view of it as a quintessentially moral activity. That, of course, is what the folkloric supports are all about. If the Twenty-Four Filial Exemplars engaged in masochistic self-sacrifice and are celebrated as culture heroes, there is a strong basis for high self-esteem in similar martyrdom.

Martyrdom takes on two distinct senses here. On the one hand, it is, as elsewhere, a powerful weapon in controlling others (as pointed out by Slote in chapter 2 of this volume). On the other hand, the martyr has the solace that he or she is the personification of what Chinese culture has chosen to sanctify as moral heroism. The importance of the resultant sense of self-righteousness is visible in its appearance in dreams and in its occurrence in religious revelations of people's cycles of reincarnation (see Jordan 1981).

Individual and Family

In the name of filiality, quite general family interests are often promoted, occasionally at the expense of the broader commonweal, and filiality becomes equivalent to legitimated, family-centered particularism. I have argued in quite a different context that the essential unit of Chinese popular religion in Taiwan is the family, not the individual. It may be the individual who suffers illness, loses money, or fails in school, but it is the family that must seek divine assistance for its misfortune in that case (Jordan 1972, 92–93). The emphatically corporate character of the Chinese family, within which there are few individual property rights and outside which there is little emotional security, militates in favor of the welfare of adults being easily identifiable with the welfare of all members of the group.

When this is taken to its logical conclusion, it can be (and frequently is) reasoned that parental welfare depends upon a broad base of family welfare (especially money); hence anything which advances the family advances the well-being of one's parents. A family member, however, is also a beneficiary of his contributions to the general welfare of the family. Filiality, while it represents self-sacrifice at the individual level, can legitimate vigorously forwarding one's own interests at the family level, and can be very self-interested indeed. Although ideology stresses the self-sacrifice of the individual actor in filiality, the actor who is able to identify his self-interest with corporate interest need experience less sense of deprivation than one who sees them as separate.[22]

In its extreme form, such a logic of filial piety can be made to rationalize nepotism, corruption, and other antisocial tendencies, so long as the family thrives from it. Chinese theories of government, proceeding from Chinese theories of ethics, accord filiality, and therefore also familistic particularism, not only a great deal of social legitimacy, but even supreme legitimacy. (Hence provisions in the legal codes of various dynasties prohibiting court testimony against family members, or providing heavy punishments for even speaking harshly to a parent.) In doing so, they set the stage for a continuing, strongly experienced, but largely unspoken tension. Despite millennia of ingenious philosophical effort to represent the nonfamilial virtues of loyalty *(jong)* and benevolence *(ren)* as the consequences of filiality (and vice versa), the tension remains latent not far below the level of consciousness of most Chinese, and presents one of the most interesting and persistent ideological issues in Chinese society. Lin Yutang has stated this quite emphatically (Lin 1968, 180):

> There is nothing wrong in all this [Confucianism]. Its only weakness was the mixing of politics with morals. The consequences are fairly satisfactory for the family, but disastrous for the state.
>
> Seen as a social system, it was consistent. It firmly believed that a nation of good brothers and good friends should make a good nation. Yet, seen in modern eyes, Confucianism omitted out of the social relationships man's social obligations toward the stranger, and great and catastrophic was the omission. Samaritan virtue was unknown and practically discouraged. . . . The family, with its friends, became a walled castle, with the greatest communistic cooperation and mutual help within, but coldly indifferent toward, and fortified against, the world without. In the end, as it worked out, the family became a walled castle outside of which everything is legitimate loot.

Mothers

A brief excursus needs to be inserted concerning the unequal roles of male and female figures in popular representations of "archetypal" filial piety. The Confucian canon presents filiality with reference to fathers and sons, which is understood as referring more broadly to children in general and parents of both sexes. In fact, however, the representation of the two sexes in folklore dealing with filial piety has apparently never been equal. Most stories about heroically filial children, for example, present us with more filial boys than filial girls,[23] but with more mothers than fathers. When the filial child does happen to be female, the person to whom she is filial is still more usually a mother than a father. Because of the strong rules of patriliny and patrilocality in China, the "mother" in question is often a husband's mother.

It normally comes as a mild surprise to Chinese informants when I point out the large number of mothers as against fathers in the *Twenty-Four Filial Exemplars* and its imitators. Although the fact is readily acknowledged when the evidence is presented, most Chinese do not seem to think of it that way. Filial piety is represented in the abstract in an all-male idiom, rationalized as referring to everyone; why then should popular stories circulating with didactic intent tend to stress the obligations of both sexes of children toward older women?

One approach would be to argue that filiality tales are designed to provide moral examples, and therefore we would predict that they would focus especially upon relationships that are inherently painful and problematic. In the case of tales of a woman's obligations toward her husband's mother, this logic seems to make sense. On the other hand, we can argue that the stories have simple entertainment value as well. In that case, we should expect to see in them expressions of the relationship where it is most heartfelt. In the case of male protagonists being filial toward their mothers, it is easy to accept this view. Unfortunately, the two lines of argument are not only different, but even contradictory.

I suggest that the reason may lie in the authors and compilers of these volumes, who are inevitably men, and who may tend to exemplify the filial piety of men and boys by means of the emotionally satisfying mother-son relationship, where filial piety "comes easy," rather than by means of the more tense, authority-related father-son relationship. But they exemplify filial piety for girls and women in an area where they feel strong moral examples are most needed, which popular opinion and sociological analysis agree is the troublesome area of relations between husband's mother and son's wife.

Recent Changes

Traditional representations of filial piety are of interest to the student of Chinese personality and culture, but equally of interest are the attempts to "reform" some of the popular tales, texts, and customs. My 1986 study found that reformed texts of the *Twenty-Four Filial Exemplars* sought to "modernize" filial piety by (among other things) avoiding tales with miraculous rewards for filial self-sacrifice. The changes are by no means intended to diminish the relevance of filial piety. The "modernized" tales are correctly claimed to have greater historicity (Wu 1979) and to provide more "credible" models for imitation by modern children (Lii 1977). It is an unexamined and possibly unnoticed result that filial piety takes on, for modern editors, a less cosmically inevitable quality and a more culturally arbitrary one.

I also found limited evidence to suggest a modernist view that filial piety as an emotion of gratitude felt toward parents (and parent surrogates) because of their earlier nurturance rather than being rather than as a duty owed to the status of parent. If so, this shift too would tend to de-emphasize universality of filiality, this time in favor of the more parochial personal experience of gratitude.

Filial piety for earlier generations of Chinese, who knew little of other lands, was a universal moral requirement of human (or anyway civilized) life. Filial piety for the international sophisticates of modern Taipei may be emerging as a Chinese tradition that one follows because one has been born Chinese. It would be going far beyond the data available to suggest that filiality in Taiwan today is moving from a moral symbol to a nationalistic one, but such a possibility was at least hinted at by my 1986 analysis.[24] The theme certainly is worthy of further study.

Conclusion

On the basis of a wide range of sources, but particularly observations by anthropological informants and an examination of popular tales intended for children, it emerges (1) that filial piety is perceived as simultaneously behavior, moral code, and emotion, (2) that it was traditionally represented as an inevitable fact of nature rather than an arbitrary social convention, and (3) that it entailed both subordination of the individual to the desires or even whims of his or her parents (or husband's parents), and also uncomplaining nurturance of those same parents. We have seen that the psychological challenge of trying to feel nurturant toward individuals for whom one must also make sacrifices may be accomplished in part through identification with the recipient's status, in part through a culturally supported sense of self-righteousness, and in part through the use filial piety as a rationalization for advancing family interests that include one's own. And we have reviewed some of the impressive (but possibly evolving) traditional supports that popular culture continues to provide to the cultural centrality of filial piety. For a core cultural symbol in Chinese society, it is surprising that so little research has centered on filial piety (although examined in considerable detail in this volume). Let us hope that its significance can be better clarified in the years ahead.

Notes

This essay began as a conference paper, which was published in full as Jordan 1986. That version considered both filial piety in Taiwan and the most popular didactic text of filial piety, the *Twenty-Four Filial Exemplars*. It also provided a discussion of variant editions created in modern Taiwan, and used them as a source for generalizations about changes in the conceptualization of filial piety today. An appendix included a full translation of the original version of the text. The present chapter is a revised version of the conference paper, omitting most discussion of the *Twenty-Four Filial Exemplars* and focusing on more general considerations. Readers interested in the text material (or in the Chinese characters associated with any of the terms used here) are referred to the earlier article.

Because of the large number of Mandarin words and names used in the original article, the system of romanization used was Gwoyeu Romatzyh ("tonal spelling"), which is more accurate than the commoner Pinyin or Wade systems. That system is maintained here for the sake of consistency between the two linked articles. All Mandarin words other than "Taiwan" *(Tair'uan)* and "Taipei" *(Tairbeei)* are rendered in this system. Note that most Taiwan informants speak Hokkien natively and Mandarin as a second language. However, in the case of the Chinese terms in this chapter, the two languages usually present exact cognates, and only Mandarin transcriptions are included here. When usage differs, I have noted it.

I am grateful to Suzanne Cahill, Ying-hsiung Chou, Stephen Eyre, Walter Slote, Audrey Spiro, Marc J. Swartz, and the participants in the original conference for their advice at various stages of the development of the manuscript. Errors that remain are my own responsibility.

1. This article is about Taiwan. There is reason to believe that at least some of these observations about filiality apply equally well to Chinese living in other areas or at other periods. I have tried to signal this by referring to "Chinese" rather than "Taiwanese" much of the time. Note, however, that reference to China and the Chinese throughout this article excludes Chinese under the Communist government, whom I have not studied.

2. A portion of the material for this paper was collected in 1984–85 while I was a Language and Research Fellow under the joint sponsorship of the Committee on Scholarly and Scientific Exchange with the United States, Academia Sinica, Republic of China, and of the Inter-University Program for Chinese Studies [Stanford Center] in Taipei. Material was also collected in 1976 during a sabbatical leave partially funded by the Chinese Cultural Center, New York. This financial support is most gratefully acknowledged.

3. *Jong, shiaw, ren, ay, shinn, yih, her, pyng.* The English glosses of these individual characters are more traditional than precise, but the semantic details do not concern us here, and I have retained them because they are better *aides-mémoire* than more innovative translations would be.

4. This passage is from "The Illustrated Book on Returning to the True Nature *(Faanshinq twu),* a mainland text of 1876. This and the following two texts are revelations by planchette *(fwuji).* See Jordan and Overmyer 1986.

5. This passage is from the *Golden Basin of the Jade Dew (Yuhluh jinparn),* a text apparently first published in 1880 on the mainland, but now widely circulating among Taiwan sectarians.

6. The strongly unilineal character of Chinese society excludes stepfathers from cultural recognition except in cases of adoption. I have no data on the rare cases that must occasionally occur anyway.

7. Analogous kinds of subordination and respect are offered to teachers, elder siblings, and public officials, but they are only analogous, not identical, and have different names in Chinese.

8. "Shyh fuhmuu ji jiann; jiann jyh, bu tsorng, lau erl bu yuann." Legge's influential translation in *The Chinese Classics* translates the passage somewhat differently (Legge 1893, 170):

> In serving his parents, a son may remonstrate with them, but gently; when he sees that they do not incline to follow his advice, he shows an increased degree of reverence, but does not abandon his purpose; and should they punish him, he does not allow himself to murmur.

This view of the remonstrating child as stubborn to the last is not confirmed by other translators or by Chinese commentators I have read, who interpret the passage as I have translated it.

9. The Hokkien cognate, *hàu-s®un,* is also a noun naming that obedience.

10. Mistakenly writing *yeang* instead of *yanq* is the commonest mistake made by editors in the phonetic sidescripting in editions of the children's books. In colloquial Hokkien, cognates of *yeang* are freely used for both, although Hokkien literary *(Hannwen)* readings exist for the specialized sense of nurturing parents. the Hokkien colloquial words are, depending upon dialect, *iáng* or *ióng* (formal) and *iú*ᵃ (informal) for Mandarin *yeang; i®ang* and literary *i®ang* or *i®ong* for Mandarin *yanq.* A possible survival of the "lower-going tone" reading may survive in the homonymous verb *i®ang,* meaning "to carry [a person] on one's back" (no standard writing), which is used both for children and of adults carried on the back.

11. The American folk expression "payin' for his raisin' " refers normally to tending the infantile needs of the next generation. It would be unlikely in American English to use it to refer to tending elderly parents. In the Chinese context, in contrast, that is the only way in which nurturance is seen as reciprocal. Ideologically, a person's reciprocal relationship with his parents is quite separate from the reciprocal relationship one has with one's own children. Psychologically, that differentiation is more ambiguous, as we shall see.

12. On the one hand, the Confucian system asserts the naturalness and inevitability of virtuous sentiments. On the other hand, it argues for one's obligation to cultivate them self-consciously throughout one's life if one is to experience them "properly," since they do not come easily. This ambiguity is pervasive in Confucianism, and filiality partakes of it. If I have understood the matter accurately, it is just this unnaturalness of what is claimed to be nature that provided the entering wedge for traditional Taoist opposition to Confucianism as philosophy.

13. This has been so since earliest times. For example, a Hann dynasty lacquerwork box—the famed "Lehlanq Basket"—temporarily "missing" but believed by some to be stored in the museum of Pyongyang, includes representations of over ninety traditional heroes, including filial children (among them Ding Lan, a character still celebrated in Taiwanese children's books).

14. The *Classic of Filial Piety* is traditionally attributed to Tzeng Shen (Tzeng Tzyy, 505–436? B.C.), a disciple of Confucius especially noted for his filial piety (and himself one of the twenty-four filial exemplars!). Other, less common, traditional attributions include Confucius himself and his grandson (and Tzeng Shen's student) Koong Jyi (Tzyy-sy, 492–431 B.C.). For a modern English translation of the *Classic of Filial Piety*, see Makra 1961.

15. Some of these are listed in Jang Chyi-yun 1973, 564 (§250.57). It is not clear to me that no one preceded Guo in making a collection of twenty-four exemplars, and the particular stories he selected do not make their first appearances in his collection. However, at the time of this writing, I do not have clear knowledge of any earlier collection of the same name, let alone quite the same content.

16. There is nothing static about the theme. As I type I am listening to a cheap tape cassette "Twenty-Four Filial Exemplars in Song," issued in Taiwan in or about 1986.

17. It is difficult to distinguish gracefully in either English or Chinese between the two senses of "child" as "offspring" and as "immature person." In the ideology of filial piety, there is, of course, no difference. Psychodynamically, the picture is probably more complicated than that. In the next few paragraphs it is the adult "child" that I principally have in mind, for it is to the middle-aged, not the very young, that care of the elderly normally falls. The cultural system, however, emphasizes that the situation is identical and the obligation constant.

18. This would not be so if nurturance could be aggressively construed, but for Chinese that seems rare, at least in this context.

19. Intergenerational role continuity may make this functional in any premodern society. If so, the longevity of the Chinese adaptation makes its presence in China unsurprising in evolutionary perspective.

20. The situation is somewhat more complex in the case of daughters than it is for sons, since their primary filial duty as adults is to parents-in-law rather than parents

as such. In principal, a woman is as naturally filial to her husband's parents as she would have been before marriage to her own (although she also retains residual filial obligations to her natal parents). In fact, however, the relationship between a woman and her father-in-law has a distance that is quite unlike her relationship with her father, and her relationship with her mother-in-law is notoriously troubled, at least in common stereotype. The psychodynamics of extending filial sentiments from parents to husband's parents would be fascinating, but no psychological study of this phenomenon has come to my attention.

21. I am grateful to Walter Slote for pointing this out. The point is not so obvious as it might at first seem, since the requirement of filiality is incumbent on all, and even children seek at times to act nurturantly. In the absence of a specific age at which a child takes responsibility for parents, the process of needs makes heavy use of individual nurturant acts that serve as private symbols of growing adult responsibility.

22. It can even happen that an elderly parent is abused or ignored in the "filial" pursuit of "family" interest. In one case in my notes an old man in Taiwan was confined to a tiny room, on a different street from the rest of the family house/shop, to avoid his interfering with family advancement. The "unfilial" character of this "filiality" was not lost on the neighbors, who criticized the son for this treatment of his father.

23. This is so much the case that some authors write instructions specifically aimed at daughters and excluding sons altogether (e.g., Wang 1972), although I know of no authors that deliberately do the reverse.

24. Some mixed evidence unsurprisingly suggests that this change in conception is not shared by all elements of Taiwan society, but may be limited to an educated elite, including the editors of children's books.

References

Hsu, Francis L. K. ([1970] 1972). *Americans and Chinese*. Garden City, NY: Doubleday Natural History Press.

Jang Chyi-yun, ed. (1973). *Jongwen dah tsyrdean*. (Encyclopedic dictionary of the Chinese language.) Yangmingshan: Jonghwa Shyueshu Yuann.

Jordan, David K. (1972). *Gods, Ghosts, and Ancestors: The Folk Religion of a Taiwanese Village*. Berkeley: University of California Press.

————. (1981). "Causes and Effects: Tales in Sectarian Revelation." *Proceedings of the International Conference on Sinology*, Academia Sinica, August 15–20, 1980, Section of Folklore and Culture, 73–99. Taipei: Academia Sinica.

————. (1986). "Folk Filial Piety in Taiwan: The 'Twenty-Four Filial Exemplars.' " In *The Psycho-cultural Dynamics of the Confucian Family: Past and Present,* ed. Walter H. Slote. 47–105. Seoul: International Cultural Society of Korea.

Jordan, David K. and Daniel L. Overmyer. (1986). *The Flying Phoenix: Aspects of Sectarianism in Taiwan.* Princeton: Princeton University Press.

Legge, James. (1893). *The Chinese Classics,* vol. 1. Oxford: Oxford University Press.

Lii Yih-yuan. (1977). "Shiaw tzay shiannday shehhuey tueishyng jy daw" (The Way to Promote Filiality in Contemporary Society). *Lianher Baw,* April 5, 1977. Reprinted in his 1978 *Shinnyeang yeu wenhuah* (Belief and Culture). Taipei: Jiuhliou Twushu Gongsy.

Lin Yutang. ([1939] 1968). *My Country and My People* (rev. illustrated ed.) Taipei: Mei Ya Publications.

Makra, Mary Lelia, trans. (1961). *The Hsiao Ching.* New York: St. John's University Press.

Solomon, Richard H. (1971). *Mao's Revolution and the Chinese Political Culture.* Berkeley: University of California Press.

Su Shanq-yaw. (1978). *Ibae haohairtzy guhshyh* (One Hundred Stories of Good Children). 10 vols. Taipei: Wenhuah Twushu Gongsy.

Tzeng, Wen-hsing and Jing Hsu. (1972). "The Chinese Attitude Toward Parental Authority as Expressed in Chinese Children's Stories." *Archives of General Psychiatry* 26: 28–34.

Wang Jinn-sheng. (1972). *Neutzyy ellshyrsyh shiaw twuyeong* (The Girls' Illustrated Twenty-Four Exemplars of Filial Piety). Taipei. Privately reprinted. (First preface dated 1871; second edition prefaced 1894)

Wu Shyh-fang. (1984). *Tair'uan minjian tzongjiaw huennher-juuyih kaoyuan* (An Inquiry into the Origins of Syncretism in the Folk Religion of Taiwan). Taipei: Gaanlaan Wenhuah Jijinhuey.

Wu Yan-hwan. (1979). *Sanshyrliow shiaw* (Thirty-Six Exemplars of Filial Piety). Taipei: Gwolih Bianyihgoan.

15

Mental Illness in Its Confucian Context

Bou-Yong Rhi

Attendant Mental Health Problems

To attempt to elucidate the possible Confucian cultural factors influencing mental health in a society such as contemporary Korea is a challenging subject. The definition of the term "mental health" and the range that it covers is controversial, and historically it has given rise to complex theoretical dispute. The concept of mental health itself varies according to the standpoint of the investigator and as such denotes nothing absolute. It can be defined objectively or subjectively, by statistical standards or by a subjective judgment of what does or does not constitute the norm (Jaspers 1946).

The term "mental health" indicates, in its narrowest meaning, a state without mental illness, either as classified according to modern psychiatric standards, or in accord with some assessment of relative maturity of personality, about which there are numerous viewpoints. Thus the two concepts, "mental health" and "maturity," are not necessarily congruent; nor are such terms such as "psychopathology" or "normal development." Furthermore, what is and what is not considered mental health varies according to the culture: what may be considered normal or abnormal for one culture is not necessarily the same for another.

A second problem lies in identifying the specifically "Confucian" elements that may have influenced the mental health or the maturity of particular individuals living in a complex modern milieu. The behavior patterns of the Korean family are still predominantly determined by Confucianism, which has been the ideology governing family life and practices throughout the Chosŏn or Yi dynasty for 500 years. However, the traditional Korean culture has been influenced not only by Confucian thought but also by Buddhist, Taoist, and shamanic religious traditions, and more recently, by Protestant and Catholic

Christian beliefs and practices. Consequently, characteristics of Korean behavior and Korean family life evidence a complex religio cultural heritage. Although in general the influence of Confucianism predominates, the extent to which one tradition is more salient than another differs for each individual and each family.

As a result, in order to avoid conceptual confusion, I will begin with some general speculations about how Confucian culture is connected with psychiatric disorders. Then I will look at Confucian influences on personal motivation. Finally, I shall consider some aspects of personal conflicts and possible solutions occurring within a Confucian family as revealed in clinical case material. These examples may help to throw some light on certain stresses in the Confucian family.

Psychiatric Illness in a Confucian Culture

There have been no systematic investigations per se in Korea about mental disorders that may be precipitated specifically by Confucian ideology. Research instruments are not tuned to provide any estimate as to the particular determinants that are specifically linked to Confucianism. Some suggestions, however, have been made in this matter in the course of investigating relationships between Korean culture and particular cases of mental illness.

Hysteria

Much interest has been paid in Korea to hysterical disorders. In the 1960s Hahn (1964) reported that far more female hysterical patients were in evidence than are reported in American research, in which a predominant symptom was some form of hysterical seizure. He was not only ready to accept the common hypothesis for this hysterical symptom, namely, that it is a face-saving maneuver, but he also tried to explain it in terms of Northrop's "esthetic continuity of life" among Orientals (Northrop 1946).

Later investigations (Kim and Kim 1974, 1975) supported Hahn's position about the predominance of hysterical neuroses in Korean females. However, they reported a shift from typical seizures to that of pain as symptomatic expression that may indicate a change in the recent social atmosphere, especially in modes of social communication within Korean society (Kim and Kim 1975).

I would suggest that the frustrations experienced among Korean women after marriage into a traditional patriarchal family still play an important role in the production of conversion symptoms (Kim and Kim 1975). However, according to one investigation (Kim and Kim 1974), the focus of interpersonal conflicts which may precipitate hysterical disorders in patients seems to be changing, from direct conflicts in the mother-in-law/daughter-in-law axis to those occurring in husband-wife dissatisfaction. Others, however, contend that a mother-in-law/daughter-in-law conflict still plays an important role in precipitating psychiatric illness (K. I. Kim 1978). From my own clinical experience, I would like to suggest that additional predisposing or precipitating factors are to be found in other forms of family interaction, for example, a possible grandmother-grandson bonding and consequent conflict arising between a grandmother and daughter or daughter-in-law.

Tendencies toward somatization among Koreans have been documented in connection with cultural premises (Kim 1972). So-called *Hwa-Byung* (Hwa-illness) is defined in terms of folk medicine as a kind of angry reaction which is suffered predominantly by women. Such cases are now under investigation to establish their psychodynamics as well as to arrive at a description which fits modern psychiatric nosological terms.

Homosexual Complaints

In the 1970s, Hahn (1970) asserted that homosexuality and incest are more rarely observed at psychiatric clinics in Korea than in America. He attributed this to the strict early separation between roles for boys and girls in the Confucian tradition; the culturally sanctioned relationship among same-sex siblings in hierarchical terms; large family settings; and the strict taboos regulating sexual indulgence. These features discourage a reversed oedipal situation, which is thought by some to be an etiological factor in some cases of homosexuality.

Today, one is more inclined to assume that homosexual behavior and other sexual irregularities are simply rarely exposed to psychiatrists in Korea. The prevalence of such behavior is probably much higher than reported. There is increasingly open evidence of its presence paralleling recently increasing urbanization in Korea. However, it is well established that overt homosexual behavior remains extremely rare compared with contemporary Western societies. Is it possible that the Confucian emphasis upon harmonious family interaction has provided Koreans with alternative means of expressive contact among same-sex brothers and sisters from an extended family? Or could it be that the strength of the cultural taboo is sufficiently repressive to prohibit homosexual expression?

Alcoholism

Alcoholic psychosis or compulsive drinking is thought to be rare despite the high rate of social drinking. There are low rates of admission for alcoholics in Korean hospitals (Hahn 1971). Hahn has pointed out that the characteristic way that one drinks in Korea is while eating. Socially tolerated drunkenness is a way for effecting more efficient communication, and in some instances can serve as an outlet for relatively poorly integrated aggressive drives which usually could not be discharged due to rules of formal propriety. Drinking alone is rare.

While it is true that alcoholism is rarely observed in Korean psychiatric wards in comparison with European and American settings, a recent epidemiological survey (Lee 1988) revealed a seemingly higher prevalence rate of alcohol abuse than in America. Probably the Korean lack of concern with drunken comportment may be one reason for high rates of reporting, though other factors may also be involved.

In sum, Confucian influences upon mental illness as precipitating, predisposing, or even causative factors are not yet clear, not to mention the prevention or healing possibly effected through Confucian beliefs or practices. More direct examination of the psychological influences of Confucian values upon personality functioning is necessary.

The Korean Interpretation of Confucianism: Problems in Personality Maturation

Possibilities for Interpretive Distortion

What Confucius really said and meant as a religious-ethical mentor is not always the same as what is understood socially and adopted as a guide to behavior. Such has been the case in all religious movements throughout human history.

Since the 1970s, there has been intense debate in Korea on the merits and demerits of Confucianism, and about the validity of Confucian doctrine as adopted by the ruling powers of the Yi dynasty.

In his *History of Korean Confucianism,* Hyun (1960) pointed out the merit in teaching *gun-ja* (gentility, or reverence for ethical values) structuring human relations harmoniously, and developing a sense of respect for the pure of heart.

The demerits include: tendencies toward factional strife and corruption; class discrimination; the overestimation of family name and social status; extreme preoccupation with the classics at the expense of practical learning *(moon yak);* weakness of individual assertion due to an overestimation of the governing literati at the expense of "doers" such as military men; resistance to modernization resulting from the depreciation of commercial, technological, and marketing occupations.

Other studies have supported Hyun's opinions (cf. Academy of Korean Studies 1983). Seen positively, the Confucian emphasis on "self-training before [therapeutically] treating others," *Shu-Ki Chi-in* (Lee 1983) has been highly appreciated. Negatively, there is repeated criticism of the devaluation of material wealth and scientific technological development for the sake of moral purity and internal psychological concerns, and social withdrawal into a totally family-centered life (Shin 1983). There is neglect of personal individuation, spontaneity, a separate self-identity, and widespread nepotism and class discrimination, due to emphasis on family ties (Shin 1983).

Confucian tenets have also been criticized for teaching one-sided obedience to superiors and the consequent lack of the autonomy to act in accord with one's own inner decisions and objectives (Yun 1975). There have been those who emphasized the later distortions of original Confucian thought and therefore advocate the Confucian thought of Choong Hyo, claiming it to be a prototype of more humane interaction and a forerunner of modern democratic ideas (Cheng 1975; Choe 1975; Lee 1983; Bae 1983).

It is indeed apparent in the psychiatric cases that I am about to report that some dysfunctional aspects of Confucian family life are the result of distortions or misperceptions and the undue rigidification of potentially more flexible interactions actually accepted within Confucian thought. As I shall note, there can appear in some cases a rigid institutionalization of formalistic relationships within the family leading to various forms of psychological stress.

Childhood Socialization within a Confucian Context

In general, it may well be necessary and helpful to examine, however crudely, to what extent the Confucian view of humanity corresponds to man's true nature and can therefore enhance or direct the achievement of more adequate personality maturation as defined within a modern psychological point of view. In regard to explicit attention to personality development in psychodynamic terms, the Confucian literature provides us with only a few brief comments about child rearing, which are regarded as crucial in considering personality maturation by the psychoanalytic school (Tseng 1975).

In native Korean tradition, there was an active traditional concern with *tai-kyo,* prenatal "personality" development ("teaching the embryo"). Many customary taboos were connected with it. Folk practices even suggested how to prevent enuresis in the very young (Lee 1969). There was an early separation of sleeping arrangements for boys and girls (Hahn 1969). In general, "bad habits" were to be eliminated early; witness the proverb "The bad habit of age three continues until age eighty." There were instructional use of plays and games for children in local folk customs. Above all, there was the early involvement of the male child in reading the Confucian classics.

Whereas the Korean folk tradition apparently was very much concerned with child rearing and education, Confucian writings per se seems to have paid little attention to childhood and adolescence. Emphasis was laid upon the later half of life in fostering "self" development (Tseng 1973). There was in fact no mention of a formative adolescent period. The early recruitment of boys into adult society *(kwan lye)* in traditional Confucian culture skipped over any transitional processes occurring in subadult youth (De Vos 1973).[1] It is obscure whether or not Korean Confucianism allowed for the slower personal development and maturity as was suggested in the Chinese case (Tseng 1973). Modern society, with the development of universal education, is inclined to delay social independence by prolonging the period of school education (De Vos 1973). As discussed in other chapters in this volume,[2] preference for males within Confucian patriarchal society has influenced the patterns of personality development and maturation in Korea for both women and men (Rhi 1974).

Sex and age role expectancies elicit different attitudes from the parents toward individual children. The outcomes are complex; one must also consider the many intervening family influences, other than those directly coming from father and mother. Frequently there are parental surrogates that bear consideration when looking at patterns of experience influencing personality development. Contrary to general expectations, in many instances Korean family socialization seems to have contributed to the strengthening of a sense of self and to the enhancement of a sense of autonomy.

Personality development among Koreans seems different in some details from the much-debated classical psychoanalytic model. This is especially apparent in respect to the resolution of Oedipal relationships. It has been suggested that Oedipal conflict is not so overtly manifest in traditional Korean culture, as it is in the Western nuclear family. This difference is due to the presence of parental surrogates, the mediator role practiced by the mother in the home, and the early assignment of sex-specific roles in such a way that they prevent the Western-type of triangular closeness within the family. This leads to an atmosphere which is less vulnerable to direct rivalry within the father-son relationship (Kim 1978).

As Tseng (1973) discussed in the Chinese case, the same patterns of one-way obligations of the younger generation toward elders are practiced in Korea in accordance with principles of filial piety, *hsiao*. It is, therefore, quite probable that those coming from traditional Confucian families become especially inhibited in consciously experiencing, let alone expressing any negative personal feelings or opinions before an authoritative elderly person.

At any rate, one can not deny that the Confucian tradition of family interaction lacks an important step toward individual autonomy, namely, the integrative separation of the individual from the family in order to actualize the totality of his or her individual personality.

It is noteworthy that the concepts of "self," "personality," and "personality maturation" considered in psychoanalytically oriented theories may not be the same as those to be derived from Confucianism (Hsu 1971; King and Bond 1985). What was regarded as important for Confucianism in regard to personal maturation or the development of the self seems not to include a concern with such dynamic tensions as those considered in psychoanalysis. For example, psychoanalysis is concerned with development stages, a search for independence, and the direct experience of psychic internal conflicts that are to be resolved in the direction of a more mature integration. Yet only the latter emphasis on achieving a more mature integration expresses a point of view congenial to Confucianism.

In Confucianism, "personhood" *(Personlichkeit)* becomes possible when one moves toward the achievement of insight into one's own ethical nature and therefore toward harmonious relations with one's fellow humans. Confucianism aims at the ideal state of harmony in human relations and with the universe, in other words, the achievement of a wholeness of human existence, called in the East "Tao." To become a whole person has similarly been emphasized as an ultimate goal of psychic development by many Western psychologists and psychoanalysts, such as Horney, Fromm, Rogers, and Jung.

It must be noted that the concept of *Tao* in Confucianism is not exactly the same as that of Buddhism or Taoism. The concepts of wholeness of person, or a state of self-actualization, also differs from school to school in Western psychology.

The most important concerns of Confucianism are human interrelationships. These easily tend to become formalistic, though internally considered decisions within the self can modulate relational behavior elastically as well as rigidly, depending upon the person (King and Bond 1985). Harmonious human relations are seen as the ultimate goal of life, as if they alone represent the wholeness of life, so much so in some cases that the need for a more total actualization of the individual psyche is utterly neglected.

As a consequence, in Confucian thought the concept of the whole person, the self, is projected largely into a system of human interaction and external behavior. Thus, in this pattern of prescribed behavior, the ultimate goal of personhood is striving toward the Confucian concept of the ideal person. Rather than leading to wholeness, this search for external form, not internal experience aside from role, induces a further splitting of the conscious ego from the more unconscious aspects of the psyche residing in personal desires, instinctive drives, and emotionality.[3]

This psychic dissociation can subsequently manifest itself in mental and somatic symptoms. Hence, various types of hysterical disorders in Korean women can be understood in this way. Hysterical dissociation is not unique to the Confucian family—such absolute identification with model behavior can also occur in traditional Christianity; therefore, the proneness toward psychic dissociation is not attributable to Confucianism per se. Every culture in which collective moral attitudes are emphasized strongly has this same danger. However, I have the impression that the type of Confucianism adopted during the Chosŏn dynasty and imposed on the people has had a larger negative effect on the mental health of Korean women than has Buddhism and even shamanism, which have served as alternative religious ideologies. Further investigation of these differences is necessary. In fact, the de facto coexistence of other religious forms in Korea may have acted as a safety valve for emotional expression not permitted in the Confucian role models of propriety. Shamanic practices are especially noteworthy in this regard (see chapters 9 and 10 in this volume).

Role Conflict in the Clinic

The following case studies have been obtained from clinical practice at Seoul National University Hospital. They are a few examples of emotional disorders elicited by examining conflicts occurring within Confucian families. Some of the cases are psychiatric outpatients under my treatment. Others are inpatients of the psychiatric ward treated under my supervision. I selected for illustration those whose emotional difficulties seemed to be related to a particular Confucian role conflict which apparently predisposed them to mental illness or directly helped precipitate their emotional or psychosomatic disorder.

Family information was obtained from the patient or his or her relatives in the course of treatment. Because the interviews were of limited duration, they were not always satisfactory for analyzing family dynamics in detail. However, they are sufficient to allow me to draw attention to certain aspects of the culturally induced conflict involved. I have excluded from consideration schizophrenic and manic-depressive psychoses, for those disorders have an overly complex etiology that is difficult to consider in any brief presentation.

Mother-in-Law Relationship Problems

CASE 1. A twenty-seven-year-old married mother of two had been suffering from depression and thoughts of suicide for one month prior to consultation. She had experienced occasional epigastric discomfort for six months. The absence of physical abnormalities suggested that the dysfunction was psychogenic in nature.

About two months prior to onset she had lost a large sum of money. From that event onward, she experienced sleep disturbances so severe that she had to induce sleep by drinking alcohol every night before going to bed. While the loss of money had apparently precipitated her depression, it became evident that the patient's marital life for a number of years had been highly unsatisfactory.

The patient married her present husband seven years ago "for love." He is a thirty-nine-year-old businessman, twelve years older than she. He was the youngest of five siblings; except for the eldest sister, all have died. He lost his father at the age of two and grew up under his mother's unstinted love. He is a true *hyoja*, a true filial child, traditional in his values concerning man-woman and parent-child relationships. He takes his meals with his mother while the patient eats with the children at a separate table. He is reluctant to go out with his wife, for his mother does not appreciate being left alone. Unlike the patient, he does not enjoy buying new furniture or decorating the house, regarding such attention as a luxury.

The patient described her sixty-eight-year-old mother-in-law as cold, egoistic, and cynical. She was said to disapprove of the patient's going out of the house. Only after the onset of her illness was the patient allowed to go out once a week to prepare for her driver's license examination.

Before her marriage the patient knew she would have to live with her mother-in-law and was willing to obey her. Over the years, however, it became increasingly difficult to endure the limitations imposed on her personal life. When she suggested to her husband the possibility of living apart from her mother-in-law, he objected strongly. He declared that if she could not tolerate her mother-in-law, there would be no other choice for him but to divorce her.

The patient was treated by medication and psychotherapy under the diagnosis of an "adjustment disorder with depression." The husband was asked to participate in the therapeutic process. He was a sincere and honest man. He loved his wife, but was at a loss over what to do either about her ailments or her complaints concerning his mother.

I proposed that he express more affection towards his wife, take her out more often, and afford her a bit more freedom. At these suggestions, he immediately expressed hesitation. His primary objection was to leaving his mother home alone in order to go out with his wife. He did, however, try to help the patient as recommended. She received much more freedom to spend time as she pleased and passed her driver's license examination.

At the eighth session, after about two months of treatment, the patient felt much better and was allowed henceforth to come in for consultations at longer intervals between sessions.

The patient's illness seemed to have been caused by the strictly interpreted Confucian standards adhered to by her husband and mother-in-law. The husband's male-centeredness, his filial piety strengthened by his mother's early widowhood, and the emotional reserve directed toward his wife in the presence of older people—virtues taught by Confucian doctrine—could not be tolerated by the patient. Her illness broke the rigidity of the family's interaction, temporarily making her the center of attention. In large part, the illness became a necessity to allow for some restructuring of family relations.

The conflicts and frustrations in the patient's marital life seemed to have been at least temporarily softened after the eighth session, when the patient reported she definitively gave up any unrealistic expectations of radical change in attitude on the part of her mother-in-law and husband.

The "giving-up/given-up" complex was a term developed by G. Engel (1972) to denote a specific complex of psychosomatic patients. However, in Korean "giving up" or *che'nyom* is more synonymous with "resigning oneself to" or "yielding to" than "abandoning home." It involves relinquishing one's desires toward and expectations of others and accepting one's *p'alja* or destiny in harmony with the cosmos. The word *ch'enyom* actually has a much more profound meaning than that in common usage. *Ch'e* means truth, self-awareness, and clarification, or *satya* in Buddhist terms. *Ch'enyom* is the ancient translation of *chongsa*, "right thinking," the second component of the Buddhist Eightfold Path (Lee 1975).

She gave up confronting; rather, she withdrew from efforts to change the character of her mother-in-law or her husband. She tried to be satisfied with the increased freedom from household duties she was allowed, a compromise made by her husband and mother-in-law. Although self-deprecatory, she was better able to enjoy her available leisure time. However, she still felt guilty that she avoided her mother-in-law. She was now aware both of the necessity of recognizing personal problems arising within herself as well as developing the courage to contend with the traditional values continuing within her family setting. She turned herself from a simple "giving up" attitude to one of increased self-awareness, *ch'enyom* in the truest sense.

CASE 2. A forty-nine-year-old mother of three sons had been in continuous conflict with her husband's family for about twenty-six years. As a result, she frequently fell victim to depression, indigestion, and anxiety attacks with heart palpitations.

Nine years ago she attempted suicide after an incident in which she felt unjustly blamed by her mother-in-law. At the time she was angry at her husband for refusing to openly support her. One year later she contracted pulmonary tuberculosis but refused treatment, wanting to die. She was given intensive psychotherapy for one year during which time she reported occasional attacks of chest discomfort, depression, a feeling of impending death, and continuing emotional distress.

The patient was the eldest of nine children. Her father was a merchant in Seoul. Her relationship with her parents and siblings was said to be good. At age twenty-three, as a student of fine arts, she married her present husband following her father's recommendation. Her father had been impressed by his honest, manly appearance. However, the demeanor her husband directed toward her was brusque and noncommunicative.

In effect, he held no charm for her. From the first day of marriage she had been disappointed. He was without humor; she was bored.

Her mother-in-law was an uneducated, ill-tempered woman. She treated her daughter-in-law like a servant. Contrary to prior promises, her mother-in-law never cooperated with her wish to continue her studies. She only allowed her to go out once or twice a month for one or two hours. Her father-in-law, now seventy-nine-years old, has a diligent but aggressive, compulsive, stubborn character. Thirteen years ago he suffered a cerebrovascular accident and since then has had motor difficulties. The patient was obliged to care for him.

Her husband, now fifty-two years old and also the eldest of nine siblings, was completely absorbed in his father's business. He had no interest in his wife's personal feelings. He was deeply attached to his mother and always avoided involvement in mother-in-law/daughter-in-law confrontations. He gave money to his mother for the household expenses. As the eldest son he was dutifully responsible, caring for his brothers and sisters. The patient at first also performed her duties as daughter-in-law very affectionately, though they were not always adequately appreciated. As the eldest daughter-in-law, she regularly conducted *chesa* (ceremonial observances of death anniversaries) and other Confucian ceremonials.

When the mother-in-law died of a heart attack three years ago, the patient became more overtly devoted to her father-in-law. Recently, however, she could no longer stand the one-sided sacrifices she was making for her father-, brother-, and sister-in-law. She began openly to express her frustration, partly with the help of the therapist. Although she and her husband have slept apart for a long time, her husband became more accessible and gave her enough money for household expenses, the children's education, and so on. She now goes to a cultural center to learn calligraphy and Oriental drawing, takes swimming lessons, and is quite satisfied with her life. She is pleased with the healthy development of her children. She considers them honest and able to understand her. She has made great efforts to send them to the best universities.

Recently, she had the following dream:

> I was with the mothers of my eldest son's high school alumni group in the kitchen preparing the Korean specialty *kujolp'an,* which we were probably going to serve to someone of importance to our sons. Accidentally, the door of the kitchen opened and an unknown man of about thirty threw me something wrapped in newspaper. I took it, unfolded the old papers, and found to my astonishment, a thumb. I hurried out of the kitchen to find out who he was, but couldn't find him.

The patient's associations about the dream were as follows:

- *The mothers:* These mothers had once set up a study group for their sons to prepare more effectively for the college entrance examination. The patient had been an active member of this mother's group, which continued to meet even after its task had been successfully performed. But recently she has been reluctant to meet with them because she thinks they are too concerned with money and social prestige. They give her headaches.
- *Kujolp'an:* Type of Korean food. Nine different kinds of food put in the nine compartments of a beautiful box.
- *Thumb:* no association.

The dream indicates that, contrary to her conscious thoughts, she still unconsciously shares collective conventional attitudes with respect to social prestige, as well as her openly acknowledged maternal ambition for her children. The unknown man is probably a personification of her internal personality, an active, guiding principle in her mind, her unconscious masculine personality, or animus.[4] It threw the dream-ego a package, as if it wished to call her attention to something important. It was "a thumb." The thumb is the first, the thickest, the strongest of all the fingers. There is a proverb in Korea: "Among the ten fingers, there is no single finger which elicits no pain when bitten." Finger in this case means one's own children. The thumb as well as the fingers is also regarded by many people as possessing magical power. In colloquial Korean, "thumb" means the chief, the head of a group.

The dream seems to suggest that as the head of the family the patient should now be aware that she is the most powerful. She always appeared to the family as an extraordinarily self-sacrificing daughter-in-law. Because this attitude was unnaturally one-sided, her good deeds were suspected and not appreciated by others, as well as by herself, in spite of her laudable efforts. Now she should know that she is the head, not only of the family, but also of her own life. The thumb wrapped in paper in her dream is like an irrational *hwadu* (koan) of Zen Buddhism, a riddle posed by a master to his disciple who must carefully solve its meaning.

In the two cases considered so far, we should take into consideration whether the mental and physical ill health of the patients can be attributed only to a rigid conventional value system, an authoritarian and face-keeping male-centered culture apparently derived directly from Confucian thought. The mothers-in-law in these cases themselves do not seem to be ideal mothers-in-law in Confucian terms. They have already suffered deformations suggesting prior personality problems. Nevertheless these particular problems may be passed on from one generation to the next among women, each in turn attributing unsatisfactory relationships to the prior generation.

The degree of conflict between mother-in-law and daughter-in-law varied according to individual character traits as well as the nature of reciprocal expectations in Korea as elsewhere. When she is the "big daughter," the eldest daughter-in-law may face special role conflicts between herself and her sisters- and brothers-in-law as an additional burden.

A girl strongly attached to her parents is especially susceptible to emotional conflict. She leaves her parents at marriage and before becoming completely independent as one member of a mature couple she will undergo the "trial" of living with unknown parents-in-law. In this way, she is supposed to learn about the difficulties of life and ways of adjusting to another milieu. This period is to serve as an initiation rite of passage for the daughter-in-law. But if a new daughter-in-law does not view it as such, or if the hazing and animosity on the part of the mother-in-law is severe, conflicts are bound to arise both internally and externally.

The mother-in-law/daughter-in-law conflict is not unique to Korea, but is reported in other Confucian societies as well (Lebra 1984). In every family where the attachment of son to mother is strong, we can observe such conflicts. Outside the Confucian cultural area, such conflicts are also specifically described in the fairy tales of many cultures containing stepmother and stepchild motifs, which often demonstrate patterns of initiation or ordeal as a toughening of the character of strong women persevering through great hardship.

One Also Suffers in the Mother-in-Law Role

It is noteworthy that today not all daughter-in-laws suffer under the tyranny of mothers-in-law. On the contrary, increasing numbers of daughters-in-law who have professions enjoy benevolent mothers-in-law who care for their grandchildren during their daily absence. Today, it seems to be the mothers-in-law who feels burdened by living with their daughters-in-law, for they are suffering from their own ambivalence toward traditional values.

CASE 3. A housewife of fifty-one complained of flushing, headaches, sleep disturbance, excessive dream anxiety, and generalized muscle pain. Laboratory data revealed no physical abnormalities.

The patient is "the big daughter-in-law" of a large head family in a southern province. The family is known in the district as *yangban*, of noble status. Economically the family had no problems. The relationship between the patient and her husband was said to be average. The only complaints she and her husband had were those elicited by their eldest son and his wife. The daughter-in-law comes from a Christian family, and she planned to keep her faith after marriage. As a result, the patient was strongly opposed to the marriage of her son with this woman, because as the eldest daughter-in-law it would be her duty to conduct *chesa* at least six times a year.

The son, who loved the girl, persuaded his mother that neither he nor his future wife would go to church after their marriage. Upon this promise, the parents gave their permission for the marriage. However, the patient recently learned that her daughter-in-law secretly goes to church and that her son allows it. In addition, they have rarely participated in the *chesa* ancestor rites which are held in their native village in the country. Combined, these two stresses were sufficient to induce multiple somatic symptoms in the patient.

The patient was extremely disappointed by her eldest son and daughter-in-law. She felt deceived by her son, became angry toward both, and could not sleep well. When the family elders asked why her son and daughter-in-law were absent at the *chesa* rites, she had to lie and say that they were studying hard in Seoul. "The only face-keeping solution is sending them to America for further study. But then they may never return home!" exclaimed the patient with great sorrow.

The patient came three times to the psychiatric outpatient clinic for treatment. She took medicine without great success. Her symptoms fluctuated. She dreamt she saw her daughter-in-law praying in church. Finally, the young couple, aware of how they were aggravating her physical symptoms, begged her forgiveness and promised again to give up church. Thereafter her complaints decreased somewhat, but did not disappear entirely.

It had always been the patients' secret desire to hand over her duties as the head of the family at some point to her eldest daughter-in-law. The patient was thus driven into a dilemma which induced a somatic disorder in conjunction with reactive depression. Her illness served as an effective means of keeping face in the family and influencing her son and daughter-in-law.

Marital Tensions

Women with a modern liberal education will perhaps not realize the traditional meanings of a *shijib-sari* life, wherein husbands who shared affection with their fiancée quickly fall into an older customary role of an inconsiderate, dominating, or neglectful male shortly after their marriage.

A majority of the husbands of our female patients seemed to identify actively with the traditional role of a son of a stem family, as noted in the above cases. The typical Confucian husband in this category may strive to "keep face" even at home. These men were described as humorless and brusque at home, but active and playful when with their colleagues. These female patients, as others, complained frequently that their husbands never shared their business concerns or events with them. Such husbands seem to be adhering to the words of Confucius (*Analects,* 1.3) in not expressing affection toward their wives in the presence of elders, or indeed in the privacy of their home with or without elders present.

In addition, they may silently agree with Confucius that women are difficult to manage (*Analects*, 17.25) when complaining.

> The Master said, 'In one household, it is the women and the small men that are difficult to deal with. If you let them get too close, they become insolent. If you keep them at a distance, they complain.'

While immature men can utilize such aphorisms to avoid the mutual responsibilities of the marital bond in the Korean family, the opposite is also evident; some women today, who have problems taking on mature responsibilities, use contemporary patterns of change in an attempt to justify internal difficulties, as the following case suggests.

CASE 4. A thirty-one-year-old woman complained of chest discomfort, labored breathing, numb, trembling hands, sleep disturbance, and general weakness. She felt extremely guilty toward her husband for her inability to perform even the most simple household tasks.

Her somatic symptoms were caused primarily by agitated depression. It was induced by childbirth and has been exacerbated by chronic emotional stress in the husband's family. The patient was very dependent on her parents, and it seemed that she was not yet prepared for being a responsible mother or performing her role in her husband's family.

The family of the patient's husband is a head family (in the direct line of eldest sons) in a southern province, and her husband is the eldest son. Consequently, the patient had to play the demanding role of the eldest daughter-in-law or "big" daughter-in-law, though she did not have to serve her parents-in-law, who live in the countryside.

Her husband is a generous man. As the eldest son he brought three younger brothers to Seoul to live with him, giving them financial and emotional support while they were in school. The patient first attended to them willingly, but after having her own child felt unable to perform her task as eldest daughter-in-law, taking care of the youngest brother-in-law who was living with them. When she complained to her husband, he did not understand her feelings. He said, "How can a stream flow against its natural direction?" and insisted that she accept her fate. Her depression became worse.

After she temporarily moved to her own parent's house and her brother-in-law left to spend his summer vacation in the country, she felt much better. However, the patient's depression regained its previous intensity when her husband decided to visit his family for a *chesa*. His duty to perform the traditional sacrificial rite to his ancestors also necessitated ceremonial participation on her part. Her parents-in-law are cultivated, benevolent people, but she was apprehensive nonetheless. At such a big gathering of the family, proper performance of her role as the eldest daughter-in-law was crucial. Above all, it upset her that her husband was completely oblivious to her physical and emotional ailments.

After a quarrel with her husband on this matter she had a dream: "I was walking through a building with people of high and low rank. Evil people came in pursuit after me. I ran away and looked for a place to hide. I discovered the closed door of a room. A man of high rank told me, 'If you wish, you can look into the room; otherwise don't look inside.' I looked into the room and woke up from the dream in extreme panic, for I saw a lot of corpses with bandages covering their faces."

The patient had no associations about the dream's content. It is not clear to what extent the dream was related to her fear of participating in the *chesa*. But one thing was obvious: the patient had to confront her repressed fear represented by the image of corpses in her dream, and this was especially concerned with saving "face." Her dignity in the external world had been injured and had to be healed and reestablished.

After this dream and talking with her mother about her fears, she decided to follow her husband's wishes, which were supported by the therapist. Returning from the country, her depression was much relieved. During the *chesa* ancestral ceremony, her mother-in-law and husband had made special efforts so that she need not overly exert herself. Her mother-in-law declared that she would simplify the ancestral rites for her daughter-in-law by decreasing the frequency of *chesa* to once or twice a year. The patient responded to the kindness shown her by wishing that her mother-in-law live long enough to carry out the *chesa* regularly and consistently.

This case demonstrates the changes in traditional family life taking place in urban Korea. The role of the eldest son, who is obliged to care for his brothers and participate in the family's rites, met strong resistance from the patient who was reluctant to follow those traditional ways of life. However, in this case no ethical values of Confucianism were severely injured, for the understanding parents-in-law reduced the frequency of *chesa* for their daughter-in-law's sake and were willing to listen to her complaints about living with her brother-in-law.

In this specific case, the problem was a result of the patient's weak personality, which had never fully matured. Her weakness made her predisposed toward illness as a means of avoiding the difficulties of life.

Chesa may be perceived differently by Korean women depending on their personality, education, and religion. The Protestant church in Korea officially rejects *chesa* as idolatry and in its place recommends the Christian memorial service. The Catholic church in Korea has only recently accepted *chesa* officially, following the acculturation movement in Catholicism. Understandably, however, the Catholic church still sets love for God above that of one's ancestors. Therefore, differences in religious beliefs within a family, especially between Confucian and Protestantism, can easily elicit conflict.

CASE 5. The patient's primary complaint was her regret that she had married a passive, weak man who comes from a very complicated family that did not follow the Confucian model. Her father-in-law, a business man who died long ago, was married three times. The patient had to serve three different mothers-in-law, and there were a lot of conflicts. She ascribed the following dream partially to her attitude toward her husband's family.

> A young house maid prepared food for my father-in-law, but she laid the food dishes on paper on the floor. I was very angry about her lack of etiquette. So I took the food and went to my father-in-law's room. There I found that he was already adequately served with food. I put the food down. Then a Western man appeared. As I left the room, he followed me. I went down the stone steps of the house and stood by them with bowed head, carefully buttoned up, as if I wished to show oriental feminine modesty.

The patient's associations about the dream were as follows:

> Maid: Unknown teenager. Father-in-law: meticulous banker, died fifteen years ago at the age of eighty-two, somewhat greedy, but kind to the patient and actually a man of sentiment. The Western man: young, elegant, prominently countenanced.

The patient said she realized after the dream that she had neglected her father-in-law and his family, preoccupying herself with the thought of her three mothers-in-law. For a long time she ignored the fact that her husband's family was actually *yangban,* of noble descent. Now she realized that she should not depreciate her husband and his family, as she had been doing.

The maid in the dream may have represented an unconscious reluctance to dedicate herself to her father-in-law. When this inner resistance against traditional etiquette has been overcome and the traditional values incorporated with respect to her father-in-law, a positive change in attitude is possible. The elegant Western man might represent the more active and creative aspect of the masculine principle in her own unconscious. The dream suggests that if the creative aspect of her unconscious becomes conscious, she can reestablish a posture of Korean womanhood.

Being a university graduate in contemporary Korean society is highly appreciated by both men and women. Traditionally, the eldest son has been granted special privileges with respect to education compared with his younger brothers and sisters. However, it sometimes happens that the eldest son, feeling compelled to sacrifice for the sake of the family economy, gives up his goal of further study and gets a job instead.

Ancestor Worship and the Tensions of Internalized Role Expectations in Males

CASE 6. The patient, twenty-three, was diagnosed as suffering from irritable bowel syndrome and anxious depression.

His indigestion and bowel trouble began when he had to leave middle school because of a sudden worsening of his family's financial condition. Since that time his symptoms have fluctuated according to the stressfulness of the family's situation. Born of a wealthy landowning family, he spent a happy childhood in the country. Because his father failed in business, he had to work as a shop boy for awhile. He frequently quarreled with his parents during his middle school years. As the eldest son of five children, the patient was constantly preoccupied by the thought that he should play a more active leading role in the family during its economic crisis. He therefore entered a commercial high school and after graduating entered one of the most prestigious companies in Seoul with good recommendations. However, he soon encountered interpersonal difficulties in the office. As a result, he went into military service earlier than necessary in order to flee the uncomfortable atmosphere of family and job. There his abdominal symptoms subsided completely. He is now working as one of the founding members of a new advertising company. He said he no longer has any occupational frustration. Consciously, he has no negative feelings toward his parents and siblings. His mother worries a great deal about his emaciation and weak physical condition.

He once wanted to marry a girl who had graduated from high school, but he never did, probably because he did not have the prestige of being a university graduate. He stated that not going to college was his most painful experience. But his physical condition, his work load, and the burden of being the eldest son of the family did not allow him to study further.

He now has a girl friend, also a high school graduate, who is tender and obedient in nature. He is planning to marry her, for his parents are old enough that he should try to please them by giving them a daughter-in-law during their lifetime. Though it has not been confirmed, it is possible that contrary to his conscious desire to obey and please his parents, the patient harbors a repressed unconscious rage toward his parents, especially toward his father, who as the leader of the head family could not maintain the family's wealth and dignity.

Physiological manifestation of unconsciously repressed emotion is one psychological explanation for the irritable bowel syndrome. In a Korean proverb it is said: "When a cousin or family-in-law buys land, I get a pain in my belly." Jealousy, or a complex feeling of envy, may elicit abdominal pain in a Korean.

CASE 7. A man, age thirty-one, was admitted to the psychiatric ward for alcoholism. He had started drinking at the age of nineteen, when he began working in a district office after graduating from high school. About seven years ago, after joining a provincial education office, his drinking problem worsened. He frequently disappeared on drinking binges lasting days. The patient was born in Andong, which is in a southern province of Korea, an area well known for its traditional Confucianism. His grandfather was a large land-owner and a *sonbi*, a literary man, who kept strict Confucian family traditions. His father, sixty-three years old, used to be primary schoolteacher and is now an assistant principal in a special school for mentally retarded children. He is an outgoing person who values discipline and family tradition. The patient's mother also comes from a landowning family. She is a compulsive and some-what aggressive woman of sixty, but has always obeyed her husband. Genetic loading for alcoholism could not be elicited from the family history.

The patient's emotional conflicts began when he entered the district office at a young age. He was an able officer and wished to perform his duties according to correct principles. He could not submit to his dishonest superiors and fell into an internal struggle. Instead of confronting his superiors, he escaped into an alcoholic debauch. He stated that he though money acquired in an unjust way should be spent recklessly, so whenever he happened to receive such money he went to a bar.

The etiology of alcoholism is very complex. Genetic and constitutional factors as well as psychosocial factors may play a predisposing role. A contributing factor is his identification with the *sonbi*, the Confucian scholar, who was especially conscious of puritan justice and did not tolerate corruption. "White stork! Don't go near the black ravens," is a famous phrase from a *shijo*, a Korean ballad of the Chosön dynasty. The second issue involves the face-keeping attitude toward older people and bureaucrats promulgated by Confucianism in Korea. Open criticism of a corrupt superior was not prohibited by Confucianism,[5] and in Korean history there are examples of open protest by *sonbi* against their superiors. However, there were also many occasions in which the Confucian scholar simply withdrew from the world and retreated into his hermitage when he could not change the evil reality of the world around him.[6] Similarly, although the patient was not a real *sonbi*, he acted like one in that he withdrew from his "evil" superiors and made a bar his hermitage. The strict, traditional atmosphere of his village was a much greater burden to him. He suffered feelings of guilt, regret, and shame that, because of his drinking, he could not add to the prestige of his family.

Clinical Comments

As seen in the above cases, it is noteworthy that the mental health of Korean women is far more endangered than that of men as far as family conflicts are concerned. Characteristically, the unhealthiest family constellation appears to be the bond between mother–only son, and especially mother–eldest son. From my clinical experience, mother-in-law/daughter-in-law conflicts also play an important role in precipitating various psychogenic disorders. For the wife of an eldest son, conflicts between her and her sisters- and brothers-in-law may be an additional burden. The degree of conflict between mother-in-law and daughter-in-law varies according to their character traits and the nature of the reciprocal expectations.

Perhaps the most significant type of family conflict lies in the relationship between husband and wife; it is especially important to the latter. The maturity of the husband's personality is crucial in moderating the degree of conflict.

A majority of our female patients' husbands seemed to identify actively with the traditional role of son of a head family. The typical Confucian husband in this category may strive to maintain face even at home. These men were described as humorless and brusque at home, but active and humorous with their colleagues. Our female patients complained frequently that their husbands never shared with them their business matters or experiences that occurred outside the home. While all of the eldest sons were described as honest, filial men with great awareness of their role as head of the family, the major frustration for our female patients arose from their husbands' absent or inadequate expression of affection.

In the previous cases, we might quickly assume that the mental and physical health of the patients was disturbed by an authoritarian face-keeping, male-centered culture apparently derived from Confucian thought. However, we should also attend to the contrary; these cases are marked by the inappropriate carrying out of the original Confucian teachings themselves. The mothers-in-law in these cases were not ideal mothers-in-law in Confucian terms. They themselves suffered from their own personality problems, which caused them to rigidify their behavior, or use formality to express unconscious hostile intent.

Some of our female patients were not always able to fulfill their role as "big daughter-in-law," for their modern education did not allow them to perceive the role as meaningful. Nor were there social rewards for adhering to the traditional ways of life. As we saw in case 4, women with personality problems before marriage are exceptionally vulnerable to the emotional stress of their roles in the psychologically unprotected environment of their family-in-law's home.

Whether adherence to the traditional ways of family life can also help men mature after marriage is unknown. Certainly, marriage allows a man to identify with his role as head of the family. This may help him in his social adjustment and in assuming leadership roles. Whether he actively performs his traditional role in the family or runs away from family conflicts into social activity, he may nonetheless readily develop a blind spot. He may tend to ignore his wife's difficulties until she overtly expresses them, either verbally or through physical or emotional disorders, for he believes that through adherence to tradition that his wife should be satisfied with her devotion to her parents-in-law and husband.

Conclusion

In order to define some of the tensions that arise within Korean Confucian families, I have cited material gathered from several psychiatric patients. Brief commentaries on the psychological and cultural factors which might have precipitated their psychic or somatic disturbances were given.

Our patients' problems were precipitated primarily by family conflicts arising from mother-in-law/daughter-in-law interactions and from marital stress that can occur between an eldest son acting as head of family and his wife. The core problem of many of our female patients lies in the disappointment they feel toward their husbands and the lack of any companionate communication.

I suggested how family conflicts might be attributable to the misinterpretation and misuse of Confucian values by husbands and mothers-in-law, the inability of patients to perform their traditional roles in the family, and difficulties arising from lack of social support. Mental disturbance in some instances, however, became an opportunity for the renewal of family communication, and properly applied therapy can instigate further personal maturation in given instances.

I have also attempted to touch upon the positive and negative aspects of Confucian thought in the human maturation process. The concept of wholeness in Confucianism is similar in many respects to the maturational goals recognized in Western psychology. One of the greatest achievements of Confucianism in Korea, and probably in Oriental culture as a whole, was its emphasis on emotional control for the sake of cultivating a rational attitude in human interaction, especially in relation to elders. This "religious" attitude toward one's elders or superiors was especially vital during the politically and ethically chaotic time in which Confucius lived.

In the rise of Christianity in the ancient Near East and its spread into the Roman Empire we can observe similar religious motivation at work. It is therefore quite reasonable that as K. Jaspers (1957) and M. Weber (1966) insist, Confucianism as an intellectual moral philosophy made an important contribution to the development of man's reason, religiosity, and self-reflection in the East, as did Puritanism later in the West. Confucianism can be regarded as a religion, originating among the intellectual elite, that attempted to transmit a code of cultivated humanistic behavior, while it offered a rational, cultivated view of a cosmos free of superstition.

However, the problem with the Confucian view of man lies exactly in its emphasis upon the virtuous behavior of man. As in Christianity, the importance of reason, modesty, gentility, esthetic expression of feelings, priority of self-reflection, disciplined behavior in human interaction, suppression of personal feelings, reverence toward elders, clear awareness of good and evil, and actualization of ethical principles are emphasized as ideals. But hostility, sexual and erotic desire, power drives, aggressiveness, impulses to compete with others, active exploitative interference in the external world, belief in supernatural powers, and all the irrational aspects of man's life and personality are, for the most part, not dealt with in Confucian tradition. They were simply considered to be baser emotional states which could be transcended through good will and knowledge. Internal patterns of stress and conflict receive no direct understanding.

In the time of Confucian ideological dominance, such neglected aspects of man's mind manifested themselves in many ways, despite man's conscious "good will": In actuality people were separated into strict hierarchically layered classes, and the factionalization of Confucian *sonbi* into numerous sectarian groups led to bloody fights in the name of justice. In Korea, a rigid bureaucracy was established preventing necessary change during the Chosön dynasty.

It seems not accidental that the changes in the Korean national expression after World War II directly contradict the traditional Confucian virtues: one sees manifest aggressiveness, a tendency to show off, neglecting to save face [ch'emyon bulgo], and exaggerated extroversion. These appear instead of an emphasis on emotional control as but a few of the negative changes all too apparent in postcolonial Korea, despite its avowed adherence to a Confucian ethical philosophy as guidance for the state. Such a reversal cannot solely be attributed to the introduction of materialistic Western culture into Korea. Such tendencies have been already present in Koreans and in culture as a reaction to the one-sidedness of Confucian formalism.

As we saw in our patients, some somatization disorders of Korean women might be regarded as manifestations of the inappropriateness and inadequacy of traditional male-centered family relations. On the other hand, however, such disorders may then serve to help develop more differentiated forms of family interaction. In this sense, then, those disorders were not only illnesses but forms of attempted communication (Szasz 1974). As such, they can be an innovating force for the renewal of family relations as well as instigators of personal maturation.

Confucianism teaches the individual how to relate to the innermost roots of his psyche, namely, the world of ancestors, the historical root of mankind so neglected in modern industrial societies. The ancestral world connects man to the essential grounding of his emotional life. Their continuing presence is known as an archetypal "kinship libido" in terms of Jungian analytical psychology (Jung 1975, 224, 233, 262) and as expressed by Confucius as "brotherhood all over the world."

As I have indicated, although Confucian doctrine acts to strengthen the ego's will power and promotes self-reflection and a religious reverence for elders, the Confucian tradition of family interaction nonetheless lacks an important step toward individuation, namely, the integrative separation of the individual from the family in order to actualize the totality of his or her individual personality. It is yet unresolved how these two goals of family responsibility and self-actualization can be brought into better balance.

Self-actualization, or becoming a whole person, has been the ultimate goal of psychic maturation not only to Western psychotherapists but to Buddha, Laotzu, and Confucius as well. Wholeness from the Confucian perspective is mainly to be achieved through social interaction, although concepts such as *shu-ki chi-in,* "self-training before treating others" are highly appreciated by Confucian scholars. Marriage, family, and all other social interactions are sacred rituals representing psychic totality and social integration. In Confucian thought the concept of the whole person, the self, is projected largely into the system of human interaction and external behavior. Thus there is a tendency to externalize. Rather than leading to wholeness, this search for external form, rather than internal substance, can induce a severe splitting of the conscious ego from the unconscious psyche, personal desires, instinctive drives and emotionality.

This psychic dissociation can subsequently manifest itself in mental and somatic symptoms. Various types of hysterical disorders in Korean women can be explained in this way. Such absolute identification with model behavior can also occur in Christianity; therefore, the proneness toward psychic dissociation is not attributable to Confucianism per se. Every culture in which collective moral attitudes are emphasized strongly has this same danger. However, I have the impression that the type of Confucianism adopted during the Chosön dynasty and enforced on the people has had a larger negative effect on the mental health of Korean women than Buddhism and even shamanism have; further investigation in this area of concern is necessary.

We should not overlook the importance of the individual's reaction to traditional culture. If Confucian values lose their meaning for one person, but are still followed by others, conflicts are bound to arise between them. The conflicts experienced by our female patients were mainly of this nature.

Inasmuch as Confucianism has been the ruling ideology in Korea for the past 500 years, it has undoubtedly had an enormous influence on the personality of the Korean people. However, its primary influence has been on the aristo-cratic upper class. Most people still live in a religious environment today which is therefore quite complex: Confucianism, Buddhism, Taoism, and shamanism have all played large roles, as have Protestantism and Catholicism more recently.

It is therefore difficult to identify the specific Korean mental health problems as having their roots solely in Confucian culture, without regard to the effects of other religious cultures and their interaction within an individual's psyche, family, and society. Since mental disorders are reactions of a total personality; there is no patient whose problem is due only to conflicts caused by a single cultural tradition.

Notes

1. In chapter 17 of this volume De Vos refers to a similar quick transition to adulthood for samurai in the Tokugawa period.

2. See especially chapters 10 (Cho) and 13 (Lee) of this volume.

3. See chapter 16 for a similar discussion regarding the Vietnamese.

4. *Animus* in terms of analytical psychology: The active, masculine aspect of the unconscious of women, manifested in judgment, opinion, and wisdom.

5. *Hyo-kyong,* trans. M. S. Lee. (Seoul: Ulyumunhwa-sa, 1971), 92–94. When Tsung Ja asked Confucius whether it can be called *hsiao* if one unquestioningly follows one's father's orders, Confucius said that the father does not fall into injustice even when his son argues with him. Therefore, if a father is unjust, there is no other way to solve the problem but debate. In the same way, the retainer must debate against the king. There-fore, you should debate if you are confronted with injustice. It is not *hsiao* if one simply follows one's father's orders.

6. K. C. Lau (trans.), *The Analects (Lun-yu)* (New York: Penguin Books, 1986), 174: "The Master said, 'In serving your father and mother you ought to dissuade them from doing wrong in the gentlest way. If you see your advice being ignored, you should not become disobedient but remain reverent. You should not complain even if in so doing you wear yourself out.'"

References

Academy of Korean Studies, ed. (1983). *Ethical Viewpoints of the Korean People.* Part 1: Ethical view of the Choson Dynasty, and part 3: The Korean Personality. Seoul: Academy of Korean Studies.

Bachtold-Staubli, Hans. (1929/30). *Handwörterbuch des deutschen Aberglaubens,* Berlin: Walter de Gruter.

Cha, J. K. (1979). "A Cultural Psychiatric Consideration of 'Hyo' [Filial Piety] in Korean Legends." *Neuropsychiatry* 18: 82–90.

Cho, D. Y. (1976). "A Psychoanalytic Study of *Hsiao* [Filial Piety] in Oriental Legends of Filial Children." *Seoul Journal of Medicine* 17: 117–26.

De Vos, G. A. (1973). *Socialization for Achievement: Essays on the Cultural Psychology of the Japanese.* Berkeley: University of California Press.

Engel, G. L. and A. Schmale, eds. (1972). "Conservation-Withdrawal: A Primary Regulatory Process for Organismic Homeostasis." In Ciba Foundation Symposia 8, *Physiology, Emotion, and Psychosomatic Illness,* 71–73. Amsterdam: Elsevier.

Hahn, D. S. (1970). "Sexual Perversion in Korea" (in Korean). *Neuropsychiatry* 1.1: 25–34.

———. (1971). "Alcoholism in Korea: Korean Patterns of Drinking." *Journal of Korean Medical Association* 14.11: 833–38.

———. (1977). *A Collection of Articles.* Seoul: Department of Psychiatry, Seoul National University.

Hsu, F. (1971). "Psychosocial Homeostasis and *Jen:* Conceptual Tools for Advancing Psychological Anthropology." *American Anthropologist* 73: 23–33.

Hyun, S. Y. (1960). *History of Korean Confucianism.* Seoul: Minjung Sogwan.

Jaspers, K. (1957). *Socrates, Buddha, Confucius, Jesus.* New York: Harvest Books.

Jung, C. G. (1975). "The Psychology of the Transference. In *The Collected Works of C. G. Jung,* vol. 16: *The Practice of Psychotherapy.* Princeton, NJ: Princeton University Press.

Kim, H. W. and J. G. Kim. (1974). "A Clinical Study of Hospitalized Hysterias" (in Korean). *Neuropsychiatry* 13.4: 475–81.

Kim, K. I. (1972). "A Study of Somatization Trends of Koreans" (in Korean). *New Medical Journal* 15: 1440–43.

———. (1978). "Mother-in-Law/Daughter-in-Law Conflict among Psychiatric Inpatients" (in Korean). *Neuropsychiatry* 17: 27–32.

Kim, M. J. and K. I. Kim. (1975). "A Clinical Study of Hysterical Neurosis" (in Korean). *Neuropsychiatry* 14.1: 25–40.

King, A. Y. C. and M. H. Bond. (1985). "The Confucian Paradigm of Man: A Sociological View." In *Chinese Culture and Mental Health,* ed. W. S. Tseng and D. Y. H. Wu, 29–45. New York: Academic Press.

Lau, K. C., trans. (1986). *The Analects (Lun-yu).* New York: Penguin Books.

Lebra, T. (1984). *Japanese Women: Constraint and Fulfillment.* Honolulu: University of Hawaii Press.

Lee, C. K. (1988). "The Epidemiological Study of Mental Disorders in Korea (X): Prevalence of Alcoholism" (in Korean). *Seoul Journal of Psychiatry* 13: 15–26.

Lee, D. S. (1968). "A Consideration of Some Wisdom Related to Mental Health in Korean Culture" (in Korean). *Neuropsychiatry* 7: 37–40.

Lee, K. K. (1981). *Psychological Problems of the Korean Family.* Seoul: Ilji-sa.

Lee, M. S., trans. (1971). *Hyo-kyong.* Seoul: Ulyumunhwa-sa.

Lee, S. N. (1975). *Korean Dictionary.* Seoul: Hanso.

Lee, W. J. (1983). "Confucian Ethics Seen from Its Positive Aspects." *Ethical Viewpoints of the Korean People,* 7–43. Seoul: Academy of Korean Studies.

Lee, Z. N. (1980). "An Analytical Psychological Study of 'Hyo' [Filial Piety] in Korean Legends and 'Hyokyung' [The Teachings of Filial Piety]" *Neuropsychiatry* 19: 281–87.

Nakamura, H. (1985). *Dictionary of Buddhism.* Tokyo: Tokyo Shyoseki.

Northrop, F. S. C. (1946). *The Meeting of East and West.* New York: Macmillan.

Rhi, B. Y. (1974). "Psychological Problems among Korean Women." In *Virtues in Conflict: Tradition and the Korean Woman Today,* ed. S. Mattilli, 127–46. Seoul: Royal Asiatic Society, Korea Branch.

Shin, O. H. (1983). "The Characteristics and Limitations of Confucian Ethics during the Chosun Dynasty" (in Korean). *Ethical Viewpoints of Korean People,* 125–78. Seoul: Academy of Korean Studies.

Minjoong, Sokwan, ed. (1967). *New Etymological Chinese Dictionary.* Seoul.

Szasz, Thomas. (1974). *The Myth of Mental Illness.* New York: Harper & Row.

Tseng, W. S. (1973). "The Concept of Personality in Confucian Thought." *Psychiatry* 36: 191–202.

Weber, M. (1966). "Die Wirtschanftsethik der Weltreligion, Teil 1." *Gesammelte Aufsätze zur Religionsoziologie,* vol. 1. Tübingen: Mohr Paul Siebeck.

Yun, T. L. (1970). *Mental Structure of the Korean People.* Seoul: Hyonam-sa.

———. (1975). "Korean Mentality and Confucian Culture." Christian Academy, ed. *Structure of Korean Mentality,* ed. Christian Academy. Seoul: Christian Academy.

16

Destiny and Determination: Psychocultural Reinforcement in Vietnam

Walter H. Slote

The Sense of Life

Every society establishes certain basic tenets about the nature of life, foundational elements that determine the perspectives that all people require in order to make sense out of this very confusing world. These serve as lodestones that give comprehension to that which we do not truly understand. In the West the search for this understanding, the essence of man in the context of his social and physical environment, is the primary focus of inquiry today. In one form or another this is what basic research at the present time is all about: the attempt first to understand, and then to harness the forces that may control us if we do not control them.

Each culture begins with the premise that these forces are accessible to some kind of understanding, and that they can be analyzed and mastered. We in the West make use of a process that we somewhat euphemistically call rational (Aristotelian). Yet other societies, those that believe in the sequences and consequences of other determinations, are equally competent to deal with the unknowns in terms that certainly make as good sense to them as ours do to us. Furthermore, most cultures have an impressive commitment to their concepts of understanding and control. They are extremely protective about their particular system and often quite disdainful of others; frequently arrogant, and even combative. Rarely, if ever, is this due to conviction about the accuracy of their own approach, although it would seem so. Usually it is the product of uncertainty because no one is really quite sure of these so-called convictions, and on one level or another most members of the society sense it. What we all do know is that we have to have something to go on that explains the mysteries and the intolerable confusions of the universes with which we are constantly forced to deal, and until something else far more durable comes along, we had better stick with what we have. And if we have to fight to the death to defend our particular system—whether it be Islam or Christianity, Buddhism or Hinduism, mysticism or science, or for that matter, Scientology or Freudianism—so be it.

Psychologically we are dealing with the internalized sense of personal power and powerlessness, a matter of extraordinary significance for the individual. All who have found themselves in a situation of critical importance, or which was considered of critical importance at the time, and over which they were able to exercise—or felt they were able to exercise—little or no control, and at the mercy of what was perceived, usually unconsciously, as destructive, malevolent forces, know well what I mean. The panic, the sense of internal disorganization, and frequently the accompanying desperate scrambling for controls, plus the despair that often goes along with it, are among the most distressing of all human experiences. And the fact that others may quite sympathetically point out that in fact heaven is not falling, and that our earthly foundations are not crumbling, does not change our conviction that although their perspective may be far sounder than ours, it is irrelevant for our purposes. In its most extreme form, this is precisely the terrifying sense of flying apart that is the entering emotional quality that precedes the psychotic episode, and is the central dimension of the nightmare, two of the most terrifying experiences known to man.

The point that is being made is that after elemental biological needs are met, there is nothing more crucial to the effective functioning of the human individual than a sense of valid control over his own destiny, and nothing so disruptive than the knowledge, whether true in actual fact or not, that he has lost it. To one degree or another, this is a primary condition within every living person and is found in all cultures.

I have often been asked how I would define "security" as a psychological condition (we all know what we mean by insecurity). And after many years of fumbling around, I would now, at least for the present, be willing to say that I believe that the core element for an adult in achieving a sense of personal security is the conviction, based upon solid, demonstrable experience, that one can, at least to a major extent, determine the course of one's life in those areas that are subject to a personal determination—the capacity to exert a legitimate mastery over one's personal fate. The emphasis is upon the word *legitimate*. This does not extend to overcompensatory mechanisms and the use of devices that would be considered unethical or improper by one's fellows. The use of wile, guile, and force, are not only the product of insecurity, but add to it.

The corollary for the child would be the sense that one can depend, solidly depend, upon the love, devotion, and skill of the nurturing ones. The image is a sleeping child in the arms of a cherishing mother who is relatively free from distracting personal concerns at that moment. I believe the term is bliss—a quality, except perhaps during moments of the ecstatic experience, that man seems to lose at a remarkably early age as he finds himself increasingly on his own.

For the child it is the profound conviction that his needs will be thoroughly satisfied; for the adult it is the assurance that, at least in those areas that are most important to him as an individual, he will be able to arrange his affairs in a just, socially sanctioned manner, in such a way that he can satisfy not only his own and others' needs but his prevailing interests as well. In short, that he can make life function in a way that he would like.

We are dealing with an inner perception of ourselves in which there is a continuum wherein one extreme is the sense of powerlessness, the inability to affect one's environment to conform to one's needs and concerns—"I am a stone and I go where I am kicked" or "I am a willow leaf and I bend as the winds blow"—to the other extreme, unfortunately rather rarely found, in which there is a relaxed, profound conviction that we have the knowledge and resources to steer our own ship (through the uncharted, reef-strewn, storm-tossed seas of life, of course).

Basic Socialization Experiences

In searching for the psychological roots that underlie the belief systems that various cultures have erected to compensate for the lack of a sense of personal determination, we must look to the parent-child relationship and particularly its earliest, pre-oedipal stages—infancy and childhood. It is here that we realize how utterly critical this matter is, because it is central both for physical and psychological survival.

The human infant is totally dependent upon the parenting adult not only for its well-being and the kind of person that he/she will ultimately become, but literally for life itself; as we all know too well, neglect can and does lead to death. In other words, in the early years, the course of the child's life and thus, to a major extent, its future, is in the hands of others. Inasmuch as all infants are born helpless, and the human animal remains dependent upon the parent longer than any other, helplessness and dependency are universal conditions. The essential issue for the child is the nature of the caring that is given and the manner in which the parenting ones respond, or do not respond, to his/her needs.

The child's sense of self, as Bettelheim has pointed out in his work with autistic children, and as my own and others' experience substantiates, is directly dependent upon his capacity to exert a rational mastery over his own environment. The basis for self-respect, ego strength, the sense of "I am" is dependent upon the parents' focus upon fulfilling the child's physical, social, and emotional needs. The child's ability to direct his parents to respond to these needs, his capacity to exert a reasonable control over the parents' behavior—in other words, his ability to induce his parents to respond to him, in effect to serve as vehicles for him, is a vital determinant in his subsequent sense of a legitimate and rational self (i.e., "I matter," "I have rights, by virtue of birth, that are respected by others," "My world is a responsive and fulfilling one," "People are caring and loving," etc.—all crucial issues in establishing a sense of self-esteem and trust).

There is an additional factor that must be considered, that of consistency and its counterpart, inconsistency. In certain cultures, and Vietnam is one of them, the child is subjected to extremes in discipline and teaching; extreme permissiveness on the one hand and abrupt restraint on the other. The child's undeveloped ego, dominated by id impulses, needs to be constrained and introduced to the social parameters that every culture imposes. The parents—or the parenting figures—are the primary transmittal agents in this process. The issue here is how it is done. The mix of affectionate discipline gradually applied in a consistent manner, as the child grows and is able to comprehend and incorporate reasonable restraints, would appear to be the most constructive. In some societies, however, certain sanctions are too strict and applied too early while at the same time, in other areas, the child is free to act as his whims dictate.

Integrating these forces intrapsychically is difficult indeed and may, in fact, never be fully resolved. Thus, when I asked experienced American and European observers how they would describe the child-rearing practices of the Vietnamese, all, without exception, said that they had never known a culture which was so permissive and allowed the children so much freedom (whether they meant license or freedom was not determined). When the same question was asked of the Vietnamese about their own childhood, they universally indicated in one way or another that they perceived their parents as having been severe and restrictive. The true situation is that both sets of observations were correct: in the imposition of parental authority two levels existed which constituted a central dimension within the parent–child relationship and ulti-mate character formation. The first was that of indulgence and permissiveness. This was observed within the desultory toilet training pattern, the variable eating and sleeping schedule, the freedom to leave the house, the absence of censorship for infractions that in many other cultures would be severely dealt with, and so on. At the same time, on a far deeper level, the child was gradually subjected to rigorous absolutes in interpersonal behavior, essential modes of conduct, and a basic value system.

Preparatory training for the code of behavior and the traditional forms starts at a very early age. For example, a friend and I were looking at some objects in an antique shop in Saigon. The proprietor was waiting on us, and his wife, together with their two-year-old son, joined him. The young boy had no interest in this commercial transaction and wanted to return to the back room. When the mother quietly insisted upon staying, the young fellow pouted and became sullen. He then walked over and punched me on the knee. The parents very gently remonstrated with him, whereupon he turned and gave my friend a resounding kick in the shins. At this point the mother acquiesced to his wishes and went off with him. The point is that at a very tender age, this child already knew that it was forbidden to express any hostility toward his parents. His controls were not yet fully established, and so he vent his anger toward a stranger, which was less forbidden.

We have here two levels of behavior: the first, in which the young child is permitted an extreme amount of self-determination; the second, much deeper in terms of content and psychological impact, in which absolute obedience is enforced. In this regard the child appears to be allowed little, if any, deviation from the set social code.

The effect of this on ego and superego development requires further investigation. My impression—and an impression is all I can offer—is that on the one hand the ego is beset by an inflated sense of personal power which later proves to be unrealistic in the face of cultural and interpersonal restraints; and on the other hand, rage at eventually being squelched, at being ejected from nirvana at so early an age. The result is an ambivalent control over aggressive impulses and a perceptual distortion of socially sanctioned limitations on behavior, eventuating in a placid, pleasant external demeanor underscored by a considerable amount of repressed hostility.

Although this pattern of indulgence and constraint begins at a very young age, to a great extent the early years are essentially discipline-free. During this period, the Confucian credo is not consciously taught to the child, but it is expressed empathically. Because it is so much a part of the nature of the parent, communication flows primarily on a nonverbal rather than a verbal level, which is the way of early teaching in all societies (i.e., mother frowns, her body becomes rigid, she becomes anxious, or conversely, she smiles, makes encouraging sounds, etc., thereby communicating approval or disapproval).

At some point, somewhere around age six or seven, the sky does fall. Discipline becomes much more forceful, the social order is codified, the child is deliberately taught and infractions are punished. (I was repeatedly told, "How can you discipline a child when he is young; he is not capable of thinking"). The golden years are over. (Although the age differs slightly, this also occurs in other Confucian societies, i.e., China and Korea. As pointed out elsewhere in this volume [Slote, chapter 2], Koreans humorously refer to "the terrible sevens," because seven is the age of imposition of forceful restraint, and the children rebel. It is especially hard on the first-born, both sons and daughters, because as one Chinese father said to me, "It is the oldest that are models for all the others, and if they don't toe the line you will not be able to discipline the rest.")

The end result, however, was that both freedom and restraint were issued from above with an absolute hand. Permission was granted or withheld but the child had very little determination over which it was to be; it was at the decision, and often the whim, of the parent. At all times, however, the child knew, with an absolute certainty, that he had little control over the parents' decisions. It is not the degree of restraint or freedom in the family that is the primary determinant, but the extent to which the child can influence the parenting—or other authority—figures to fulfill his needs that later leads to a heightened sense of self-worth and ego strength, firmly integrated within the child adult's self-image.

The urgency of this matter of legitimate mastery over one's own destiny continues uninterrupted throughout life. If it is initially well integrated through loving and responsible parenting, it makes for a sense of presence, the quality of "I am" and "I matter" which is empathically recognized by others. If all goes well, in later life it is expanded and deepened through caring and supportive relationships, with work that is fulfilling, by living in a manner that one respects, and in the esteem of others.

We must, however, clearly delineate between legitimate forms of control and, for lack of a better word, illegitimate forms. The first is based upon ego strength; the second on weakness: the strong do not have to coerce, cajole, manipulate, or depend upon guile, violence, or brutality (often, unfortunately, interpreted as strength).

There are, however, cultural exceptions to this thesis. All cultures support certain stylistic forms of behavior, including the ways in which members relate to one another. Although these forms can, I suppose, be regarded as manipulative, this certainly does not mean that all who use them conceive of themselves as weakened. An example is *amai*,[1] a relatively common interpersonal form, which certainly could be considered manipulative, used by women in relating to men in Japan and Vietnam (although it is found among individuals in other societies, it is not culturally supported). This does not mean that all who employ it feel inadequate or inferior; it may simply mean that, as a social form, it works. Furthermore, in this context, I would suppose that the motivation of the person who uses it matters a great deal.

Confucian Forms of Awareness

Vietnam is a society that incorporates several ancient religiocultural forces. It is an amalgam of Buddhism, Taoism, and Confucianism, and various folk and local belief systems. Christianity has its adherents, but its effect upon the culture seems to be minimal and psychologically it does not appear to have penetrated very deeply. The code of ethical and moral conduct was primarily determined by Confucianism, and in that sense Vietnam was a nation solidly entrenched within the Sinic/Confucian sphere of influence.

The family patterning in Vietnam was based upon an historically traditional Confucian system. Filial piety, the integrity of the family, and the intensity of intrafamilial relations were primary. The authority of father, mother, teacher, elder was unquestioned, and obedience to all was absolute. Although I specifically probed, with two exceptions, none of my informants in Vietnam ever revealed any hostility whatsoever toward either a parent or family elder. Culturally it was totally proscribed; personally it was dissociated from conscious awareness. Their appraisal of the parent was always benign and always fit into the accepted cultural mold; all negative perception was instantly suppressed both toward the parent and from the parent. Parents, however, were free to admit that they were often angry with the children, "Just as you are in your country," and openly stated that they did not hesitate to spank the older children when it was considered necessary. A slight exception was that of a vigorous young student dissident whose father was an alcoholic who, when on a drunken binge, would beat the mother. The children would run away, but the mother refused to leave (the role of the martyr is highly regarded in Vietnam; it is a most effective weapon, and in this instance was used to dramatize the father's brutality). In the telling, however, it was the alcohol that was responsible, not the father.

The second case was that of a leading intellectual and author whose father had made an abortive attempt to give (probably sell) him to a wealthy landlord when he was a child. According to my informant, he deliberately behaved so badly that he was returned. He never quite resolved the rage he felt over this act of betrayal and abandonment, although he attempted to rationalize it by assigning a benign interpretation to his father's motivation (e.g., his father wanted him to have a better life than he could provide). It should be added that for many years this informant not only lived in France but was educated there and associated with some of the foremost intellectuals of the time—people who were freer to related to emotions that would be forbidden in Vietnam. It should also be noted that this pattern of repression of culturally unacceptable ideation, emotions, and perceptions tends to be modified among the young Vietnamese when they come to the United States and are exposed to a society that is considerably more accepting of anger—including anger toward parents. However, strong residuals of the underlying Confucian patterns remain, which often results in serious emotional conflict, frequently expressed in intrapunitive behavior. I have had several Vietnamese in psychoanalysis, and I found that one has to be very cautious in dealing with the issue of parent-child hostility and its sequel, separation-individuation.[2]

The Confucian family, particularly as it was found in Vietnam was authoritarian. The father's power, if he wished to exercise it, was absolute. The fact that most fathers left the rearing of the children to the mother and, for the most part, maintained a detached aloofness from the affairs of the home, in no way changed the children's and the wives' realization that it was he who governed by right and the mother by sufferance. The fact is, as in all Confucian societies, a balance of authority within the family was established—though undefined and often covert—and usually effective. This also extended far beyond the garden gate, and teachers and elders shared in the power structure.

This system not only maintained the pattern of infantile dependency and powerlessness, but massively reinforced it. Moreover, there were no alternative models for the young to adopt; in this regard all families were essentially the same, and as a result the system, as it traditionally existed in Vietnam, remained unchallenged.

Perhaps of greatest consequence was the fact that this pattern of hierarchical structuring, in which the issue of inferiority/superiority was so firmly established, became deeply imprinted within the self-image of the child and was maintained in the adult throughout life. There was a sense of ineffectualness, of being subject to the will of others without recourse to self determination within the psychic structure of all. In a very profound sense, few seemed to conceive of themselves as their own masters—regardless of age and status. Concomitantly, however, compensatory, face-saving mechanisms were relatively common.

Symbolic Analysis: The Rorschach Test

Let me demonstrate. One of my informants was the young man who led most of the major Buddhist demonstrations against the Diem government prior to 1966. He was in hiding during the time that I saw him, living in a pagoda under the protection of a politically powerful Buddhist venerable. He was highly intelligent, rather withdrawn and somber except when acting as the dashing leader of the masses, an inspired orator, and distressingly naive in his political perspectives. I gave all informants a battery of psychological tests. Of these the Rorschach probes most deeply and has always proven most valuable for delving into unconscious processes. The Rorschach responses are products of the unconscious mind expressed as symbols and metaphors and can be analyzed in the same manner as a dream, or the free associations produced in a psychoanalytic session. For purposes of economy it is necessary that we confine ourselves to the informant's responses to the first two cards (there are ten), and deal only with material that relates to his vision of himself and of his parents—his self-image and the source from which it was primarily derived.

On Card I he first sees himself as a small calf with the ears of an ass. The calf has very gentle, lovely eyes, abundant hair, and wants to be cuddled.

He then sees another animal, a little more cunning than the first, which turns out to be a three-month-old puppy. He then visualizes himself as a crystal vase held by two birds with crowns on their heads (parental images). And finally he perceives a scorpion with an open mouth, and adds that the pony is standing on a block of ice.

On Card II he first sees two hairy dogs leaning against each other and playing (parents). He then adds a composite animal. He refines the precept and one aspect of the animal evolves into a headless pig; the other into a lion who has been struggling with another animal, which subsequently becomes a second lion. the ground is covered with blood. Last, he sees the grave of a princess and steps of white marble leading to the tower where her remains are buried. He creates an allegory about the princess and a prince in which the prince competes for and wins her hand in marriage. "As the moment of happiness is nearing," a fiend abducts the princess. The prince follows and slays the demon, but before it dies it retains enough strength to destroy the palace, and a falling stone kills the princess. The prince returns her body to her parental home and builds a mausoleum that consumes all of his and her father's resources. "And afterwards the prince leaves for the deep jungle and no one ever finds him."

To return to Card I, on the outside he is a man who leads the multitudes against an oppressive and restrictive government (read this also as a transposition from family and society); on the inside he feels himself a weak, helpless calf with the ears of an ass (which in Vietnam as elsewhere represents stupidity and ignorance), and a little puppy in need of love and warmth. The calf, however, has a great deal of hair. The Vietnamese men have no body hair, and the Vietnamese women seemed admiring of the large, hairy American soldiers (or at least the Vietnamese men thought so and resented it). Therefore, this symbol probably represents potency and masculinity. Should this interpretation be true, and I believe it is, it would be a statement as to how he compensates for his feelings of being weak, immature, and ineffectual (the calf) through displays of masculinity and bravado (the hair). He then sees a crystal vase held by two crowned birds. A crystal vase is very precious, but this one is in a precarious position: if the birds drop the vase it could be shattered. Our informant is the oldest son in a Confucian family. His parents are the regal birds; he is the precious vase dependent upon them for support. He then proceeds to reveal another dimension of how he regards himself: he is a scorpion with an open mouth. Scorpions are dangerous and poisonous. And for his last response to the card he adds that the pony is standing on a sheet of ice. Ice is slippery, it constitutes a very unstable base. It is also cold—and our informant means emotionally cold. The pony/puppy that needs cuddling finds that his world is loveless and unreliable.

On Card II he proceeds to tell us how his damaged ego came into being. At first he produces a proper, Confucian image of the parents—two playful dogs, innocent, without guile. He then reveals a deeper, repressed perception of his parents: his mother and father are tightly bound together (the composite animal), inseparable but locked in mortal combat. His mother a headless pig (mindless, faceless); his father a raging lion that attacks the mother. However, the mother is not without her own capacity for aggression and destructiveness, because she becomes a lion too. But the father is by far the stronger; the ground is covered with her blood, not his.

He ends with a tale of loneliness and despair in which he strives to find love but is defeated. He may be able to conquer the fiend but he cannot overcome its destructive power. He buries his lost hopes, the affection and caring that he needs so much but which he is convinced can never be his. He goes off, alone, where no one can find him.

The Experiences of Power

The Vietnamese operate upon the premise that there are forces, external to themselves, that are very influential in determining their destiny. They believe this with conviction, and it provides a philosophical base to their lives that serves as a substratum to their psychology. It is true that other cultures also live with the certainty of external determination—God, Christ, Mohammed. What is unique about the Vietnamese is the nature of their beliefs, the power that is assigned to the forces that govern their destiny, the panoply of elements that combine to determine fate, and the high degree to which these external forces are internalized within the conscious and unconscious life of the Vietnamese people.

The consequence is that the Vietnamese to a great, although far from an absolute extent experience themselves as being in the hands of a destiny that is determined by forces beyond their command. The intrapsychic reaction is such that it confirms and reinforces the sense of impotence that arises from a childhood spent in an authoritarian family, where conforming to the social code and obeisance to the absolute domination of the parent is the pattern.

The feeling of helplessness is deeply repressed. As such it exists within the unconscious strata of mental life; one senses that conscious awareness would be too traumatizing for the individual to experience overtly. Inasmuch as it is one of the most devastating of all psychodynamic forces, man has created certain ego-defense mechanisms to handle it, both individual and cultural. Aside from the personal modes of coping that serve to reduce anxiety and that are universal to all mankind (i.e., detachment, withdrawal, denial, obsessive-compulsive mechanisms, etc.), the Confucian societies have devised a series of religiocultural belief systems that mesh with these powerful individual human forces. In Vietnam, they are *phuc duc,* astrology, geomancy, and the spirit world.

Individually, these serve a complex set of psychological and cultural purposes, but common to all are three primary functions: they support, they justify, and they explain. They provide a codified system for understanding the forces that beset man, and they lighten and frequently remove the onus of personal responsibility for what happens in life. They are an affirmation of man's global sense of inferiority and inadequacy: tacit testimony to the belief that there are powers which are essentially beyond individual control that govern one's destiny, and the perception of man as a pawn in a great cosmic arrangement.

This is a direct extrapolation from the situation found in the Vietnamese home where the child is subject to the will of others. His fate, the quality and nature of his life are determined elsewhere—by father, mother, elder, socioreligious code, and so on. If one transposes from hearth to heaven, we find an identical dynamic: man is weak and ultimately powerless in the face of overwhelming forces, and the best he can do is to negotiate, plead, cajole (but never demand) in the hope that these powers will prove more benign than malevolent. Thus the authoritarian interpersonal relationships found within the Vietnamese family and reflected in village and nation are, in turn, converted into a belief system that recapitulates precisely those conditions that exist in the home.

Although all four of these tenets are interrelated and tend to mesh in the minds of the Vietnamese (the spirit world somewhat less a presence among the more sophisticated), all play important roles in the ideation of the people and their approach to life. Geomancy and the spirits are, to a limited extent, manipulable: one can change the position of the grave of an ancestor or the direction that one's house, bed, or chair faces; one can negotiate with the spirits, or deceive them, or even bribe them (all spirits have a quasi-human dimension). On the other hand, *phuc duc* and astrology are not subject to personal determination: the stars are relentless, and the behavior of one's ancestors, whether virtuous or sinful, is beyond anyone's capacity to change; one's destiny has been set, and the best that can be hoped for is that other forces will intervene and modify the course of life.

Of the four, *phuc duc*[3] is most uniquely Vietnamese and is of particular importance because it affects not only the individual and the family, but the structure of society as well. Although related forms are found elsewhere, the stylistic format and the particular nature of *phuc duc,* in addition to its broad social consequences, appears to be culture specific and places it in a very special category. There is very little published literature on *phuc duc* and, therefore, I shall confine my discussion to it.

Phuc duc refers to the merit that an ancestor has acquired through virtuous deeds that is then passed on to succeeding generations, and the merit that a member of the present generation passes to future generations as yet unborn. It is quantified (reference is made to "a lot" or "much" *phuc duc*). Based on the manner in which one lives one's life, it can be a force for evil *(vo phuc)* as well as good. It is considered influential over a span of five generations. Thus, the nature of one's *phuc duc,* together with one's horoscope (the confluence of the stars), and geomancy (the influence of the forces of the earth) determines the course of life. The individual can exert a limited personal influence, but the primary pattern is set external to the self. Those acts that constitute a virtuous life follow the Buddhist-Confucian code of meritorious conduct. The *Gia huan ca,* a famous fifteenth-century poem, defines with great specificity those acts that gain merit and those that do not. The definition and the teaching of the virtues have remained essentially unchanged to this day. The young woman who was translating the poem for us repeatedly remarked that her mother's instructions as to proper behavior were precisely the same as those set forth in the text.

The primary determinant, however, is not the act itself, it is the motivation beneath the act. Thus in the great epic poem *Kim van Kieu,* Kieu, a girl of particular charm, beauty, accomplishment, and morality, sells herself as a minor wife to an unscrupulous scholar in order to redeem her father who has been beset by ill fortune. The scholar, a man devoid of virtue, turns out to be the husband of the madame of a brothel and Kieu is forced into prostitution. Under these circumstances, Kieu's sacrificial act brings much *phuc duc.* On the other hand, were she to have become a prostitute for profit alone, she would have been condemned, her family would have suffered, and future generations would have born the penalties. In a parallel sense Kieu's misfortune, inasmuch as her life had been thoroughly virtuous, could be ascribed to bad *phuc duc* visited upon her because of the transgressions of some ancestor.

Coupled with the nature of the motivation that serves to precipitate the act is the issue of sacrifice. An act that is performed easily brings far less reward than an equivalent action that is difficult and involves suffering. To stay with the previous example: were Kieu to have enjoyed the sexual experience of prostitution she would have diminished the family' *phuc duc.* Instead, she found it revolting, and when her fortune later changed and she was reunited with the man she loved, to whom she had originally been betrothed, she renounced sex with her husband and, with his reluctant concurrence, established a morganic marriage.

Both *phuc duc* and astrology provide a rationale wherein responsibility for personal acts can be avoided, and this is supported by the belief that the *phuc duc* that parents acquire does not affect their own children. It skips a generation and is visited upon the grandchildren and beyond. At dinner one evening, a Vietnamese professional and his wife said that their seventeen-year-old son was behaving badly. His grades in school were poor, he had become increasingly rebellious, and he was not showing proper deference to his parents. During the ensuing discussion I asked the father if he felt that he had done anything to contribute to his son's problems. Vehemently he answered, "Not me. If I have done my best to educate my children and they turn out badly, then why should I feel responsible? Nonsense!" His wife remained silent but nodded vigorously in agreement. Somewhat tangentially I pursued the issue on a considerably more abstract level and asked what explanation he would offer if a child became stubborn and intractable. Firmly he answered, "It is fate, it is due to his horoscope." The wife remonstrated and said that perhaps it was because the child was scared, embarrassed, or insecure. When I asked where that might come from, she answered, "It is due to the influence of other people." The husband interjected, "No. It is due to the child's horoscope—100 percent!" He then went on to develop the theme that a horoscope, cast by a good astrologer, will incorporate the child's *phuc duc*. The point is not the ascription—*phuc duc,* astrology, or whatever—the issue is that someone else or some condition beyond the person is responsible.

Inasmuch as *phuc duc* is essentially a mystical concept and is determined pragmatically by figuring backward (e.g., if life goes well one has good *phuc duc,* if it goes badly one has poor *phuc duc*), it can be used as a rationalization for unacceptable behavior. My own sense was that when it was used in this manner it was received by others with a degree of skepticism. The ascription was not challenged, but neither did the behavior gain acceptability. *Phuc duc* is complemented by *giao duc,* the influence exerted on a person's life through guidance and education. The term carries the connotation of ethical direction, the teaching of morality. Although the Vietnamese may claim that they, as parents, exert little or no influence upon the way their children's character is formed and the manner in which their lives evolve, in practice they do not act as if this were the case. The Vietnamese instruct, direct, and discipline their children as do parents everywhere. And being a Confucian society, the proper forms are taught forcefully, especially as the child grows older. If all were predetermined, then instruction of the young would be irrelevant—and this is certainly not how the Vietnamese parent acts.

It is difficult to determine the relationship between *giao duc* and *phuc duc;* people do not conceptualize belief systems—they just act them out. And so it is with the Vietnamese. It is particularly difficult because one hears very little about *giao duc* and the term is infrequently used. However, to the best of my ability to determine, in the minds of the Vietnamese, *phuc duc* and the astrological signs establishes a person's character and the major events in his life. These are foreordained, and nothing can be done to change them. *Giao duc* refers to the socialization process, the instruction of the young in the ways of the culture. Thus *phuc duc* and *giao duc* complement each other, with *giao duc* considered of far less importance.

The acquisition of *phuc duc* is primarily, although not exclusively, the responsibility of the women. This makes the choice of a bride a crucially important issue because the future of the family depends upon the *phuc duc* that she brings, and later creates. Not only is it necessary that she possess the proper womanly virtues, such as humility, industry, and subservience, but it is essential that she bring propitious *phuc duc* and that her horoscope complement that of her betrothed. The wealth and status of her family matters but, especially in the past, it was secondary. The result was a leveling of class structure. A poor but virtuous woman of good heritage and blessed at birth by the heavens, who would increase the family's fortune and ultimate destiny, was a most desirable bride. And of course when marriage was arranged between a poor but virtuous girl and a son of a wealthy family, the girl's family also usually benefited. Inasmuch as all Vietnamese share the same morality, an identical code of proper conduct, and a common religiocultural belief system, movement either up or down the class ladder could be relatively fluid. To a large extent, *phuc duc* has been influential in maintaining class unity and social homogeneity.

With the responsibility of acquiring *phuc duc* assigned primarily to the women, a double standard has been created. Whereas the women are constrained, the men, if they choose, are relatively free to act in ways that are scarcely designed to build *phuc duc*. It is thus that many men rationalize activities that by any Confucian standard would be considered highly improper, such as gambling, cheating, and whoring. On the other hand, there are men who contribute heavily to the building of *phuc duc* for the family. On several occasions, I heard elderly men referred to as living saints, a position that carried great esteem.

The women did, of course, capitalize on the status their *phuc duc* brought, but at the same time it was a mixed blessing because it left them vulnerable to attack if the affairs of the family did not go well. On one occasion, I was interviewing the elderly, formerly affluent parents of an Americanized Vietnamese woman who was married to a European journalist. The old gentleman had monopolized the conversation, pontificating at great length, and although I had directed several of my questions specifically to the mother, he was allowing no interruptions. However, at one point she did break in, whereupon he angrily turned to her and said that their misfortunes could only be due to her lack of *phuc duc*. A shocked silence ensued at this very improper behavior in front of a stranger. I could see the mother debating as to how she would handle this delicate situation so as to preserve her dignity and yet answer in such a way that her husband would not lose face. After a moment's hesitation she quietly, but forcefully, said that perhaps had it not been for her *phuc duc* they both would have been dead. Her husband did not respond, but from that time forth he permitted her greater participation in the proceedings.

Phuc duc, by its very nature, lends itself to manipulation. It can be used as a metaphor in the service of many emotions: hostility, competitiveness, defiance, self-sacrifice, guilt, control, and so on—all of which, in one form or another, are power maneuvers. But although it can and often is used quite consciously in this manner, this does not detract from the deeper meaning that it carries, the mystical awe in which it is held.

One also has the sense that for many Vietnamese, *phuc duc* is resorted to as justification when all else fails: when a Vietnamese-American son is unfilial and the parents have exhausted their ability to control him; when a distinguished elder feels lost and ineffectual in this strange and daunting new world; when one is beset by misfortune and is unable to reverse it. But again, although on occasion it certainly is used in this manner, it does not diminish its underlying significance.

The origins of *phuc duc* are difficult to derive. My own sense is that it is a magical, prelogical folk belief that has evolved as a cultural rationalization for an unresolved psychological dynamic, a useful concept that justifies and helps reduce the anxiety provoked by some very disturbing repressed emotional conflicts.

Be that as it may, *phuc duc* would appear to be loosely related to both filial piety and ancestor worship, from which it most probably arose. Both reinforce the Confucian code of moral conduct, which, in turn, serves as the matrix for the society—although it has been argued elsewhere that filial piety is itself the matrix, a position that I would not challenge. Within this constellation, *phuc duc* performs a most significant function: through a combination of rewards and punishments, it constitutes the equivalent of a legal system. Moreover, in a culture that is particularly sensitive to shame because of the importance of the family, and where one's personal conduct reflects upon all others, the censorship provided through *phuc duc* is particularly effective. In the West, guilt, which is related to shame, is essentially a personal matter; in Vietnam, one's transgressions have both a horizontal and a vertical dimension: they affect both the nuclear and extended family in the current generation and the well-being of the family for generations to come. Not only is this a powerful deterrent to improper behavior, more important, it is a glue, a bonding agent (although not the only one) that holds the society together.

The accountability that *phuc duc* places upon the Vietnamese, in terms of the implications that it carries for personal conduct, is awesome. It is difficult enough being responsible for oneself and one's personal nexus of family and friends, but for this to extend for generations forward is a heavy load indeed.

Phuc duc does place stringent limits on the extent to which the Vietnamese feels he is his own master. Yet at the same time, it provides a coherent sequence of cause and effect. It postulates an orderly universe, and if one accedes to the conditions that this universe imposes, one can work out a modus vivendi—if not in this incarnation, then in the next.

A straight reading of *phuc duc,* geomancy, astrology, and the spirit world phenomena might lead one to conclude that the Vietnamese consider themselves helpless pawns in the grip of an unremitting fate over which they have little or no control. This is, of course, far from true. Were it so, this, and other cultures that have similar beliefs, would not be able to function; they would be immobilized with hopelessness and despair. For the answer as to why this is not so, one has to examine first the total social milieu and second, the capacity of the ego to synthesize, to incorporate disparate input into a functional mode.

Phuc duc and other related forms have to be considered within the context of other prevalent religiocultural systems. In a Confucian Buddhist society, an internalized sense of power is derived from many sources: age, knowledge, family, maleness, mother-in-lawness, grandmotherness, affluence, status, the anticipation of a better life after death if one lives or dies in a virtuous manner, and so on. All know that eventually they will be in a position of authority and power: sons will someday be fathers, daughters will become mothers, daughters-in-law will be mothers-in-law. And all young women know that at some point they will be grandmothers, a position that carries great influence and respect, just as becoming an elder brings for the men.

The self-determination that is granted to the children is also of psychological significance. Although a mixed blessing in the face of later expression, it does have positive qualities that appear to carry over throughout later life. The stored subconscious memories of the glorious omnipotent years appear to buttress the ego, to add measurably to the feeling of self-worth and intrapsychic power.

We must also consider the impressive capacity of the ego to integrate conflictual demands and the versatility and effectiveness of the defense system. The Vietnamese, as is true of those of many other societies, are skillful in compartmentalizing, in separating and isolating discordant forces, both internal and external. They, and others, also make good use of dissociation, the ability to detach one's self from the conscious awareness of distressing inner forces, to live "as if" they do not exist. One pays a price for this, but life usually becomes far more bearable. The Vietnamese have other intrapsychic coping mechanisms, but these appear to be relatively universal, whereas others are idiosyncratic.

A Contrast to the West

The Vietnamese assignment of power to forces that are outside one's personal determination is in sharp contrast to the conceptual mode found in the West, wherein the locus of power resides within the self. Although there are extensive variations to this theme, the essential image is that man determines his own destiny. This is modified, of course, by realities external to the individual over which he may have little or no control such as wars, political disruption, socioeconomic factors, and so forth. But intrinsic to the concept of the self, one's internalized image, is the conviction that man has the power and the freedom to act as the central agent in the organization of his life. In Vietnam the inverse holds true. The essential difference is that one primarily looks within the self and the other essentially looks outside and beyond.

Notes

The basic field data for this study was collected during two research seasons in South Vietnam, in 1966 and 1967. It was continued in France, 1970, and in the United States, with Vietnamese émigrés, 1976–79. From 1978 to the present, I have had a number of Vietnamese in psychoanalysis to whom I am very indebted; they have been a particularly rich source of data. From 1984 to the present I have been involved in two studies in South Korea: one relating to the psychocultural dynamics of the Korean family; a second on child rearing. Both have contributed comparable data and have helped to put the Vietnamese research in perspective.

Although much of this study was done in the past, I have taken the liberty of presenting it as though the research had been recently completed— thus the occasional use of the present tense. I found that any other approach was simply too awkward.

1. An ingratiating manner practiced by women which combines subservience, subtle sexual provocation, and seeming dependency.

2. The initial research on *phuc duc* was conducted in conjunction with Stephen Young and Hoa Young. Their sensitivity and commitment were invaluable, and I am deeply appreciative of their dedicated collaboration.

References

Doi, T. (1981). *The Anatomy of Dependence*. Tokyo/New York: Kodansha.

———. (1995). *Amae no shiso.* 1st ed. Tokyo: Kobundo.

Eber, I., ed. (1986). *Confucianism: The Dynamics of Tradition*. New York: Macmillan; London: Collier Macmillan.

Johnson, F. A. (1993). *Dependency and Japanese Socialization: Psychoanalytic and Anthropological Investigations into Amae*. New York: New York University Press.

Slote, Walter. H. (1972). "Psychodynamic Structures in Vietnamese Personality." In *Transcultural Research in Mental Health,* ed. W. P. Lebra. Vol. 2: *Mental Health Research in Asia and the Pacific.* Honolulu: University of Hawaii Press.

―――. (1986). "Metaphor, Imagery, and Fantasy: The Symbolic World of the Vietnamese." *Journal of Psychoanalytic Anthropology* 9.3.

―――. (1986). "The Intrapsychic Locus of Power and Personal Determination in a Confucian Society: The Case of Vietnam" In *The Psycho-Cultural Dynamics of the Confucian Family: Past and Present,* ed. W. H. Slote. Seoul: International Cultural Society of Korea.

―――. (1988). "Separation-Individuation as a Central Issue in Psychoanalysis with Patients from Confucian Societies." American Psychoanalytic Association, Montreal. Session on Transcultural Issues in Psychoanalysis: The Confucian Societies.

―――. (1992). "Oedipal Ties and the Issue of Separation-Individuation in Traditional Confucian Societies." *Journal of the American Academy of Psychoanalysis* 20.3.

17

Confucian Family Socialization: The Religion, Morality, and Aesthetics of Propriety

George A. De Vos

For many the concept of religion entails some emphasis on the supernatural, or at least concerns itself with the origins of life or the eventual destiny of man. Traditional Confucian thought as developed in Japan during the Tokugawa period from 1600 on was a guide to practical moral behavior buttressing Japanese premodern institutions of family and government. It was focused on the here and now, and a sense of continuity marked neither by beginning nor end. Little concern, even among Confucian specialists, was directed toward a vague concept of "heaven" or a cosmos extending beyond. What was stressed was a sense of belonging and the moral cultivation necessarily attendant upon particularist sentiments of fealty and reverence directed toward family lineage and temporal authority. Confucian doctrine in Japan as in China was concerned with ethical imperatives directing the individual toward a development of self in social role.

While there is reverence for ancestry and a mythology of a golden age where temporal society was just, harmonious, and well governed, in Confucian writings there is little concern with any philosophical or mythological transcendence beyond human time or space. For many Western students of religion, vague references to "heaven" or metaphysical discussions about unity or duality in a first principle do not qualify Confucian doctrines for consideration as a "religious" system.

Whatever the technical definitions used to justify such a judgment, I would argue to the contrary. For many Asians, past and present ethical preoccupations and moral guides to propriety as considered in Confucian thought and practice were and are sufficient for them to encompass the social and psychological functions of religion. The sense of reverence and awe the experiences of deep love and gratitude for many entail a supernatural source or intervening divine intentionality. Others, however, experience such feelings without positing the existence of a realm beyond nature or relationships that transcend humanity. The religious sense of a practicing Confucianist in my judgment can be as complete as that of a Hindu, Buddhist, Muslim, Jew, or Christian. There are psychological, if not technical reasons for this assertion about religious belief and practice that will become clearer in the course of my discussion.

Indeed, following my reasoning, the Japanese family may be considered a quasi-religious institution. In what follows I shall try to delineate how the heritage of Confucianism continues quite unconsciously in today's Japan by remaining visible in the manner in which one inhabits given social roles, and experiences interpersonal sentiments about gratitude and reverence.

I shall argue that to understand the traditional Japanese family as bound together as a religious entity, it is necessary to examine the ritualized forms of deference practiced toward older family members, and the sense of reverence and gratitude experienced in respect to progeniture which obviates for many the experience of such emotions directed toward the divine as occurs in the West.

In the case of the Japanese I would further argue that although Confucian thought has not been explicitly taught as such for some time, the interpersonal attitudes of belonging to a quasi-religious family have been continued in spite of the disappearance of Confucian dogma from the surface of Japanese social consciousness. What I say for the Japanese family as an institution that satisfies in its members some inherent human needs of a religious nature, also applies, given some cultural differences in each instance, to Chinese, Koreans, and to the Vietnamese.

Ancestor worship, which remains more directly related to Confucian thought among Koreans or Chinese, is more characteristically officiated by Buddhist specialists in Japan. Yet there is Confucian continuity despite the almost total absence today of any form of explicit adherence to formal Confucian dogma and ceremony. Confucian sentiments remain in a basic Japanese sense of social propriety to be explained as gratifying, at the same time fulfilling moral and aesthetic needs. Behaviorally they are actualized in role behavior within the family.

Confucian thought and feeling are engendered during the early socialization of children. Japanese as other inheritors of the Confucian tradition are socialized within a primary family to defer gratification as they come to follow internalized directives to realize the self through responsible moral-social behavior throughout the life trajectory. The purpose of this chapter is to attempt to explain certain aspects of childhood socialization and their consequences within a Confucian psychocultural context.

Looked at from a psychodynamic perspective I would argue that ritual, even secular in origin, can become "sacred," because it becomes moral to perform when it is imbued with meanings of loyalty or fealty to proper authority and it can become immoral not to do so. There is one further contention I would make, namely, there is an unconscious but strong associative link between morality and aesthetics in the socialization of humans. I plan to support these generalizations by tracing out how basic religious-moral feelings are integrated as part of the experience of self.

The Locus of Power Related to
Self-Development in Confucian Thought

One of the issues raised in respect to the social and psychological effects of childhood training within a Confucian family is whether or not such training characteristically leads to passivity and resignation to circumstances, or conversely, to a sense of initiative in assuming one's social expectations. Is one a passive respondent to uncontrollable circumstance, or is one prompted to seek out whatever instrumental means are available to bend circumstances to one's own advantage?

Is passivity and resignation, when it appears, due to the internalization of *Confucian* teaching per se, or to other social or personal factors occurring in given individuals? A stereotype about Confucianist "Oriental fatalism" is no longer in evidence given the economic and social change now evident in East Asia. Nevertheless, patience and forbearance in the name of long-range purpose is sometimes misconstrued as passivity, as is recourse to magic when other means of resolving a problem is lacking. As Jordan has argued in examining the magical practices to which Chinese have recourse in geomancy or in divination, what may be cited as magical procedures used to improve one's fate can also be read as active instrumental behavior based on shared folk beliefs that are used to ward off any easy acquiescence or resignation to fate, rather than indications of a passive resignation to it. Seen psychologically, recourse to magic usually entails an instrumental or active practice to achieve some need or desire.

Among the Japanese there are at times seeming acts of acquiescence to circumstances or acts of resignation in which the person uses the term *akirameru.* One must note that this is a term borrowed from Buddhism that literally means "to become enlightened." It is actually the Buddhist tradition in Japan— not the Confucian heritage—that permits one to "drop out" of worldly endeavor. Prayer for some Christians or Buddhists is a form of meditation, but for many is a more helpless supplication for outside assistance due to a deep sense of inner insufficiency. Confucianism does not use prayer in supplication. It is not a tradition that allows one passively to put one's fate in the intervening hands of a supernatural benevolence.

The Japanese distinguish between forms of religion in which individuals appeal to outside power, *tariki,* and religious activities employing *jiriki* or power from within. Appeal to the mercy of Amida is *tariki.* Zen practices of meditation are *jiriki*. Confucian concepts of social role actualization are also *jiriki*. The resignation found in a Confucian adherence to one's role does not result in inactivity, rather it is a sought-for resolution between what is termed "selfishness" and the proper active, but more selfless carrying out of one's expected role. Proper assumption of an expected role implies hard work and self-discipline— not resignation or withdrawal from challenge or an appeal to external power to help one's fate.

As I shall shortly discuss, belief in magic can be related to forms of mechanical precausality found in children in which the locus of power is in some manipulative activity, either on the part of oneself or on the part of a specialist who knows how to cause change in line with what is desired. This is different from prayer, which acknowledges a sense of inner helplessness and the need for the intercession of an outside intentional power to amend one's fate.

This training results in self-discipline—not passivity or appeals to outside power. One learns to put off present gratification, but with future social purpose and future social and occupational mastery in mind. A sense of mastery in respect to the events occurring in the world about is the goal of Confucian self-development *defined within one's prescribed social role*. One senses *internally* an active potential. One seeks to enhance an active locus of control *within*. Causality is ultimately moral, but morality is related to inner will and to emotional intensity in *ki* or *kokoro*, not to some submission to a potentially wrathful deity. This concept of *kokoro* for a Japanese implies active will, heart and mind, or in Western psychological terminology, a combination of conation-will, affect-motion, and cognition or causal thought, interfused with one another in social behavior resulting from our inner nature.

As I have already mentioned in chapter 6 on Tokugawa Confucian thought, there are discussions in the Neo-Confucian literature whether or not *ri*—as a first principle of order and the interactional causality inherent in all nature, as well as inherent in man—is distinct from *ki* or *kokoro*. This is not the place to take on again such philosophical discussions of Confucian specialists, rather let us turn to a more psychological investigation of the early experience of power occurring in infancy and childhood in humans and consider how these experiences are transmuted into a concept of a still remaining Confucian social self in Japan.

Precausality in Children and the Experience of Belonging and Mastery

Psychosexual Development, Social Resonance, and Religious Compassion

The newborn's information-processing system at first cannot distinguish the locus of stimulus and response and only gradually begins to define a sense of separateness, distinguishing what is inside from what is outside the experiential self; what is "I" and "not I," what is "we" and "not we." The boundaries established by ego mechanisms become progressively more congruent with the boundaries of the physical body.

In Western social values individuation and autonomy are goals. The self is to become a distinct experience separated off from social roles. However, in some societies the "self" concept remains more interactional, more embedded in social role behavior than in others (Hsu 1985). Through various forms of continuing social attachment, one maintains a sense of security. The experiential self in a Confucianist context tends to remain interactive and transactional. One is a belonging member of an entity larger than oneself. Rather than being concerned with the boundaries of one's "individuality" or becoming distinct from one's primary social attachments, as in the Western individualistic goal, Confucianist self-definition is found in the behavior that unites one with others as well as in activities that distinguish the "we" from the "they" (De Vos, Marsella, and Hsu 1985).

In the earliest development phase, the human child is presumed to experience little or no sense of separateness from its primary caretaker, usually the mother. The early infant as yet distinguish his inner experiences from those of the external world in experiencing the source of sensation. The maternal breast as such is not experienced as distinctly separate from the child. The universe and the baby are at this point one and the same. The maternal breast, body warmth, and protection constitute a self-contained sense of infantile paradise.

This sense of paradise is interrupted from the beginning. From the very first, the quality of contented oneness is not continuous, there are also periodic experiences of malaise and discomfort. Biologically the infant is equipped with a capacity for crying. Vocalization is in effect an early establishment of a locus of power; the act of crying itself is related causatively to a desired remission of malaise. When relief follows crying, a sequential association is established in which the crying has caused a change. Crying is both the earliest form of beseeching and the earliest form of command.

The so-called "oral" period in psychoanalytic reconstructions of childhood experiences is not just one of concern with being fed; it is one emphasizing body contact, closeness, and warmth. The human mammal needs warmth as well as feeding. Moreover, mammals including humans are resonant animals. There are "aliments" of experience that are taken in through all the senses and responded to in the body as well, leaving residues to be digested and integrated within the developing mind. All the senses and the total body are involved in the experience of parental care.

From a religious standpoint, one finds the earliest stages of experience prior to the sense of individual separation represented in later religiously defined experiences of closeness, even mystical oneness. In some religious experience, there is an intense sense of togetherness, closeness, and belonging.

Tracing back the motoric experiences in ritual as I shall presently attempt, one must attend to this progressive development of patterns of bodily resonance in human beings. Such development is part of an inherited mammalian capacity for "emotional responsiveness"—involving the adaptive release of physiochemical agents guiding responses within the social environment of animals through which antagonism or sexual receptivity is perceived (De Vos and Suarez-Orosco 1987). Adaptive learning occurs through resonant interplay.

When I perceive with my eyes the posture of another person or the smile on a face, something happens inside to resonate and to cause a similar or complementary response. One "knows" (Ekman 1973) what the other person is feeling because ones own motoric response can be "read" and brought into conscious awareness. Examined kinesthetically any social interaction involves perceptions automatically communicated to the musculature, which is resonantly reading the postural display of others. These readings can be selectively ignored or brought to attention depending on a complexity of factors (Birdwhistle 1970).

Mammalian empathic resonance is inherent in the mental mechanism of "introjection," and gradually this capacity is transmuted into identification on a conscious level into social identity. This mechanism insures a cultural continuity of social behavior from generation to generation. Humans possess a complex capacity to "internalize" all forms of social experience and communicated thought. In a religious context, empathic resonance is the origin of the human capacity for compassion. We can comprehend psychological malaise as well as physical hurt in others.

The early infantile origin of the human capacity for compassion is graphically represented with direct insight on a giant mural in the original postwar Supreme Court chambers in Tokyo. Three major Japanese virtues are personified in the figure of Shotoku Taishi, the prince responsible for early juridical reforms based on both Confucian and Buddhist teachings. To represent compassion Prince Shotoku is depicted as a small babe in the arms of his mother.

Human capacities for social attachment and communication, the feeling of good will and compassion, start early and are diffused out into human relationships within one's social group. The transcendence of too immediate social boundaries is one of the recognized tasks of religious development. Human interaction starts in close contact. Feelings are imparted through the body first and then more distantly through the eyes and through the ears so that all the senses are employed at progressive distances, but what is outside at a distance can still be experienced as inside and incorporated as part of the self or the social entity with whom one identifies.

The so-called oral stage is indeed primarily one of physical-tactual closeness of the body to an encompassing "social" warmth. There is gradually established a causal sequence in which crying, an oral act, precedes resultant nursing, closeness, and the reestablishment of a sense of well-being. But from the beginning, the infant is also "commanding," to gain satisfaction, the first sense of inner intentionality directed out toward an as yet imperfectly separated-off outside. While there is suffusion inward—an introjection of satisfaction—this sequential satisfaction is imperfectly realized. The infant comes to perceive that there is not always a direct correspondence between a need and a resulting satisfaction. Progressively, there is an increased ability to bind the tension between crying and anticipated result.

As I shall subsequently discuss, physiological capacity increases and intentionality also becomes related toward one's own musculature. A sense of willful control becomes directed toward one's own motility, the hand-mouth focus broadens out into more agile locomotion. There is an increasing awareness of "muscular causality," an automatized intentional voluntary control over one's sphincters as well as other musculature.

Some sense of power also becomes progressively located in an inner awareness of social communication. There is good evidence to suggest that there is increasing inner control of what starts out as automatic, inherited patterns of facial gesture such as smiling, frowning, and disgust. These gestures become a controlled part of intimate communication in parental bonding (Ekman et al. 1972; Ekman 1973). A child learns progressively to voluntarily manipulate his gestural capacities to induce resonant feeling states in observers.

Early omnipotence is weakened with the gradual realization that one cannot always control or cause what is desired. Concomitantly, a sense of helplessness and insecurity also gradually develops. There is an increasing realization that control and force are frequently external and subject to an outside, often unpredictable will. One must relate to this outside volition for satisfaction and security. This sensing of external power and intentionality arises out of emotional states in which power is experienced as lost due to a sense of separation from its source, increasingly located outside the self (see Slote, chapter 16). Sebastian De Grazia (1948) has related the Freudian concept of separation anxiety to the use of societal religious and political beliefs as "security systems." These systems of thought and forms of social participation are attempts to reestablish an early sense of belonging by group participation. As I shall further discuss, for the Japanese, and perhaps for many Confucianists, the family, not a church or political entity, is both the primary and the ultimate belonging.

The Experience of Divine Intentionality

A religious sense of power in deity can be represented in various forms. Causal interference in the sequence of human events can be attributed to a single deity, or manifest through the actions of different deities. Humans employ a variety of representations of the intentionally directed consequences of supernatural power. Even in theoretically atheistic Buddhism there has been developed a pantheon with various Buddhist representations of a hell and afterlife. These were historical additions, allowing for popular representations of power in divinity. As the present head monk at Mt. Hiei expressed it to me, most adherents of religious sects are, through reassuring belief, seeking for external succor and assistance. For others however, true religion is seeking inner enlightenment, a realization of inner capacities as well as limitations. The power of God sought outside is really within.

Reestablishing a fusion with external power is a primitive, universally utilized, psychological mode of coping with a need for security. Satisfaction is, at least momentarily, gained through attempts at attachment to, or introjection of, outside power. A fear of possible separation becomes a significant part of parental interaction paralleling some maintenance of a defensive belief that it is one's own vocalization and gesture that influences the outside parent to provide needed security.

As already indicated, experiences in infancy are at first inextricably confused in relation to outer objects. Various coping mechanisms (1) either introject and digest, (2) exclude from awareness attendant affective states, or (3) expel unwanted or dangerous affectively suffused thought (De Vos 1984). From early on there is also developed a capacity to "project," that is, what is occurring internally is perceived as occurring outside. Instead of an empathic, proper reading of outside stimuli, intense internal emotionalized states can cause concomitant internal postural tensions to be improperly read as responses to outside stimuli. For example, destructiveness as part of one's own intentionality can be projected out as an experience of malevolence directed at one from an outside power. Neutral or even positive behavior in actual encounters with another can be quickly misinterpreted as hostile or destructive in intent. Such constantly occurring processes can become quite complex or convoluted. An outside destructiveness can be confused with one's own response to it and can become intertwined and reintrojected in what are termed depressive states (Freud 1917, 243–58).

As noted, not only is there command, but fearful supplication in the act of crying. When the initial separation of the self comes to be more harshly experienced, power must be sought from projected external, intentional willful beings, and potential anger and destructiveness must be avoided. To the extent that one comes progressively to experience the "reality" of inner helpfulness, one seeks benign engulfment—reattachment—or one can come symbolically to seek or "ingest" power. Acts of commensual communion are found in religious ritual enactments cross-culturally (De Vos and Suarez-Orosco 1987).

Separation can result in overwhelming anxiety because it often occurs regardless of volition. An intense feeling of helplessness begins to alternate with a still continuing optimism that one's internal intentionality may still bring on satisfaction.

One is powerless to prevent loss, but the infant comes to experience and define his own separateness as assuageable by social reattachment. With physiological maturation, the infant is turning into a child. The prone infant is becoming a crawling child. While body motility is sensed as progressively coming under one's voluntary or "willful" control, there is also sensed selective outside approbation and disapproval of efforts to move about, and outside appraisal of how one uses one's body. Indeed, the outside intentional beings even require and force certain forms of internal muscular control into what will later be perceived as patterns of motoric propriety.

There may result a battle of wills. The anal sphincter can become symbolically in Western culture not only an erogenous focus of positive and negative feelings, but also a symbol of conformity and submissiveness or defiance and rebellion. In infancy the awesome realization that pleasure and security is subject to the will of another intentional individual can be devastating because the "other" does indeed "go away," potentially leaving one helpless. The experience that this outside source can be destructive and/or the fear of losing this "almighty" source of goodness, constitute the first sense of true human horror or overwhelming "separation anxiety," as we have discussed above.

As the boundaries of separateness become increasingly evident, the infant especially senses the horror of isolation from the source of pleasure, protection, and comfort. To the degree the child comes to experience his own separateness, the parents have become endowed with extraordinary powers. As the child experiences that the source of comfort is not solely within himself but is shared with his parents, they then become omnipotent. They *are* intentional power.

Satisfaction (the breast that brings food, the body that brings warmth and protection) which was experienced earlier as intimate and inseparable begins, with the increasing sense of separateness, to be experienced as subject to an outside, sometimes hostile intentionality demanding obedience—even a complete capitulation of "will"—the conative in human experience. Yet the early stage of omnipotent intentionality, located within, leaves a profound residue in the human mind.

As the boundaries between the developing self and the external world make the sense of separateness evident, the child projects into the external universe his own life, animation, and tendencies, which often continue to interparticipate with his own wishes, thoughts, and gestures. The child who once experienced the cosmos as an intimate continuity, now animistically endows it with life and intent which still can be controlled through the manipulation of proper formulae.

Human thought during early childhood is characterized by a continuing lack of precise differentiation of internally stimulated intentionality as distinct from the outer mechanical energies of the external world. Mechanism and intention, either in the self or in other living beings, can only be separated from one another after further maturation, given the culturally available forms of conceptual thought making such separation possible. There remains a tendency in contemporary Western science, religion, and philosophy no matter how well developed, to fuse these forms of causality or subordinate one to the other.

An essential aspect of all thought is interaction, a dynamic flow of interchange which is conceptualized as causality—whether between beings or objects. Some experiences of causality are temporal in that the flow is from prior conditions to subsequent ones. Other experiences of causality are interactive in spatial as well as temporal dimensions.

Adults as well as children alternate subjectively between experiences of power and powerlessness. As the child grows, he begins to establish his own separated position in the complex world of natural forces and human social events.

Jean Piaget (1930, 237–305) has elegantly analyzed the development of causality in the child. Early thought is characterized by Piaget as being permeated by the "realism of perception." Early on, subjective perceptions are taken as given. The child is tyrannized by a far from perfect human perceptual apparatus. The perceptual distortion that the moon "moves" as he does, is indeed taken very seriously. "Realism" as Piaget uses the term refers to the child's construction of the universe as animate and participating with his own actions, thoughts, wishes, and gestures. During the sensory-motor stage (approximately the first eighteen months of life), the infant's thinking is dominated by egocentric perceptions rooted in an incapacity to precisely judge from where causality is empowered, whether part of the self or part of the outside world. Thinking at base remains hopelessly "animistic" as well as "magical." Rocks move because they are "alive." The child who experiences his own musculature in movement, projects it into the inanimate world, endowing it with life. In Japan, Shinto beliefs continue to endow nature with vitality and soul. Mt. Fuji is awesome and treated with reverence. Japanese turn their sense of reverence and awe out onto nature.

A sense of awe and reverence for power may find both natural as well as human exemplars that become objects of worship. The Japanese concept of *Kami* in some respects resembles what has been described as *Mana* in Polynesia (Firth 1940; Levy 1973, 154ff.). In some cases it adheres to individuals. Some humans such as Sugawara, the Heian courtier-calligrapher, are enshrined. The Kitano shrine in Kyoto is to this man-become-*kami,* whose wrath was feared as causing pestilence and other disasters after his wrongful exile and subsequent death.

Piaget discusses how in primitive psychological precausality, thinking itself is powerfully "efficacious." The initial confusion between the self and the external world gives the child the illusion that a great source of power remains located within the self. What is not discussed in Piaget's writings is the awesome, possibly traumatic nature of the sense of power which becomes part of magical and religious representations in all cultures. There are potential psychopathological traumas that can be rigidified into a future neurosis when the child senses that his or her own ideas cause hurtful things to happen, that is, should an accident happen during a period of enmity, the child's interpretation might be that his evil wish, which can be conscious or unconscious, might have caused a sibling to be hurt. Egocentric experiences are not easily to be undone in the development of a sense of guilt over one's own destructive wishes. Thoughts, gestures, or wishes of a sexual as well as destructive nature might prove so devastating that they create profound propensities for guilt that is later represented in religious imagery in relation to a potentially wrathful supernatural force.

One can seek to influence or to alter divine will by being "pleasing" to a deity. One also learns from childhood various culturally available notions of negotiation used as means of interacting with a powerful external being should help be needed. Concepts of early social negotiation in childhood, as well as later forms which can be observed as occurring between adults, remain as paradigms for influencing action in others. This very human perception of negotiation with the supernatural is most evident in various forms of ritual sacrifice (De Vos and Suarez-Orosco 1987).

With the maturational growth of a "self," the source of power begins to be more precisely and discreetly located in the intentional energy of powerful humans, in nature, in the belief in supernatural intervention, or in the control exercised over one's own body by directed thought. One's culture instructs one in how to envision power in harmony with those of one's own group.

There continues into adulthood the experiential context of the child's own musculature in which power has been experienced. There is continual progressive experiential observation of the body and the growing self, as well as the natural world. Since the experience of power and the attribution of power, in most instances, is mediated through some social context, the perception of a moral universe as it is envisioned in Confucianism is quite understandable. It is not simply the product of childish adherences visible in adult thought.

For some groups nature continues to be considered as having intentional qualities. For some, nature is benevolent and nurturant; for others, it is harsh toward humanity rather than impartial. As man worships aspects of nature, they are sometimes imbued with intentional force. Thus thunder may come to either punish or bring needed rain; the arrival of spring is given to man and can excite a sense of gratitude for the new life springing from the earth and the fruitfulness of each yearly cycle. In this sense, nature itself can be perceived as divine. Divinity is seen by man as a source of blessing. Reverential gratitude is a basic religious feeling that needs outlet, that needs objectification in some symbolic representation.

Among the Japanese reverence and gratitude can continue to be expressed religiously within the family system, or toward a *sensei* who guides one's efforts toward mastery. Objects of revered benevolence remain the mentor, as well as the mother and father. A supernatural image may not be necessary. The sense of deep gratitude need not be attributed to a figure such as Jesus or a nurturing Virgin Mary.

The figures of Amida and Kannon, derivative of popular Buddhism, have been used by some Japanese as objects of gratitude, but others with the same emotions to express do not transcend the family. The fact that the deepest gratitude need not be expressed toward a supernatural object can be related to the preempting of such emotional states by Confucian teachings in which the focus remains in the social world. Such feelings of gratitude are not diverted out onto a realm of supernatural benefactors.

In the Confucian five relationships, gratitude is diffused throughout these human social transactions. The ultimate virtues to be cultivated in feeling good about life are all directed toward humanity, not divinity. They are *gen* or in Japanese *gi,* propriety, wisdom, good faith, and righteousness.

Bellah (1957, 77), in his study of Tokugawa religion, directly includes Confucianism as a religion. It is a religion for Bellah, as it is in my judgment, because spiritual cultivation brings a person to oneness with the universe in sensing a suffusion of goodness. Two main types of *religious* action according to Bellah, as well as myself, are the deep reverence with which a Japanese Confucianist returns *on,* or gratitude, and the dedication to self-cultivation in social interaction as a goal of human life. Japanese Confucians were vigorous in practicing activism and attacking quietism that remove a person from responsible participation in society. (Bellah 1957, 77ff.).

The only difference between my approach and Bellah's approach to the religious sense expressed in the Japanese is a matter of focus. I have described the sense of gratitude for sacrifice engendered within the family (De Vos 1960, 1984), whereas he searches out the outer moral-social atmosphere as it was engendered in the Tokugawa period, not only by Confucianism, Buddhism, and Shinto, but also by other religious movements. He sees asceticism and selfless labor in the fact that some Japanese see restraint of selfish desires for hedonistic consumption as closely related to the obligations felt to sacred and semisacred superiors, which is stressed in all Japanese religions. I have sought out on a psychological level more directly how *on* is a reverential repayment to parents. He has sought out how Japanese come to experience a state of selfless identification with ultimate nature as a religious concept to be found not only in Confucianism but in other forms of religious development heavily influenced by Confucianist thought (Bellah 1957, 196).

The Moral Implications of Causality

As we have been discussing, there is a justifiable concern in Confucian thought with how to reconcile natural mechanisms which have been explored by Western-derived science, and moral causality viewed as inherent within the total Confucian cosmos.

The universe described by Western science is not a moral universe. It is no longer homocentric. Yet Western Judeo-Christian thought grew out of an all-encompassing religious system that defined the beginning and end of all existence with a god as first cause, and man's moral nature as of central concern to this god. Only with great difficulty has scientific thought freed itself from formal religious doctrine and philosophical systems derivative of such doctrine. Now the problem has become how to reintroduce moral concerns into the contemporary's social world without retreat into some irrational form of fundamentalist dogma.

Science as positivism is an outgrowth transcending its origins in magical manipulation. It reaches toward an objectification of mechanical causality, stripped of the encumbrances of any intentionality interfering with the natural world. Scientific theory now works well to explain the physical universe and the natural-ecological environment surrounding humanity. Positivism within the social sciences has also allowed us greater understanding of the history and prehistory of human groups, their political, and economic systems, human social organization, even the psychological structures operative in the human mind.

What science is hard pressed to do, however, is to examine human consciousness and morally considered human behavior as a social, even physical force, having interactive effects on the physical world. Intentionality exists as a serious, irreducible determinant of individual human behavior and collective human history. How should one approach scientifically the very socialization practices that continue a society? What is necessary is to develop forms of sociological and psychological analysis that credits consciousness with its own force.

There is within Western thought a tendency to grant the impersonal in nature priority over the personal. This was the perceptive suspicion of Confucianist scholars. There is an absolutist tendency in Western thought to push toward an ultimate unitary explanation in mechanical terms. A concept of balance would seek better to delineate how the appearance of self-consciousness in a life form makes intentionality a new causative motive force influencing the natural world. Human will in its early beginnings was indeed subject to nature. But now human understanding has penetrated into subatomic depths, and into the genetic mechanisms that cause the transmission of life itself. Causative sequences in those areas where human intentionality now intervenes cannot be reduced to mechanical explanations.

Human volition is, by its very nature, moral. That is to say, one who possesses intentionality knows that behavior, whatever its form, has consequences. Morality is simply knowledge of intentional causality, that is, knowledge of the consequences of behavior within the self. To understand the determinative effects of human moral development, and why religious thought is inescapable in one form or other in human society, is to know that moral-social considerations cannot be superseded by morally neutral scientific observation. As observers, however, let us turn again to some psychological discussion of psychosocial development as explanatory of human moral nature. This will help explain why Confucian thought, regardless of its total or relative exclusion of the supernatural, is nevertheless, deeply religious.

Magic in Precausality as a Need for Control

Religion and science, or if you would prefer, moral and rational thought, are parallel developments within the human mind. From their earliest appearance, however, they are intertwined and never become completely analytically separated in the inner experience of most individuals. In several contexts I have already referred to this interpenetration of experience of will and mechanism in complex causal explanations. Magic is the expression of an instrumental need for control employed to ward off the fears engendered by an unpredictable environment. Any expressive social concerns that enter into magical thought are secondary. Magical beliefs and practices are based on institutionalized precausal protoscientific formulae controlling predictive change. The practices of alchemy in the Middle Ages gradually were objectified into the explanatory regularities of chemistry. Note, however, that chemistry is generally free of attribution of intentionality. Chemical processes are not interactive with human destiny, although magic potions continue to exist.

The same is not true for the thought that continues the entire system of astrology as a form of magic. The development of astronomy as objective science has not ruled out the continuance of protoscientific explanations of how the influence of the planets and stars on humans are supposed to differ depending upon one's date of birth!

With difficulty, and never completely, the magical precausality of childhood becomes objectified, detached from human desire, and is transmuted into instrumental rational-scientific thought. Suffice it to say that a need for control is an apparent motive in both magic and science. Western man has successfully implemented his search for both understanding and control over nature. In society as a whole, at present, there is increasing awareness of our awesome control over destructive power.

Morality in Early Psychological Development

As already discussed, a sense of volitional control *within* starts very early in the human infant. If an infant vocalizes long enough, it will command and change the world about it. Once discrete language is learned, more specific words cause more specific results. As Piaget described it (1930), the word adheres to the object named. To be able to name is to be able to control. If one learns the right word one gains control over the named object. In many groups, as in the case of the Jews, the name of one's tribal god was kept secret. Should one's enemy learn the sacred name, the god could be controlled, and the group vanquished (Graves 1947). Such institutionalized forms of early prelogical thought are patently magical in nature. Proper magical use of words is an instrumental extension of a subjectively experienced volition out into the social world.

There may not be any immediate moral involvement in the desire for control. A moral sense becomes evoked only later when one develops awareness of the social consequences of one's desire to control or to destroy. At first, there is a split between good and bad outer objects (Kernberg 1975). What is experienced as "bad" also tends to be projected outward. "Good" as far as possible is kept within. Only when there is developed a capacity to take conscious inner "responsibility" does the moral necessity to anticipate the consequences of behavior manifest itself.

Wicked individual wishes when too dangerous are not allowed to come or to remain in conscious thought. They are repressed after their occurrence. Projection on an individual or a group basis can be used to avoid inner responsibility for one's unconscionable sexual or destructive wishes. The fallabilities within one group can be displaced as the vices of the enemy or the outsider.

The development of a human "conscience" or "superego," which allows one to assume responsibility for one's intentionality, is part of the phylogenetic evolution of the human forebrain. The forebrain frees us from being bound to the immediate present. Increased storage capacities and complex networks allow us to draw on memory input as in a computer. We can predict the future. The human brain extends us in time and space without having to move close physically. We can quickly test out the consequences of alternative paths before taking action. The results of pursuing a given desire become visible ahead of time. Morality is knowledge of intentional causality. We come to know sin, individually, in hurting another by our willful behavior, or collectively, by using science to create new capacities for destruction. We become responsible for anticipating the future. This capacity develops from early childhood on.

Egocentrism

Piaget (1932) in his interviews with children was able to delineate an egocentric phase in cognitive and moral development that precedes a stage in which one is maturationally capable of autonomy. He does not examine why difficulties arise in the actualization of autonomy in so many individuals. We witness today much social "anomie" and personal alienation in all modern societies (cf. my discussion of alienation in Japanese suicide, De Vos 1973), that space does not permit us to enter here.

A child in the stage of early egocentrism can only see things from his own point of view. Interesting tests have been devised to demonstrate that a child at this stage cannot imagine how something looks from another physical angle, let alone another social perspective. He cannot give equal value to other points of view, or even comprehend how something could possibly be viewed differently.

Piaget traces out how egocentric thought as a maturational phase gradually gives way to capacities for reciprocity, relativity, and objectivity. Egocentrism in children is governed by what Piaget termed "realism"—what is experienced subjectively is what exists.

In science the subjective experience of a flat earth has given way to a theory of governing all positions in the universe. Maturation in the recognition of relativity is a developing capacity to move from conceptions that start from one's internal "realism," into a recognition of interactional causality in which one can appreciate the point of view and valid perceptions of others. Motives are perceived as mutually directed. Reconciliation demands that some equal weight be given to the desires and intentions of others.

Such recognition places equal value on both participants in *reciprocal* relationships. Morality becomes understood in reciprocal terms; not only as an extension of one's values or inner needs directed toward another person. Responsible moral reciprocity can appear in either horizontal or vertical status relationships. Both sides have moral responsibility. One finds parallels to this concept of reciprocity in Confucian conceptions of moral development.

Objectivity is the capacity to distance oneself from our subjectively governed perceptions. There is a developmental capacity in morality enabling us to see that things are reciprocal because we can objectify an experience by getting out of it, both spatially and temporally, and observing oneself in our interactions spatially with others and anticipating temporally what the distant results will be.

Ethnocentrism in some of its aspects is an extension of egocentrism into the social level. There lacks the development of a capacity to evaluate different culturally derived perspectives with any objectivity. There is no extension of reciprocity and certainly little capacity to become somewhat relativistic in our perception of the moral organization of people differing from us in their own traditions.

Legislative Morality

Piaget exemplified his early study (1932) of progressive stages in the moral judgment of children by describing the sense of rules involved in how children, at various ages, engage in the game of marbles. At the earliest level there is imitative play with no comprehension of the rules. The very smallest tots play at marbles without knowing what they are doing. As I shall discuss presently, such motoric play can be an efficacious form of learning. Rote learning has been well utilized in some traditional educational systems in the imparting of religious lore or artistic mastery. Children gradually become aware of the rules governing play. In the first phase of this awareness they learn to obey the rules in the presence of older children, but cannot exercise them independently. Progressively the rules are actually "internalized." They are first taken in as sacred and fixed. The child has entered what Piaget describes as a "heteronomous" stage of development. Regulation is through the inculcation of exterior norms. This is a transitional phase in childhood during which codes of behavior can only be comprehended as immutable. One could say that the rules of the game are divinely ordained, not to be questioned. Heteronomy is an unquestioning adherence to rules of behavior. Regulations are imposed from above to be obeyed. Rules are not related to people; they have an independence from human tampering. This period contrasts with what Piaget sees as the later development of "autonomy," or self-regulation according to one's internally perceived moral sense.

In the game of marbles the players gradually leave their heteronomous stage to enter what one could call a "legislative" phase in their play. They reciprocally begin to change the rules to make up new games so as to enhance mutual enjoyment. Experimentation takes the place of immutability. There is comprehension that the game of marbles exists for the benefit and enjoyment of the players, and can be changed when there is agreement to do so.

Piaget cannot tell us what happens afterward, for children reach an age where they no longer play marbles. If one moves from the game of marbles to human society generally, Piaget's empirically derived metaphor can be seen to have wider implications. Humans could achieve a conceptual-moral level of political democracy in marbles even at a time when they still believed in the divine right of kings.

Judgment of what is moral must go beyond what has been defined in the past. Societies have been governed by sacred kings and sacred scriptures. But can entire moral codes become avowedly legislative? The American society bypasses this issue by maintaining a separation between religion and the secular state. Morality is left to private enterprise. Heteronomy remains a problem faced by all major religions. The immutable nature of past ritual and past hierarchy concerns both Confucianists and those brought up in the Christian tradition. Can we evolve a stable religious-moral humanism as a legislative process?

Vicissitudes in Heteronomy and Motoric Learning

Obedience versus Propriety

Starting from a Western cultural perspective in psychoanalysis, interpretations concerning the so-called "anal period" in childhood development has been too focused upon the control of defecation and the ensuing battle of wills occurring between parent and child. When the vicissitudes of this period in early childhood is approached cross-culturally and normatively, rather than clinically in terms of problems that may arise in any culture, one finds it more generally to be a period of the development of "will" or conation, a period when one learns a social balance between inner guided motor control and response to outside social cues.

Early on, when one is highly dependent, one learns to take cues from the outside to guide behavior. One begins to make judgments on the basis of outside cues and to draw upon these in governing one's own behavior in a social context. As I have noted from a Piagetian perspective, there can be rote behavior without inner comprehension. But as I have also noted, the period of learning control is a period during which one seeks, albeit magically, to maintain internal volition. In other terms, a child seeks, to some degree, to maintain a locus of control within the self, and gradually develops some confidence about being able to use one's own body, as well as one's thoughts, to judge outside events. Depending on prevailing practices of parenting and an increasing capacity for mastery, there can be progressive shifts in balance between outer and inner regulation and finally, a movement toward autonomy.

Examined clinically, there are a number of rigidified imbalances resulting in what are usually termed neuroses, which result from particular psychosexual disturbances occurring at critical periods in development. So called "character traits" can be set; there can develop strong rebellious propensities, or overly compliant attitudes. Rigid defenses can occur both motorically and conceptually.

During World War II some psychological anthropologists attempted to understand patterns of behavior prevalent among the Japanese suggesting psychological rigidity and self-righteousness (Gorer 1943; Le Barre 1945). Their efforts were ill-founded, as later evidence proved. These earlier attempts at describing a "national character" had directly applied Western-derived psychoanalytic theory heavily dependent on Western clinical observations. They were not based upon sufficient observation of actual Japanese socialization practices.

The general consensus resulting from direct studies (e.g., Lanham 1956) is that toilet training in Japan was never imposed with any of the rigor characteristic of some groups observed in traditional Western child rearing. In Japan, what is controlled very early by direct manipulation of the body, rather than any use of guiding words, is proper bowing and other deference behavior directed toward important outsiders. There is a continued sensitivity aroused from early on about properly controlled motoric behavior. Can we relate this part of early childhood experience in Japan to a moral sense located in the musculature? and to the pleasures of propriety? In these following sections I shall attempt to do so.

Social relationships are symbolized in proper posture, which is as important as the verbal deference also practiced from early on. A Japanese mother's concern with social compliance, or with other consequences of a child's behavior, is not about obedience or disobedience, but about how a child may hurt the feelings of others and hence do poorly socially. If a behavior is too directly aggressive, the child will be isolated (Lanham 1956, 1962).

Obedience in itself is not the desired goal, but what is sought for is an awakening in a child of an awareness of the potentially negative consequences of behavior (cf. Miyake et al. 1986). The potential for hurting one's family, not only oneself, is learned fairly early. Behavior can cause collective harm a long time distant. Vigilance becomes part of a future time orientation, while the child's sense of self remains embedded within his family. There is a socialization of achievement motives not individualistically, but collectively defined (De Vos 1973). Social or occupational failure produces guilt for hurting those deserving gratitude (De Vos 1960). The parent becomes the sacrificial figure rather than a more distant divinity (De Vos 1984).

Maternal discipline in Japan avoids a test of wills. Japanese mothers are more likely to appeal to a child's awareness of consequences (Azuma, Kashiwagi, and Hess 1981). The child is made aware of his potential for injuring objects as well as people. This is a form of moral inculcation, rather than a tempering of contentious wills as is parent-child interaction in the United States.

Japanese children are quickly made sensitive to their capacity to arouse negative feelings in others. As compared in systematic studies by developmental psychologists, American mothers are more apt to make desired behavior, whether toilet training or other forms of compliance, a question of obedience to the will of the mother (Azuma, Kashiwagi, and Hess 1981). The Japanese mother avoids any such confrontation. She "gets with the child" and uses her closeness to move the child toward compliance with her wishes without making them a direct issue.

The Absolute versus the Situational

Taking a Piagetian perspective, motoric training of early behavior precedes comprehension. It is preparatory to a sensitivity to the intentionality of others in the actual social world. In the West there is institutionalized in religious training an immutable set of requirements divinely ordained, codes of behavior in regard to sexual and aggressive behavior set down by a potentially wrathful or suffering deity. Hence from a Western religious perspective Japanese moral thought has been considered more socially situational rather than based on universalist absolute principles. It is only directed toward persons with which one has actual social contact. In the traditional culture one could avoid moral responsibility for those outside one's social network. (Today in Japan one notes a widening of concern with universalizing of the concept of human rights being taught in the schools.)

With this emphasis on behavioral consequences rather than abstract principles, Japanese moral training is potentially more "legislative" and negotiable. Indeed, rather than concern with statutes, equity plays a much more important role in Japanese legal practice and in court decisions.

Field Dependence versus Field Independence

There are a considerable number of cross-cultural studies of the cognitive development of children related to school performance (De Vos 1982). One such series of inquiry concerns itself with whether in making perceptual judgments a child is "field dependent" or "field independent." There is a developmental progression from field-dependent judgments toward field-independent ones (Witkin 1967; Witkin and Berry 1975). To explain the meaning of these terms and the type of observations on which they are based, one can cite one task given to subjects placed in a dark room. They are shown a rod in a frame that is lit up at one end of the room. The frame can be tilted slightly, or the rod may be placed in other than a vertically upright position. The subject is asked to judge when the rod is upright, and when it is not.

Subjects can be separated into those who tend to judge the upright position in terms of the frame in which it is placed, and those who use their own body posture sitting on a chair as the basis for judging the rod. This test and other test results were correlated and differentiated between Mexican-American children who do relatively poorly in school and "Anglo"-American children who do relatively better in their studies (Kagan 1974; Kagan and Buriel 1977). Mexican children tend to remain more field dependent while

Anglo children become more quickly field independent. Conversely, Mexican children tend to be more cooperative and socially sensitive, whereas the Anglo children tend toward individualistic competitive behavior (Madsen 1967; Madsen and Shapira 1973).

Drawing on related studies with Black and Mexican ethnic minorities in the United States, there is a tendency in the resulting discussions to see traits of cognitive independence and social compliance as inversely related. Traits emphasizing social compliance are considered to be due to patterns of child training emphasizing authoritarian forms of discipline and hierarchical status positions in the family. The locus of power remains prevailingly external in such individuals. Heteronomous fear of authority remains, not to be superseded by a more internalized superego.

Cues for acceptable behavior are part of a sensitivity to the norms of "significant others" or a dominant reference group (see the discussion of the role of peer reference groups in ethnic minorities in De Vos 1978). Such individuals are "other directed" (Riesman et al. 1958). Inferentially, they cannot use their own bodies with confidence for perceptual verification.

However, how are we to consider the fact that Japanese children tend to be field independent on the one hand, but socially sensitive and compliant on the other, brought up in families emphasizing hierarchy in both language and social gestures? Japanese field independence in the cognitive, perceptual realm confounds generalizations made on the basis of American studies, just as generalizations in American psychology (McClelland 1961) about "need achievement" being inverse to affiliative and nurturant needs are confounded by the more family-oriented definitions of achievement found in the fantasies of Japanese when they are tested with the same tests given American subjects (De Vos 1973).

Most field-dependent compliant children remain present-oriented. The time dimension of many Mexican children is relatively brief and present-oriented (F. Kluckhohn 1953). They do not develop the extended future time orientation so evident in the Japanese. Anglo children show a future time orientation, but they are less constrained by it, for they do not envision that possibly contentious or openly competitive behavior will be damaging to future goals. They are less guided by social sensitivity in their behavior than are Mexican or Japanese children.

I have discussed in more detail elsewhere (De Vos 1982) that, when considered comparatively, Japanese children manifest in their cognitive development forms of "field independence" that indicate on a cognitive level, at least, they maintain a locus of power within. In Japanese this is consonant with the internalization of moral directives emphasizing forms of family responsibility depending on social sensitivity and social compliance. In the Japanese context, cognitive independence is coupled with compliant receptivity to teachers or other mentors allowing for better adaptive learning. In the American pattern, cognitive independence is coupled with social and psychological competitiveness and individualistically oriented internalizations. Lower-class American children not interested in formal learning feel psychologically free to more or less openly defy the teacher in the school situation.

American children generally are not compliant at school. In fact, the amount of defiance and disrespect displayed toward teachers has produced a present crisis in the public schools. A good number of teachers are leaving the profession, not due solely to the relatively low salaries provided teachers (itself a symptom of social disrespect), but due to the direct physical as well as status violence directed toward them in the classroom. One observes that such irreverent behavior toward a teacher is very rarely in evidence among Asian-American children, who continue to treat a teacher with respect.

In Japan at present there are some signs of unrest in the schools, but by and large, Japanese internalization still appears to emphasize a type of socialization that stresses an anticipation of the consequences of behavior to family as well as self. Compliance is not simply on the basis of obedience to a potentially frightening authority. Japanese children show more immediate social sensitivity and concern with the opinion of others, but they also manifest an awareness of behavioral consequences in a future time orientation that can envision alternative future consequences resulting from present behavior.

In other words, Japanese children are socialized toward present social sensitivities, but these are to be understood in the context of a future time orientation. They are socialized toward group compliance, but not by stern measures instilling a fear of authority, rather through a form of maternal guidance that instills a reverence for authority reinforced ritualistically by verbal and physical gestures of deference. On a cognitive level there is less frightened repression of consciousness, and more behavioral restraint. Constraint in behavioral expression demands the *suppression* of thought and affect rather than severe *repression* of either. Many Japanese children do not become cognitively blocked, although some do. More characteristically, there is no retardation of an internalized potential for self-guided cognition that can continue to be used from an inner locus of control. From childhood on, Japanese learn severe behavioral constraint maintained for social purposes. There is a compliant intake of knowledge imparted by hierarchical figures acting in the status of parent.

Age Grading and a Sense of Mastery

Rote Learning versus Verbal Explanation

Before turning to a direct concern with the morality and aesthetics of propriety, there are two final points to consider in comparing the social be-

havioral implications of the Japanese cultural emphasis placed on present compliance for future mastery as compared with American learning patterns.

As I have been discussing, a Japanese cultural mode of socialization is the
direct use of the child's body in patterning expected behavior. In more extreme cases there can be a molding of the child in an emotional closeness that
gratifies dependency as a means of control. One can note some lack of development of clear ego boundaries separating mother and child when such dependent bonds are maintained (Doi 1973). Considered from a clinical standpoint
one can see how such a continuing dependent relationship may cause a number of psychological disturbances. Suffice it to say that excessive attachment to
a controlling mother can be a source of considerable personal malaise in Japan,
as elsewhere.

Generally speaking, autonomous or willful behavior is neither a threat
nor a goal. From the very beginning Japanese mothers when compared with
their American counterparts communicate through close body contact (Caudill
and Weinstein 1966). American mothers treat their infants as independent
objects; verbal communication is emphasized from early on.

In Piagetian terms, a motoric stage in both cognitive and moral perception is implicitly acknowledged and long utilized in Japanese concepts of
training whether in social comportment or in artistic skills. A child or an
apprentice is expected to learn through pliant behavior before he understands
what he is doing or why. This is very apparent when one looks at traditional
patterns of schooling and apprenticeship in Japan. It also appears in the learning of the martial arts.

A most recent successful example of such a method of training is the
Suzuki method of teaching children the violin. There are certain elementary
pieces where everyone plays together from the youngest on up. The more
adept are not excused from the elementary exercises; they play along with the
little tots. There is a participatory togetherness that creates willingness to
practice in those less skilled and stimulates an optimism about being able to
reach the next difficult level of behavioral performance playing next to those
who have already done so. Learning is social and behavioral, not individual and
conceptual.

Rote repetition and memorization as well as behavioral participation in
ritual has been used in a number of traditions to inculcate sacred scriptures.
Note that such a pattern seems to be appropriate in the imparting of a literate
religious tradition because it is not the expectation that children are to examine critically the beliefs derived from sacred sources. Secularized scientific
investigation is based on the contrary notion that all present knowledge is
based on theory that must receive continuous critical examination with a
willingness to doubt current orthodoxy. The current arguments in pedagogy
are about how much is to be imparted first before the learner becomes
sufficiently equipped to be able to start to use a critical approach with merit.

In understanding traditional plastic and dramatic art forms in Japan, one must note how rote behavior long continues on the long road taken toward eventual mastery. There is no presumption that every practitioner will eventually come to full comprehension. Francis Hsu (1985) has written with considerable insight into the continuity in art due to the tradition of the *iemoto*. An *iemoto* is the sole unchallengeable master of a tradition. Upon death this tradition is passed on to a successor. He is the only one who can modify or change anything. All others, trained or being trained, are subject to his final authority. Religious and philosophical traditions as well as Noh drama, Kabuki, schools of flower arrangement, all have an *iemoto*. In the Noh tradition, for example, only an experienced true master knows the meaning of the cryptic codes that describe the state of mind to attain in attempting a particular role. The master doesn't attempt to impart such knowledge or secrets except to his immediate successor.

Lack of knowledge, or even lack of belief, does not exclude someone from becoming part of a group created around a tradition. This is especially true for religious organizations. In contrast, in the West those seeking to become a convert to a religious body are to be tested to see whether they have proper comprehension and proper adherence to the essential beliefs of the group before they are formally admitted. Helen Hardacre (1985) describes how she was asked to join Reiyuukai, a new Japanese religion she was studying. She demurred that she did not share the beliefs of the participants. This was of no matter she was told. By doing things together she would come to understand and to comprehend.

Age Grading and Optimism in Future-Oriented Confucian Societies

In considering authority and social status among adults, contemporary American society has not worked out a comfortable distinction between vertical relationships that are temporary as in age grading, and those that are due to status differences of a more permanent nature. Present-day Western societies, in their efforts at democratization, are progressively attempting to do away with concepts of seniority among adults, regardless of age. In the United States this effort has been extended to "children's rights" as something to enforce legally, especially should parents be considered too authoritarian.

In contrast, much emphasis in deference behavior in Asians is related to age-graded offices. Such deference behavior causes less social resentment than that required by social class or ethnic differences. It is difficult for a contemporary American, looking at social hierarchy in a Confucian society, to understand the emotions attached to age grading and its complex relationship to both mastery and dependency. For Americans, deference behavior readily demeans the person. It is interpreted as submissiveness and possible weakness of character, or a form of deviousness. It would seldom be considered as marking a future time framework, a form of nondemeaning patience informed by an optimistic consideration of future possibilities.

I shall not enter into the topic of the problems of continuing manipulative dependency *(amae),* well discussed by Doi (1973), practiced by subordinates toward their superiors. Note that dependency in Japanese does not lead to any general social passivity, but may be related in some instances to vigorous social striving and occupational success (Vogel 1963; De Vos 1975). Nor are dependency and deference congruent concepts. One refers to the continuing receptive need for gratification from some one in a position to bestow benefits, the other, is an expression of respect, even reverence to someone superior in status.

To properly understand age grading, one must examine more fully the concept of self-development in traditional Confucian education, whether it is that of an artisan apprentice, a would-be artist, or scholar. An anticipation of future power is at the heart of the concept of apprenticeship in Japan as elsewhere (De Vos 1975). Theodore Reik (1941), analyzing "moral masochism," offers an excellent description of the mentality of the apprentice, who by submission, gains eventual mastery. One doesn't submit to comply; one submits to gain power. The sense of endurance itself may become pleasurable in enhancing an internal sense of "being able to take it," furthering the anticipation of one's future goals. "Patience" is not passive in nature, rather the individual is already actively engaged in a future purpose.

Patience is an instrumental virtue not demeaning to those who practice it. Others recognize it as a legitimate deferment of future goals. The Japanese could, when proved necessary, submit to the American occupation without losing all sense of honor. They could outlast it. When one knows that one has kept one's inner capacities despite tribulation, there is assurance that the proper energy will be there to realize one's goals at a future time. Things are going to change if one can hold on and endure.

In the past, farm families apprenticed their children to merchants and artisans in the city. Second sons and third sons were sent in from the rural countryside. First sons succeeded to the farms. A dynamic population flow in Tokugawa society was based on this continual urbanization into the townsmen culture by eager new arrivals (Wagatsuma and De Vos 1985).

The apprentice worked very hard for little pay. In the past in Japan, an apprentice worked up to fourteen hours without any right to complain. Maids were their counterparts. Young girls were in this sense apprenticed to learn domestic duties in a higher-status household. A complainer, male or female, would be sent home in disgrace, where the family would berate the "failure." An apprentice knew if he worked hard enough he could even have a *"noren wake,"* symbolically a splitting of the cloth designed with a house emblem that was strung across the doorway of a traditional establishment. The boss would "split" functions with him, making him a branch or a subsidiary master, or if he was quite successful, he might even marry the boss's daughter.

In such a system of thought one is tempering oneself to overcome future obstacles. The moral muscles are being exercised to strengthen oneself to triumph over future competition. The lifting of daily burdens strengthens the spirit, even if the flesh must be sacrificed. This is the Japanese virtue of endurance (Wagatsuma and De Vos 1985). This virtue is exercised by both men and women. Young mothers exercise it with their children at home; younger fathers practice it in their occupations.

The Japanese made a virtue of endurance (Wagatsuma and De Vos 1985). Men practice it in their professions; women inside the family. The young man is in no better status than is the young bride. In entering a company at the bottom or in becoming an apprentice, one must submit to a system to be rewarded only with time. Today there are wage scales and about forty-five hours a week officially, but often one is required to work overtime. The young man, either as a worker or a member of management, is still required to work very hard for relatively little pay. Wage labor has eroded this tradition in Japan without completely doing away with the concept of age grading in modern industry.

Apprenticeship is almost totally a thing of the past in American society. There is insistence on being paid equally for work, regardless of age. There tends to be an all or none concept in American systems of thought: all authority is bad, especially any rule by the elderly gerontocracy; we should not have to wait to be gratified; let us push aside the old fogies who stand in our way. Verticality in any form is bad. This is the "now" generation. Everything has to be leveled and made more equal because equality is good.

The growing tension over gender differences in the West has been due to the past withholding of some of equal respect and other features of full adulthood from women on the basis of their imputed immutable inferiority. The leveling of equality between the sexes for many implies congruence with no idea of a remaining complementarity in family roles.

Asian women, while now insisting increasingly on greater economic parity as well as parity of respect, are not as insistent on congruity in social roles within the family as their American counterparts are. They still espouse some role complementarity. They do not tend to see a woman's role in the home as relatively powerless as do many American women.

To understand this difference, one must note how the age grading of women's roles in admittedly formally patriarchal Asian societies, as discussed by Cho in chapter 10, can mitigate feelings of powerlessness or a sense of inferior status. By exercising patience, a younger woman can achieve the domestic power she sees exercised by older women. Women in Japan, or in Korea, sense how with time, as a mother, one eventually moves into a higher status. A husband or son make one an object of dependency needs. A woman desiring control learns how to manipulate such needs.

In sum, in considering hierarchy in a Confucian social context one must emphasize that ideally, at least, the system is not demeaning to those in lower positions. The optimistic inner religious message of Neo-Confucianism is one of self-development through the better exercise of one's social role. Rather than an emphasis that in changing status one becomes a greater success the message points toward achieving personal satisfaction through self-improvement.

Within the family, therefore, the mother does not try to compete with the role of father because it is seen as a higher role. The goal is to become the mother of a successful man or men. Hierarchy in age as an ideal is reassuring. Automatically aging, one knows with patience respect and status will be accorded. There is no such assurance in American society. There is no security in aging. On the contrary, one faces the problem of Willie Loman that at some future time one will be dispensed with when no longer useful. This implicit message is explicit when one looks at sports, where during the period of peak success one is rewarded, but one is quickly discarded when injuries or infirmities make one no longer useful.

Mentorship: The Role of the Sensei

For the Japanese, mentorship is religious. The Confucianist sentiments of reverence and gratitude that are supposed to be expressed to the still living previous generation can only be understood in terms of the sacred. Being made into an object of veneration or gratitude can be discomforting for a Westerner. Such behavior is sometimes decried by secularized Japanese as well, who prefer "dry" to "wet" emotional attachments, as it is recently phrased. The actual benefits bestowed do not explain the intense symbolic value of mentorship. One can almost consider some adolescent Japanese, like ducklings, going through a phase wherein they can become "imprinted" by a teacher, or *sensei*—a person "born before." Some retain throughout their careers a veneration of a master. There remains for many a romanticized image of the *sensei*, somewhat akin to the youthful image of a first love.

An American agricultural specialist, Wm. Clark, visited Hokkaido during the time when Hokkaido University was being established as a pioneer institution specializing in modern agriculture and fishing. After a visit of several months, he casually remarked when leaving, "Boys, be ambitious." He forthwith became a symbol for the zeal felt by this first generation of students. They built a statue to him and took his words as the school motto. They embodied the undying gratitude felt toward Clark *sensei*.

Being accepted into a mentoring situation is considered very important for one's career by young Japanese. The contemporary sense of alienation felt by many Japanese college students attending large classes is intense. The sought-for direct contact with a teacher cannot be realized. Radical students quickly change their ideology once they are taken into an organization after graduation and put into the hands of older members of the organization for in-house training. In Japanese culture, the mentor remains a transcendence of the parental relationship in providing vocational guidance. It was even customary for merchants during the Tokugawa period to send their sons out to learn by being apprenticed to another shop, rather than receiving all their training at home.

Mentorship is a two-way relationship. In its Confucian context it is as important to the sense of self-dignity and accomplishment of the master as it is to the pupil. Erik Erikson (1959), in describing various stages of the life-cycle, sees a successful aging process as involving a sense of generativity turned toward continuity into the next generation. Many aging Japanese are as concerned with such a successful bestowal, as they were with receiving when young, from parents or from a mentor.

This sense of continuity is deeply felt in all religions, whether it is contained in a belief in the personal continuity of one's individual soul as in the Christian and Muslim traditions, or as a belief in the continuity of a family lineage or occupational tradition as is fostered in Confucian thought.

This generational continuity is found in the occupational world in Japan as a direct transcendence for the nurture that was supposed to be given as parents to children. The emotional tone between older and younger is what makes a sense of hierarchy bearable, even desirable, for those raised within a Confucian family wherein role harmony ideally reigns. In this cultural atmosphere, equalizing relationships is not a goal. One equalizes basically only with friends of the same age.

There is present-day mythology in Japan about the ideal company president. He is a folk hero who exemplifies the ideal exercise of power and control for the benefit of his workers, as well as producing a product that will benefit the populace at large. The purpose of gaining power as head of a company is to become a benevolent figure. Power is not for its own sake but to help others. Realizing ambition is not an individualistic achievement; it is to be able to bestow favors on others. One becomes a boss or *kacho* to be a "sage" advising the younger people coming up through the firm (cf. description of fantasies elicited by TAT pictures in De Vos 1973). In Japanese fantasy, older men are not only teaching younger men, but taking care of them.

What is to be bestowed, and the manner of bestowal, in the perception of Americans would be considered a kind of "maternal" benevolence. These qualities were attributed to the emperor as part of the prewar mobilization of

Japan around his divinity. Indeed, Robert Bellah (1969) once described the emperor as a "maternal symbol."

There are indeed those who seek to actualize this culturally shared fantasy. There is gratification to be derived from playing such a role. It is a repetition of an idealized family setting in which parents take care and provide, even to the point of self-sacrifice, for their children. The biggest gratification to be attained is to make enough money to be a philanthropist in the original meaning of the word. Periodically such figures can be found in Japanese industry. Beliefs in this pattern are thereby reinforced. Contrary to the emphasis that is put by some observers on the situational ethic of Japanese, actual ethnological observation of an urban community convinced Wagatsuma and myself how much public service is present in some urban Japanese communities.

The Role of Successful Elders in Voluntary Organizations

Many older Japanese do get beyond immediate concern with their own family. They do get involved with social causes. We were examining community activities related to delinquency in Arakawa ward in northwest Tokyo, a district of petty artisans and merchants. We could not attend to them all, but concentrated on those concerned with the prevention or diminution of delinquency. There were a plethora of voluntary organizations joined both by men and women.

One such activity will illustrate. A number of men over fifty-five became *hogoshi,* voluntary probation officers, looking after from two to four delinquent youth remanded to their charge by the formal probation officer. This was not simple surveillance; sometimes a mentoring relationship was established. The recidivism rate of youth working with *hogoshi* was relatively low. Because these *hogoshi* came from the same ward as their charges, they knew their life pattern and could closely interact with them. Big Brother was indeed watching, but with a benevolent form of control.

Leisure time for many older Japanese is utilized for such social causes as neighborhood betterment. The social atmosphere constrains one to join a number of organizations. In fact, we are of the firm impression that Japanese today are greater joiners than middle-class mainstream Americans. Roger Barker (1968) completed a very detailed study comparing a Midwest town in the United States with a town of the same population in Britain. He examined all the voluntary organizations, whatever their purpose, and found that Americans are greater joiners than the English.

If someone did a similar systematic present-day comparison of the United States and Japan, I am certain that the Japanese would be found to spend more time in community activities than their American counterparts. Among so-called salarymen, it is mainly their housewives who are so occupied. In the merchant and artisan groups, men are also drawn in. It is obvious in some instances that it is the network that forces them to enter a number of these "voluntary" groups. The Japanese too, have their "Rions" and they roar together with their fellow boosters as they do in the United States. The Kiwanis organization co-sponsors exchange programs for youth. The Japanese, even in large city neighborhoods, have local organizations resembling small-town America.

Collectively, volunteers are bestowing some good on the community. This development in Japan may not be directly Confucian in origin, but is important to consider the type of self-actualization related to responsible status that engenders such activities.

Compared with the United States, the Japanese family and local community are maintaining better coordination, despite the individuating and socially isolating features of modern mass society everywhere. There are many difficulties increasingly faced by the aged in Japan which we cannot here consider, but the Confucian concepts of the past have prevented the isolation of the aged apparent in modern urban America. Respect has not completely disappeared.

Vicariousness and Generational Continuity in Women

I have already discussed above how social sensitivity is engendered in Japanese primary socialization. Related to this quality of sensitivity is how a capacity for identification is further developed as part of a woman's role, whereas men, while remaining dependent upon them, in contrast, are not supposed to identify, openly at least, with women inhabiting an inferior role.

But, as also noted above, in age-graded situations there can be a vicarious identification with inferiors by superiors, a maternal nurture of younger by elder. Instrumental contracts bind labor in the West. Hierarchical exploitation breeds alienation as Marx well described it. There are mitigating features in Japanese age-graded social inequality that prevent such class alienation from becoming a primary social concern. Subordinates identify with the success of the company to which they belong rather than feeling exploited by others who achieve wealth and status at their expense.

The capacity to endure in order to succeed and to measure success through some form of identification reaches its apotheosis in Japanese mothers. Success is experienced jointly in the family unit as part of the complementarity of family roles between men and women. Vocational success is the role of the man. Aiding this accomplishment is the role of the wife-mother.

I have described elsewhere (De Vos 1975) how the boy's success gives pleasure to the mother. Supposedly, the husband's success also gives pleasure to the wife. There is here, however, a remaining underlying tension in the Japanese family over wife, mother-in-law relations. The mother-son tie is often maintained into adulthood and marriage. As a consequence, the younger wife turns more to her children than to her husband in realizing herself within a marriage. In many contemporary families in Japan women are not as apt to feel gratified as wives of salarymen on a treadmill. As mother she turns to the education of her children as hope for future accomplishment.

In American society vicarious identification is most readily pleasurably fulfilled in those who follow team sports. They feel enhanced by the victory of their team. They gain physical empathic excitement in watching their team play. Within the American family parents do feel gratification when children succeed, but they indulge children toward the realization of what have been personal goals rather than family goals. The degree of complementary empathic involvement between spouses in either society is difficult to determine. The American relationship may in many cases be no closer than the Japanese, even though the American ideal relationship is supposed to be a more companionate one, rather than the mutual performance of roles so emphasized in Japan. The American ideal is horizontal intimacy rather than the harmonious maintenance of family hierarchy in the realization of future family goals. Nevertheless, capacity for empathy depends more on individual psychological maturation than on culturally desirable norms.

The heart of Confucian endeavor is the achievement of harmony in society. This can only be accomplished when each individual inhabits his or her role properly. Metaphorically harmony occurs when everyone in an orchestra plays the same opus, united in common purpose. Let us now explore the possible aesthetic as well as moral pleasure possible through the Confucian religion of the family.

One learns to harmonize by practicing self-discipline. The very concept of self is a relational self in which what one is, or what one is to be, is defined by relationships. One gains both purpose and pleasure out of one's placement in the orchestra. There is a future time orientation in the realization of pleasure. Much practice is necessary before skillful harmony results. Pleasure occurs with the aesthetic refinement of a skill. It is not crude and direct. Sensuality that can be immediately gratified has much less value. Refined pleasures are transmuted into aesthetic forms. The Italians have learned to appreciate the taste of bitterness in Campari. Past generations of Japanese have taken the bitterness of life and distilled a moral virtue out of it.

In the past nothing was wasted, either materially or spiritually. In Arakawa ward, Tokyo, waste dealers recycling what others could no longer use were still to be found in the 1960s. Refined moral masochists, many Japanese learned not to waste suffering, but rather than diffuse it expressively in lamentation, they have used it instrumentally to fuel efforts toward future purpose, and by so doing, increased their own self-regard.

The Relationship between Aesthetic and
Moral Gratification in the Exercise of Confucian Ritual

In various discussions of the resolved tensions, needs for security or gratifications of social belonging, that is, the functions of religion from a psychological perspective (De Vos and Sofue 1986), too little attention is paid to the direct involvement of the body as well as the mind in belief and ritual. The religious value of body comportment is central to why I consider Confucianist family practices as satisfying some religious needs that therefore do not have to be met in religious practices outside the family.

The Westerner can understand Confucian espousals of the Golden Rule of moral reciprocity, since cautions about not hurting others are to be found in other religious teachings as well. But what may be difficult to understand is what is to be gained religiously by so much time and emphasis spent in the concern with proper ritual. Although ritual plays a heavy role in all established religions, Confucian ritual may seem to some to be "religiously" empty since it does not seem concerned with the worship of a supernatural deity. The *Book of Rites* was one of the major traditional texts—and yet rituals outside those directly related to ancestor worship or ritualized deference and propriety between family members have little relevance today.

This traditional central concern with ritual—as opposed to dogma— is not something that people can intuitively appreciate right away in looking at Japanese family practices. While religions recognize austerities and abnegation as training for self-control, these practices are more characteristically seen as part of a direct relationship to a deity. They are not simply part of regulation directed toward fellow humans. However, in Confucian practice just as in Western religion, keeping the rules can lead to a sense of self-righteousness. Unfortunately, as in the case of the Japanese extreme, self-constraint can also lead to the denigration of those seemingly incapable of exercising sufficient self-control. Japanese, in their relationships with outsiders, during the militarist period, arrogantly assumed the moral superiority of *Yamato damashi,* the Japanese spirit. Extreme self-denial was not the only component of Japanese fanaticism, but a social atmosphere of severe inner constraint can conduce to seeking for explosive release externally as happened toward the Chinese in Nanking, and periodically in the treatment of war prisoners.

Religious exercises, if properly conducted, also impart a sense of aesthetic gratification that cannot be separated from the experience of propriety in gesture. Seen psychologically, propriety can be morality. This is very difficult for Westerners to understand. It is sometimes reported, however, especially by more self-conscious converts to a traditional religion that by practicing individual or group religious exercises one finds not only reassurance but a sense of aesthetic gratification. There can be no clear line drawn psychologically between the experiences of morality in belief and that felt in ritual.

Some Catholics claim what really attracted them to Catholicism is the ritual, which they found to be aesthetic and moving. For nonbelievers this does not quite jibe with what one is supposed to derive from the Catholic faith. However, participation in ritual has strong attraction for some people. We must look at ritual behavior as carrying *meaning* in religious experience.

There is some transformation of the correctness and the delicacy of body movements into an aesthetic pleasure which at the same time imparts a sense of morality. Having the proper self-discipline and control over oneself permits proper participation. A practicing member of a religion is behaving, as well as thinking, in religious terms. Psychologically, it is difficult for people to understand without some stretch of their ordinary sensibilities, either the pleasure to be obtained from the constraint of Japanese Noh drama, or the pleasures to be obtained from the tea ceremony. In both these instances, the tensions in the body, which can be interpreted aesthetically when the practice of movement is well performed, are of a very refined and subtle nature. Only those who submit themselves to a severe discipline can appreciate the expression of the aesthetic standards contained in traditional movements. The Confucianist courtier must have also gained a sense of aesthetic pleasure from the performance of propriety in courtly manners and in the self-containment and self-control of behavior regardless of circumstance. These traits are no longer appreciated in the modern world. Pleasure is, for some, more to be gained from the breaking of rules, from the excitement that breaks through forms of propriety in the direction of license. In periods of change, license is more easily understood by people in every culture than the pleasures of propriety and self-restraint when they are well executed.

Regularity and Order in the Aesthetic and the Moral

Aristotle and other philosophers of ancient Greece did not distinguish between what is moral and what is beautiful. They were participating in a developing cult of beauty not yet completely removed from its religious origins. They remained conscious of how music, drama, and the plastic arts were directly derivative of religious beliefs and practices, and so remained expressive of deeply religious sentiments. I would suggest that in Japan such a connection is still being transmuted from early experiences, although examples of such instruction are becoming increasingly less common. In the early 1950s I directly observed how the mother would often teach by moving the child's body into correct motoric postures. "Proper" motoric learning instilled early enough, as already discussed, maintains an inseparable aesthetic and moral component that tends to remain implicit in feelings about body comportment throughout life. This was a culturally consistent pattern with the later learning of aesthetic traditions through the manipulation of the body by the teacher or *sensei*.

It has been incomprehensible to Western observers who visited premodern schools in China or Japan, how learning could take place through such rote methods. Learning would be instilled by group recitation of what was to be learned without any attempt to explain what one was reciting. Comprehension was not an immediate goal. One would learn the meaning of the words later. Such forms of recitation are now only practiced in sacred or semisacred contexts in Western settings. In all schools from early childhood one learns to recite the Pledge of Allegiance to the American flag in a rote manner. In Catholic schools in the United States during my childhood, the "Our Fathers" and "Hail Marys" as well as the "Apostles' Creed" were recited without any attempt at explanation of the words. During my early years of Catholic education I never learned in school what was meant by "Blessed is the fruit of thy womb, Jesus." The words were sacred and were to be repeated—not to be comprehended. It has been equally baffling to Western observers how the "imitative" Japanese, who started modernizing by emulating Western industrial patterns exactly and rigidly, could ever hope to compete successfully in modern manufacturing. Again, they were doing first and comprehending later. In the learning of an artistic tradition from a teacher, comprehension was supposed to come eventually from the continual exercise of correct behavior. One comprehends eventually what one is doing. This form of learning is contrary to the American principle in education to explain everything so that the learning individual knows what he is doing. This "intellectualizes" learning. The "grace" of proper doing is not considered.

The traditional Japanese modes of instruction remained more moral and aesthetic and even magical. Langdon Warner (1958) describes how the master swordmaker learned and imparted the art of properly tempering steel through ritual acts that measured the proper timing to be used.

Emotions engendered ritually could be experienced without being totally understood. Reverence and awe were to be encouraged in the teaching situation. Everlasting gratitude was the feeling to be experienced in the teacher-student relationship. The moral authority of the teacher was reinforced by the family, instilling a sense of reverence for the *sensei*—the one born before.

A "practicing" member of a religion is behaving as well as thinking in religious terms. There is deep expressive gratification to be realized in ritual, and perhaps for some others, there is a sense of malaise engendered in failing to follow prescribed forms of ritualized or routinized behavior. For example, some Japanese are truly workaholics. They feel uneasy during the weekends.

Motoric learning from very early childhood on creates patterns that when followed produce a reassuring sense of morality. Following specified patterns ritualistically can impart a sense of aesthetic rightness and also a moral satisfaction of orderliness, ultimately giving the individual a sense of general orderliness and predictability. Proper gestures can be magical gestures insuring a controllable, predictable world.

Ability to believe in an orderly predictable world, which can be improved to run even more properly, is one of the deepest needs which an ideology or a religious system seeks to satisfy. Security is not only found in belief, but proper motoric behavior is necessary to ensure belief. Strict adherence to politeness, still practiced in the proper bringing up of Japanese children, continues to perpetuate patterns of propriety that have a moral tone even though the direct ideological or religious referents to Confucian dogma are not used consciously. Being critical of proper family authority, gesturally or verbally, is a breach of the unquestioned sacred as much as reviling God would be to a Western believer.

In the West, religious sensibilities are not tied to behavior expressed toward real parents, but in Christendom are only directed toward "the Holy Family." One no longer ties morality to behaving gracefully toward others. American children have not been disciplined toward respectful deference. By Asian standards, both parents and children behave crudely. Parents are prone to use physical punishment, yet children are not really taught to properly defer without continually questioning or testing the intention of parents in various situations. Motoric constraint per se is not an issue. American parents are often indulgent of willful behavior expressed toward outsiders.

In modern times Western artists in various media have been in revolt, trying to be innovative by breaking through established forms. What occurs, rather than transcendence of a discipline, is sometimes revolt for its own sake. Instead of being disciplined and then receiving satisfaction out of creative transcendence, there is pleasure in the rebellious, even assaultive flouting of expectations. In one sense the practice of art takes the form of Tantric exercises reversing or negating propriety. They are antireligious in intent. They continually seek to test the limits of social acceptability. What is sanctioned, what is not sanctioned? Their practices are symbols of undoing the restraints of early socialization, even to the extent of reveling in incontinent disorder.

An individual may seek to rebel against ambivalently experienced authority by forms of almost ritualized disorder. A struggle to avoid "socialization" takes place not only on the level of belief but is often very deeply symbolized motorically. These patterns too, can lead to ill-defined malaise. At Berkeley I have observed how deeply rebellious students, who have been in a state of emotional turmoil, have subsequently attempted to resolve their malaise by joining a religious sect that reinforces strict behavioral codes and ceremonializes collective, repetitive, almost automatic words and gestures. Seeking out the possible appeal of the particular expository dogma used by the sect would fail to explain belonging. It is the reassurance of ritual which calms disturbing, errant thoughts for new adherents.

Religious conversion does more frequently occur among the antireligious than among those more truly secular. Some eventually seek out some form of religious resolution that satisfies a need for the restoration of regulation, or that assists in the maintenance of self-regulation. One notes the not too infrequent occurrence of religious conversion among artistic and political radicals; sometimes they join sects that demand absolute submission to a ritualized regime.

In my judgment, many of the anomic attempts at aesthetic experimentation are directly opposite to the aesthetic elements found in Confucianism or in other religious rituals. They are against generational continuity in any form. They are against belonging. Consider the malaise apparent in Western art: Is it not a true reflection of a prevalence of social anomie and individual alienation, rather than an expression of personal autonomy? What is the survival value of such attempts? One questions how long individuals can live with so much disorder about them. One must ask if there is not something basically unhappy and unstable about living in disorder. Ultimately, an aesthetic sensibility cannot tolerate disorder.

The Pleasures of Self-Constraint

To repeat, if we look at the localization of the sense of power, the causality within Confucianism, we must not assume that functioning in a social hierarchy creates a sense of powerlessness in the individual. On the contrary, the Japanese sense of pleasure in accomplishment comes out of the ability to exercise one's role to the optimum regardless of one's position in society. In our interviews in Arakawa, Wagatsuma and I were very impressed with the number of individuals who were in lowly positions who nevertheless had a sense of themselves as doing their job well. They identified with their work rather than being alienated from it. According to Marx, alienation is a consequence of becoming a worker in an industrialized society. Contrary to this, we found that many individuals, rather than thinking of themselves as being constrained or pushed into a lowly position, were able in some way to actualize themselves despite their lowly positions. Therefore, the sense of powerlessness that is often attributed to individuals of lowly positions, or to women vis-à-vis men in hierarchical gender situations, does not necessarily become the inner experience of the person in that position. The sense of propriety in role delivers to the individual certain forms of pleasure in accomplishment and a realization of self that is hard to understand for people imbued with an egalitarian philosophy that says that those beneath are failures, and the only way to realize oneself is to become a relative economic success in a competitive society.

Moreover, an emphasis on social role does not make the individual fatalistic, because embodied in the Confucianist tradition, as Tu (1985) has well explained in his writings, is a sense of continuous self-development so that the older individual has a greater sense of accomplishment in this regard than those who are more youthful. The reverence for age in a Confucian society deals with the fact the individual has had more time to travel toward a sense of self-realization and greater wisdom.

It is our egalitarian ideal that constrains us to see that the only way to feel or to sense one's self in low-status positions is to feel a frustration of the sense of power. This is a reading into others, a projection, of how we would feel if we are imbued with an egalitarian philosophy and we would find ourselves in a hierarchical situation. We would perhaps have less capacity to examine the pleasures of accomplishment within such a constrained role.

The Japanese best seller several years back, *Kokotsu No Hiso*, would be almost incomprehensible for an American audience. In this work, a woman comes to devote herself entirely to an irascible, childish, demanding, senile father-in-law. The ultimate degradation is that this demanding unpleasant old man has to have his diapers changed when he becomes incontinent. What is hard for a Western audience to see is how any woman would turn herself into a voluntary slave to such a person. In the West we are very quick, once the aged become physically incapable or bothersome, to send them off to a facility for the aged where attendants are paid to take care of the daily unpleasant tasks. Very few Americans individually take care of an incapacitated person, much less an in-law. The idea of voluntarily taking on the burden of a senile in-law, but more than that, finding a sense of self-realization in such a dedication, is incomprehensible to us. Perhaps the closest that some Americans understand such dedication is found in a mother taking care of a seriously incapacitated child, and by so doing, completely emptying her life of other meanings or possibilities.

It is the subtle sense of self in social role, related to the moral performance, albeit sometimes in a ritualistic way, that is the greatest difficulty for Western understanding. One finds even in those of the newer generation of Japanese increasing incomprehension of this type of attitude. In the search for *shiawase*, happiness, the Japanese is giving us his understanding, and on various levels, the religious meaning of endurance.

As I have indicated, the discussion in the psychoanalytic literature that comes the closest, in my judgment, to the understanding of how in the past self-sacrifice could become a central meaning is to be found in Theodore Reik's (1941) discussion of masochism. The pleasure to be derived from pain is in the anticipation of an ultimate triumph. In Christianity it is the reassurance that "the meek shall inherit." The act of endurance is almost an eroticization of the future—taking on of certain roles whether it is that of a nun

totally devoted as a "bride of Christ" or a Japanese mother totally devoted to
a child. For the individual, so seeking meaning from these roles can become
a total avowal and a source of gratification to sacrifice the self for a larger
cause. Among religious practitioners in the West, only among those considered
would-be saints does one find equally tolerated, or equally espoused, such a
seeking of a meaningful sense of accomplishment in dedication.

Formalism versus Development

There can be an empty use of gestures just as there can be an empty use
of words which are no longer a part of one's belief. There can be hypocrisy
in gesture or behavior, as there is hypocrisy in words. Humans not only believe
what they say and do—they learn to manipulate and act. There is the expediential in proper behavior, as there is the expediential in proper words. All
behavioral propriety in Confucian practices, no more than that of other religious behavior, represents a serious internal religious purpose. Confucian practice, no less than Jewish or Christian ritual, can reflect an interior emptiness.
Empty ritual per se is not conducive to inner development of responsible
social behavior in any tradition.

For some, propriety is a defense either against external or internal threat.
Deviation from a prescribed behavioral code can create an internal sense of
chaos and disorder. For others, propriety in religious behavior or artistic appreciation is meeting the expectations of one's social status, or the social
presentation of proper sophistication. Some foreigners or Japanese might find
sitting through a Noh drama a trial, but not admit this to others. Social
considerations cause them to sit still and be polite. They may not understand
the lyric poetry inaccessible to them. Attending to art can be necessary to
manifest status. Individuals pretend to feel what they don't feel when it is
expected of them, because it's proper to their status to experience things this
way. These usages of propriety do not negate the fact that others derive
religious satisfaction out of the same activities. What does body propriety have
to do with an inner sense of power or powerlessness? I would submit that
constraint and propriety enhances a sense of moral ascendancy. This sense of
self-worth can be relatively independent of external social status. Those in
lowly positions, by doing their job the best way possible, preserve a sense of
personal worth. They may not have any social power, but they maintain a sense
of self-regard. If one does one's own assigned job well, some self-satisfaction
is possible. This is hard to comprehend by members of some minority groups
who refuse jobs because they are considered demeaning.

The Asian minorities in the United States could not be demeaned by
the work assigned them within the host society as immigrants. They maintained their sense of personal worth within their family relationships. Respect

within the family sustained them against outside discrimination. They could not be alienated in a Marxian sense. Their work did not become purposeless or without meaning. They were sustained by a religion of the family.

Surveys in Japan indicate that over 90 percent of the Japanese say they're middle class. What does it mean to be middle class? The concept of social class does not work in a Western sense in Japan. There is hierarchy, but there are no alienated antagonistic classes. The janitor at Asahi Press does not belong to a janitor's union, the janitor at Asahi wears an Asahi button and so does the president of the firm. They all belong to Asahi, belonging within a hierarchical structure that Nakane Chie described as a "frame" society, in which all the members, whatever their respective status, belong. They are not alienated. This is the opposite of what Marx told us would happen to industrial workers.

At 8:30 in the morning in downtown Tokyo one can observe people doing exercises and singing together. This is bodily movement, mobilizing the self in a social role. Movement in concert, belonging to their occupational group. Technically not a prayer or religious ritual, nevertheless an act of belonging, creating some sense of relevance to their lives. Modern secularized individuals may be very impatient observing such collective behavior, but it is of consequence to those whose occupational destiny may be working in a department store or on an automobile assembly line.

Confucianism as Religion:
Family Continuity, Reverence, and Gratitude

Religious Functions Realized in Confucian Family Continuity

This chapter about Confucianism as religion is a continuation in more detail of a more general, previous presentation of the functions of religion in East Asia (De Vos and Sofue 1986). In this conclusion, I should like to recapitulate why I insist that Confucian beliefs and practices within the family fulfill many, if not all, of the possible basic functions of a religious system.

To recapitulate, the primary function of any religious system is to assure a sense of psychological continuity for an individual or a social group. By such assurance, the belief system opposes death and dissolution (cf. De Vos and Ross 1982; also Lifton 1970). A sense of continuity need not be individual as it is in Western religions. Religious reassurances of continuity may be focused on the social group, or on the family as is the case for practicing Confucianists. Continuity can be achieved by emphasis on one's sense of belonging to a social group which persists even though individual members disappear.

Viewed temporally, religious beliefs are representations of a collective sense of purpose and continuity. The group in which the person lives is *self-consciously* related insofar as its members share in a collective sense of past and future. Religious representations continue to give temporal direction to human purpose. In Confucian ritual practices, there is a central focus on a symbolic assertion of family continuity.

A social structural approach to religion in the Chinese family as it interacts with family definitions and roles is well exemplified by Suenari (1986), who discusses a pattern found in a contemporary Taiwanese village wherein there is a continuity of traditional ancestor worship. Suenari provides for us a description of how ancestor worship operates as part of this pattern. The worship of the dead can also be viewed as a pattern of distribution of goods.

In this Taiwanese case, religious practices are also forms of instrumental cooperation to achieve a common purpose in the lineage unit. There is economic sharing; the shares within any cooperative enterprise are carefully calculated. In effect, in Taiwan there is little difference in how a business and a religious venture are conceptualized.

Suenari attempts some structural comparison between the Chinese family observances and those of Japan and Korea. He finds obvious differences in the forms taken by ancestor worship in the three societies. The Japanese corporate *ie* household assumes most of the functions which may be handled disparately in Taiwan. The *ie* is a religious unit of worship and also the unit of life-crisis rituals. The so-called *dozoku,* which appears in parts of Japan as main and branch family relationships, is quite different from the compound fraternal units of the Chinese family in Taiwan. In northeastern Japan, for example, it is only the main household that is responsible for ancestral ritual. The descendants of branch households send a representative to attend the ritual at the main household rather than seeing this ritual as directly pertaining to their own ancestors of the branch household, who are not considered as direct ancestors of the main household. Suenari perceptively notes that relationships with the ancestors in Japan are based more on a continuity of emotional feelings than on instrumental contracts. Ancestors are worshipped even though secular gain is not implicitly promised, as it is in Taiwan. The traditional Japanese, with primogeniture, did not emphasize sharing in ancestral worship. The Chinese still do since inheritance is equally distributed among children.

Suenari notes that the Korean situation, at first glance, seems to resemble that in Japan. However, in the Korean instance, there still is much more direct emphasis on Confucian formalism than was found in the typical Japanese household, which now uses Buddhist services. When Koreans gather at the household of the eldest son for rituals of commemoration celebrating the anniversary of dead ancestors, the responsibility for the ceremony is that of the eldest. This was also true for the Japanese, but there is sharp difference to be noted in the consciousness of the participants. In the Korean case, the ancestor is seen as an ancestor of all those assembled rather than only as ancestor of the main household.

Comparing the three Confucian cultures, Suenari sees the Korean as adhering most closely to the prescribed official Confucian manners to be observed by the living toward the dead. The Koreans, in other instances, are intermediate between the Japanese and the Taiwanese in observed practices. As for the Japanese, both yesterday and today, the emotional incentives for participation as a quasi-religious act of *belonging* per se seem more important than the instrumental economic purposes which characterize the Chinese household. The Chinese and Japanese are further apart in formal religious terms. The Chinese family is a symbolic summation of relationships at various levels, including those beyond the immediate domestic one, whereas the Japanese do not formalize as religious units beyond the immediate household or *ie*.

I have discussed in detail elsewhere (De Vos and Sofue 1986) how, seen developmentally in human psychology, the various motives and interpersonal concerns reflected in religious expression start with the universal human experience of helplessness as an infant and the initial experience of separateness arising with the dawn of consciousness. The progressively more self-conscious human never overcomes a need for some form of dependence on outside powers for nurturance. This deep need for nurturance is also reflected negatively in an existential fear of nonexistence, that is, the basic sense of death— a threat to the continuous existence of the self—which is an early conscious experience.

There is also a deepening awareness of how one's own helplessness is juxtaposed to the presence of external power, be it conceptualized naturalistically or in supernatural terms. Some of the early childhood representations of fearful power, whether thunder, or fire, or the aggressive behavior of giant adults, remain embedded in religious representations throughout life (Spiro 1986). From childhood, the human consciousness begins to locate power as an attribute of awesome outside objects or beings. This sense of awe starts early and humans never completely overcome a need to relate to such external powers as a means of assuring personal security.

A religious sense of power in deity can be represented in various forms. The conceptualization of power never becomes completely secularized in most explanatory systems. It is conceptualized in instrumental terms as ultimate authority and control as well as in expressive terms as ultimate love as closeness and benevolence.

A belief in divine benevolence affords deep emotional security and comfort for most human beings. Conversely, the potential of evil force in the supernatural causes one to seek divine protection. Early animistic representations of power are found in various folk beliefs. In the Japanese case, *kami* is vaguely conceptualized as representations of power in sacred mountains, impressive trees, or other unusual manifestations of nature. Deity can be represented in vague concepts of fertility, generativity, sometimes personalized and sometimes not. Power also becomes represented in particularly awesome individuals who become deified objects of worship.

Some forms of security are gained in the process of cognitive growth by a developing sense of instrumental control through knowledge. The seeking out of explanations for the workings of nature are means of assuaging anxiety. However, the cognitive system of causal knowledge provided within a culture remains inseparable from religious thought except when secularization processes provide more critical alternative modes of thought. A religious system blending magic and science gives the individual some sense of regularity in experiencing the outside world, and affords some hope for control over the awesome powers of nature as well as modes of relating to them in supplication.

Religious concepts suggest instrumental means of maintaining relationships with awesome powers, whether conceptualized as impersonal or personal. When personalized, religious practices are, in effect, acts of submission and entreaty to sway, divide, will, or purpose. Humiliation of the self or ascetic practices are means toward having one's humble wishes granted. Confucian thought has transcended the supernatural referents in practices of austerity. For a Confucianist, austerity is for self-development and the enhancement of self-esteem not as a mode of supplication to please a deity. The lack of supplication in Confucian practices makes it seem less of a religion to Western observers.

When we look at various societies, we note that the type of control and security obtained through development of knowledge of the world can become heavily secularized. Explanations are progressively developed in naturalistic terms and lose their religious representations as modes of explanation. In some systems, such as that developed under Confucianism, the immediate influence of the supernatural becomes of secondary concern to human control and regulation. Confucianism maintains its providence in the realm of moral and ethical problems, that is to say, in regard to the type of causality that exists in human not supernatural interaction. The proper exercise of one's family role is made central to moral behavior, not the pleasing of a potentially judgmental deity.

Family is less central in Buddhism. The individual may seek for separate religious resolution, leaving the family and its obligations in order to realize personal religious salvation.

The seeking out of knowledge acts as a means of security when one is dealing with the most awesome experiences of human life, namely, birth, sexuality, inexplicable illness, and death. These very emotional experiences when witnessed must be given some kind of representation which aims at regulating them. Experiences of this nature are never free from a sense of individual incapacity and anxiety.

Religion functions to bolster a sense of personal adequacy as well as assuaging fear of failure, in the achievement of life goals. The individual often senses himself to be inadequate, and in his own sense of imperfection seeks out means of assistance from the supernatural in reaching toward what he conceives to be the ideal level of competence. Prayer takes two forms: it is used to request deity to aid or intervene when personal insufficiencies make one helpless. It can also take the form of a request for confidence so that one finds the inner resources to function more adequately.

Moreover, individuals, to varying degrees within any religious system, feel themselves incapable of becoming fully responsible socially. They seek help in internalizing social directives and acquiring self-control so as to be able to act morally. In the Confucian system, there is a great deal of emphasis upon attaining a satisfactory level of self-control and responsibility as part of self-development. There is, however, no recourse to prayer to a deity to help in this effort.

In the domain of emotional needs, religious representations in some contexts take on a deeply affiliative meaning. They represent a search for deepening intimacy and understanding, and act as an assurance for the individual against isolation and neglect. In Christianity a "church" is a religious brotherhood that transcends or even supplants family ties. In Confucian thought, there is no religious representation of a nonkin-centered group. This is counter to Western conceptions that religious individuals may find represented in their religious practices which constitute bonds of closeness as they share in their mutual worship of the supernatural. One finds closeness bonded with others who are adherents of shared beliefs. In the Western tradition there is a common sense of social belonging that unites the religious community expressively as well as instrumentally as they seek a joint purpose. A need for belonging and group identity is assured by common religious practice. In East Asia such ceremonies take place within the family; in the West under Christianity they are more individualistically conceived or they may be realized in a church congregation of fellow believers. In ancestor worship, the affiliative bond remains within the family. In Christianity the so-called Christian brotherhood of the church is religiously more important than individual family units. Monasticism is a type of affective withdrawal that comes in conflict and, therefore, must be reconciled with the family as an institution (Koh 1986).

In Western individualistically oriented traditions, the problems of human isolation are given very direct representation. It is expected that religious conversion can be used to assuage a deep sense of alienation and problems of loss of meaning which are usually associated with a loss of intimate forms of human attachment. The relation of the Christian to his god is manifestly separate from his relationships to others within his family. The resolution of a sense of alienation or isolation is more often resolved in Asian traditions by a symbolic reincorporation of the individual within the family (De Vos 1973, chapter 18).

Religions have an evaluative dimension by which one judges oneself emotionally in reference to one's own standards of self-acceptance as well as in reference to standards of social acceptability. One's behavior is evaluated positively or negatively in respect to religious regulation. There are a variety of conceptualizations that define acceptability. The most pervasive are the concepts of purity and pollution, a topic I considered in detail elsewhere (De Vos and Wagatsuma 1966). Behavior is evaluated as bringing one closer to a possible communication with the deity, or making one unworthy of contact and constraining others to reject one as being in a state of pollution. In Confucianism, the individual who fails to fulfill social obligations is seen as reprehensible and, if all efforts at reform fail, worthy of social ostracism.

All religions regulate aggression; they regulate how or under what conditions there can be proper expression of hostility and destructiveness. Conversely, they promise the eventual attainment of forms of harmony and peace that are considered an expressive need in all societies. One sees represented in religious beliefs concepts of ideal harmony as well as representations of the sources of discord and unhappiness among individuals. Every religious system embodies taboos on killing or intragroup destructiveness, whereas they may condone destructiveness directed outside the group under religiously nonpolluting circumstances. The religious system gives moral justification to certain forms of aggression while proscribing others. In this sense, all religious systems regulate harmony and discord on an expressive as well as on an instrumental level, setting up regulations for cooperation and competition within and between societies. The ultimate ideal of Confucian thought is harmonious social regulation.

Religions set boundaries on sexual expression, defining degrees of relatedness in the family. Religious beliefs enforce incest taboos and define the times and occasions and age of maturity at which sexual practices are condoned. Various forms of pleasure come under social regulation. As already discussed above, religious beliefs offer explanations, giving meaning to suffering. Religion often seeks to provide a sense of purpose for the enduring of affliction.

In brief, both bodily pleasure and malaise are religiously defined. Religions impose regulations on the individual, but also provide periodic release from regulation. There is a differential emphasis in Asian religions concerning the tolerance of emotional expression through religious conceptualizations. Whereas Confucianism aims in its concepts of self-regulation toward the establishment of harmony within society, Buddhism is more concerned with internal experiences and the causes of suffering for the individual or the collectivity. Buddhist concepts in this sense are more concerned with emotional expression and self-regulation, whereas Confucianist concepts are more related to the instrumental aspects of social responsibility.

I shall not herein discuss whether Confucian practices by themselves offer *sufficient* forms of release for all. Note that in any social group, Confucian practices are never found without some forms of alternative folk practice appearing that offer supplementary possibilities for those seeking outer emotional release or providing promises of divine intervention in the form of assistance or protection not to be provided within the more constraining and demanding dimensions of Confucianist practice (cf. Kendall 1986).

Some Cultural Differences in Japanese Family Relations

In the religious teachings of the great traditions that developed in China and spread to Korea and Japan, what is the ultimate relationship of the individual to the family in Japan? What is the conceptualization of the self as related to the family and how is this relationship viewed as part of religious meaning within the individual? What is the relationship of family membership to religious practice and dogma? What is the relationship of Japanese family membership to psychological security and other functions provided by religious adherence and belief? Looking at relations within the family structure, what is the interaction between given forms of religious belief and the family as an institution? Does religion support the family as an institution, or in seeking for religious answers and purposes, is the individual brought into conflict with the family?

Confucian answers to such questions and the traditional use of Confucian ideas in China and Japan reflected basic differences between these two cultures. Bito (1986) rather succinctly summarizes some incisive thoughts relating the family as a social institution to the forms and ideas of Neo-Confucianism as they were accepted, rejected, or modified in Japanese past usage. His main point is that scholars of Confucianism in Japan without explicitly raising the issue almost invariably denied a basic proposition of the Chu Hsi school. Whereas Chu Hsi emphasized the absorption of basic principles into the self in order to discover one's basic nature, the Japanese philosophical commentators saw that the outer behavior "residing in reverence" accomplished all of one's moral training. The so-called penetrating principle of going into the self was not considered because it is enough to unconditionally devote oneself behaviorally to the given social norm and the role to which one dedicates oneself in the feudal service of one's lord. This espousal of proper behavior as the ultimate expression of virtue is still found today reflected in Morita therapy (Reynolds 1976), a specific form of psychotherapy developed out of Zen Buddhist principles. It is not considered important therapeutically to resolve the inner experience of malaise; rather, what is resolved is an incapacity to act properly in accordance with one's role expectations. The measure of proper virtue is behavior, not thought. Thought can interfere. One learns as well as possible to be "selfless" in one's expected behavioral role, whatever one's errant thought might be.

Bito notes that the Japanese concept of the family has not changed since the eighth century. He contends that the *ie* system is basically different from the conception of family espoused in the Chinese lineage system. The *ie* as a unit of social organization and social morality in Japan is not based on concepts of strict kinship but displays many of the characteristics of an artificially contrived social organization formed to preserve the household occupation rather than to continue it directly through blood lineage. Bito points out how it is possible for a nonkin member to succeed in the continuity of the *ie* so that, in given circumstances, the first son as head of the household is circumvented when his succession would be to the detriment of family business or property. The corporate concept of the Japanese family has as its requisite the appointment of an appropriate heir who will maximize the functioning of the *ie* rather than the automatic succession of someone strictly on the basis of birth. Kinship is a principle of family continuity that can be modified in given circumstances. One does not acquire, according to Bito, the qualifications of a member merely by being born into a family. One becomes a full member only after some form of achievement and actualization.

Looked at anthropologically, the religious family, strictly speaking in Japanese conceptions, is characterized not only by status acquired by birth but by a combination of acquired and achieved status. In China, in contrast, one is born into a family and thereby given rights and obligations which become the basis of all social activity. The realization of self is not specifically in the continuity of a given occupation; rather the individual has some choice as to how to actualize himself, which may take a different form from that previously taken by other family members. What is required is obedience to the father to ensure the lineage rather than the continuity of a corporate household defined occupationally or professionally. It is relationships that are respected rather than one's ability or qualifications. Bito, interestingly, points out how in Japanese the very concept of filial piety itself has to be expressed by a Chinese-derived loan word. There is no "Yamato" language word for it. Bito paraphrases Tsuda, a prominent scholar of history and thought, who argued that the reason the Chinese regard filial piety as the basis of morals is because they view all morality as based on the dyadic relationship between individuals. He contrasts this with the Japanese view in which it is the individual's relationship with the group that is the prime consideration. The basis of morality in respect to the *ie* lies in the performance of one's designated role within the group.

Bito describes how the samurai developed the concept of a pattern of loyalty. It must be noted that the samurai differed basically as administrators from the gentry of China. Japanese feudalism developed in a way different from the continuity of power in China. Bito speculates that the shift from Buddhism to Confucianism in the Tokugawa period was due to the fact that the attempted centralization that occurred under the Tokugawa regime led to some functional similarities to the bureaucratic system extant in China.

During the early part of the Tokugawa period, it was not necessary for samurai to devote themselves to any Confucianist study. However, those who had some special interest in learning or wanted to be scholars themselves had access to Confucianist scholars. These Confucianist scholars as well as Zen priests with their aesthetic as well as ascetic practices were the teachers and mentors of members of the samurai class. Studying Confucianism became useful for acquiring a position but was not essential to the acquiring of an administrative post, as was true in China with its examination system. Learning for the samurai was somewhat irrelevant to actual politics but helped validate status in the Weberian sense (Weber 1947). Confucian ethics could be used also as validation of an ethical code which gave some expression to the religious sensibilities of an individual. Such a code gave him a sense of purpose and regularity in the performance of duty, permitting actualization of the self through the exercise of social duties and roles.

Tu (1986) distinguishes cogently between the state of being religious and religion as an institution with objectifiable dogmas. The sense of being religious involves a sense of self-identification and of self-purpose in relationships and interaction with others. It is the characteristic of the Chinese sense of a self located, not in a structure or a normative concept of the individual, but more in a sense of process in which the self is continually transformed and developed in social interaction. The "self-transformation," therefore, is transactional rather than located in some kind of "individual" entity that takes on new structural characteristics. In both China and Japan, self relates to social role.

Ancestor worship remains a principal feature of religious sensibilities in East Asia. It is found embedded in indigenous cults, but with the coming of literacy, ancestor worship was preempted by Confucianist writings in which ancestor worship as a religious practice became more concerned with social reverence of the living than with a benevolent relationship with the powerful dead or a deity that judges or provides. In indigenous religion there was a great concern about possible malevolent consequences should ancestor worship be neglected. Under Confucianism, ancestor worship becomes a moral imperative maintaining the social forms and symbolizing inheritance practices within lineage structures. Whereas ancestor worship in China and Korea became and remained Confucianized, in Japan concern with ancestral tablets became attached to Buddhist memorial practices offering respect to the dead. In effect, ceremonially Buddhism now plays the same functional role in Japan as the more direct, self-consciously organized Confucianism does in Korea and China.

Reverence and Gratitude

As I have discussed at length in this chapter, basic to Japanese Confucian-inspired religious thought is respect and gratitude. There is a gratefulness for what is received and a need to return the gratitude by some acts on one's own part, be they morally defined in terms of good and bad action, materially in terms of a bestowal upon others, or as an ascetic sacrifice of pleasure to achieve greater purpose. Some form of responsible behavior is deemed repayment for what is received. The Japanese concept of *on*, therefore, seems to be consonant with, if not derived, from, Confucian thought. *On* as benevolent giving from elders to be repaid came to be heavily imbued with this reverential sense of something so precious and, indeed sacred, that it can never be totally repaid. This sense of reverence related to incurred benevolence need not be related to a supernatural being such as Amida Buddha, although it can be. More characteristically, it remains localized within the human social realm. It can be directed toward the person of superiors, although it is first related to the gratitude felt toward parents.

In looking at these basic elements of Confucianism, we see that concepts of reverence and gratitude are the essence of religiously directed social interaction. They are based on *kokoro*, this Japanese concept of "heart," combining reason, will, and feeling, united in social action. Without concern with the supernatural, Confucianists nevertheless insist on the maintenance of some superordinate ethical principles governing the behavior of man that could not be reduced to the material forms of causality found in Western science.

There are indeed what one might deem "mystical" concepts of ultimate unity in the thought of many Confucianists who do not take recourse to a concept of deity governing life. Wang Yang-Ming considered innate knowledge of the good as forming one body with all things. Integrity is the principle of "Heaven" applied to everyday things.

References

Azuma, H., K. Kashiwagi, and R. Hess. (1981). *The Influence of Maternal Teaching Style Upon the Cognitive Development of Children*. Tokyo: University of Tokyo Press.

Barker, R. (1968). *Ecological Psychology: Concepts and Methods for Studying the Environment of Human Behavior*. Stanford, CA: Stanford University Press.

Bellah, R. (1957). *Tokugawa Religion*. New York: Free Press.

———. (1969). *The Emperor as Maternal Symbol*. Berkeley: University of California Press.

Birdwhistle, R. (1970). *Kinesics and Context.* Philadelphia: University of Pennsylvania Press.

Bito, M. (1986). "Confucian Thought during the Tokugawa Period." In *Religion and the Family in East Asia,* ed. G. A. De Vos and T. Sofue. Berkeley: University of California Press.

Caudill, William and Helen Weinstein. (1966). "Maternal Care and Infant Behavior in Japanese and American Urban Middle Class Families." In *Yearbook of the International Sociological Association,* ed. René Konig and Reuben Hill. Switzerland: Broz.

de Grazia, S. (1948). *The Political Community: A Study of Anomie.* Chicago: University of Chicago Press.

De Vos, G. A. (1960). "The Relation of Guilt toward Parents to Achievement and Arranged Marriage among the Japanese." *Psychiatry* 23.3: 287–301.

———. (1973). "Role Narcissism and the Etiology of Japanese Suicide." In *Socialization for Achievement: Essays on the Cultural Psychology of the Japanese,* ed. H. Wagastsuma and G. A. De Vos. Berkeley: University of California Press.

———. (1975). "Apprenticeship and Paternalism." In *Modern Japanese Organization and Decision Making,* ed. E. Vogel. Berkeley: University of California Press.

———. (1982). "Adaptive Strategies in American Minorities." In *Minority Mental Health,* ed. E. E. Jones and S. Korchin. New York: Praeger.

———. (1984). *The Incredibility of Western Prophets.* Amsterdam: University of Amsterdam Press.

———. (1985). "Dimensions of Self in Japanese Culture." In *Culture and Self: Western Perspectives,* ed. A. Marsella, G. De Vos, and F. Hsu. London: Methuen.

De Vos, G. A., A. Marsella, and F. Hsu. (1985). "Introduction: Approaches to the Self for a Psychocultural Perspective." In *Culture and Self: Asian and Western Perspectives,* ed. G. A. De Vos, A. Marsella, and F. Hsu. London: Methuen.

De Vos, G. A. and L. R. Ross. (1982). *Ethnic Identity.* Chicago: University of Chicago Press.

De Vos, G. A. and T. Sofue. (1986). *Religion and the Family in East Asia.* Berkeley: University of California Press.

De Vos, G. A. and M. M. Suarez-Orosco. (1987). "Sacrifice and the Experience of Power." *Journal of Psychoanalytic Anthropology,* vol. 10, no. 1, pp. 34–64.

De Vos, George. (1993). "A Cross Cultural Perspective: The Japanese Family as a Unit in Moral Socialization." In *Family, Self, and Society: Towards a New Agenda for Family Research,* ed. P. Cowan, J. Filed, D. Hansen, M. Scolnick, and G. Swanson. Hillsdale, NJ: Erlbaum Assoc.

De Vos, G. A. and H. Wagatsuma. (1966). *Japan's Invisible Race.* Berkeley: University of California Press.

De Vos, George. (1978). "Selective Permeability and Reference Groups Sanctioning: Psychocultural Continuities in Role Degradation. In *Major Social Issues—A Multi-Community View,* ed. Milton Yinger. Free Press. pp. 9–24.

Doi, Takeo. (1973). *Anatomy of Dependence.* Tokyo: Kodansha, 1973.

Durkheim, Emile. (1947). *The Elementary Forms of the Religious Life.* Glencoe, IL: Free Press.

Ekman, P. (1973). "Cross-Cultural Studies of Facial Expressions." In *Darwin and Facial Expressions: A Century of Research in Review,* ed. P. Ekman, 169–222. New York: Academic Press.

Ekman, P., W. V. Friesen, and P. Ellsworth. (1972). *Emotions in the Human Face.* New York: Pergamon Press.

Erikson, E. H. (1959). "Identity and the Life Cycle: Selected Papers." *Psychological Issues.* 1.1: 1–171.

Firth, R. (1940). "The Analysis of Mana: An Empirical Approach." *Journal of the Polynesian Society* 49: 483–510.

Freud, S. ([1917] 1957). "Mourning and Melancholia." *Standard Edition* 243–58. London: Hogarth Press.

Gorer, G. (1943). "Themes in Japanese Culture." *New York Academy of Science* 5: 106–24.

Graves, R. (1952). *The White Goddess.* London: Faber and Faber.

Hsu, F. L. K. (1985). "The Self in Cross-Cultural Perspective." In *Culture and Self: Asian and Western Perspectives,* ed. G. A. De Vos, A. Marsella, and F. Hsu. New York: Tavistock Publications.

Kagan, S. (1974). "Field Independence and Conformity of Rural Mexican and Urban Anglo-American Children." *Child Development* 45: 765–71.

Kagan, S. and R. Buriel. (1977). "Field Dependence-Independence and Mexican-American Culture and Education." In *Chicano Psychology,* ed. J. Martinez. New York: Academic Press.

Kendall, L. (1986). "Korean Shamanism: Woman's Rites and a Chinese Comparison." In *Religion and the Family in East Asia,* ed. G. De Vos and T. Sofue. Berkeley: University of California Press.

Kernberg, O. (1975). *Borderline Conditions and Pathological Narcissism.* New York: Jason Aronson.

Kluckhohn, F. (1953). "Dominant and Variant Value Orientations." In *Personality in Nature, Society, and Culture,* ed. C. Kluckhohn, H. A. Murray, and D. M. Schneider. New York: Knopf.

Koh, H. (1986). "Religion and Socialization of Women in Korea." In *Religion and Family in East Asia*, ed. G. De Vos and T. Sofue. Berkeley: University of California Press.

Lanham, B. (1956). "Aspects of Child Care in Japan: Preliminary Report." In *Personal Character and Cultural Milieu*, ed. D. Haring. Syracuse, NY: Syracuse University Press.

————. (1962). "Aspects of Child-Rearing in Kainan, Japan." Unpublished Ph.D. dissertation, Syracuse University.

Le Barre, W. (1945). "Some Observations on Character Structure in the Orient." *Psychiatry* 8: 319–42.

Levy, R. I. (1973). *Tahitians: Mind and Experience in the Society Islands*. Chicago: University of Chicago Press.

Lifton, R. J. (1970). *History and Human Survival*. New York: Random House.

Madsen, M. (1967). "Cooperative and Competitive Motivation of Children in Three Mexican Subcultures." *Psychological Reports* 20: 1307–20.

Madsen, M. and A. Shapira. (1973). "Cooperative and Competitive Behavior or Urban Afro-American, Anglo-American and Mexican Village Children." *Developmental Psychology* 9: 16–20.

McClelland, D. (1961). *The Achieving Society*. Princeton, NJ: Van Nostrand.

Miyake, K., S. S. Chen, and S. S. Campos. (1986). "Infant Temperament, Mother's Mode of Interaction, and Attachment in Japan: An Interim Report." In *Monographs of Society for Research in Child Development*, ed. I. Bretherton and E. Waters.

Piaget, J. (1930). *The Child's Conception of Causality*. London: Kegan Paul.

————. (1932). *The Moral Judgment of Children*. London: Routledge and Kegan Paul.

Reik, T. (1941). *Masochism in Modern Man*. New York: Grove Press.

Reisman, D., R. Denny, and N. Glazer. (1958). *The Lonely Crowd: A Study of the Changing American Character*. New Haven, CT: Yale University Press.

Reynolds, D. (1976). *The Quiet Therapies*. Honolulu: University of Hawaii Press.

Spiro, M. (1986). "Some Reflections on the Family and Religion." In *Religion and the Family in East Asia*, ed. G. A. De Vos and T. Sofue. Berkeley: University of California Press.

Suenari, M. (1986). "The Religious Family in Central Taiwan." In *Religion and the Family in East Asia*, ed. G. De Vos and T. Sofue. Berkeley: University of California Press.

Tu, Wei Ming. (1985). "Selfhood and Otherness in Confucian Thought." In *Culture and Self: Asian and Western Perspectives*, ed. A. Marsella, G. De Vos, and F. L. K. Hsu. New York: Tavistock Publications.

————. (1986). "On Neo-Confucian and Human Relatedness." In *Religion and the Family in East Asia,* ed. G. De Vos and T. Sofue. Berkeley: University of California Press.

Vogel, E. (1965). *Japan's New Middle Class.* Berkeley: University of California Press.

Wagatsuma, H. and G. A. De Vos. (1984). *Heritage of Endurance: Family Patterns and Delinquency Formation in Urban Japan.* Berkeley: University of California Press.

Warner, L. (1958). *The Enduring Art of Japan.* New York: Grove Press.

Witkin, H. A. (1967). "Cognitive Styles across Cultures." *International Journal of Psychology* 2: 233–50.

————. (1969). "Social Influences in the Development of Cognitive Style." In *Handbook of Socialization Theory and Research,* ed. D. A. Goslin. New York: Rand McNally.

Witkin, H. A. and J. W. Berry. (1975). "Psychological Differentiation in Cross-Cultural Perspective." *Journal of Cross-Cultural Psychology* 6: 4–87.

Witkin, H. A. and D. Goodenough. (1977). "Field Dependence and Interpersonal Behavior." *Psychological Bulletin* 84: 661–89.

Contributors

Haejoang Cho is a full professor in the Department of Sociology, Yonsei University, Seoul, Korea. She received her Ph.D. in 1979 from the University of California, Los Angeles. Her earlier research focused on gender studies with special interest in Korean modern history. Her current work focuses on cultural studies in the global/local and post-colonial context. She is the author of *Women and Men in South Korea* (Seoul, 1988); *Reading Texts, Reading Lives in the Post Colonial Era,* 3 volumes (Seoul, 1992, 1994), and *Children Refusing School; Society Refusing Children* (Seoul, 1996).

George A. De Vos is both a clinical psychologist and anthropologist trained at the University of Chicago. An emeritus professor of anthropology, University of California at Berkeley, he is author of twenty books and 180 articles documenting his forty-five years of cross-cultural field experience and research in the United States, East Asia, and Western Europe. From a comparative perspective, he has integrated a European derived sociological approach with psychoanalytically oriented American anthropology and psychology.

He has specialized in the use of psychological tests cross culturally *(Oasis and Casbah: Algerian Culture and Personality in Change - 1960; Symbolic Analysis Cross Culturally: The Rorschach Test - 1989).* In psychological anthropology, he has written and edited: *Responses to Change: Society, Culture and Personality 1976; Culture and Self: Asian and Western Perspectives 1985; Status Inequality: The Self in Culture 1990).*

He also has written extensively on Japanese cultural psychology *(Socialization for Achievement - 1973);* religion *(Religion and The Family in East Asia 1986);* social problems, e.g., delinquency *(Heritage of Endurance: Family Patterns and Delinquency Formation Japan 1984);* and minority group issues, including the plight of the former outcastes of Japan *(Japan's Invisible Race - 1966, Koreans in Japan - 1981; Social Cohesion and Alienation: Minorities in the United States and Japan - 1991).*

John B. Duncan is an associate professor in the Department of East Asian Languages and Cultures at the University of California, Los Angeles. His primary professional interest is in Korean historical cultural adaptation. Forthcoming from the University of Washington Press is *The Origins of the Choson Dynasty*. He has also written on the formation of the central aristocracy in early Koryo, the social background to the founding of the Choson Dynasty, and Confucianism in the late Koryo and early Choson periods. His current projects involve a study of neo-Confucian orthodoxy and the civil service examination in Choson Dynasty Korea and protonationalism in premodern Korea.

Born November 2, 1924 in Cho Lon, South Vietnam, *Nguyen Ngoc Huy* combined scholarship with political leadership. Under the pen name of Dang Phuong he was an accomplished poet as a young man. In 1948 he was elected to the central leadership of the Dai Viet Quoc Dan Dang nationalist political party opposing both French colonialism and Communism. Forced into political exile after 1955 by President Ngo Dinh Diem, Huy graduated from the political science faculty of the University of Paris in 1958, received a degree in law and economics from the same university in 1959 and a PhD in political science from the Sorbonne in 1963.

He published a study of elite leadership in traditional China, a two volume work of political theory, Dan Toc Sinh Ton, and a study of human rights in traditional China and Vietnam (Virtue and Law; Yale University; Southeast Asian Studies); translated Han Tei Tzu's writings into Vietnamese, translated the Le Dynasty Law Code of 1433 into English (Quoc Trieu Hinh Luat, Ohio University Press), and wrote numerous articles.

From 1965 to 1975 he taught political theory at the National Institute of Administration, Saigon. From 1975 to 1990 he was a Research Associate, East Asian Legal Studies Program, Harvard Law School. He formed the Tan Dai Viet political party in 1964, the Progressive Nationalist Movement in 1967, and the Alliance for Democracy in Vietnam in 1975. Professor Huy is now deceased.

Francis L. K. Hsu was born in China, and received his Ph.D. from the London School of Economics in 1940. After teaching at Columbia and Cornell Universities, he joined the Northwestern University Department of Anthropology in 1947. His thirty-one year tenure included seventeen years as Chairman of the Department. Now Professor Emeritus, Dr. Hsu is a specialist in psychological anthropology and the cultural anthropology of large literate civilizations. Past President of the American Anthropological Association and a member of the Academia Sinica, Dr. Hsu's many publications include *Under the Ancestor's Shadow, Clan, Caste and Club, The Study of Literate Civilization, Religion, Science and Human Crises, Iemoto: The Heart of Japan* and *Americans and Chinese: Passage to Differences.* He is also the Editor of and a contributor to *Psychological Anthropology: Approaches to Culture and Personality.* Dr. Hsu has written numerous articles for professional journals including the *American Journal of Sociology, The American Sociological Review, The American Anthropologist, Psychiatry, and the International Journal of Social Psychiatry.* Dr. Hsu currently resides in Marin County, California.

David K. Jordan is both a professor of anthropology at the University of California, San Diego, and the Provost of Earl Warren College, UCSD. His fieldwork encompasses extensive studies in Taiwan and China, with emphasis on Chinese popular religion. He has published widely, including seven books on anthropology, Taiwanese folk religion and sectarianism, and Esperanto—a particular interest.

Eddie C. Y. Kuo (PhD, Minnesota) is the founding Dean (since 1992) of the School of Communication Studies at Nanyang Technological University, Singapore. He was formerly Head of the Sociology Department (1986–90), Director of the Centre for Advanced Studies (1986–88) and Director of the Mass Communication Programme (1990–95) at the National University of Singapore.

A sociologist by training, Professor Kuo's research interests include communication policy and planning, information technology, cultural policy and national integration, and the sociology of multilingualism. He has authored/edited 10 books, including: *Language and Society in Singapore* (1980), *Communication Policy and Planning in Singapore* (1983), *Information Technology and Singapore Society* (1990), *Mirror on the Wall: Media in a Singapore Election* (1993), and *Videotex Development in the Asia-Pacific* (1995).

Professor Kuo is the founding co-editor of the *Asian Journal of Communication* (Singapore). He also serves in the advisory boards of the *Journal of Asia-Pacific Communication* (USA), the *Journal of Development Communication* (Malaysia), the *Journal of International Communication* (Australia), and the *Chinese Journal of Communication* (Hong Kong). He is also a board member of the International Center for Communications (USA).

Takie Sugiyama Lebra is Professor Emeritus of Anthropology, University of Hawaii. Her research and teaching have concentrated on psychological and social anthropology with primary focus on Japan. Her publications include *Above the Clouds: Status Culture of the Modern Japanese Nobility* (1993: Winner of the Hiromi Arisawa Award from the Association of American University Presses), *Japanese Women: Constraint and Fulfillment* (1984); *Japanese Patterns of Behavior* (1976); Editor, *Japanese Social Organization* (1992). Among the benefactors that have supported Lebra's research are the John Simon Guggenheim Foundation, the Fulbright Award, the Social Science Research Council, the Wenner-Gren Foundation, the Japan Foundation, and the National Science Foundation. Currently Professor Lebra is working on Japanese selfhood in a comparative perspective.

Kwang-Kyu Lee is a professor in the Department of Anthropology at Seoul National University in Korea. He was granted the Presidential Award for academic work in 1997. His earlier research dealt with topics relating to cultural and social issues, with particular emphasis on the Korean family. More recently he has been conducting a worldwide study of Koreans living abroad. His current publications include: *Overseas Koreans in the Global Context* with Walter H. Slote (1993); *Koreans in China* (1994); *The Korean Community in the Russian Far Eastern Area* (1995); and *Koreans in the World*, Volume 7, Europe (1996).

Bou-Yong Rhi was professor of Psychiatry at the Department of Psychiatry, Seoul National University, College of Medicine from January 1969 until his retirement from the university in August 1997. He is a psychiatric specialist and a leading Jungian analyst in Korea, trained at C. G. Jung Institute Zürich, Switzerland. He served as president of the Korean Society for Analytical Psychology from 1978 to 1987 and since 1986 has been the publisher of the Journal : Shim Sŏng Yongu (Research of the Mind). He is currently president of the Korea Research Institute for the Analytical Psychology of C. G. Jung.

As an invited fellow of the East West Center in Hawaii in 1971 he participated in the Culture and Mental Health Program in Asia and the Pacific at the Social Science Research Institute, University of Hawaii, USA. With his colleagues he founded the East Asian Academy of Cultural Psychiatry and became the first president in 1987. He has engaged in many national and international academic activities in the field of mental health.

He has published numerous articles in cultural psychiatry, mental health issues, analytical psychotherapy, and Korean traditional culture. He is the author of: Analytical Psychology (1978), Depth Analysis of Korean Folktales (1995) and co-author of Korean personality (1980), Origin of Korean Thought (1976), and Studies of Folktales (1982).

Dr. Rhi has received awards from the American Society for Psychopathology of Expression in 1995, and the American Association for Psychosocial Rehabilitation 1996. He received the Dr. Wunsch Medical Prize in 1995 from the Korean Academy of Medical Science and the Pyŏkbong Prize in 1992 from the Korean Neuropsychiatric Association.

Walter H. Slote is a Senior Research Associate at the East Asian Institute, Columbia University, where for many years he taught the advanced doctoral seminars on psycho-cultural dynamics and was a founding member of the Center for Korean Research. He is both a practicing psychoanalyst and a psychoanalytic anthropologist, and from 1988 to 1995 he was co-chair of the Colloquium on Psychoanalytic Methods in Anthropological Fieldwork of the American Psychoanalytic Association. His research includes: a study of the north central Quechua in Peru in conjunction with Cornell University; an extensive study of the rebel and the revolutionary in Venezuela in conjunction with MIT and the Universidad Central de Venezuela; a psycho-cultural study of the Vietnamese and an extension of the rebel and revolutionary project in conjunction with MIT; and a continuing study of Korean personality structure and child rearing practices. He has written extensively on topics relating to his field research and its implications for both psychoanalysis and anthropology.

Tu Weiming was born in Kunming, China and educated in Taiwan (B.A. at Tunghai University) and North America (M.A. and Ph.D. at Harvard University). Before joining Harvard University as professor of Chinese History and Philosophy in 1981, Dr. Tu taught Chinese intellectual history at Princeton University and University of California at Berkeley. He has also lectured on Confucian humanism at Peking University, Taiwan University, Chinese University in Hong Kong, and University of Paris. He is the author of *Neo-Confucian Thought: Wang Yang-ming's Youth, Centrality and Commonality, Humanity and Self-Cultivation, Confucian Thought: Selfhood as Creative Transformation,* and *Wang, Learning, and Politics: Essays on the Confucian Intellectual.* A member of the Committee on the Study of Religion at Harvard, the chair of the Academia Sinica's advisory committee on the Institute of Chinese Literature and Philosophy and a fellow of the American Academy of Arts and Sciences, Professor Tu Weiming is currently interpreting Confucian ethics as a spiritual resource for the emerging global community. He assumed his tenure as the Director of the Harvard-Yenching Institute in January 1996.

Dawnhee Yim is professor of History and Dean of Women's Affairs at Dongguk University in Seoul, and president of the Korean Society for Cultural Anthropology. She is the co-author of *Ancestor Worship and Korean Society* (Stanford University Press, 1982) and *Making Capitalism: The Social and Cultural Construction of a South Korean Conglomerate* (Stanford University Press, 1993).

Born on November 2, 1945, *Steven B. Young* graduated magna cum laude from Harvard College and cum laude from Harvard Law School. He served in the Republic of Vietnam with the Agency for International Development from 1968 to 1971. With Nguyen Ngoc Huy he wrote Virtue and Law, a study of human rights in traditional China and Vietnam (Yale University: Southeast Asia Studies Program). He has written on Le Dynasty property law and the political cultures of Vietnam, China and Thailand. With Nguyen Ngoc Huy in 1986 he founded the International Committee for a Free Vietnam. In 1966 Young discovered the UNESCO World Heritage site on Ban Chiang, a bronze age community in northeast Thailand. Young was an assistant dean at the Harvard Law School, Dean and Professor of Law at Hamline University School of Law, and taught Vietnamese history at the University of Minnesota, Faculty of Liberal Arts.

Subject Index

Author Index
and Mentioned Terms